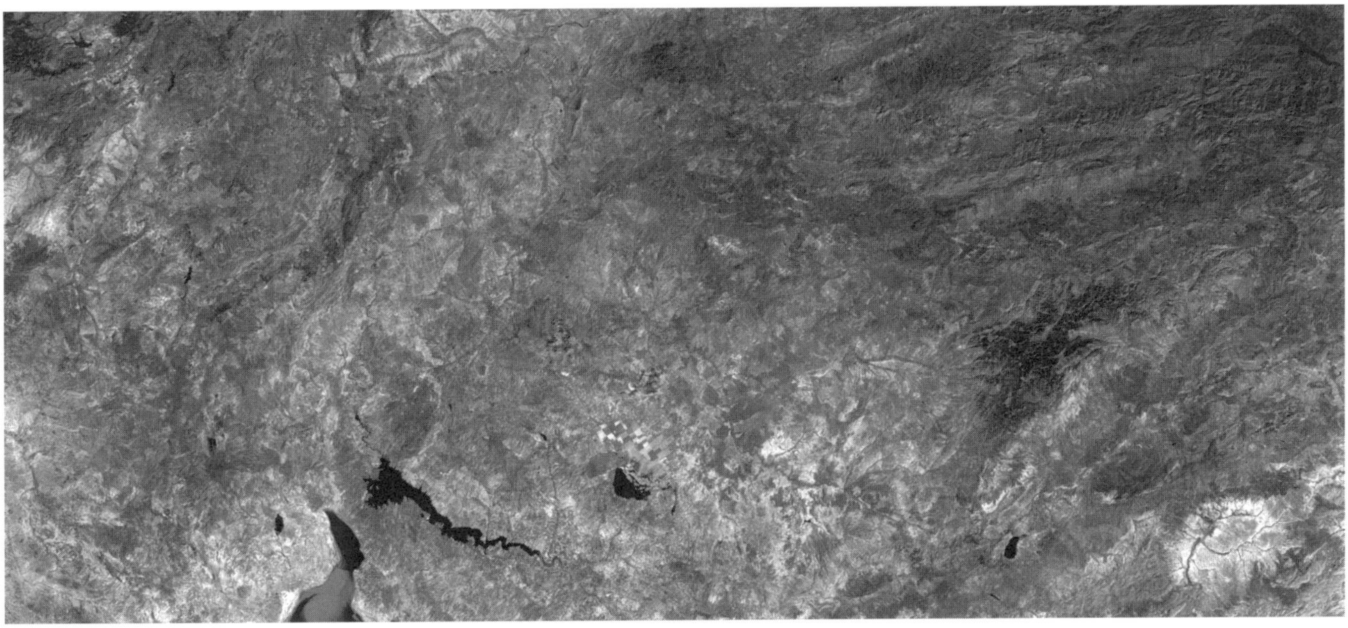

Across the Anatolian Plateau

READINGS IN THE ARCHAEOLOGY OF ANCIENT TURKEY

THE ANNUAL OF
THE AMERICAN SCHOOLS OF ORIENTAL RESEARCH

Volume 57 (2000)

Series Editor
Nancy Lapp

Billie Jean Collins
ASOR Director of Publications

Across the Anatolian Plateau

READINGS IN THE ARCHAEOLOGY OF ANCIENT TURKEY

Edited by
David C. Hopkins

American Schools of Oriental Research • Boston, MA

Across the Anatolian Plateau

READINGS IN THE ARCHAEOLOGY OF ANCIENT TURKEY

Library of Congress Cataloging-in-Publication Data
Across the Anatolian Plateau: Readings in the Archaeology of Ancient Turkey
edited by David C. Hopkins.
p. cm. — (The annual of the American Schools of Oriental Research; v. 57)
Includes bibliographical references and index.
ISBN 0-89757-053-7
1. Turkey—Antiquities. 2. Hittites—Turkey
3. Excavations (Archaeology)—Turkey.
I. Hopkins, David C., 1952- II. Series.
DS101 .A45 vol. 57
[DR431]
939′ .2—dc21
2002005288

Printed in the United States of America
on acid free paper. ∞

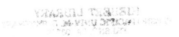

Contents

Preface

This volume of readings in Anatolian archaeology owes its existence to the foresight, advocacy, and energy of Dr. Ronald Gorny of the University of Chicago. Nearly two decades ago, Gorny was concerned that new developments in the archaeology of Turkey and, especially, the vast legacy of the Hittite culture remained the purview of a circle of specialists yet demanded a prominent place before the broader archaeological community as well as the general public. His vision resulted in the publication of special issues of the journal *Biblical Archaeologist* (now *Near Eastern Archaeology*) in 1986 and 1993. This volume incorporates most of the articles from those two issues. Chapters originally published in 1986 have been thoroughly updated by their authors. This group focuses on the Hittite Empire and presents synthetic historical and literary analyses of the multitudinous data provided by archaeological endeavors. It includes contributions by Gary Beckman, Ronald Gorny, Greg McMahon, and Ahmet Ünal. Five pieces from the 1993 issue of the journal published in honor of Peter Neve present data and analysis of a much wider range of Anatolian archaeology. Chapters by Henrickson, Nesbitt, Singer, Yener, and Zimansky reappear from that special issue with only minor changes. Close to one-half of the chapters collected here consist of studies solicited expressly by Gorny for this volume. These seven essays, by Cahill, Dusinberre, Matney, Neve, Ratté, and Voigt, make their first appearance in print. Especially noteworthy is P. Neve's chapter on the great temple at Boğazköy, which makes available in English for the first time the excavator's description of this massive and extraordinarily well-preserved complex of Hittite cultic buildings.

The constellation of chapters assembled in this volume spans the Anatolian plateau and then some, ranging from Sardis and Aphrodisias in the west to sites of the Urartian kingdom close by Lake Van in the east. Its temporal dimension stretches between the medieval period settlement pattern of Gordion and the domestication of plants ten thousand years BP. Along the way, chapters display a host of research methodologies and techniques: palaeobotany, metallurgical study (lead isotope analysis), architectural analysis, remote sensing technology, iconographic analysis, as well as the study of ceramic manufacturing processes, urban layout, and domestic assemblages. An array of archaeological analyses unrolls the panorama of ancient Anatolia.

Many had a hand in the creation of this volume. The format of the chapters follows that realized by the artistic director of the 1993 issue of *Biblical Archaeologist*, Bucky Edgett. Lyle Rosbotham contributed his design skills to the layout of the refreshed 1986 chapters and those appearing for the first time. Monica McLeod brought the whole together. Ellen Rowse Spero and Rebecca Scheirer worked on the manuscripts in the editor's office, Ruth Kent helped to gather the index, and Dr. Billie Jean Collins, ASOR Director of Publications, managed the final stages of editing and production. The authors, of course, contributed their expertise, their effort in reworking the older manuscripts and checking edited versions, and their patience as the road to the appearance of this collection stretched out longer than anyone might have anticipated.

David C. Hopkins
January 2002

Anatolian Archaeology: An Overview

By Ronald L. Gorny

People in antiquity referred to Modern Turkey by several names. The term Asia Minor comes from the Greek and was probably first used in the fifth century CE. Use of the term Asia may ultimately go back to *Aššuwa*, the Hittite designation for a part of the western peninsula. The term Anatolia is also derived from Greek, as a reference to the east. It is, however, a rather late toponym, probably first used by a Byzantine writer in the tenth century CE. Both terms are now used as rather general appellations for the peninsula occupied by the modern nation of Turkey, with Anatolia the more common because of its preservation in the modern Turkish form *Anadolu*.

The history of the Anatolian peninsula has been long and colorful. Over the centuries, Hittites, Phrygians, Persians, Greeks, Romans, and Turks—to mention only a few—have all made the land their home. These peoples left indelible marks on the face of the peninsula, the meanings of which are only now becoming fully understood. Although scholarly literature has long since offered a skeletal outline of the region's historical development, the archaeological process of fleshing out this outline is still in its infancy. The archaeology of Anatolia remains, in fact, still a developing discipline, but its bloodlines run deep. As the offspring of two prestigious progenitors—biblical and classical studies—it can claim an illustrious lineage.

The eastern origins of Anatolian archaeology lie in the early study of the Bible (Ramsay 1907; Ceram 1956:22–45; Mellink 1966:113–15). Because the geographical setting of Asia Minor formed the backdrop for so much of the New Testament, ancient biblical scholars developed a keen interest in it, traveling across the land and describing it in detail. Modern archaeologists continue to draw insight and inspiration from these early explorations. In the west, Anatolian archaeology was grounded in a longstanding interest in classical studies (Mellink 1966:111–13), a discipline rooted not only in the literature of native writers, such as the historian Thucydides, but also in the spectacular ruins of classical cities scattered across Asia Minor. From this forum came attempts to vindicate Homeric tradition and ultimately Heinrich Schliemann's (1875, 1884) discovery of Troy.

In view of this parentage, it is not surprising that scholars initially viewed Anatolia as peripheral to both biblical and classical studies, and research on Anatolia long remained subservient to both. The early years of work in Turkey focused on the acquisition of museum pieces from the region's rich supply of classical monuments. As such, Anatolian studies did little more than help illuminate the historical events of its "foundational" traditions. Even though the biblical and classical traditions had intermingled at Anatolian sites such as Ephesus, Sardis, and Pergamon (Yamauchi 1980), these contacts were generally viewed in terms of a confrontation between secular Greek traditions and sacral Bible traditions. Anatolia remained in the background. There was little discussion of the native culture into which the two traditions had been implanted.

Several events influenced the subsequent development of Anatolian archaeology. One was Schliemann's discovery of the stratified remains of Troy. Further work at the site by W. Dörpfeld (1902) and C. W. Blegen (1963) revealed Troy to be the center of a native Anatolian culture. The first stratigraphic excavations at Alişar Höyük in central Anatolia followed. There was also excavation work in the preclassical lands of Lycia, Lydia, and Phrygia, largely undertaken by archaeologists whose fascination stemmed from a background in classical studies (Mellink 1966b: 112–13). More recently, southeast Anatolia has been opened for intensive work as the result of salvage operations along both the Tigris and Euphrates Rivers. This has encouraged scholars with a Syro-Mesopotamian background to lend their expertise to the field and has begun to illuminate the important borderlands between Anatolia and Syria. One discovery, however, has had the greatest impact of all: the discovery of Ḫattuša, the Hittite capital, in central Turkey.

The German Archaeological Institute's excavation of Ḫattuša, proved to be a landmark in the archaeology of both Anatolia and the whole ancient Near East. Located on the central plateau at the site of modern Boğazköy/Boğazkale, Ḫattuša was a native Anatolian city of monumental proportions. The vestiges of its material culture recovered from the ruins provided ample evidence of its former glory. Cuneiform records found at the site supplied a literary touchstone against which discoveries in other areas of the ancient world could be measured. They documented an indigenous Anatolian culture that had once been a major world power, effectively providing Anatolian archaeology with a central focus. More significantly, the discovery of this important capital city led to the active involvement of Turkish archaeologists who adopted the Hittites with a sense of national pride and whose leadership fashioned Anatolian studies into an independent field of research. The discovery of Ḫattuša must, therefore, be considered the single most critical element in the emancipation of Anatolian archaeology from its early identification with the biblical and classical traditions, releasing it to develop an identity of its own.

The discovery of the Hittites, however, created new problems. One of the most troubling difficulties concerns the nomenclature used to define the discipline. The grandiosity of Ḫattuša elevated Hittite studies to great prominence within Anatolian history and archaeology, implying a kind of Hittite archaeology. This is a critical issue because the contemporary definition of Anatolian archaeology has become intertwined with the problematic understanding of the term *Hittite*. This problem has plagued both philologists and archaeologists since the discipline's inception (Mellink 1956:2–55; Güterbock 1957:223–39; Hoffner 1973:197–200). Even after decades of research and discussion, philologists (Steiner 1981, 1990) and archaeologists (Mellaart 1981) are still trying to come to grips with the issue.

The emphasis on Hittite Anatolia can obscure the fact that Anatolian archaeology transcends the bounds of both the Hittite capital and its empire. Thus, a critical task for future Anatolian scholars is to define more precisely the role of *Hittite archaeology* within the framework of the overall discipline. By what criteria do we decide to classify something as Hittite? Where is the dividing line between Hittite and Anatolian? This problem is not unlike that which faces those attempting to define the role of biblical archaeology within the context of Syro-Palestinian archaeology (Toombs 1982:89–91; Dever 1982:103–7).

One productive means of addressing the issue of Hittite archaeology may lie in viewing the emergence of the Hittite empire within the theoretical framework of the French *Annales* school of social and economic history.

In this way, the process of Hittite centralization takes its place in a much broader understanding of social and economic change in the region. The Hittites appear on the scene as just one manifestation of cultural adaptation in a cyclical pattern of recurring empires within what Braudel described as a *longue durée* (Braudel 1972, see Lamberg-Karlovsky 1985; Hodder 1987; Knapp 1992). The application of this Braudelian concept to Anatolia helps to place the Hittites in a broader Anatolian context and interprets Hittite domination as a single peak in an ongoing process of integration-disintegration that is repeated over and over again with different players (e.g., Hittites, Phrygians, Byzantines, and Ottomans). In other words, Hittite history cannot be isolated from other events that have occurred in Anatolia throughout time. The Hittites represent but one cast of players appearing at different times on a common stage (the Anatolian plateau) with identical props (the physical setting) or what Braudel calls *structures* (1972:231–75). We may, therefore, hope to understand Hittite social and political formation better by viewing it as a second millennium response to the pervasive underlying power of the *structures* that influence long-term history in Anatolia. This, in turn, provides a certain degree of explanatory potential for various similarities found in the many imperial ventures that coalesced within ancient Anatolia's physical and environmental constraints.

Like any new discipline, Anatolian archaeology has suffered through a period of growing pains. Methodologically, the discipline is still in the process of maturation. Great strides have been made, however, and Anatolian archaeology has undergone a substantial transformation since its inception. Recent years have witnessed a changing perception within the ranks of archaeology as a whole (Dever 1987) that is beginning to spread through the ranks of Anatolian archaeologists as well (Bittel 1980:276). Basic to this change is the understanding that individual sites are more appropriately understood in the context of complex societies that emerged under the influence of an intricate set of internal and external forces (compare Kohl 1978). This realization has also led to changes in the excavator's research goals, the theory and methodology of excavation, the management of data, and the synthesis of all aspects of the data into well-rounded published interpretations. Such changes, however, have not occurred across the board: individual institutions and their excavators have adopted them in varying degrees. In past years, divergent approaches among the principal investigators of various Anatolian projects often resulted in a disparity between expectations and results. Recent efforts by the Turkish Department of Monuments and Museums to coordinate excavation efforts more effectively have served to moderate inconsistencies among the various international projects while maximizing the overall results.

Perhaps the greatest development in the method and theory of Anatolian archaeologists in recent years has been the trend towards a more science-oriented, interdisciplinary approach (first noted by Kurt Bittel 1980:276). Current excavations now make use of a whole host of technological advances ranging from Electronic Distance Measuring to satellite imagery. Most of this high-tech equipment is linked to advances in computer technology which, over the last twenty years of archaeological investigation, have opened up a multitude of new possibilities. The computerization of archaeology has allowed for more efficient data processing, but also for advanced graphic illustration and the reconstruction of archaeological monuments through virtual reality. Though this virtual aspect is just being introduced into Anatolian circles, it is already being applied successfully in other areas of the ancient Near East with spectacular results, and one can expect it to appear soon as a major element in the overall strategy of key excavations in Turkey.[1]

The most widely applied of the new computer-related technologies are remote sensing practices such as resistivity and magnetometry (see both Matney and Ratté in this volume). The application of these ground radar systems, especially when used in conjunction with Geographic Information Systems (GIS) and Global Positioning Systems (GPS), allows the researcher to locate and map specific points accurately, as well as to create visual three-dimensional representations of what lies beneath the ground before excavation work even begins (Summers and Summers 1999a, 1999b; Summers et al. 1998; Matthews 1998). Needless to say, this option presents archaeologists with a much less invasive means of exploration, and though limited by the depth of cultural deposits (it works best on single-period sites lying directly below the surface), the process limits the destructiveness of excavation in that it allows archaeologists to make subtle determinations before breaking ground about where they might gather the most useful data.

The underlying motivation for the application of such an interdisciplinary, science-oriented approach is the realization that an excavation is capable of revealing more than fragmented historical accounts and ceramic sequences. It should, in fact, reveal as fully and closely as possible the dynamic relationship between the inhabitants of a site and the world around them. This aims at no less than an understanding of human behavior and how cultural processes take place. A final analysis of this relationship must include the integration of a variety of data into interpretation data, which archaeologists in the past relegated to addenda and appendices. Of particular note here is the ability to evaluate the role of environment in determining the nature of civilization and culture. A premeditated determination to identify environmental data (e.g., soil analysis) and include them in the synthesis allows the archaeologist to prepare excavation strategies capable of revealing the underlying, often intangible relationships that are not readily apparent in the gross material remains. In practical terms, this methodology often calls for a more problem-oriented approach especially designed to gain access to specific data that will make these relationships discernible. Such research in Anatolia is relatively recent and the scale at which it can be applied is heavily dependent on financial resources. The results of this integrated approach are only beginning to appear (Marfoe 1979, 1987; Zimansky 1985; Hodder 1996; Algaze 2001; Yakar 2000). Renewed excavations by the British at Çatal Höyük (Hodder 1996; Matthews 1998a), the Germans at Troy (Korfmann 1997), along with the efforts of Japanese excavators at Kaman Kalehöyük (Omura 1999, 2000) represent three dramatic examples of archaeological projects that—despite their somewhat different methodologies—are moving towards more precise interpretations by successfully implementing broad multidisciplinary strategies. One hopes that in the future such research will prove to be the rule rather than the exception.

Note

[1] See web sites such as that of Sam Paley www.learningsites.com/NWPalace/NWPalhome.html for the Neo-Assyrian palace of Assurbanipal. Also compare the work done by Kerkenes Dağ project at www.metu.edu.tr/home/wwwkerk/.

Bibliography

Algaze, G.
2001 The Prehistory of Imperialism: The Case of Uruk Period Mesopotamia. Pp. 27–84 in *Uruk Mesopotamia and its Neighbors: Cross-Cultural Interactions and their Consequences in the Era of State Formation*, edited by M. Rothman. Santa Fe: School of American Research.

Bittel, K.
1980 The German Perspective and the German Archaeological Institute. *American Journal of Archaeology* 84:271–77.

Blegen, C. W.
1963 *Troy and the Trojans*. London: Thames and Hudson.

Braudel, F.
1972 *The Mediterranean and the Mediterranean World in the Age of Philip II*. Translated by S. Reynolds. New York: Harper and Row.

Ceram, C. W.
1956 *The Secret of the Hittites: The Discovery of an Ancient Empire*. New York: Alfred A. Knopf.

Dever, W. G.
1982 Retrospects and Prospects in Biblical and Syro-Palestinian Archaeology. *Biblical Archaeologist* 45:103–7.
1987 The New Archaeology. *Biblical Archaeologist* 50:150–51.

Dörpfeld, W.
1902 *Troja und Ilion: Ergebnisse der Ausgrabungen in den vorhistorischen und historischen Schichten von Ilion*, 1870–1894. Athen: Beck and Barth.

Güterbock, H. G.
1957 Toward a Definiton of the Term Hittite. *Oriens* 10:233–39.

Hodder, I.
1996 *On the Surface: Çatal Höyük 1993–95*. London and Cambridge: McDonald Institute for Archaeological Research and the British Institute of Archaeology at Ankara.

Hodder, I., ed.
1987 *Archaeology as Long-Term History*. New York: Cambridge University Press.

Hoffner, H. A.
1973 Hittites and Hurrians. Pp. 197–228 in *Peoples of the Old Testament*, edited by D. J. Wiseman. London: Oxford University Press.

Knapp, A. B., ed.
1992 *Archaeology, Annales, and Ethnohistory*. Cambridge: Cambridge University Press.

Kohl, P.
1978 The Balance of Trade in Southwestern Asia in the Mid-Third Millennium B.C. *Current Anthropology* 19:463–92.

Korfmann, M.
1997 Hisarlik und das Troia Homers. Pp. 171–84 in *Ana shadi Labnani lu allik: Beiträge zur altorientalischen und mittelmeerischen Kulturen* (Festschrift für Wolfgang Rollig). Kevelaer und Neukirchen-Vluyn: Verlag Butzon und Becker und Neukirchener Verlag.

Lamberg-Karlovsky, C. C.
1985 The Longue Durée of the Ancient Near East. Pp. 55–72 in *De L'Indus aux Balkans*, edited by J.-L. Hout, M. Yon, and Y. Calvert. Paris: Maison de L'Orient.

Marfoe, L.
1979 The Integrative Transformation: Patterns of Sociopolitical Organization in Southern Syria. *Bulletin of the American Schools of Oriental Research* 234:1–42.
1987 Cedar Forest to Silver Mountain: Social Change and the Development of Long-Distance Trade in Early Near Eastern Societies. Pp. 25–35 in *Centre and Periphery in the Ancient World*, edited by M. Rowlands, M. Larsen, and K. Kristiansen. Cambridge: Cambridge University Press.

Mellaart, J.
1981 Anatolia and the Indo-Europeans. *Journal of Indo-European Studies* 9:135–49.

Mellink, M.
1956 *A Hittite Cemetery at Gordion*. Philadelphia: University Museum of the University of Pennsylvania.
1966 Anatolia: Old and New Perspectives. *Proceedings of the American Philosophical Society* 110:111–29.

Omura, S.
1999 A Preliminary Report on the Thirteenth Excavation at Kaman-Kalehöyük (1998). *Anatolian Archaeological Studies* 8:178. (Japanese.)
2000 The Eleventh Excavation at Kaman Kalehöyük in Turkey (1996). *Bulletin of the Middle East Culture Center in Japan* 11:51–91.

Ramsay, W. M.
1907 *The Cities of Saint Paul–Their Influence on his Life and Thought: The Cities of Asia Minor*. New York: A. C. Armstrong and Son.

Schliemann, H.
1875 *Troy and its Remains*. London: John Murray. Reprint. New York: Arno Press, 1976.
1884 *Troja: Results of the Latest Researches and Discoveries on the Site of Homer's Troy*. London: John Murray. Reprint. New York: Arno Press, 1976.

Summers, G. D. and Summers, M. E. F.
1999a Kerkenes Dağ 1997. *Araştırma Sonuçları Toplantısı* XVI/2:121–51.
1999b *Kerkenes New/Kerkenes Haberler 2*. Ankara: METU Press.

Summers, G. D., Özcan, M., Branting, S., Dusinberre, E. R. M., and Summers, M. E. F.
1998 Kerkenes Dağ 1996. *Kazı Sonuçları Toplantısı* XIX/1:627–61.

Steiner, G.
1981 The Role of the Hittites in Ancient Anatolia. *Journal of Indo-European Studies* 9:150–73.
1990 The Spread of the First Indo-Europeans in Anatolia Reconsidered. *Journal of Indo-European Studies* 18:185–214.

Toombs, L.
1982 The Development of Palestinian Archaeology. *Biblical Archaeologist* 45:89–91.

Yakar, J.
2000 *Ethnoarchaeology of Anatolia: Rural Socio-Economy in the Bronze and Iron Ages*. Monograph 17. Tel Aviv: Tel Aviv University.

Yamauchi, E.
1980 *The Archaeology of New Testament Cities in Western Asia Minor*. Grand Rapids, MI: Baker Book House.

Zimansky, P.
1985 *Ecology and Empire: The Structure of the Urartian State*. Studies in Ancient Oriental Civilization 41. Chicago: The Oriental Institute.

Plants and People in Ancient Anatolia

By Mark Nesbitt

Plant products have always played a vital role in the Near East, most importantly as food, but also as fuel, building materials, medicines, and for a host of other uses. In the past, the cultivation of crop plants was the major occupation of most of the population, which literally lived or died by its success in food production. Given the status of crop production as the major economic activity in pre-industrial societies, clearly it must form a central part of any study of ancient civilizations. Equally importantly, study of plants in the past will illuminate the daily life of the villagers who formed the great bulk of the people.

Until the 1960s archaeologists showed little interest in such topics, in part reflecting the priorities of art history and text-based history in determining the objectives of excavations; in part reflecting practical difficulties in recovering and studying plant and animal remains from archaeological deposits. Major changes in archaeological thinking occurred in the late 1960s—the "New Archaeology"—with two major consequences for archaeological practice. First, there was a shift to thinking about past societies as interlinked processes—"systems"—in which all the elements were important and in which individual sites or historical events could not be studied in isolation. Secondly, the basis of how we recover and interpret the archaeological record became a topic in its own right for questioning and discussion. Agriculture and diet were seen as integral to an understanding of the past, and there was a resulting keen interest in sampling methods for biological remains.

New techniques of flotation for collecting plant remains and dry-screening for bones were developed and as an ideal, if not in practice, results were integrated with studies of soil, pollen, and landscape history. Archaeologists working on excavations in Turkey were at the forefront of these developments in archaeological science, and my purpose in this article is to survey what has been achieved after thirty years.

Archaeobotany in Turkey, Past and Present

The study of plant remains from archaeological sites is known as archaeobotany or, more often in North America, as palaeoethnobotany (the two words are synonyms). The materials studied cover a wide range: from wood, seeds, tubers, and other plant parts, to pollen and phytoliths. All these types of remains require a common approach: Using techniques based in the biological sciences to identify and interpret plant remains, but addressing questions rooted firmly in an archaeological framework (Hastorf and Popper 1988; Greig 1989; Miller 1991; Nesbitt 1993a, in press; van Zeist and Casparie 1984). Originally, archaeobotanical services were often provided by botanists to archaeologists, but today archaeobotanists are archaeologists just as much as trench supervisors or specialists in ceramics and are usually working in archaeology or anthropology departments.

The earliest reports on plant remains from Turkey (indeed, one of the earliest anywhere) were published in the 1880s by the Berlin botanist L. Wittmack (1880, 1890, 1896) on crop seeds from Heinrich Schliemann's excavations at Troy and the Koertes' work at Bözhöyük. This pioneering effort did not result in any continuing interest, and few plant remains were collected until the 1950s, when the dynamic Danish archaeobotanist, Hans Helbaek, began working on Near Eastern sites. A stream of reports followed, on sites of every period, which established the framework on which all future work has been based. In Turkey, Helbaek worked with James Mellaart at Beycesultan, Çatal Hüyük, and Hacılar (Helbaek 1961, 1964, 1970), and with the Braidwoods on the Amuq plain (Helbaek 1960). In the late 1960s, Willem van Zeist from the Netherlands and Gordon Hillman from England began working in Turkey (Hillman 1972, 1978; van Zeist 1979/80; van Zeist and Bakker-Heeres 1975; 1982; van Zeist and Buitenhuis 1983). Although interest in archaeobotany has been strong since the 1960s, a shortage of trained staff was a major factor in limiting the number of excavations at which large-scale sampling was carried out. Even today, as archaeobotany becomes better integrated into university courses in archaeology, fewer than twenty archaeobotanists work in the Near East as a whole.

Archaeobotany in Practice

The archaeobotanist's work takes place in three arenas: in the field, in the laboratory, and at the computer. In the field, the initial tasks are to build a flotation machine and to supervise the collection of samples from the excavation trenches for flotation. Sampling strategy depends both on the nature of the excavated deposits, and the research questions posed for the site. When not engaged in flotation, the archaeobotanist will be found studying the local flora and talking to villagers about their crops and wild foods. Back in the laboratory, the time-consuming task of sorting the "flots" under a stereoscopic microscope begins. Each sample contains a mixture of different types of plant remains, including seeds and charcoal,

The Raw Materials of Archaeobotany

Ash heap outside a current-day house near Lake Van, eastern Turkey. Such middens are often found outside excavated houses. Resulting from the accumulation of dumping ashes, bones, and broken pots over many years, these are a valuable archaeological resource. *All photographs by Mark Nesbitt except as noted.*

Plant remains fall into two classes. *Macroremains* are large enough to be visible to the naked eye and include seeds and wood remains. *Microremains* must be viewed with a microscope and include pollen and phytoliths. The two classes enter the archaeological record in quite different ways and are sampled and interpreted differently.

Macroremains

In truly arid areas, such as the Egyptian desert, plant remains will often survive intact in archaeological deposits. However, in most of the Near East, including Turkey, winters are wet, and any plant materials will soon be consumed by animals or fall victim to rot. To survive, botanical remains must be in a biologically inert form that is not susceptible to decay. Charring is one of the most important routes to preservation. Seeds, wood, or other plant parts that come into contact with fire will often burn to ash, but much will not burn completely and ends up charred—black, but retaining much of its original dimensions and appearance. Although largely composed of carbon, other organic material does survive within, and lipids and DNA have both been successfully extracted from charred seeds (Brown, Allaby and Brown 1994; Brown et al. 1993; Hillman et al. 1993; McLaren, Evans and Hillman 1991). Residues of food and other organic substances can also be charred, and chemical analysis shows promise for identifying these (Heron and Evershed 1993; Mills and White 1989).

Contact with fire can occur in two ways: when houses burn down (a relatively common event in prehistory), or through the everyday disposal of household refuse into hearths and ovens, and the eventual disposal of their cinders into middens and pits—the garbage cans of antiquity. Obviously, there is a big difference in the type of samples that will be preserved by each of these routes, and this in turn will affect sampling strategies. In burnt destruction levels the contents of pots, silos, and other stores will be burnt *in situ* often well preserved by an overburden of fallen roof material. These primary deposits will easily be found in excavation of the debris resulting from the fire, and sampling simply involves recording their location and bagging the seeds. Household refuse is more complicated. As every household had at least one fireplace, the center for all cooking and heating activities, very large amounts of plant remains became charred and were incorporated into the archaeological record. Although ovens and hearths usually do contain some ashes, they were often cleaned out and their contents deposited elsewhere—in pits, in alleyways, or on the edge of settlements. As middens accumulated, ashes and other refuse became mixed with soil and decayed mudbrick. When excavated, this type of deposit often gives the misleading impression of sterile earth that does not contain plant remains. Here, flotation is essential to release charred plant remains from the soil matrix. Prior to the development of flotation techniques in the 1960s, it was often thought that plant remains did not survive except in destruction levels.

A wide range of plant materials can be preserved by charring, including seeds, chaff, tubers, straw, and wood.

Microremains

Pollen grains are tiny spores that fertilize the female part of the flower and are often distributed by wind or insects. The outer coat or exine of pollen is resistant to decay in anaerobic conditions such as in lake beds and bogs. Difference in the appearance of pollen grains allows their identification, usually to family or genus level. By examining the changing proportions of different pollen grains in cores from lake beds, changes in vegetation through time can be identified. Pollen analysis is an important tool for looking at vegetation on a regional scale (Bar-Yosef and Kra 1993; Bintliff and van Zeist 1982; van Zeist and Bottema 1991). Pollen grains survive poorly in typical archaeological deposits in the Near East and are therefore not usually sampled from archaeological contexts (Bottema 1975).

Phytoliths are silica bodies that form within certain plant cells. After plants die and decay, phytoliths are deposited in archaeological soils, from which they can be extracted in the laboratory. Phytolith analysis is a young field, but first results suggest this will be a useful tool once identification techniques are further developed (Mulholland, Rapp and Gifford 1982; Rapp and Mulholland 1992; Rosen 1987, 1989, 1991). Possible uses of phytolith analysis include the identification of plants under-represented in charred plant remains and, in conjunction with studies of soil micromorphology, studying the detailed histories of archaeological deposits (Matthews and Postgate 1994).

The Flotation Revolution

Flotation at Aşvan Kale, eastern Turkey in the early 1970s. One of the first flotation machines, its bulky design has been replaced by more compact flotation tanks that can easily be operated by one or two people. *Photo courtesy of Gordon Hillman.*

Flotation works on a simple principle: soil particles sink, charred plant remains float. The idea of immersing archaeological soil in water and floating off the plant remains into a sieve was pioneered in the mid-1960s in North America and by Hans Helbaek (1969) at Ali Kosh in Iran. However this flotation was carried out on a small-scale with buckets, and had a limited impact on the quantity of plant remains recovered. In the late 1960s the flotation machine was devised, by which large quantities of soil—up to 1000 liters—can be processed each day. Originally a cumbersome device that required several operators (French 1971), a version of this based on a 40-gallon oil drum (ubiquitous in the Near East) is now widely used (Williams 1973; Nesbitt 1995).

Water is pumped through a valve halfway down the tank. Once the tank is full of water, soil from an archaeological deposit is poured gently into the tank. As the lumps of soil disaggregate, silt drops to the bottom of the tank and plant remains float to the top and are carried by the water flow through a spout and into 1 mm and 0.3 mm sieves. The flot from each sample is wrapped in cloth and gently dried in the shade before bagging up for future study. A 1 mm plastic mesh (widely sold in Turkey as mosquito screen) lines the top half of the tank, and catches heavy items as they sink. This *heavy residue* will contain a range of bones and artifacts and offers an excellent check on their recovery from the site. At early or coastal sites the ability of the flotation machine to recover tiny bones from fish and wild animals and small artifacts such as microliths and beads is just as important as its role in collecting plant remains. The contents of the heavy residue are also a good indicator as to whether any of the plant remains are sinking—a particular problem with dense seeds such as nuts and pulses.

Charred seeds and charcoal flow out of the flotation tank into two sieves. Disaggregation of archaeological soil in water ensures that as little as possible of the fragile charred material is damaged during the recovery process.

The large capacity of the flotation machine means that a wide range of deposits can be sampled without slowing down excavation. It is important that enough soil is processed from a deposit, as the density of plant remains is often low. Soil volumes for a sample might range from 50 liters at a typical Bronze or Iron Age settlement mound to 500 or 1000 liters at a Palaeolithic or Neolithic site, where seed densities are much lower. The key ability of the flotation machine is that it achieves a good yield of material from virtually all sites. Furthermore, it is cheap (about $200 for the machine) and flexible. If water is in short supply, a recycling tank can be used. If electricity is not available, a petrol pump can be used. Any blacksmith can build a flotation machine, and they are long-lasting.

and these must be separated into categories and identified.

Identification works on the simple principle of comparing ancient, unknown seeds to modern, known seeds collected from carefully classified modern plants. The "seed reference collection," often numbering several thousand specimens, is the core of an archaeobotanical laboratory. Once the seeds have been named, counted, and the results entered onto a computer scoresheet, interpretation can finally begin. It is this step, when we move from the "laundry list" of names and numbers to what they mean about human behavior in the past, that is the most exciting and most challenging part of our work.

What Mean These Seeds?

Interpretation of plant remains from a burnt destruction level is relatively straightforward. Such deposits often come from crops cleaned for storage: for example, a silo of wheat grains or a jar of lentils (Jones et al. 1986). Interpretation hinges on accurate recording of each deposit, sometimes a tricky procedure in the tangle of ashes and collapsed roofs typical of a burnt level. For example, a single room burnt at Sardis by invading Persians in the mid-sixth century BCE was found to contain seven deposits of barley, two of bread wheat, one of chickpeas, and one of lentils. In some cases the seeds were found in their original jar, but most were probably stored in sacks that have not survived burning, leaving heaps of seeds on the floor. A group of garlic cloves was found at the base of a wall; it may have fallen from a hanging shelf. Overall the finds suggest a diet in which barley was most important, and a relatively small number of crops formed the staple foods. However such a deposit is only a snapshot of what was found in one room on one day.

Ethnoarchaeology

How do we bridge the gap between identifying seed assemblages from archaeological samples and deciding what these mean in terms of human behavior? Archaeobotanists are fortunate in being able to visit villages where traditional farming is still practiced, and where we can directly observe agricultural activities and their resulting effects on the material world. It is the focus on material culture that separates ethnoarchaeology from social anthropology: we cannot interview our prehistoric subjects, and we must therefore enable their material remains to speak for them (Jones 1983).

Current day farmers are a valuable source of information. These villagers in the Pontic mountains have excellent recall of agricultural practices from the days before tractors and chemical fertilizers.

In the early 1970s Gordon Hillman spent four excavation seasons at the village of Aşvan in southeast Turkey, destined to be submerged by the Keban dam in 1974. By observing farming activities, collecting samples of crops during processing, and talking to villagers, he was able to show that the composition of seed assemblages was diagnostic of the processing that farmers had undertaken (Hillman 1973, 1981, 1984a, 1984b, 1985). These processes are complex, ranging from husbandry activities such as irrigation and weeding, to the sequence of crop processing by which the plants growing in the field are harvested and prepared for cooking. The crop-processing sequence for cereals such as wheat and barley is a multi-phase process, involving threshing to break up the ears, winnowing, and a series of sievings. Each of these steps generates a distinctive waste by-product assemblage as well as the main crop component destined to pass to the next phase of processing.

A failure to appreciate the effects of crop-processing can lead to major misinterpretations. A simple example is the presence of weed seeds in a sample. Processing of a single sheaf of wheat would result in a final end-product—clean wheat grains—but also by-products composed of light weed seeds and chaff from winnowing; large, heavy weed seeds and chaff from sieving with a large mesh; and small weed seeds and chaff from fine sieving. It would be a mistake to interpret the lack of weed seeds in the end-product as meaning the original crop had no weed infestation, while it would also be wrong to regard the mixture of weed seeds and chaff in a sieving by-product to be typical of ancient diet.

Bulgur-making in progress. A seten is used to remove the bran from boiled wheat grains. The pressure of the vertical millstone on moistened grain causes the bran to slide off. We still know all too little about food preparation in antiquity. As food rarely enters the archaeological record, we must rely on interpreting food-related artifacts.

Archaeobotanists are using the ethnoarchaeological results from Hillman's work and that of later projects in Greece and elsewhere, combined with statistical techniques, to establish the nature of each of their samples before tackling wider questions of interpretation. Ethnoarchaeology has been used to look at other aspects of daily life such as the use of stone grinding tools and the functions of different types of ovens. Decision-making in traditional agriculture is another important line of enquiry, with implications for how we interpret changes in agricultural practices in the archaeological record. Wild plants are still an appreciated food supplement, and their use can give insights into the diet of pre-agrarian hunter-gatherers, as well as farmers' use of gathered plants as supplemental foods.

Rural life is changing fast in the Near East, and there is an urgent need for more ethnoarchaeological work while traditional crops and techniques are still in use.

In contrast, flotation samples from hearths, middens, pits, and other such contexts offer a much broader picture of plant use. This is because the ashes in these deposits usually accumulated from a number of activities. Sardis is a good example of how flotation samples from redeposited seed assemblages can give different but complementary results to seeds from burnt levels. Flotation of a series of unburnt floor levels adjacent to the burnt level showed that barley was present in all the samples, while bread wheat was present in sixty percent of samples. Compared to the burnt level, these results confirm the importance of barley but suggest bread wheat was under-represented in the burnt room. A further five crops were found in the flotation samples that were absent from the burnt level: millet, grass pea, bitter vetch, grape, almond, and flax. Additionally, weed seeds and chaff were present—highly informative classes of plant remains totally lacking from the cleaned storage samples. It is significant that garlic was not found in the flotation samples—herbs and spices rarely enter the archaeological record because they are used in small, carefully husbanded quantities. Such plant products are most often found in burnt levels and other exceptional contexts, such as shipwrecks (Haldane 1990, 1991, 1993).

Unlike a potsherd or coin, plant remains carry no obvious indication of their age and must be dated using evidence from careful stratigraphic excavation. The recent development of Accelerator Radiocarbon Dating has allowed individual seeds weighing a hundredth of a gram to be radiocarbon dated—a valuable check, especially with contentious early material (Harris 1986).

The Origins of Agriculture

One of the great successes of archaeobotany has been unravelling the early history of farming. The development of agriculture is a critical turning point in the development of human society (Harlan 1995; Harris and Hillman 1989). After the origin of agriculture, there is a rapid increase in population and spread of farming villages, and later on agriculture underpins the development of the first literate civilizations in the early cities of Mesopotamia. Yet, until recently, there was little hard evidence that could be used to explain this remarkable human invention. Plant remains or bones had hardly been collected from pre-agrarian or early agricultural sites.

Interdisciplinary, integrated research projects have been essential in understanding the dynamics of early agriculture and the preceding hunter-gatherer cultures. Botanists have demonstrated that the wild ancestors of crop plants such as wheat, barley, lentils, and chickpeas grow only in the Near East, showing that they must have been taken into domestication in this region (Zohary and Hopf 1993). Excavators, using radiocarbon dating, have shown that the earliest Neolithic villages—settlements based on farming—occur in the Near East, at about 10,000 years ago. As one moves away from the Near East, the earliest farming settlements are later in date—consistent with the spread of farming from its central area of origin. Archaeobotanists have shown that Near Eastern sites dating more recently than 10,000 years ago have domesticated crops, while earlier sites only have remains of gathered, wild plants (Miller 1992; van Zeist 1980).

In outline the picture is reasonably clear. In the upper Palaeolithic,

Excavation of a typical round house at Hallan Çemi, southeast Turkey. These solid architectural remains, combined with a rich material culture and biological evidence, point to year-round occupation of these pre-agrarian villages by foragers eating a wide range of wild plants and animals.

Fields of wild cereals in oak woodland near Hazar Lake in southeast Turkey. These dense stands of wild einkorn, wild emmer, and wild barley may resemble the landscape exploited by hunter-gatherers prior to the beginning of agriculture 10,000 years ago.

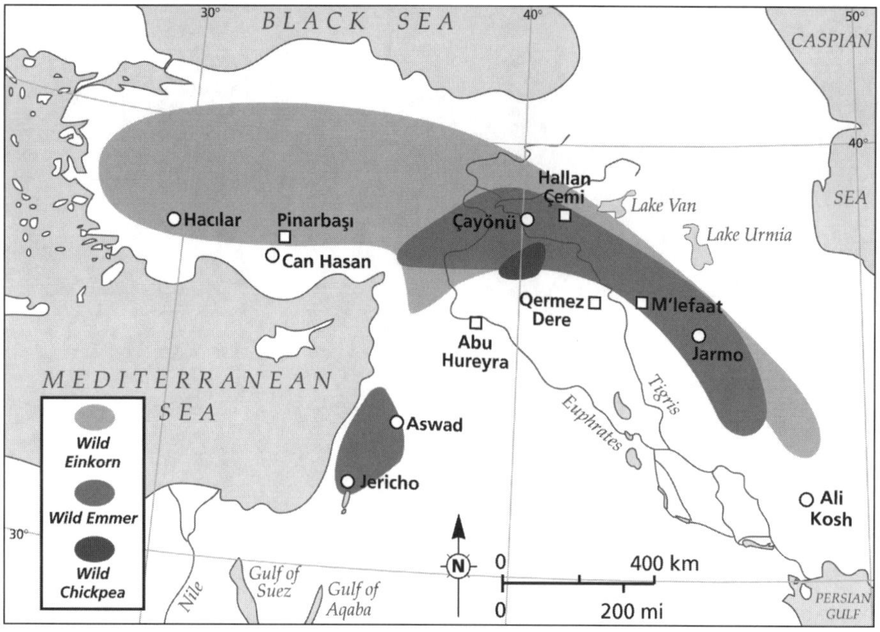

Early sites and the distribution of selected wild ancestors of crops. Squares indicate pre-agrarian sites; circles indicate early farming villages. The arc of low mountains that stretches from the Levant, through southern Turkey and northern Syria to Iran is rich in the wild ancestors of crops, and the origins of agriculture certainly lie in this area.

humans gathered the wild plants and hunted the wild animals of their environment. At a site in oak forest, such as Hallan Çemi on a tributary of the Tigris in southeast Turkey, the diet included wild almonds and *Pistacia* nuts, wild pulses, and the seeds of riverside plants such as club-rushes (*Scirpus maritimus*) and knotweed (*Polygonum*). A thick layer of charred fruits of a tumbleweed (*Gundelia tournefortii*) was also found, perhaps the remains of an unsuccessful attempt at extracting the oily fatty seeds (Rosenberg and Davis 1992; Rosenberg et al. 1998). At sites such as Abu Hureyra and M'lefaat farther to the south, in the steppe woodland of northern Syria and Iraq, fewer forest plants were used (Hillman, Colledge, and Harris 1989). Large quantities of wild cereals, wild pulses, and terebinth nuts (*Pistacia*) were collected, as well as an extremely diverse range of other plants—at Abu Hureyra from about 130 different species. Some of these hunter-gatherer villages contained well-built houses and were probably occupied year round.

About 10,000 years ago, somewhere within the "fertile crescent" that is so rich in these wild ancestors of crops, foragers began to collect and sow the seeds of wild plants they had previously simply gathered. During harvesting, the first farmers unconsciously imposed selection pressures on wild plants that led to domestication. Most importantly, crops lost their ability to disperse their seed without human intervention. Cereal ears, for example, remained intact at maturity rather than shattering and scattering the seeds. The advantage of such changes to farmers is obvious—seeds stay on the ear during harvesting, rather than falling to the ground (Hillman and Davies 1990; 1992).

It is still unclear exactly where in the Near East the first steps to agriculture were taken. Some of the wild ancestors of the "founder package" of crops that appears at most Neolithic sites grow all over the hilly flanks of the "fertile crescent;" some are more restricted. Wild barley, lentils, and peas are widespread all over the fertile crescent. Wild emmer wheat grows widely but is much more abundant in the Levant; wild einkorn wheat mainly grows in southern Turkey and adjacent areas; chickpea is restricted to a narrow region of southeast Turkey. Most likely, we will never know exactly where or over how wide an area of the Near East agriculture originated, as farming techniques probably spread very quickly, and crops would have been domesticated in different areas, quickly merging to form a founder "package" of Neolithic crops. It is also likely that the distribution of wild ancestors has changed with time. However, in view of the evidence for early settlement and its wealth of wild ancestors of crop plants, it is likely that Turkey played a crucial role in the origins of agriculture.

Why hunter-gatherers began farming is a topic of hot debate. In the two thousand years before farming began, global environmental changes occurred as the ice age came to an end. Pollen diagrams show that a wetter and warmer climate in the Near East led to the spread of forest into the steppic interior of Anatolia and other large land masses (van Zeist and Bottema 1991). It seems likely that these changes caused instability in existing hunter-gatherer life, perhaps leading to increased population, and that increased demand for food led to the first experiments in agriculture. A major barrier to a better understanding of this period is the paucity of known early sites. These are often low mounds that are difficult to locate by archaeological surveys. At present only two such sites from the period immediately preceding the Neolithic have been excavated in the interior of Anatolia: Pinarbaşı and Hallan Çemi. The situation is similar for the earliest Neolithic: a few more sites are known, but plant remains have been published from only one early farming village, Çayönü, dating between 7500–6000 BCE (van Zeist and de Roller 1991/92). Further advances in studying agricultural origins will hinge on finding more early sites and on ensuring that excavators undertake the full recovery of plant and animal remains.

Changing Crops, Changing Cultures

How should we interpret the waning and waxing fortunes of different crop species? Even on the broad scale of Turkey as a whole, major changes through time are apparent (Hubbard 1980). Are these simply chance variations, or can we relate these changes to wider economic patterns? Observation of farmers' decision making, whether in a Near Eastern village or on the North American prairies, shows that decisions on what is grown and how it is grown are directly linked to market forces—whether these are responses to consumers, or imposed by central government. Choice of crops is not a matter of chance, and it would not have been in the past. But how can we apply this insight to archaeological plant remains?

Einkorn wheat and emmer wheat make a good case study. These archaic cereals are distinct from most other wheats in having seeds enclosed by a tough husk, the glumes (Charles 1984; Harlan 1967; Samuel 1989; 1993). This characteristic means that vigorous pounding is required to release the seeds, but it also protects them from pest damage while in storage. Emmer and einkorn were among the Neolithic founder species, appearing at the earliest farming sites, and spreading west as far as the British Isles and east to India and beyond. Today these wheats are on the verge of extinction, their cultivation restricted to remote mountainous areas scattered across Europe, southwest Asia, India, and Ethiopia. Archaeobotanical evidence from Turkish sites shows that up to about 3000 BCE they are grown alongside other cereals such as macaroni and bread wheats and barley. However, at the beginning of the Early Bronze Age, about 3000 BCE, both emmer and einkorn wheat abruptly disappear from the archaeological record in southeast Turkey, never to reappear (van Zeist and Bakker-Heeres 1975; author's unpublished data from Aşvan).

Wild pea. A wide range of wild pulses are found at pre-agrarian sites, only a few of which were domesticated. The beginning of agriculture saw a narrowing of the food base from a hundred or more wild species to fewer than ten crops. *Photo courtesy of Ann Butler.*

Why did this happen?

Fortunately emmer and einkorn still grow in a few villages in the lush Pontic mountains of northern Turkey. I was able to travel to the Pontic mountains with Dr. Delwen Samuel, a specialist in the history and use of emmer wheat from Cambridge University, and to talk to farmers with first-hand knowledge of these archaic crops. We found that emmer and einkorn are still grown because they are uniquely resistant to fungal diseases such as stem rust that flourish in the wet, warm summers of the Pontic mountains. Emmer and einkorn are also prized because of their high quality as chicken feed and, for human food, as bulgur, a popular cracked wheat food. However today their area of cultivation is in steep decline, often restricted to one field in a village.

Are there any parallels between this steep decline now and that of the Early Bronze Age? Farmers told us that there were two main reasons why cultivation of bread wheat was increasing at the expense of emmer and einkorn. Firstly, government subsidized fertilizers were available and bread wheat responded better to these. Secondly, grain merchants would buy bread wheat, but were not interested in minority crops such as emmer and einkorn. Thus, even though bread wheat is susceptible to disease and fared poorly in their fields, it was better integrated into the modern cash economy.

Returning to the Early Bronze Age, in southeast Turkey this period is characterized by a large increase in settlement density and a shift from a landscape of small villages to a more hierarchical system with villages centered on large towns (Whallon 1979). A plausible hypothesis is that increasing demand from a larger, more urban population encouraged farmers to shift production to crops that responded better to increased manuring and that were easier to process once harvested, such as bread wheat and macaroni wheat. Ways of testing this idea are currently being explored, including

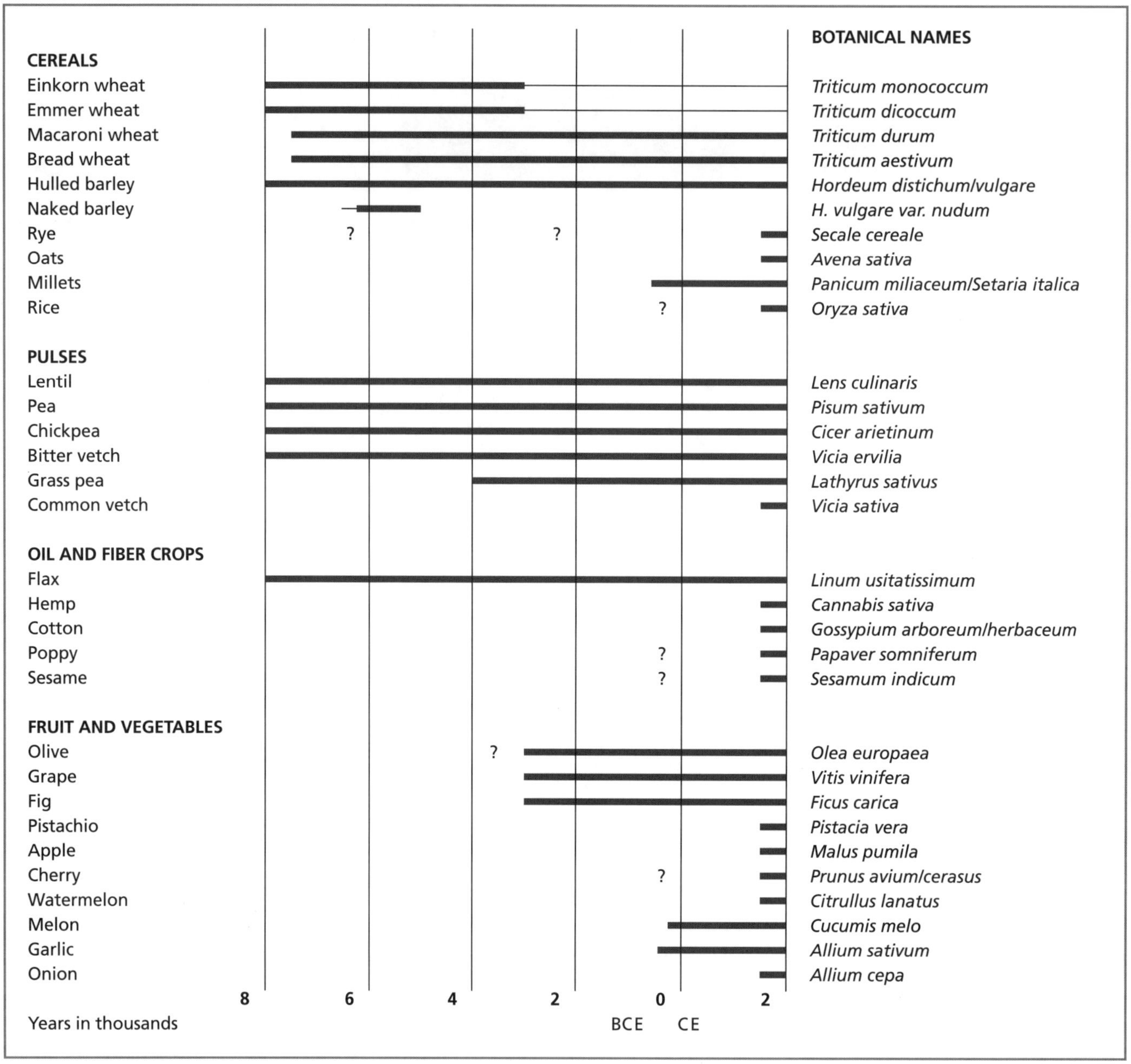

Timechart of major crops in Turkey. Thick lines indicate periods of widespread cultivation; thin lines represent cultivation limited to small areas. Question marks indicate likely periods of introduction. It is likely that cultivation of some crops began in the Classical or Byzantine periods, but this cannot be documented owing to lack of archaeobotanical data for these periods.

experimental cultivation of different wheats under different manuring conditions, analysis of weed seeds as indicators of changed husbandry practices, and searching for parallel evidence of intensification in animal husbandry.

Similar large scale changes in settlement patterns and economies over the Near East as a whole may account for the sudden appearance of fruits such as grape and fig as perennial crops at the beginning of the Early Bronze Age (Rivera Nunez and Walker 1989; Runnels and Hansen 1986; Stager 1985). For later periods, the sporadic recovery of archaeobotanical material means that patterns are less clear cut. However we have enough data to hint at major changes in agrarian practice: the introduction of summer season crops such as millets in the Iron Age (Nesbitt and Summers 1988); the possible arrival of fruits from further east such as cherry and peach in the Classical period; the still unresolved question of whether such major crops as cotton, rice, and opium poppy were cultivated in Anatolia prior to the Islamic period (Canard 1959; Faroqhi 1979; Watson 1983), and the post-Columbian diffusion of Mesoamerican crops (Andrews 1993). Linking changes in crop species and crop husbandry techniques to the major long-term changes in settlement patterns that can be identified by detailed archaeological surveys (e.g., Whallon 1979; Wilkinson 1988) is a major opportunity and challenge for archaeobotany.

The great range of topography in Anatolia makes for wide diversity in farming systems, ranging from the classic Mediterranean olive and vine cultivation of the coast, to the wheat and barley fields growing high on the Anatolian plateau (Erinç and Tunçdilek 1952). Much of our archaeobotanical evidence comes from central and eastern Turkey because that is where most prehistoric excavations have been carried out. As we learn more about ancient farming in western Turkey, with its Aegean contacts, and in regions at lower altitudes, the more diversity in ancient agriculture we can expect to find.

A Pontic Mountain village, near Kastamonu. A typical landscape of northern Turkey, with village houses constructed of wood. Emmer and einkorn wheats are grown here on an ever decreasing scale.

Similar changes have occurred in dietary preferences. Barley is overall the most common cereal in archaeobotanical deposits from Turkey. Today, we think of barley as an animal feed or for malt (Sams 1977), but there is good archaeological evidence for its role as human food. At Sardis and Gordion, pots of barley husks were found amongst the ashes of catastrophically burnt rooms dating to the mid-first millennium BCE. These are the by-product of making pearl barley by stripping off the grain's silicaceous, inedible husks. This tedious dehusking is not necessary for animal feed and must represent preparation of barley for human food. Allied with evidence from classical texts for the importance of barley as a human food, it is likely that ancient barley remains represent human food just as much as ancient wheat. Barley is sporadically noted as a food in Turkey in the present, but it is unclear when it ceased to be an important food for humans. The pulse group offers two further cases: bitter vetch and grass pea. Both are widely grown today in Turkey as fodder crops and, as their seeds contain toxins, they are not obvious human foods. Nonetheless, both are abundant in archaeobotanical samples from the Neolithic period onwards and have been found in kitchen contexts. It is highly likely that both were used for food. Provided they are adequately cooked and eaten as part of a mixed diet, both make good foodstuffs (van Zeist 1988). Clearly we must be careful not to project modern ideas of foodstuffs into the past in an uncritical manner.

Opium poppy. Still widely grown for morphine around Afyon, in western Turkey, and for poppy seeds all over Turkey. It is still unclear whether this crop plant was grown in Turkey before the Medieval period, although it is common in the Aegean Late Bronze Age.

Fuel

Fuel is an essential commodity for cooking and for heat during the long winter of the Anatolian plateau. Given the role of fire in preserving plant remains, it is not surprising that fuel remains make up a large part of most archaeobotan-

Piles of dung cakes, on the shores of Lake Van in eastern Turkey. These large stacks are an essential store of fuel for the winter. Archaeobotanical samples from excavation near the village show that dung was in use here in the Early Bronze Age—an indicator of deforestation.

ical samples. A wide range of plant products is still used as fuel in villages today. Where wood is available it is, naturally, the favored fuel (Horne 1982). Strict laws protect Turkey's forests, but brushwood can still be collected, and large areas of eastern Turkey are covered by *enerji orman* ("energy forest"), woodland of oaks coppiced for fuel. Small bushes and other woody plants, such as the tragacanth (*Astragalus*) in the Taurus mountains, are also collected.

However, in large areas of Turkey cutting and grazing have led to extensive deforestation, particularly in areas such as the central Anatolian plateau, where climatic conditions are rigorous (McNeill 1992; Willcox 1974; 1992). In these areas animal dung (Turkish *tezek*) is an important source of fuel. Dung of domestic animals is collected from stables and fields and buried in pits for several months. Over this time the dung becomes dry and odorless. When it is dug up, it is mixed with water and straw and molded into cakes that can be stacked up for use through the winter months. Dung cakes burn well and cleanly and are a favored fuel.

Today, the use of dung as fuel correlates closely with lack of woodland, and the presence of dung in archaeobotanical samples is therefore a useful indicator of ancient deforestation (Miller 1984; 1985; 1990; Miller and Smart 1984). Identification of dung in ancient samples is also important because seeds of grazed plants pass through the animal, end up in the dung and enter the archaeological record as charred seeds. This can contribute a significant number of seeds to archaeobotanical samples and results in a very different seed assemblage from that which is derived from crops and crop-cleaning.

Archaeology and Texts: the Case of Hittite ZIZ

There is a tendency for archaeologists working in historical periods, for which texts survive, to assume that the written sources already contain all the information they need. This has led to a real neglect of archaeobotanical or zooarchaeological recovery from sites in the Late Bronze Age onwards. Unfortunately, not only do the documents rarely contain the type of information we need for understanding the dynamics of farming economies, but translation of terms for crops is highly problematic.

For example, in the Hittite period many tens of thousands of tablets have been excavated at Boğazköy, the Hittite capital. Almost all of these deal with diplomacy, law, religion, or myth. Even if we had perfect understanding of these texts, they would offer us virtually no quantitative information on Hittite agriculture. In any case, translation of the Hittite crop terms has proved almost impossible. Philologists have, however, assumed that Sumerian words used as shorthand by Hittite scribes bore the same meaning as in Mesopotamia.

One of the most frequently used term for a crop is ZIZ, generally translated as emmer wheat in its original Mesopotamian context and assumed to mean the same in the Hittite texts (Gurney 1990; MacQueen 1986). Some years ago Hoffner (1974: 68–69) suggested that archaeobotanical data for the decline of emmer wheat before the Late Bronze Age meant that ZIZ must either refer to bread wheat or be a general term for wheat. Recent archaeobotanical analysis of samples from Kaman Kalehöyük, a Hittite town, confirms that emmer is present only in tiny amounts. Bread wheat is by far the most common wheat, supporting Hoffner's identification (Nesbitt 1993b).

While the Hittite texts do contain some interesting data on crop plants and agricultural techniques, they are best used in combination with archaeobotanical data. Exactly the same point applies to the Classical and Medieval periods (Humphreys 1991:284–308; Sallares 1991; Watson 1983). It is certain that new crops entered Turkey and major agricultural changes occurred, yet these are poorly documented in the historical texts. Only with the inception of the Turkish Republic in 1924 can documentary sources and ethnography be said to replace archaeobotanical data.

Conclusions

Archaeobotanical research in Turkey and the rest of the Near East is at an early stage. The small but ever increasing number of scholars in the field are still working on basic techniques of seed identification and questions of interpretation; few major assemblages of seeds have been recovered and even fewer published. Large-scale recovery programs for plant and animal remains are taking place at a mere seven or eight of the dozens of current excavations in Turkey.

The early stages in the development of a discipline are an exciting time; every fresh bag of plant remains from an excavation is likely to hold important new finds. I have tried to show how archaeobotany can illuminate every period of the human past; whether in prehistory, at the dawn of agriculture, or during the literate civilizations since the development of writing. Successful archaeobotanical analyses depend on a wide range of techniques: making decisions about sampling in the field; understanding the modern flora; identifying seeds under the microscope; and carrying out ethnographic work with current day farmers. Most of all, the future of archaeobotany hinges on the use of its ability to address major archaeological questions, as one of a range of techniques on a modern, integrated project.

Çayönü, an early agricultural village in southeast Turkey. The large scale of the famous "cell-plan" buildings is a good indicator of much higher productivity of agriculture compared to foraging. *Photo courtesy of Gordon Hillman.*

Bibliography

Andrews, J.
1993 Diffusion of Mesoamerican Food Complex to Southeastern Europe. *Geographical Review* 83:194–204.

Bar-Yosef, O. and Kra, R. S., eds.
1993 *Late Quaternary Chronology and Paleoclimates of the Eastern Mediterranean.* Tucson, AZ: Radiocarbon.

Bintliff, J. L. and van Zeist, W., eds.
1982 *Palaeoclimates, Palaeoenvironments and Human Communities in the Eastern Mediterranean Region in Later Prehistory.* BAR International Series 133. Oxford: British Archaeology Reports.

Bottema, S.
1975 The Interpretation of Pollen Spectra from Prehistoric Settlements (with Special Attention to Liguliflorae). *Palaeohistoria* 17:17–35.

Brown, T. A., Allaby, R. G., and Brown, K. A.
1994 DNA in Wheat Seeds from European Archaeological Sites. Pp. 37–45 in *Conservation of Plant Genes II: Utilization of Ancient and Modern DNA*, edited by R. P. Adams, J. S. Miller, E. M. Golenberg, and J. E. Adams. Monographs in Systematic Botany 48. St. Louis, MO: Missouri Botanical Garden.

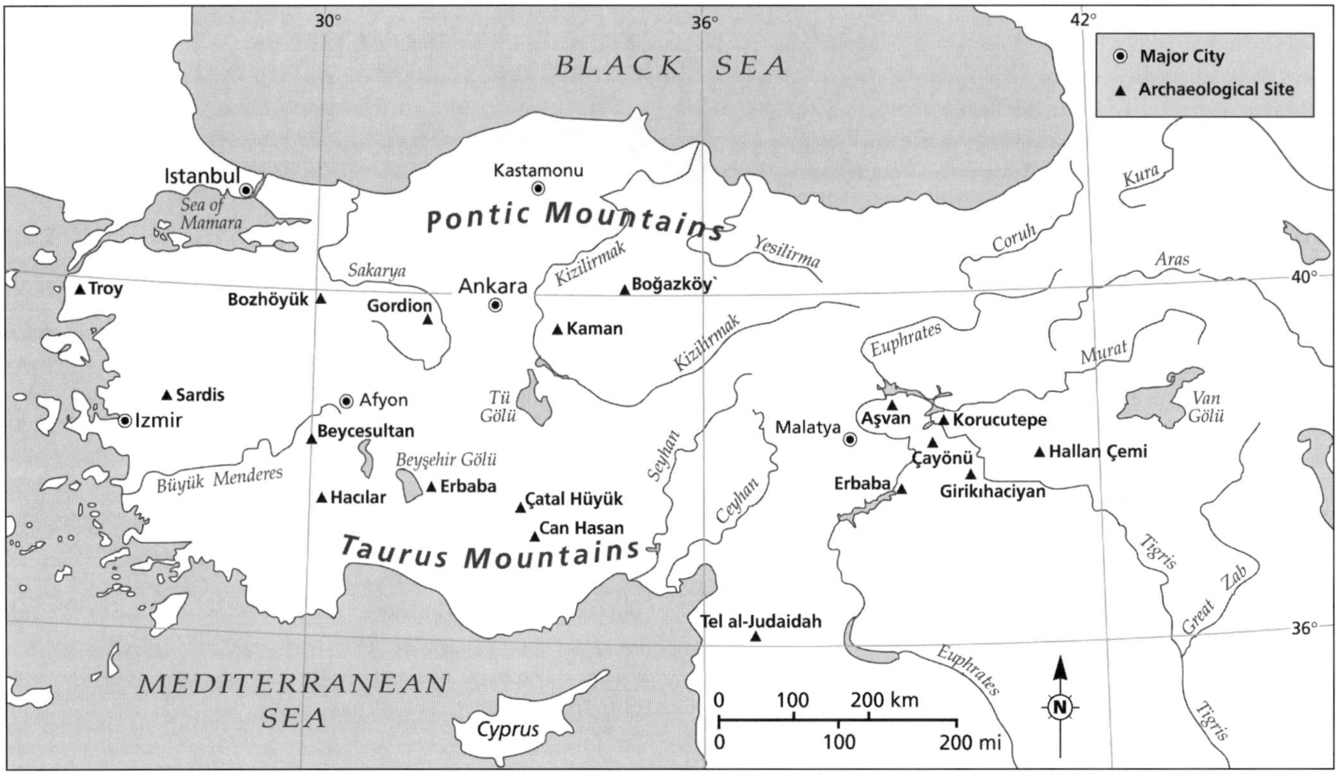

Sites with archaeobotanical reports that are mentioned in the text; note the concentrations of sites on the central plateau and southeast Turkey. These reflect biases in fieldwork, and complicate any attempt at comparing regional patterns.

Brown, T. A., Allaby, R. G., Brown, K. A., and Jones, M. K.
1993 Biomolecular Archaeology of Wheat: Past, Present and Future. *World Archaeology* 25:64–73.

Canard, M.
1959 Le riz dans le proche orient aux premiers siècles de l'Islam. *Arabica* 6:113–31.

Charles, M. P.
1984 Introductory Remarks on the Cereals. *Bulletin on Sumerian Agriculture* 1:17–31.

Erinç, S. and Tunçdilek, N.
1952 The Agricultural Regions of Turkey. *Geographical Review* 42:179–203.

Faroqhi, S.
1979 Notes on the Production of Cotton and Cotton Cloths in Sixteenth- and Seventeenth-Century Anatolia. *Journal of European Economic History* 8:405–17.

French, D. H.
1971 An Experiment in Water Sieving. *Anatolian Studies* 21:59–64.

Greig, J.
1989 *Archaeobotany*. Handbooks for Archaeologists 4. Strasbourg: European Science Foundation.

Gurney, O. R.
1990 *The Hittites*. 4th edition. London: Penguin.

Haldane, C. A. W.
1990 Shipwrecked Plant Remains. *Biblical Archaeologist* 53:55–60.
1991 Recovery and Analysis of Plant Remains from Some Mediterranean Shipwreck Sites. Pp. 213–23 in *New Light on Ancient Farming*, edited by J. M. Renfrew. Edinburgh: Edinburgh University Press.
1993 Direct Evidence for Organic Cargoes in the Late Bronze Age. *World Archaeology* 24:348–60.

Harlan, J. R.
1967 A Wild Wheat Harvest in Turkey. *Archaeology* 20:197–201.
1995 *The Living Fields: Our Agricultural Heritage*. Cambridge: Cambridge University Press.

Harris, D. R.
1986 Plant and Animal Domestication and the Origins of Agriculture: the Contribution of Radiocarbon Accelerator Dating. Pp. 5–21 in *Archaeological Results from Accelerator Dating*, edited by J. A. J. Gowlett and R. E. M. Hedges. Oxford University Committee for Archaeology Monograph 11. Oxford: Oxford University Committee for Archaeology.

Harris, D. R. and Hillman, G. C.
1989 *Foraging and Farming: The Evolution of Plant Exploitation*. London: Unwin Hyman.

Hastorf, C. A. and Popper, V. S., eds.
1988 *Current Paleoethnobotany: Analytical Methods and Cultural Interpretations of Archaeological Plant Remains*. Chicago: University of Chicago.

Helbaek, H.
1960 Appendix II. Cereals and Grasses in Phase A (Hassuna period). Pp. 540–43 in *Excavations in the Plain of Antioch I*, edited by R. J. Braidwood and L. Braidwood. Oriental Institute Publications 56. Chicago: University Press.
1961 Late Bronze Age and Byzantine Crops at Beycesultan in Anatolia. *Anatolian Studies* 11:77–97.
1964 First Impressions of the Çatal Höyük Plant Husbandry. *Anatolian Studies* 14:121–23.
1969 Appendix I. Plant Collecting, Dry-Farming, and Irrigation Agriculture in Prehistoric Deh Luran. Pp. 383–426, pl. 40–41 in *Prehistory and Human Ecology of the Deh Luran Plain. An Early Village Sequence from Khuzistan, Iran*, edited by F. Hole, K. V. Flannery, and J. A. Neely. Memoirs of the Museum of Anthropology 1. Ann Arbor, MI: University of Michigan.

1970. The Plant Husbandry of Hacılar. Pp. 189–244 in *Excavations at Hacılar*, edited by J. Mellaart. Edinburgh: University Press.

Heron, C. and Evershed, R. P.
1993 The Analysis of Organic Residues and the Study of Pottery Use. Pp. 247–84 in *Archaeological Method and Theory 5*, edited by M. B. Schiffer. Tucson, AZ: University of Arizona.

Hillman, G. C.
1972 The Plant Remains. Pp. 182–88 in *Papers in Economic Prehistory*, edited by E. S. Higgs. Cambridge: Cambridge University Press.
1973 Agricultural Resources and Settlement in the Aşvan Region. *Anatolian Studies* 23:217–40.
1978 On the Origins of Domestic Rye-Secale cereale: The Finds from Aceramic Can Hasan III in Turkey. *Anatolian Studies* 28:157–74.
1981 Reconstructing Crop Husbandry Practices from Charred Remains of Crops. Pp. 123–62 in *Farming Practice in British Prehistory*, edited by R. Mercer. Edinburgh: Edinburgh University Press.
1984 Interpretation of Archaeological Plant Remains: The Application of Ethnographic Models from Turkey. Pp. 1–41 in *Plants and Ancient Man*, edited by W. van Zeist and W. A. Casparie. Rotterdam: Balkema.
1984 Traditional Husbandry and Processing of Archaic Cereals in Modern Times: Part I, the Glume-Wheats. *Bulletin on Sumerian Agriculture* 1:114–52.
1985 Traditional Husbandry and Processing of Archaic Cereals in Modern Times: Part II, the Free-Threshing Cereals. *Bulletin on Sumerian Agriculture* 2:1–31.

Hillman, G. C., Colledge, S. M., and Harris, D. R.
1989 Plant Food Economy during the Epipalaeolithic Period at Tell Abu Hureyra, Syria: Dietary Diversity, Seasonality, and Modes of Exploitation. Pp. 240–68 in *Foraging and Farming: the Evolution of Plant Exploitation*, edited by D. R. Harris and G. C. Hillman. London: Unwin and Hyman.

Hillman, G. C. and Davies, M. S.
1990 Measured Domestication Rates in Wild Wheats and Barley under Primitive Cultivation, and their Archaeological Implications. *Journal of World Prehistory* 4:157–222.
1992 Domestication Rate in Wild Wheats and Barley under Primitive Cultivation: Preliminary Results and Archaeological Implications of Field Measurements of Selection Coefficient. Pp. 113–58 in *Préhistoire de l'agriculture: nouvelles approches expérimentales et ethnographiques*, edited by P. C. Anderson. Monographie du Centre de Recherches Archéologiques 6. Paris: Éditions du CNRS.

Hillman, G. C., Wales, S., McLaren, F. S., Evans, J., and Butler, A.
1993 Identifying Problematic Remains of Ancient Plant Foods: A Comparison of the Role of Chemical, Histological and Morphological Criteria. *World Archaeology* 25:94–121.

Hoffner, H. A.
1974 *Alimenta Hethaeorum: Food Production in Hittite Asia Minor*. American Oriental Series 55. New Haven, Conn.: American Oriental Society.

Horne, L.
1982 Fuel for the Metal Worker. *Expedition* 25:6–13.

Hubbard, R. N. L. B.
1980 Development of Agriculture in Europe and the Near East: Evidence from Quantitative Studies. *Economic Botany* 34:51–67.

Humphreys, R. S.
1991 *Islamic History: A Framework for Inquiry*. London: I.B. Tauris.

Jones, G.
1983 The Ethnoarchaeology of Crop Processing: Seeds of a Middle-Range Methodology. *Archaeological Review from Cambridge* 2:17–24.

Jones, G., Wardle, K. A., Halstead, P., and Wardle, D.
1986 Crop Storage at Assiros. *Scientific American* 254(3):84–91.

McLaren, F. S., Evans, J., and Hillman, G. C.
1991 Identification of Charred Seeds from S.W. Asia. Pp. 797–806 in *Archaeometry '90: Proceedings of the 26th International Symposium on Archaeometry, Heidelberg, 1990*, edited by E. Pernicka and G. Wagner. Basel: Birkhäuser.

McNeill, J. R.
1992 *The Mountains of the Mediterranean World: An Environmental History*. Cambridge: Cambridge University Press.

Macqueen, J. G.
1986 *The Hittites and their Contemporaries in Asia Minor*. London: Thames and Hudson.

Matthews, W. and Postgate, J. N. with Payne, S., Charles, M. P., and Dobney, K.
1994 The Imprint of Living in an Early Mesoptamian City: Questions and Answers. Pp. 171–212 in *Whither Environmental Archaeology*, edited by R. Luff and P. Rowley-Conwy. Oxford: Oxbow.

Miller, N. F.
1984 The Use of Dung as Fuel: An Ethnographic Example and an Archaeological Application. *Paléorient* 10:71–79.
1985 Paleoethnobotanical Evidence for Deforestation in Ancient Iran: A Case Study of Urban Malyan. *Journal of Ethnobiology* 5:1–19.
1990 Clearing Land for Farmland and Fuel: Archaeobotanical Studies of the Ancient Near East. Pp. 71–78 in *Economy and Settlement in the Near East: Analyses of Ancient Sites and Materials*, edited by N. F. Miller. Masca Research Papers in Science and Archaeology, Supplement to Volume 7. Philadelphia, PA: University Museum.
1991 The Near East. Pp. 133–60 in *Progress in Old World Palaeoethnobotany*, edited by W. van Zeist, K. Wasylikowa, and K.-E. Behre. Rotterdam: Balkema.
1992 The Origins of Plant Cultivation in the Near East. Pp. 39–58 in *The Origins of Agriculture: An International Perspective*, edited by C.W. Cowan and P. J. Watson. Washington, D.C.: Smithsonian.

Miller, N. F. and Smart, T. L.
1984 Intentional Burning of Dung as Fuel: A Mechanism for the Incorporation of Charred Seeds into the Archaeological Record. *Journal of Ethnobiology* 4:15–28.

Mills, J. and White, R.
1989 The Identity of the Resins from the Late Bronze Age Shipwreck at Ulu Burun (Kaş). *Archaeometry* 31:37–44.

Mulholland, S. C., Rapp, G., and Gifford, J. A.
1982 Phytoliths. Pp. 117–37 in *Troy: The Archaeological Geology*, edited by G. F. Rapp and J. A. Gifford. Supplementary Monograph 4. Princeton: University Press.

Nesbitt, M.
1993a The Archaeobotany of Turkey: A Review. Pp. 329–50 in *Proceedings of the Fifth OPTIMA Conference, Istanbul 1986*, edited by H. Demiriz and D. Phitos. Istanbul: Istanbul University.
1993b Ancient Crop Husbandry at Kaman-Kalehöyük: 1991 Archaeobotanical Report. Pp. 75–97 in *Essays on Anatolian Archaeology*, edited by T. Mikasa. Bulletin of the Middle Eastern Culture Center in Japan 7. Wiesbaden: Harrassowitz.
1995 Recovery of Archaeological Plant Remains at Kaman-Kalehöyük. In *Bulletin of the Middle Eastern Culture Center in Japan 8*. Wiesbaden: Otto Harrassowitz.
in press Archaeobotany. In *The Archaeology of Anatolia: An Encyclopedia*, edited by K. Sams.

Nesbitt, M and Summers, G. D.
1988 Some Recent Discoveries of Millet (Panicum miliaceum L. and Setaria italica [L.] P. Beauv.) at Excavations in Turkey and Iran. *Anatolian Studies* 38:85–97.

Rapp, G. and Mulholland, S. C., eds.
1992 *Phytolith Systematics: Emerging Issues.* New York: Plenum.

Rivera Nunez, D. and Walker, M. J.
1989 A Review of Palaeobotanical Findings of Early Vitis in the Mediterranean and of the Origins of Cultivated Grape-Vines, with Special Reference to New Pointers to Prehistoric Exploitation in the Western Mediterranean. *Review of Palaeobotany and Palynology* 61:205–37.

Rosen, A. M.
1987 Phytolith Studies at Shiqmim. Pp. 243–49, pl.8.1–8.3 in *Shiqmim I: Studies Concerning Chalcolithic Societies in the Northern Negev Desert*, edited by T. E. Levy. BAR International Series 356. Oxford: British Archaeology Reports.
1989 Microbotanical Evidence for Cereals in Neolithic levels at Tel Teo and Yiftahel in the Galilee, Israel. Mitekufat Haeven (*Journal of the Israel Prehistoric Society*) 22:68–77.
1991 Phytoliths as Indicators of Ancient Irrigation Farming. Pp. 281–87 in *Préhistoire de l'agriculture: nouvelles approches expérimentales et ehnographiques*, edited by P. C. Anderson. Monographie du Centre de Recherches Archéologiques 6. Paris: Éditions du CNRS.

Rosenberg, M. and Davis, M.
1992 Hallan Çemi Tepesi, an Early Aceramic Neolithic site in Eastern Anatolia: Some Preliminary Observations Concerning Material Culture. *Anatolica* 18:1–18.

Rosenberg, M., Nesbitt, M., Redding, R., and Peasnall, B.L.
1998 Hallan Çemi, Pig Husbandry, and Post-Pleistocene Adaptations along the Taurus-Zagros Arc. *Paléorient*, 24(1):25–41.

Runnels, C. N. and Hansen, J. M.
1986 The Olive in the Prehistoric Aegean: The Evidence for Domestication in the Early Bronze Age. *Oxford Journal of Archaeology* 5:299–308.

Sallares, J. R.
1991 *The Ecology of the Ancient Greek World.* London: Duckworth.

Sams, G. K.
1977 Beer in the City of Midas. *Archaeology* 30:108–15.

Samuel, D. J.
1989 Their Staff of Life: Initial Investigations on Ancient Egyptian Bread Baking. Pp. 253–90 in *Amarna Reports V*, edited by B. J. Kemp. London: Egypt Exploration Society.
1993 Ancient Egyptian Cereal Processing: Beyond the Artistic Record. *Cambridge Archaeological Journal* 3:276–83.

Stager, L. E.
1985. The First Fruits of Civilisation. Pp. 172–88 in *Palestine in the Bronze and Iron Ages: Papers in Honour of Olga Tufnell*, edited by J. N. Tubb. Occasional Publication 11. London: Institute of Archaeology.

Watson, A. M.
1983 *Agricultural Innovation in the Early Islamic World: The Diffusion of Crops and Farming Techniques, 700–1100.* Cambridge: Cambridge University Press.

Whallon, R.
1979 *An Archaeological Survey of the Keban Area of East Central Turkey.* Memoirs of the Museum of Anthropology, University of Michigan 11. Ann Arbor: Museum of Anthropology.

Wilkinson, T. J.
1990 *Town and Country in Southeastern Anatolia. Volume I. Settlement and Land Use at Kurban Höyük and Other Sites in the Lower Karababa Basin.* Oriental Institute Publications, 109. Chicago: Oriental Institute of the University of Chicago.

Willcox, G. H.
1974 A History of Deforestation as Indicated by Charcoal Analysis of Four Sites in Eastern Anatolia. *Anatolian Studies* 24:117–33.
1992 Timber and Trees: Ancient Exploitation in the Middle East: Evidence from Plant Remains. *Bulletin on Sumerian Agriculture* 6:1–31.

Williams, D.
1973 Flotation at Siraf. *Antiquity* 43:288–92.

Wittmack, L.
1880 Antike Samen aus Troja und Peru. *Monatsschrift des Vereines zur Beförderung des Gartenbaues in den Königlich Preussischen Staaten und der Gesellschaft der Gartenfreunde Berlins* 23:120–21.
1890 Samen aus den Ruinen von Hissarlik. *Zeitschrift für Ethnologie* 22:614–20.
1896 Untitled. [Prehistoric seeds from Bözhöyük]. *Sitzungsbericht der Gesellschaft Naturforschender Freunde zu Berlin* 3:27–30.

van Zeist, W.
1979/80 Plant Remains from Girikihacıyan, Turkey. *Anatolica* 7:75–89.
1980 Aperçu sur la diffusion des végétaux cultivés dans la région méditerranéenne. Pp. 129–45 in *La mise en place, l'evolution et la caractérisation de la flore et de la végétation circumméditerranéenne.* Naturalia Monspeliensia, Hors Série. Montpellier: Colloque de la Fondation L.Emberger.
1988 Some Aspects of Early Neolithic Plant Husbandry in the Near East. *Anatolica* 15:49–67.

Mark Nesbitt studied at the Institute of Archaeology, University College London. He has spent time as a Research Fellow of the British Institute of Archaeology at Ankara. Nesbitt has worked as an archaeobotanist at sites in Turkey, Iraq, Bahrain, and Turkmenistan. His research interests include early agricultural and pre-agrarian use of plants, the ethnoarchaeology of wild and cultivated foods, and the study of long-term agricultural change in the Near East.

van Zeist, W. and Bakker-Heeres, J. A. H.
1975 Prehistoric and Early Historic Plant Husbandry in the Altınova Plain, Southeast Turkey. Pp. 221–57 in *Korucutepe, Final Report, Volume 1*, edited by M. N. van Loon. Amsterdam: North Holland.

van Zeist, W. and Bottema, S.
1991 *Late Quaternary Vegetation of the Near East.* Beihefte zum Tübinger Atlas, Reihe A, 18. Tübingen: Reichert.

van Zeist, W. and Buitenhuis, H.
1983 A Palaeobotanical Study of Neolithic Erbaba, Turkey. *Anatolica* 10:47–89.

van Zeist, W. and Casparie, W. A., eds.
1984 *Plants and Ancient Man: Studies in Palaeoethnobotany.* Rotterdam: Balkema.

van Zeist, W. and de Roller, G. J.
1991/92 The Plant Husbandry of Aceramic Çayönü, SE Turkey. *Palaeohistoria* 33/34:65–96.

Zohary, D. and Hopf, M.
1993 *Domestication of Plants in the Old World.* Second Edition. Oxford: Clarendon Press.

Urban Planning and the Archaeology of Society at Early Bronze Age Titriş Höyük

By Timothy Matney

For decades, scholars worked with a model of social complexity that viewed the northern plains of Syria, Iraq, and the comparable region of southeastern Anatolia (hereafter "Syro-Anatolia") as a cultural backwater peripheral to the more advanced civilization of southern Mesopotamia during the Early Bronze Age (ca. 3200–2000 BCE). This perspective has recently started to change as a result of spectacular finds of administrative or elite goods in Syria, e.g., at Tell Mardikh (Matthiae 1980), Tell Mozan (Buccellati and Kelly-Buccellati 1988), Tell Chuera (Orthmann 1986), and most recently at Tell Banat (Porter and McClellan 1996). Moreover, increasing evidence from southeastern Turkey in the third millennium BCE suggests that Syro-Anatolia, rather than a peripheral backwater, was a center of indigenous development where vigorous local polities thrived in a social milieu of marked internationalism.

One such local polity was Titriş Höyük in the Sanliurfa province of southeastern Turkey, a small mid-late Early Bronze Age (EBA) city state that has been the subject of six seasons (1991–1996) of archaeological survey and excavation (Algaze et al. 1992; Algaze and Misir 1994, 1995; Algaze et al. 1995; Matney and Algaze 1995). Within this context of internationalism, one of the principal research questions addressed by the excavations at Titriş Höyük has been the role of the southern Mesopotamian polities in influencing the urbanization process of their northern neighbors in the EBA. This chapter continues the assessment—started in an earlier publication (Matney and Algaze 1995)—of the relationship between the indigenous EBA polities of Syro-Anatolia and those of southern Mesopotamia.

Depas cup (TH11855) found in 1995 excavations. This Troy II style vessel exemplifies the imported goods that demonstrate interregional communications at Titriş.

Traditionally, archaeologists exploring cross-cultural relationships between regions have used the presence of imported raw materials and trade goods to demonstrate far-flung economic and political connections. This approach has been successful at Titriş, where materials from the Aegean, southern Mesopotamian, eastern Anatolian, and Transcaucasian regions found at Titriş suggest that the site served as an important trading station within an extensive exchange network that moved goods and commodities across thousands of kilometers during the third millennium BCE. More specifically, contacts with southern Mesopotamia appear in a number of glyptic or inscribed objects uncovered at Titriş. Two cylinder seals found in good domestic contexts and one badly preserved seal impression showing an ED III contest scene come from the current excavations. Additionally, two contest scene cylinder seals were discovered in partially plundered graves excavated in 1981 by Hauptmann (Algaze et al. 1992:47; Hauptmann 1993). A one *mana* weight—now in the Sanliurfa Museum—inscribed in Old Akkadian with the name of an official of the king Shu-durul, the penultimate ruler of the Agade dynasty, is also reported to have come from Titriş. Titriş also produced three Karaz ware vessels, characteristic of sites in eastern Anatolia and the Caucasus, found in a cache during magnetometry test sounding at the site in 1994 (Algaze et al. 1995:fig. 37). Similarly, numerous small marble violin-shaped figurines, usually associated with the Aegean, western Anatolia, and the eastern Mediterranean, have been found in mid-EBA contexts and burials at the site (e.g., Algaze et al. 1992:fig. 17; Algaze et al. 1995:fig. 35). Also from the same regions, or possibly from southwestern Anatolia, are three Troy II style *depas* vessels emerged from late EBA contexts. Two of the *depas* vessels were associated with living surfaces in private residences and one turned up within a late EBA burial associated with houses.[1]

Important as the evidence outlined above may be in terms of the breadth and extent of commercial contacts at Titriş Höyük, a second category of data—architecture—can also provide clues as to the cultural interaction spheres of Titriş and of southern Mesopotamian houses. These correlations are vital to viewing southeastern Turkey as an integrated element of a wider cosmopolitan world in the Early Bronze Age. While trade goods demonstrate a certain level of cultural contact, similarities in architectural form suggest much stronger ideological ties and provide clues to the impact of the societies of southern Mesopotamia on the indigenous societies of Syro-Anatolia. Unlike the movement of luxury materials and locally-unavailable raw materials, the importation of canons of architectural design strikes at the core of many social behaviors.

Viewing architecture as both a product of human invention and construction as well as a powerful influence on subsequent human behavior (following Giddens' structuration theory in the study of architecture), means the adoption of building plans from distant regions involves not only the importation of artifacts, materials, and technology, but also the diffusion and adoption of powerful structural and ideological mechanisms for influencing the way individuals relate to one another and to the outside world (Giddens 1979; see Donley-Reid 1990 for a particularly good elaboration of the role of structuration theory). Architecture structures the space used in domestic and extra-domestic contexts, creating rooms, corridors, closets, stairs, and other work spaces and corridors of movement, and thereby strongly influences subsequent behavior. Appropriate behavior is cued contextually from the architecture itself, from non-portable features within the architecture and from the portable artifacts used to transform an empty construction into a working environment.

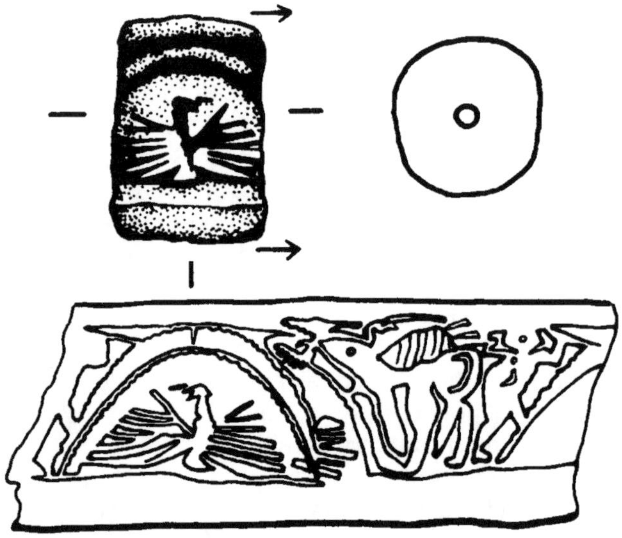

A Mesopotamian-style cylinder seal (TH8537) found in a domestic context.

The adoption of a specific ground plan or a set of architectural design elements signifies more than the borrowing of an aesthetic canon. The placement, size, and ordering of a building reinforces and, in some ways, even dictates appropriate action. The modern traveler to rural southeastern Turkey who has spent time being entertained in the formal reception room—placed adjacent to the entrance of many traditional homes—will be fully aware of the strength of such structuring principles. In this way, the very ordering of day-to-day existence would be affected by cultural contact and the borrowing of architectural traditions as a result of cultural contact. The *nature* of interregional connections suggested by the adoption of specific architectural conventions is markedly different than if the connections were illustrated simply by the presence of a few high-status trade goods or a few aesthetic motifs.

This chapter is divided into four parts. First, it offers a brief description of the archaeological site of Titriş Höyük and the excavations conducted there since 1991, with an emphasis on two seasons (1994–1995) that have focused on domestic architecture (also see note 2). Second, it presents data from the Outer Town of Titriş demonstrating concepts of urban planning at the site in the late Early Bronze Age. Third comes an outline of architectural parallels with the site of Tell Asmar in the Diyala Valley of Iraq intended to demonstrate the existence of widely shared conceptions about the ordering of space and its use, linking the Syro-Anatolian plains and southern Mesopotamia. Finally, the chapter suggests some social implications of urban planning canons in late EBA contexts at Titriş.

Project Background

Early Bronze Age Setting

Across ancient southwestern Asia, the Early Bronze Age was a time of tremendous social change. By the second half of the third millennium BCE in northern Syria, northern Iraq, and southeastern Turkey, one of the most significant changes was the appearance of numerous small city-states comprised of subsidiary towns and villages centered around larger regional capitals. Over the past three decades, excavations have been conducted at a number of these regional capitals, e.g., Tell Mardikh, Tell es-Sweyhat (Zettler 1996), Tell Leilan (Weiss 1983, 1986, 1990), Tell Brak (Oates and Oates 1989), Kazane (Wattenmaker and Misir 1994), and Tell Mozan (Buccellati and Kelly-Buccellati 1988), providing ample evidence for considerable cultural sophistication in the region during the third millennium BCE.

Location of Titriş

The archaeological site of Titriş Höyük represents one of these Early Bronze Age regional capitals. Located approximately 45 km north of the modern city of Sanliurfa alongside the Tavuk Cay, a small seasonal tributary of the Euphrates River in southeastern Turkey, Titriş occupied a central position in a small agricultural plain within a lowland from northern Mesopotamia and the fertile Harran Plains of modern-day Turkey northwest across the Euphrates ford at Samsat and into southwestern and central Anatolia. Regional survey by Wilkinson has shown that the agricultural land surrounding Titriş was probably insufficient to support the population of the city at its maximum size, about 43 ha (Wilkinson 1994). From this it may be concluded that the emergence of the city within an agriculturally peripheral area was due, at least in part, to its location along this important overland route (Algaze et al. 1992, 1995; Matney and Algaze 1995; Wilkinson 1990).

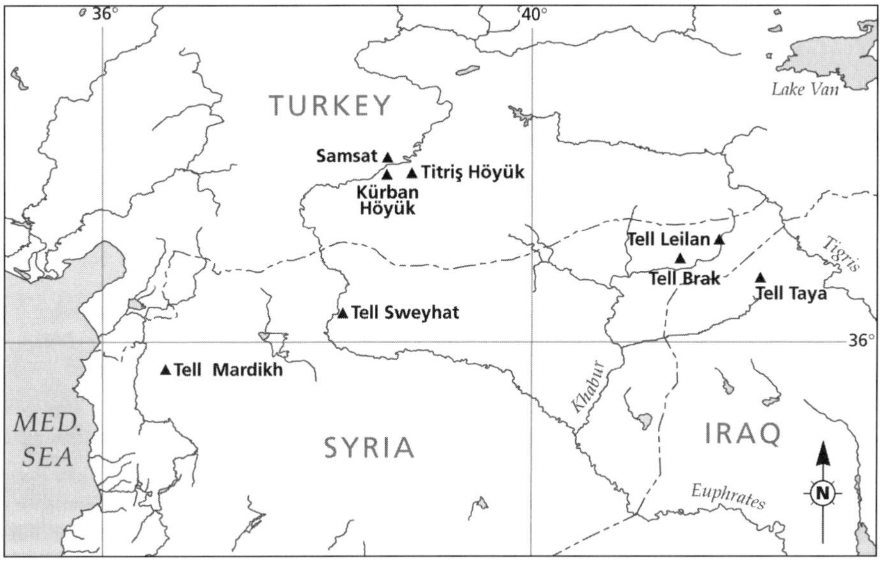

Early Bronze Age sites mentioned in the text.

Morphology of Titriş

Initial archaeological investigations of the site revealed the presence of five distinct morphological areas that formed the city at its apogee: a 22 m high High Mound; two long rises adjacent to the High Mound following the course of the Tavuk Çay, referred to collectively as the Lower Town; an extensive Outer Town located due north of the High Mound and Lower Town; a Suburb area defined by patchy surface scatters of artifacts outside the limits of the Outer and Lower Towns; and an Extramural Cemetery located about 400 m northwest of the Outer Town. The city proper was delineated by the course of the Tavuk Çay on the south, a now-dry *wadi* running the length of the northern and western limits of the city and on the east by a city wall and defensive ditch which has been partially excavated in two places (Algaze et al. 1995).

Titriş Settlement History

Titriş is a multi-period site. Occupation on the High Mound itself covers a long span of time from the beginnings of the EBA through the Medieval period (Algaze et al. 1992:39–40). Middle Bronze Age, Iron Age, Classical, and Medieval occupation, however, is largely limited to the High Mound while the other areas of the site (i.e., the Lower and Outer Towns, Suburbs and Cemetery) date almost exclusively to the mid-late EBA. Our current reconstruction is that around 2600–2500 BCE, the small EBA settlement of Titriş underwent an exponential growth, expanding from a village of few hectares to a city of 43 ha. After a prosperous period of some three to four hundred years, Titriş appears to have collapsed as a regional center in the Upper Euphrates basin and never again achieved urban status.

Excavations in the Outer Town sector of the city allow us to distinguish two architectural building and ceramic phases within this time frame: a mid-EBA (corresponding to

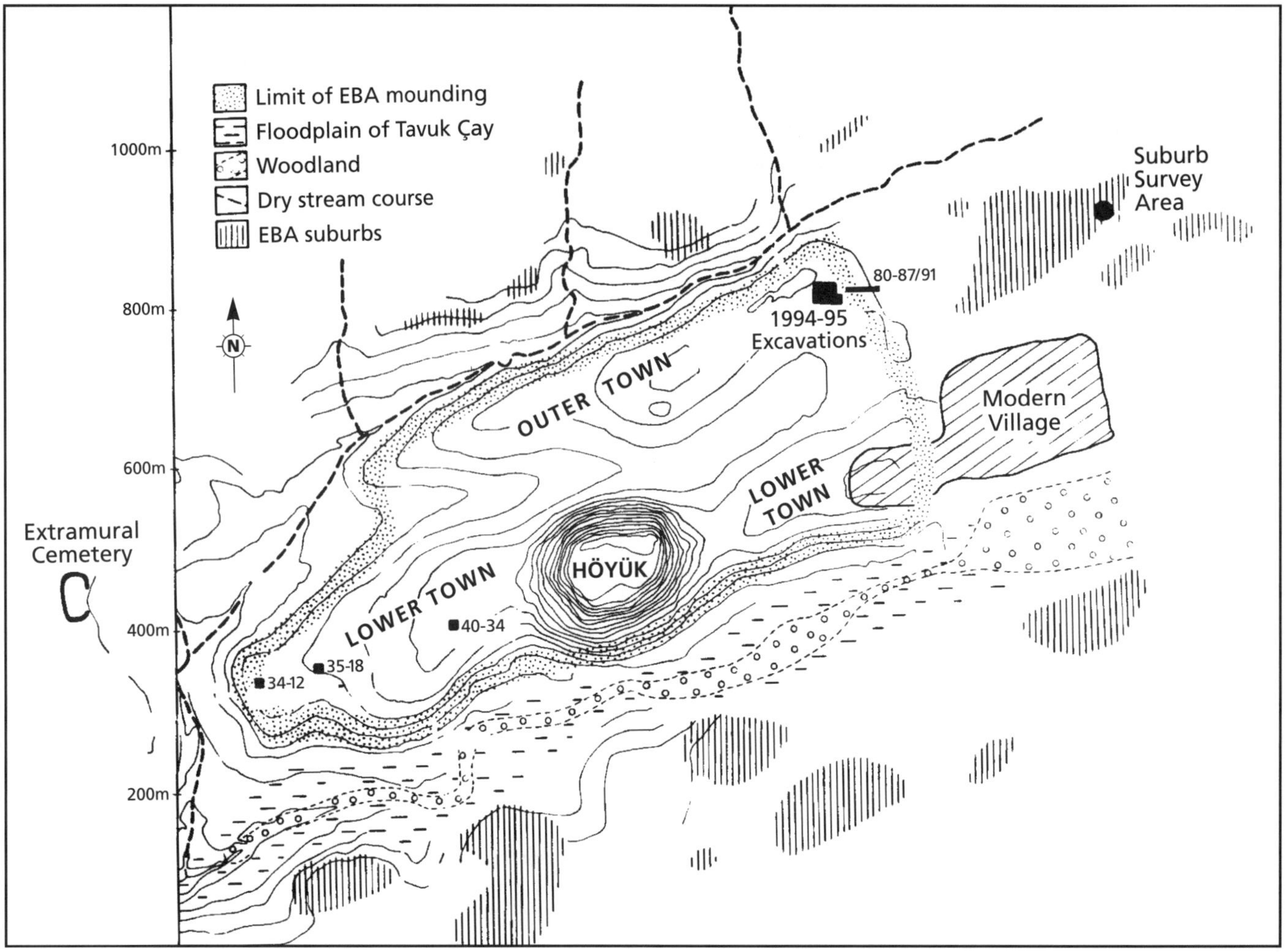

Contour map of Titriş showing the principal sectors of the city and the location of the 1994–1995 excavations. The 1996 excavations expanded on the small test sounding in Trench 34/12 at the western edge of the Lower Town.

Period IVC-B at Kürban Höyük) and a late EBA (corresponding to Period IVA at Kürban Höyük; Matney and Algaze 1995; Algaze 1990). As noted above, the location of the site along an important overland trade route is key to understanding the genesis and collapse of the site, which we believe was heavily reliant upon the constant demands of the southern Mesopo-tamian markets. As such, the rise of the city is probably tied to the emergence of a vigorous city-state system in southern Mesopotamia during the course of the Early Dynastic period. The collapse of Titriş, similarly, likely relates to the impact of the weakened Mesopotamian political and economic strength at the end of the historically-documented Sargonid (Gadd 1971).

Project Goals

Scientific explorations started at Titriş Höyük in 1991 under the direction of Guillermo Algaze of the University of California-San Diego. The initial project goals were to establish a basic chronology of the site and to assess the site's morphology and functional use patterns of its different areas. To these ends, probes and small-scale clearances located in various parts of the site were started in 1991 and detailed remote sensing magnetic surveys were conducted from 1992 to 1994. These two methodologies have produced a fairly complete magnetometry map of the ancient city, as well as well-defined ceramic sequence of the region from the mid- and late EBA. An "interpretative" plan was created by tracing the outlines of features defined by very highly magnetic signatures representing roads constructed or paved with sherds as well as highly fired areas such as kilns, and heavily non-magnetic features representing wall foundations, typically made with dressed and undressed pieces of limestone. From this magnetometry data, a clear general structure emerges of long, planned streets directly fronted by residential structures of modest size. This street system also delineates clear blocks of architecture that formed coherent spatial units or "neighborhoods" within the EBA city (see plan on p. 25).

In 1994, utilizing our knowledge of site morphology to organize a study of non-elite residential patterns in the EBA, we initiated large-scale horizon-

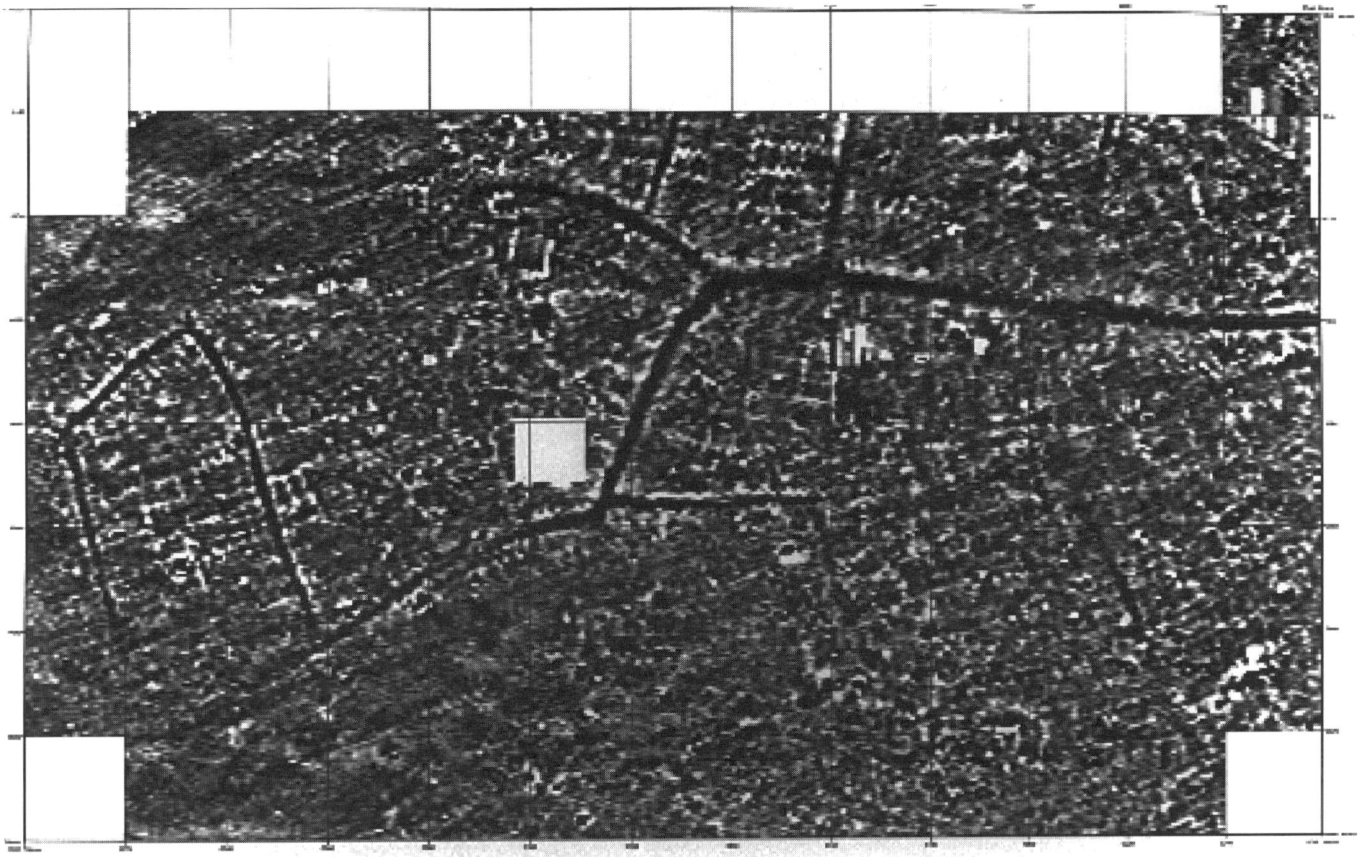

Above: Magnetometry map of western sector of the Lower Town. Dark areas represent features with high magnetic signatures, such as streets paved with pottery sherds and kilns. Light areas represent features with low magnetic signatures, like limestone wall foundations. The well-defined "neighborhood" in the far west was partially excavated in 1996. Each grid square is twenty meters on a side.
Below: Interpretations of magnetometry map shown above showing lines of streets and wall foundations. This area is characterized by dense rectilinear structures of a modest size. Most represent domestic dwellings.

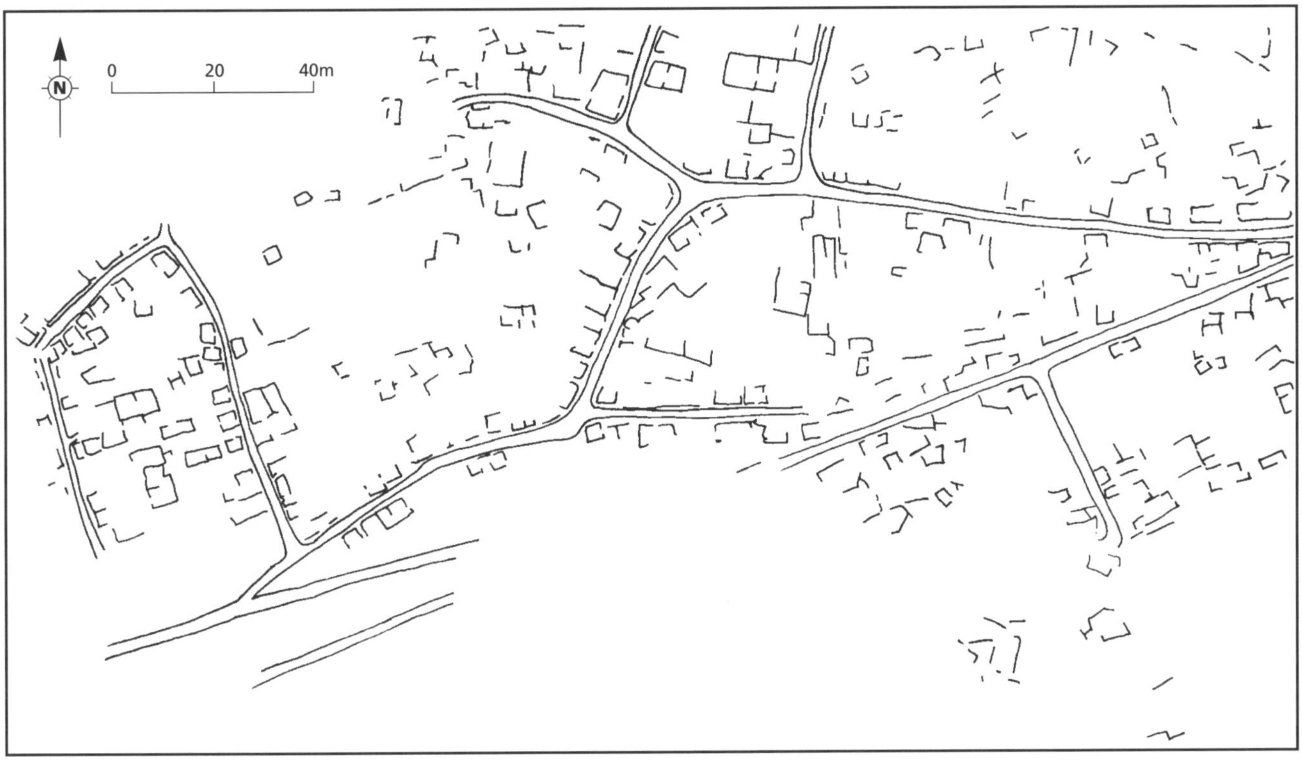

Radiocarbon dates established for the Outer Town at Titriş Höyük

LAB NO.	LOCUS	CONTEXT	SAMPLE NO.	BP DATE	INTER-CEPTS	1 SIGMA CALIB. (68.3%)	PERCENTAGE OF PROBABILITY	2 SIGMA CALIB. (95.4%)	PERCENTAGE OF PROBABILITY
SITE SECTOR: OUTER TOWN									
Beta-80446	79–85: 031	Floor	TH 6162	4260± 170	2886 BCE	3076–2611 BCE	3086–3060: .04 3044–2586: .96	3357–2409 BCE	3359–2453: 1.0 2421–2406: .00
Beta-80449	80–85: 015	Street	TH 3771	3860± 180	2315 BCE	2568–2035 BCE	2564–2523: .07 2501–2093: .85 2090–2037: .09	2877–1776 BCE	2872–2800: .04 2777–2713: .02 2708–1877: .93 1834–1822: .00 1795–1788: .00
Beta-80447	79–87: 046	Floor	TH 8267	3630± 60	1972 BCE	2113–1890 BCE	2111–2089: .10 2038–1895: .90	2141–1780 BCE	2173–2168: .00 2141–1871: .93 1842–1778: .07
Beta-80448	79–87: 047	Floor	TH 8274	3860± 70	2315 BCE	2457–2197 BCE	2452–2424: .12 2404–2273: .65 2255–2204: .23	2490–2048 BCE	2487–2132: .98 2076–2048: .02
Beta-95287	81–85: 065	Floor	TH 12161	3770± 60	2190; 2160; 2145 BCE	2281–2045 BCE	2281–2127: .83 2080–2045: .17	2398–1980 BCE	2399–2376: .02 2355–2015: .96 2006–1979: .02
Beta-95289	79–87: 042	Supra-floor	TH 12560	3860± 70	2315 BCE	2457–2197 BCE	2452–2424: .12 2404–2273: .65 2255–2204: .23	2490–2048 BCE	2487–2132: .98 2076–2048: .02
SITE SECTOR: LOWER TOWN									
Beta-95288	34–12: 010	Supra-floor	TH 15038	3860± 70	2315 BCE	2457–2197 BCE	2452–2424: .12 2404–2273: .65 2255–2204: .23	2490–2048 BCE	2487–2132: .98 2076–2048: .02

tal clearance of a domestic unit in the northeastern sector of the Outer Town. Here, via magnetometry, it was possible to locate well-defined, coherent residential complexes, and, because there was little later overburden, it was feasible to excavate the area on a fairly large scale. These excavations were extended in 1995 and, to date, approximately 1,200 square meters of contiguous architecture have been uncovered in the Outer Town, mostly dating to the late EBA (Matney and Algaze 1995). This project supplements existing databases and previous excavations at other contemporary sites that have often focused largely on temple, palace, or elite residential areas.[2]

Late EBA housing in the Outer Town of Titriş Höüyuk. *Courtesy G. Algaze.*

Urban Planning at EBA Titriş Höyük in the Outer Town

Soundings and broad horizontal exposures (ca. 1,200 square meters) of the eastern portion of the Outer Town revealed two primary occupational phases of the Outer Town. The underlying phase, exposed only in small soundings, was built directly over virgin soil and dates to the mid-EBA. A single radiocarbon date for this phase suggests a date in the twenty-fifth century BCE.[3] The overlying phase, exposed within

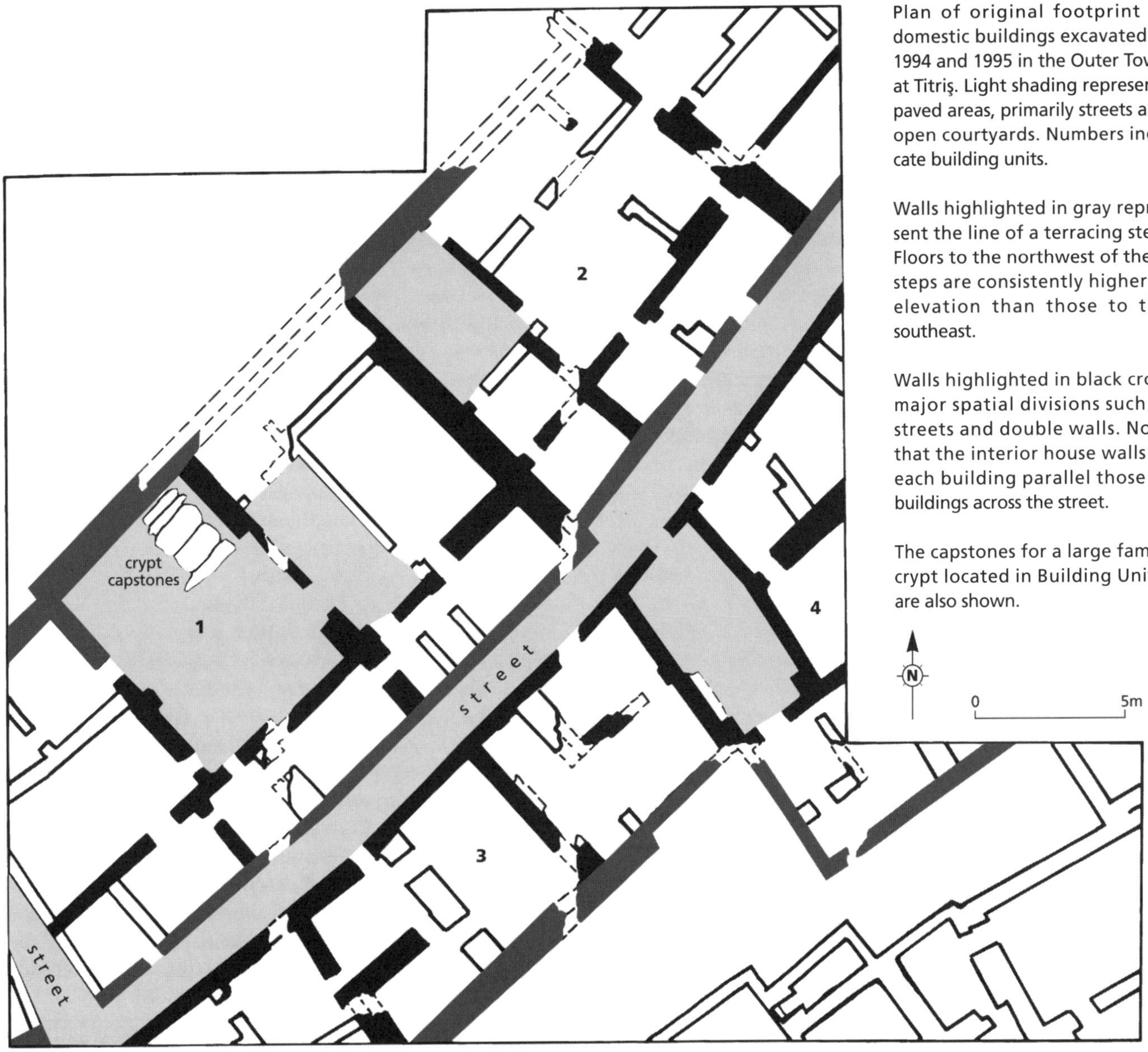

Plan of original footprint of domestic buildings excavated in 1994 and 1995 in the Outer Town at Titriş. Light shading represents paved areas, primarily streets and open courtyards. Numbers indicate building units.

Walls highlighted in gray represent the line of a terracing step. Floors to the northwest of these steps are consistently higher in elevation than those to the southeast.

Walls highlighted in black cross major spatial divisions such as streets and double walls. Note that the interior house walls of each building parallel those of buildings across the street.

The capstones for a large family crypt located in Building Unit 1 are also shown.

a broad area of some 1,200 square meters, dates to the late EBA. Seven radiocarbon dates have now been obtained for this phase. Five of the seven available dates (Beta-80448, -49, 95287, -88, and -89) form a very tight cluster suggesting a date in the twenty-fourth to twenty-third centuries BCE for the late EBA at the site (see also Matney and Algaze 1995:38, table 1).

From available soundings in the Outer Town, as well as from trenches elsewhere at the site, it is possible to present some broad comparisons between the two periods. There is a marked difference in architectural styles and construction between the mid-EBA and the late EBA domestic structures in the Outer Town. During the mid-EBA, builders constructed the domestic architecture of the Outer Town with carefully-masoned stones forming the foundations for mudbrick superstructures. Sunk into virgin soil, these foundation stones were often of massive proportions and rooms were small relative to the wall thicknesses (Matney and Algaze 1995:39, fig. 5). In contrast, occupants of much of the Outer Town in its late EBA phase built more modest domestic structures directly on top of the mid-EBA walls. These late EBA walls are much smaller than those of the mid-EBA and are frequently built with rough field stones, although they do on occasion utilize cut stone in their foundations. In general, the mid-EBA and late EBA walls do not share a similar alignment, further illustrating the clear break between the periods. At the moment, insufficient horizontal exposures of mid-EBA architecture prevent us from detailing changes in the function of the structures in the Outer Town between the mid-EBA and the late EBA. We hope to correct this sampling problem in future seasons of work at the site.

The extensive remains of late EBA structures in the Outer Town provided considerable evidence for urban planning at the site. Excavations have revealed the remains of over fifty rooms from at least four separate building units. Although patterns and the degree of cooperation in construction between neighboring building units—seen, for example, in the use of party walls and the extension of wall lines beyond the limits of individual buildings—suggest that city planners laid out this section of the city according to well-established principles of architecture and with supra-household organization of space in mind.

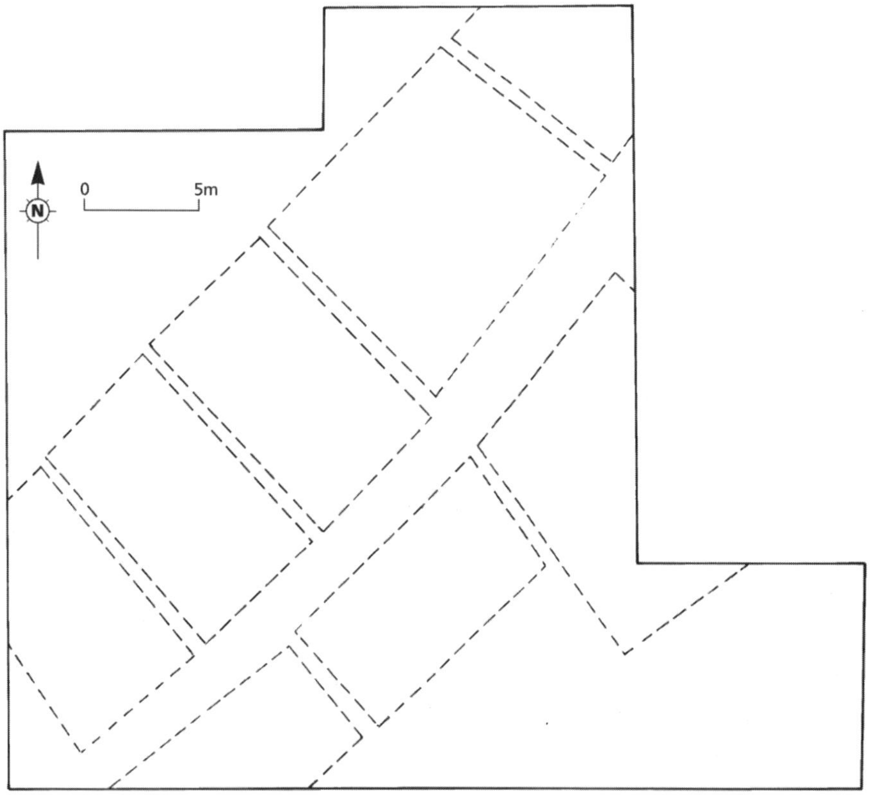

Outline of plots. Using the double walls at the site to represent conceptual boundaries, this figure shows the lines of the original building plots. Actual houses often incorporated more than one of these basic plots.

our analysis of the architecture is only in a preliminary stage, several striking spatial patterns provide some insight into the organization of social space during the EBA.

The late EBA domestic architecture excavated in the Outer Town represents the original architectural footprint of a portion of a residential neighborhood. The regularity and symmetry of the buildings, the presence of coherent subfloor drainage site terracing, and street access clearly influenced the expression of the spatial rules. Similarly, as inhabitants used these structures over a span of many generations, they made significant modifications and rebuilt these structures. Despite this variability, it is still useful to consider the regularities seen in the original architectural footprint.

Current evidence suggests that this part of the Outer Town of late EBA Titriş Höyük was a planned community. It is important to note that while initial building plans followed certain rules, there was still considerable individual variation within the actual structures, which becomes increasingly pronounced with each successive subphase after initial construction. Considerations such as the availability of unoccupied space,

Four observations illustrate town planning: the regularity and longevity of the street system; terracing; the use of a uniform plot size for construction; and the alignment of walls and major architectural divisions. Each of these sources of evidence is briefly outlined below.

Street Systems

From the magnetometry survey, it is clear that Titriş Höyük in the EBA had a well-planned street system. Major streets appear as long linear features on the magnetometry map, often running for several hundred meters. Numerous test probes and excavations, both across the Outer and Lower Town sectors of the settlement, have confirmed their identification. Available probes into some of these streets showed that they were long-lived, since the street deposits varied from 0.60 meters to 0.90 meters in depth. Moreover, it seems that the street system of the site did not grow by slow accretion but was instead deliberately laid out. Builders constructed streets by cutting linear foundation trenches into virgin soil and lining their subsurfaces, first, with small limestone boulders and, then, with compacted layers of small river pebbles. Probes indicate that streets were laid before the houses on either side were constructed because, in places, house builders cut the foundation trenches for the house walls into the street.

Our expansive horizontal clearance in the Outer Town recovered a long, well-preserved, east–west running street, which served as an artery for traffic throughout the entire late EBA, despite considerable modifications and alterations within individual houses surrounding it. Near the southwestern edge of our excavated area, this street intersected a second north–south running street of roughly the same size and construction. Servicing a number of different domestic units, these streets formed an irregular grid within which the remainder of the Outer Town structures were placed. The basic features of the architecture and streets (alignment, construction, and so forth) remained constant throughout the late EBA.

Terracing

The domestic architecture in this section of the Outer Town occupied a moderate natural slope from the northwest to the southeast. To create horizontal areas for the buildings, a series of wide terraces took shape behind long parallel retaining walls that encircled the natural rise. These terrace walls also served as the foundations for the mid-late EBA architecture. Excavations uncovered three of these terracing "steps." In each case, the floor level or ground level of the unit to the southeast was lower than that of the adjacent unit to the northwest. In one case, the terracing step followed the main east–west street, in another, it occurred around an open communal "midblock" between structures. The midblock served essentially as a shared "backyard," possibly with no access from the street, except through one or more of the domestic units. The placement of the terracing steps, their size, as well as their shared natures, manifest a degree of planning above the level of the individual household.

Uniform Plot Size

One of the most striking patterns observed in the field at Titriş was the presence of very uniform-sized plots of land. These plots appeared to represent recurring *measures of space*. Archaeologists recognized two standard shapes within the exposed area: rectangular plots and square plots. Rectangular plots were 7 x 12 m in extent and varied in their orientation. Three rectangular plots to the north of the main street, for instance, were all oriented downslope, while two opposing plots on the south side of the street were oriented across slope. Square plots were approximately 11 m per side. Two such plots faced each other across the street within the exposed area. Save for a single exception, the use of double walls marked the separation of plots. That is, between the plots, two walls, both with good interior and exterior faces, abutted each other lengthwise.

While the plots were recurring measures of space, they did not appear to be the primary unit of domestic organization in the late EBA architectural phase. Doorways connecting different plots allowed us to distinguish four larger discrete interconnected units. These building units varied in size, depending on the number and orientation of the plots they incorporated. That some degree of variation should exist, even within a highly structured built environment, is hardly surprising. As Nicholas David has noted, "societies do not have a norm for structures but a graded series appropriate for corresponding social and functional configurations" (1971:111). The challenge for the archaeologist is to recognize and define those social and functional rules governing the appropriate layout and use of domestic space.

Alignment of Walls and Architectural Divisions

Finally, some sort of supra-household urban planning is clearly shown by the observation that the walls on one side of the main east–west street align exactly with those on the other side of the street and, furthermore, that this alignment crosses the boundaries separating building units. In other words, wall lines running both parallel and perpendicular to the main street continue across all real (physical) boundaries, thus marking them as important *conceptual* elements in the organization of space in the late EBA Titriş Höyük. The principal walls are aligned consistently with those across the street and across large double walls dividing plots and building units.

The spatial effects of these conceptual lines create a register of shallow rooms parallel to the main street and, in general, make uniform-size rooms. The plans of these rooms are reminiscent of the Akkadian clay tablet showing an architect's plan for domestic houses found at Tell Asmar, in which long walls also create orderly registers of rooms (Delougaz et al. 1967:pl. 65). The extreme regularity of this alignment argues again for an initial, conscious planning of the neighborhood prior to construction. It would seem that all these domestic units were built as part of a single constructional effort, and, while not necessarily built according to a "master plan," the house plans followed strong canons of spatial ordering.

To summarize, the Outer Town at Titriş Höyük exhibits a supra-household level of organization in its overall architectural footprint during the late EBA. The regularity of the streets, terrace walls, and the walls dividing plots all testify to this coherence. An extreme regularity in the size and shape of plots also contribute to this suggestion of supra-household organization. We believe these plots represent basic conceptual divisions of land measurement. However, actual building complexes often incorporate more than one plot into a coherent building. Thus they are not limited by the plot divisions, but are guided by a set of well-defined architectural principles. Further analytical work is needed to recover the specifics of these principles. A similar organization is seen in the architecture recovered in 1996 from soundings on the western edge of the Lower Town (see note 2).

Architectural Parallels

Having established that the excavated structures in the Outer Town at Titriş were planned and that they follow a set of principles for organizing space, it is necessary to relate these observations to one of our overall project goals noted above, namely, understanding the relationship between the southern Mesopotamian heartland and the independent city-states of the Syro-Anatolian plains to the north. The most direct method of validating or invalidating a relationship would involve the recognition of similar (or dissimilar) principles in the organization of domestic architecture found at other sites of the same age. Unfortunately, efforts here are hindered by a general lack of data pertaining to non-elite residences in ancient southwestern Asia, the result of decades of archaeological research focusing on palaces, temples, and wealthy households. Nevertheless, a few sites are obvious candidates for such a comparative study (e.g., Ur, Tell Asmar, Tell Taya).

A brief comparison of the basic morphology of two domestic structures—Building Unit 2 at Titriş Höyük and House II (the "Arch House") in Level IVa at Tell Asmar, in the Diyala area of southern Mesopotamia (Delougaz et al. 1967)—offers one opportunity. What is striking from this comparison is the extreme similarity in plan, orientation, and construction between these two structures (see illustration). These factors argue that similar principles for organizing domestic space were shared across a wide geographic region. While a single material parallel, no matter how striking, hardly constitutes proof of social interaction, it does provided a starting point for such an argument. The presence of Mesopotamian and Mesopotamian-influenced artifacts at Titriş, as well as the use of cuneiform writing (Algaze 1990: 344–45), suggests that architectural

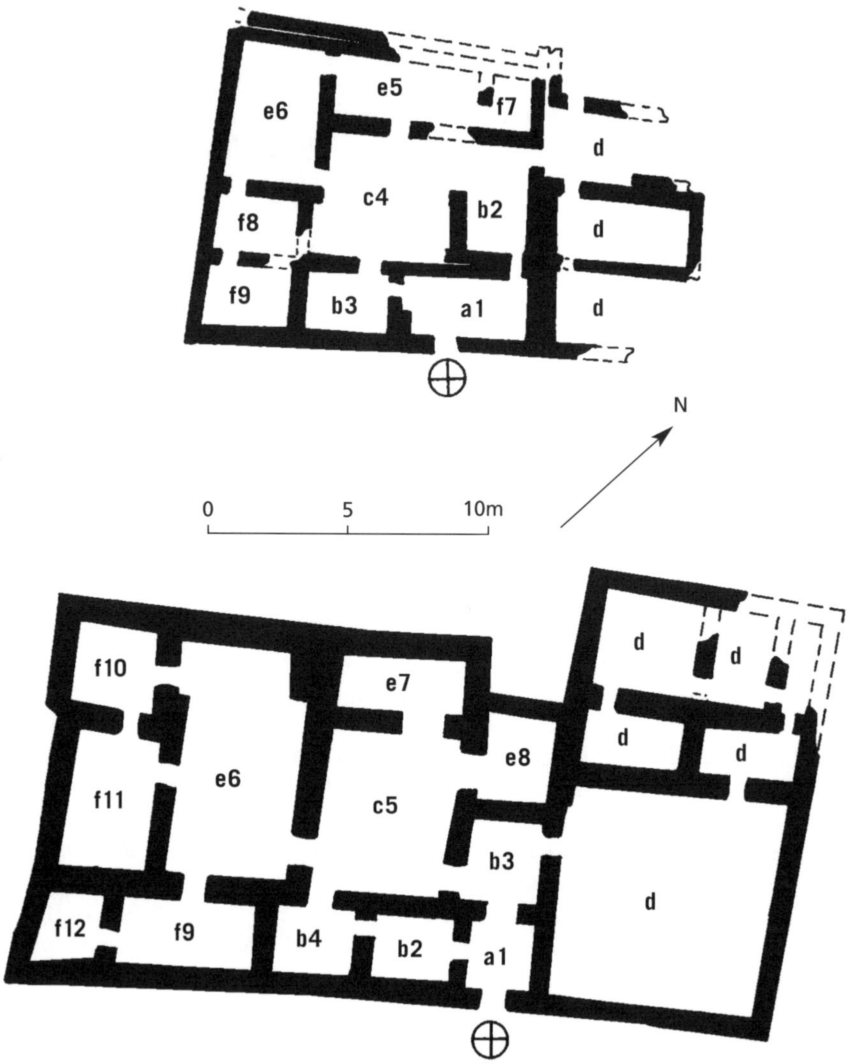

Comparison of Titriş Building Unit 2 (top) and Tell Asmar IVa, Building II (bottom). Each plan is drawn at the same scale and orientation. The Asmar house is redrawn from Delougaz et al. (1967:pl. 28).

concepts described below may have been part of a suite of cultural practices shared between the two regions.

Both houses are located off small streets in essentially residential districts of more or less contemporary late third millennium cities. Both thoroughfares were stable throughout the latter part of the EBA (Hill in Delougaz et al. 1967), and both areas were terraced along a moderate slope. Both houses had subfloor drainage systems. House II at Asmar is slightly larger, but both structures are built on a similar scale. The longevity of the Private House Area at Tell Asmar was noted by Hill:

> The separation of occupation levels into strata presented difficulties peculiar to the houses. The continuity of occupation of the area was unbroken by any general destruction to mark a division into periods. Rather, each house had its own history, not necessarily paralleled by that of its neighbors (1967:143).

This statement also holds true for the domestic structures of the Outer Town at Titriş.

Hill reports that House II at Tell Asmar was in use, with modifications, from the Asmar Level Vc

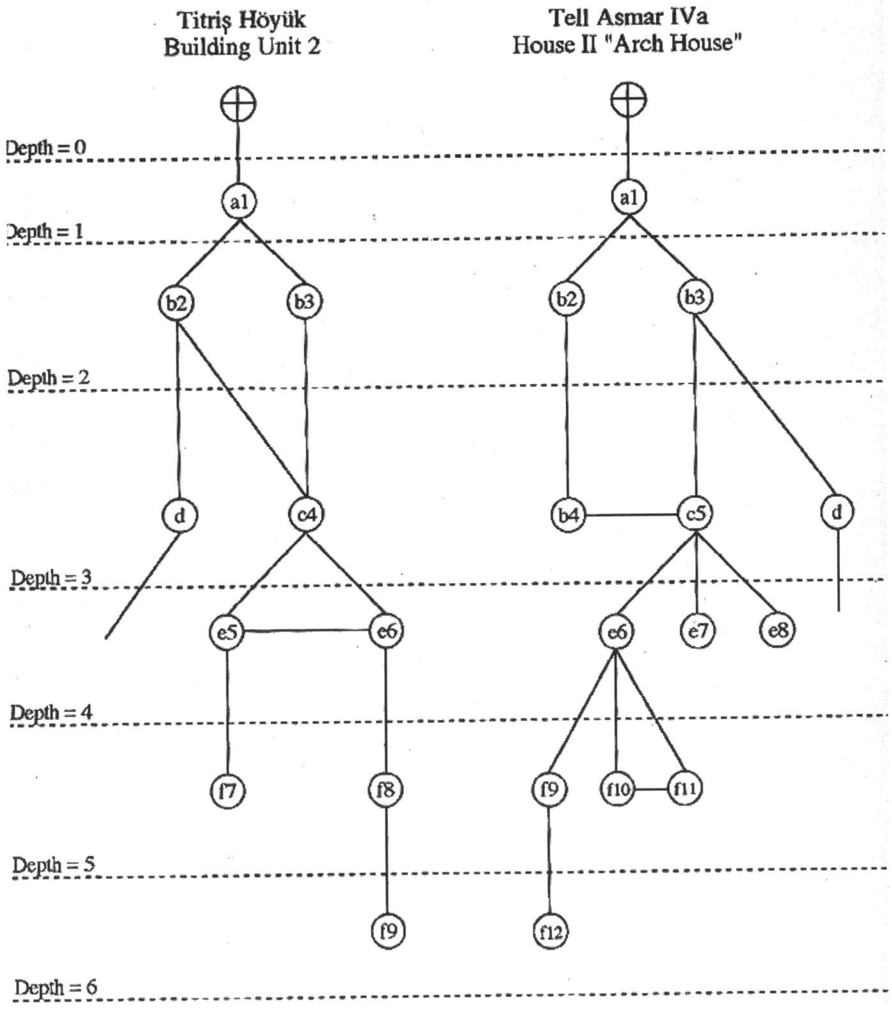

Justified permeability maps of Titriş Building Unit 2 and Tell Asmar IVa, Building II. "Depth" indicates the distance from the exterior carrier (street). The exterior carrier is indicated by a circle enclosing a cross. Rooms are indicated by circles and doorways by connecting lines.

(Early Dynastic III) through Level I (Larsa)—a life span of nearly a millennium (but see Gibson 1982:533 on the dating of the Asmar houses). Since the Outer Town at Titriş was abandoned at the end of the late EBA, there is no parallel for such extensive re-use of Titriş Outer Town Building Unit 2. The detailed comparison of the architectural plans made below focuses on the contemporary Asmar Level IVa, dated by the excavators to the Late Akkadian period by means of a seal impression of Shu-durul, one of the last Sargonid kings (Hills 1967:144). This dating agrees with the dates for the late EBA architecture at Titriş determined via radiocarbon measurements and ceramic typologies (Matney and Algaze 1995:51, note 2; table 1). As noted earlier, an inscription thought to be from Shu-durul's reign was plundered from the extramural cemetery at Titriş (Algaze 1990:344–45).

In both cases, it is difficult to assign precise functions to rooms due to a lack of distinguishing architectural features. The presence of various categories of small finds (e.g., spin whorls, grinding stones, etc.) is also difficult to interpret at Tell Asmar, while work on the Titriş small finds, pottery, and other occupational debris is still in progress. Still, as seen below, simple spatial placement is an important factor in understanding the use of space, as all societies have rules governing the definition and appropriate placement of various functional areas: bedrooms; kitchens; public spaces; and so forth. The analysis that follows relies primarily upon the morphology of the EBA buildings themselves.

The entrance to both buildings is from the street through an entryroom (a) near the southeastern corner of each building (letters in parentheses refer to the top plans on p. 28). This represents the only known entrance for these two structures from an exterior space, providing easy control over access from outside. From here, doorways allow passage into two sets of rooms (b). While House II at Tell Asmar has three rooms marked (b), Titriş Building Unit 2 only has two such rooms, although one later modification to the Titriş structure was the addition of an east–west wall dividing the northernmost room (b) into two small rooms, thereby creating a closer parallel with the Asmar house.

At both Titriş and Tell Asmar, one of the (b) rooms offers access to a complex of rooms marked (d), located to the east of the main building. A detailed comparison of the (d) complexes through the analysis of small finds must await complete excavation of the corresponding area of Titriş, although these two complexes do appear to be of similar scale, location, and accessibility. Hill has suggested the Asmar house represents a combination of public and private parts, with the (d) complex being a public space where household business was conducted. Alternatively, both sets of (b) rooms also access a centrally-placed room (c). This space is a central node for communication, leading to four or five rooms. From this, one would expect this room to be heavily trafficked. It is interesting to note that neither (c) room is an open courtyard, as might be expected from the stereotype of the modern Near Eastern courtyard house formed by a central unroofed courtyard flanked on each side by smaller roofed subsidiary rooms (Hill 1967:149).

The surrounding rooms (e) are only accessible through the central room. The most private spaces of both complexes (f), are removed from the outside world by four intervening spaces. Prior to any determination of the use to which residents put any of these spaces, our initial typology is based purely on the circulation patterns of the two buildings.

Justified permeability maps of these two buildings (following Hillier and Hanson 1984) show the pattern of movement through the buildings. Beginning with the outside street, each horizontal band of rooms is reached by passing through an equivalent number of rooms (i.e., rooms in the first horizontal band are entered directly from the street, rooms in the second horizontal band require passage through one intervening space, rooms in third horizontal band require passage through two intervening spaces, etc.). These maps are a graphic representation of the floor plans of the two buildings compensating for differing room size and cardinal orientation. Simple visual inspection of the justified permeability maps confirms a number of parallels noted above, e.g., the constriction of movement through a controlling space (c) and the relative inaccessibility of the rooms (f).

More important than the visual analysis of such graphics, however, is the conversion of the information they contain into numerical measures that can be discussed statistically (Hillier and Hanson 1984:143–75). A detailed statistical analysis for these buildings lies outside the scope of this paper. However, to confirm further the similarity of these structures and as an illustration of the theory of spatial syntax proposed by social theorists Bill Hillier and Julienne Hanson, a very abbreviated analysis of these two structures is given below.

Hillier and Hanson have extensively studied the social dimensions of spatial patterning in terms of both settlements and individual buildings. They have provided a wide range of graphical and numerical measurements that allow for the precise comparison between different settlement and building layouts (Hillier and Hanson 1984). Simplifying their complex arguments, Hillier and Hanson study the social dimensions of space by providing a series of analytical tools that allow architectural constructions and, indeed entire built environments, to be viewed as a series of laws or transformations acting on a limited number of types of basic spatial units ("cells" in their terminology). These cells can be combined mathematically (i.e., via laws that can be expressed as mathematical formulas) in a nearly infinite number of ways. However, each society has a limited that strictly govern the use of these spatial units. These laws determine the form and content of the final spatial product. One goal of this spatial analysis is to discern and quantify local and global morphological features through a descriptive theory of spatial patterning (Hillier and Hanson 1984:xi). The importance of such a *spatial syntax* is that the spatial patterning that results from such lawful behavior and that can be visibly seen in architecture, carries a social content; it has meaning and value in transmitting and perpetuating cultural information and norms. If one understands the spatial syntax governing a built environment, Hillier and Hanson argue, then it is possible to understand the "spatial content of social patterning" as well. That is, it is possible to get at why different cultures use different spatial forms.

In developing their theory of spatial syntax, Hillier and Hanson use three essential "principles" that allow them to generate a series of laws for any given spatial form. These principles are: symmetry/asymmetry, distributed/nondistributed, closed cell/open cell (Hillier and Hanson 1982:52–81). I will deal with only the first of these principles in this example. Symmetry is achieved when space A has the same relation to space B as space B has to space A. Asymmetry occurs when this relationship is not true. Two rooms placed side-by-side with a common wall and passage between them illustrate symmetry; a large

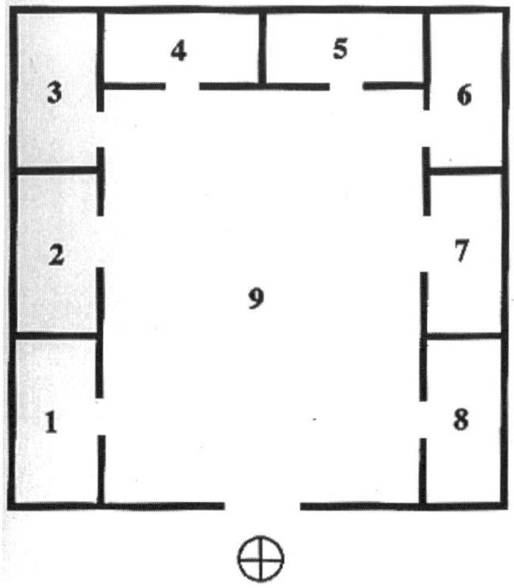

Hypothetical architectural plan of house.

room with passage to the outside that encloses a second smaller room that only has passage to the larger room illustrate asymmetry.

Relative asymmetry (RA) is a statistical measure of the degree of symmetry or asymmetry that a building (or other construction) possesses. One theoretical extreme is a case in which each space leads only to one additional space, forming a long, unilinear sequence. To get to the space furthest from the entrance, one would have to pass through all the other spaces. At the other extreme is a construction in which every space contains a passage to outside (Hillier and Hanson 1984:15). These are the "deep" and "shallow" extremes of the principle of

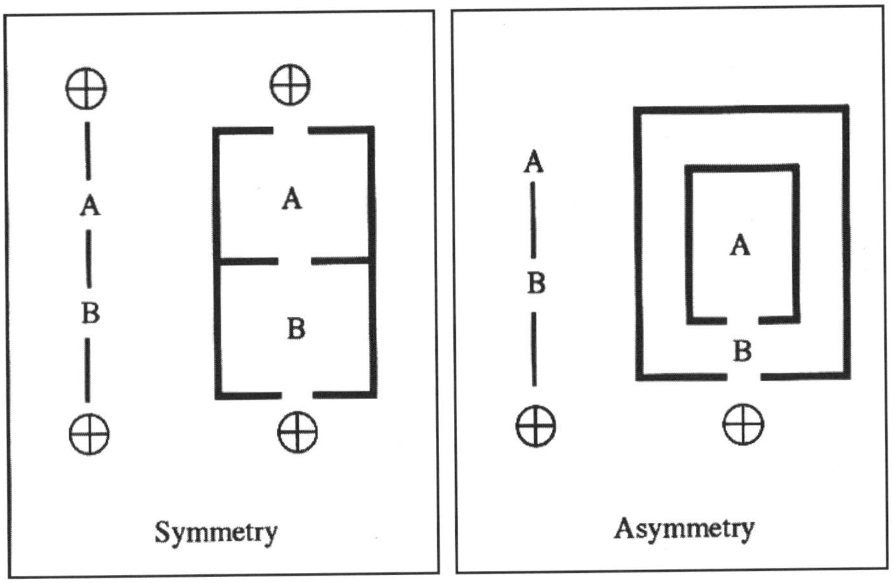

Diagram illustrating the principle of symmetry/asymmetry.

Relative asymmetries of rooms in Titriş Höyük, Building Unit 2 and Tell Asmar IVa, House II

Titriş Höyük, Building Unit 2

ROOM NO.	DEPTH	RA
0	0	0.639
a1	1	0.417
b2	2	0.306
b3	2	0.306
c4	3	0.194
e5	4	0.278
e6	4	0.250
f7	5	0.500
f8	5	0.417
f9	6	0.639
MEAN	3.556	0.395
SD	1.667	0.157

Tell Asmar IVa, House II ("Arch House")

ROOM NO.	DEPTH	RA
0	0	0.485
a1	1	0.318
b2	2	0.333
b3	2	0.227
b4	3	0.242
c5	3	0.136
e6	4	0.182
e7	4	0.303
e8	4	0.303
f9	5	0.318
f10	5	0.333
f11	5	0.333
f12	6	0.485
MEAN	3.667	0.308
SD	1.497	0.100

symmetry/asymmetry. Relative asymmetry measures where a given construction falls between these two extremes, characterizing relations of depth from an outside carrier. A deep construction, like the long unilinear chain of spaces noted above, would have a value of 1; a shallow construction where all spaces connect to the outside world would have a value of 0. The formula for calculating relative asymmetry is given by: RA = 2(MD - 1)/ k - 2 where "MD" is the mean depth of the structure and "k" is the number of spaces in the system (see Hillier and Hanson 1984:108–40 for details on deriving and calculating this statistic).

The justified permeability map for Titriş Höyük enables one to calculate the RA for the outside space quite easily (leaving aside for the moment the [d] complex). As seen from the outside, there is one room (a) that has a depth of 1; two rooms (b2) and (b3) that have a depth of 2; one room (c4) that has a depth of 3; two rooms (e5) and e6) that have a depth of 4; two rooms (f7) and (f8) that have a depth of 5; and one room (f9) with a depth of 6. The mean depth (MD) of these values is 3.556. The number of total spaces in the system (which includes the outside) is 10. Therefore: RA = 2 (3.556 - 1) / 10 - 2 = 0.395.

This figure represents the relative depth of the system, as viewed from the outside. This process can be repeated by drawing a new series of justified permeability maps using each room in the building as the starting point. Rooms that have strong centralized symmetric relations, e.g., central courtyards, have low RA values, while room that gave strong asymmetric relations, such as secluded storerooms, have high RA values.

Perhaps the most important point to recognize when comparing the RA values for each room in Titriş Höyük Building Unit 2 and Tell Asmar IVa House II (excluding the complex of rooms represented by "d") is that the mean depth of these two structures viewed from the outside is very similar. This similarity exists despite the fact that the Titriş building has three fewer rooms than the Asmar example. The difference in the two values of 3.556 ad 3.667 is not statistically significant within one standard deviation. In other words, in terms of the accessibility of the various spaces from the outside, as measured by RA, these two structures are comparable. A similar situation holds for the mean relative asymmetry for the buildings. Titriş Building Unit 2 has a mean RA of 0.395 with a standard deviation of 0.157, and Asmar House II has a mean RA of 0.308 with a standard deviation of 0.100.

By themselves, these statistics are insufficient to formulate a first rule of spatial syntax for EBA domestic architecture. However, they do allow us to differentiate this building "type" from other morphological types. For example, a "courtyard" hypothetical house plan would have a mean depth of 1.889 (S.D. = 0.333) and a mean RA of 0.200 (S.D. = 0.070). This house type, then, falls outside the range established by the Titriş and Asmar buildings and would, by this criteria, be categorized as a separate construction type.

More useful for our immediate comparison is an inspection of the RA values for each individual room. As suggested above, spaces such as entrance ways and deep storage rooms showed the greatest asymmetry. Titriş (f9), Asmar (f12), and both exterior spaces fell outside the range of one standard deviation from the mean RA with significantly higher values. Similarly, the central spaces Titriş (c4) and Asmar (c5) feel significantly below the mean plus standard deviation. This supports the observations made above by simple visual inspection of the ground plans. All other spaces in both complexes, with one exception, fell within the expected range of one standard deviation from the overall mean RA. The exceptional space was Asmar (e6) with a RA value of 0.182, which is below the range established for the Asmar complex. Its initial labeling as a type (e) room was perhaps mistaken, as it has a numerical characteristic more similar to the two (c) rooms, Titriş (c4) and Asmar (c5), with values of 0.194 and 0.136 respectively. How can this be interpreted?

The most parsimonious syntactic explanation for this apparent anomaly is that in terms of the principle of symmetry/asymmetry, Asmar (c5) and Asmar (e6) share similar spatial functions. If one accepts that Titriş (c4) and Asmar (c5) are both communication nodes, then Asmar (e6) is also a communication node. Why build two communication nodes (i.e., Asmar [c5] and [e6]) side-by-side? One possible explanation has to do with the generative nature of spatial syntax proposed by Hillier and Hanson. If the spatial syntax for this type of EBA domestic structure is meant to allow for the real construction of a building with a minimum of, say, nine rooms (like the Titriş example), but no set maximum, then one way of adding rooms onto the basic plan is to add additional communication nodes with connecting rooms into the heart of the complex. In the Asmar example, this is seen spatially by the addition of Asmar (e6) (and probably either Asmar [f10] or Asmar [f11] or both). This is significant since one is often tempted to think of house additions as "modular" where expansion needs are met by adding a "new wing" onto the exterior of an existing plan.

A further caveat to the rule that additional rooms are created through the construction of more communication nodes might be that these nodes must be adjacent to one another. These two rules, then, might conceivably be part of an EBA spatial syntax for domestic architecture. This hypothesis must be checked by testing it against domestic architecture from as many contemporary locations as possible, including comparable domestic architectural complexes at Titriş itself. What is important here, however, is the observation that—on present evidence—these two structures represent simple transformations of the same basic building type. Morphological differences can be explained by reference to a simple rule of spatial syntax.

Conclusions

Although we need substantially more analysis of the material—we have only scratched the surface—the similarities between the two domestic structures from two sites separated by hundreds of kilometers and forming part of different cultural and political spheres argue for the existence of a pan-Mesopotamian idea of urban planning and organization of space, one that is shared across otherwise independent, and perhaps even competing, polities. The attempt to define a spatial syntax for EBA architecture is hardly new. In the original Tell Asmar excavation report published thirty years ago, Hill made a similar type of observation, noting that the size of houses might be determined by the practicalities of roofing. When a larger house was required, part or all of a similar unit was added, rather than enlarging the existing structure. Or, in a similar vein,

> we can only observe the ideals toward which the builders seem to have been striving in their adaptations of the plans governing conditions and note whether variations from what would seem normal planning are explained by the wall below (Hill 1967: 145–46).

The improvement that the current analysis makes, and that the application of Hillier and Hanson's spatial syntax offers in general, is the explicit formulation of the process by which spatial rules are constructed and limited. By viewing architecture as a set of restrictions on the randomized process of cell aggregation, it becomes possible to describe the built environment in a fresh, powerful manner and, by observing statistical patterns in such computations as relative asymmetry, to compare cross-culturally the use of domestic space. In terms of the relationship between peripheral city-states such as Titriş Höyük and those sites more directly within the Mesopotamian heartland, the initial analysis of domestic architecture suggests a shared canon of spatial organization, with similar laws in operation and important common modes of social organization. Future work will examine how a common domestic spatial ideology came to be shared by independent polities located hundreds of kilometers from one another.

Notes

[1] Cylinder seals from current excavations are TH8537 and TH64025. The former is published as Algaze et al. (1995:fig 9). The seal impression is TH2097. The Karaz vessels are TH10501, TH10502, and TH10503. The two *depas* vessels from living surfaces are TH132 and TH65077; the one vessel from a late EBA burial is TH11855. TH132 is published as Algaze et al. (1992:fig 16). TH11855 is published as Algaze et al. (1996:fig 7, center).

[2] At the time of the final preparation of this chapter, the 1996 field season had just finished. The results from this season revealed a similar series of domestic residences within the Lower Town of the site. Approximately 900 m^2 of architecture were uncovered for the 1996 season. As in the Outer Town, the architecture of the Lower Town consists of small rooms grouped into moderately large structures of eight to fifteen rooms each. Houses are aligned along a well-constructed street, which is clearly visible on the magnetometry map and share many morphological features with the Outer Town structures, including significant evidence for town planning. A preliminary report on the 1996 season appeared in the journal *Anatolica*.

[3] Matney and Algaze (1995:table 1). Beta-80445 had a one-sigma range of 2553–2350 BCE with an intercept of 2467 BCE.

Bibliography

Algaze, G., ed.
1990 *Town and Country in Southeastern Anatolia, II: The Stratigraphic Sequence of Kurban Höyük.* Oriental Institute Publications 110. Chicago: Oriental Institute of the University of Chicago.

Algaze, G. and Mısır, A.
1994 Titriş Höyük: An Early Bronze Age Urban Center in Southeastern Anatolia, 1993. *Kazi Sonuçlari Toplantisi* 16(1):107–20.

Algaze, G., Mısır, A., and Wilkinson, T.
1992 Sanliurfa Museum/University of California Excavations and Surveys at Titriş Höyük, 1991: A Preliminary Report. *Anatolica* 18:33–60.

Algaze, G., Beyer-Honça, D., Goldberg, P., Matney, T., Misir, A., Rosen, A., and Schlee, D.
1995 Titriş Höyük, A Small EBA Urban Center in Southeastern Anatolia: The 1994 Season. *Anatolica* 21:13–64.

Buccellati, G. and Kelly-Buccellati, M.
1988 *Mozan I: The Soundings of the First Two Seasons.* Bibliotheca Mesopotamica 20. Malibu: Undena.

David, N.
1971 The Fulani Compound and the Archaeologist. *World Archaeology* 3:111–31.

Delougaz, P., Hill, H., and Lloyd, S.
1967 *Private Houses and Graves in the Diyala Region.* Oriental Institute Publications 88. Chicago: The Oriental Institute of the University of Chicago.

Donley-Reid, L.
1990 A Structuring Structure: The Swahili House. Pp.114–26 in *Domestic Architecture and the Use of Space: An Interdisciplinary Cross-Cultural Study*, edited by S. Kent. Cambridge: Cambridge University Press.

Gadd, C. J.
1971 The Dynasty of Agade and the Gutian Invasion. Pp. 417–63 in *The Cambridge Ancient History, Vol 1, Part 2*, 3rd ed., edited by C. J. Gadd, I. E. S. Edwards and N. G. L. Hammond. Cambridge: Cambridge University Press.

Gibson, M.
1982 A Re-evaluation of the Akkad Period in the Diyala Region on the Basis of Recent Excavations at Nippur and in the Hamrin. *American Journal of Archaeology* 86/4:531–38.

Giddens, A.
1979 *Central Problems in Social Theory: Action, Structure and Contradiction in Social Analysis.* Berkeley: University of California Press.

Hauptmann, H.
1993 Vier Jahrtausende Siedlungs-geschichte am mittlere Euphrat. *Archäologie in Deutschland* 1:10–15.

Hill, H.
1967 Tell Asmar: The Private House Area. Pp. 143–209 in *Private Houses and Graves in the Diyala Region*, edited by P. Delougaz, H. Hill, and S. Lloyd. Oriental Institute Publications 88. Chicago: The Oriental Institute of the University of Chicago.

Hillier, B., and Hanson, J.
1984 *The Social Logic of Space.* Cambridge: Cambridge University Press.

Matthiae, P.
1980 *Ebla: An Empire Rediscovered.* London: Hodder and Stoughton.

Matney, T. and Algaze, G.
1995 Urban Development at Mid-Late Early Bronze Age Titriş Höyük in Southeastern Anatolia. *Bulletin of the American Schools of Oriental Research* 299–300:33–52.

Oates, D. and Oates, J.
1989 Akkadian Buildings at Tell Brak. *Iraq* 51:193–211.

Orthmann, W.
1986 The Origins of Tell Chuera. Pp. 61–70 in *The Origins of Cities in Dry-Farming Syria and Mesopotamia in the Third Millennium BC*, edited by H. Weiss. Guilford, CT: Four Quarters Publishing.

Porter, A. and McClellan, T.
1998 The Third Millennium Settlement Complex at Tell Banat: Results of the 1994 Excavations. *Damaszener Mitteilungen* 10:11–63.

Wattenmaker, P. and Mısır, A.
1994 1992 Excavations at Kazane Höyük. *Kazi Sonuçlari Toplantisi* 15(1):177–87.

Timothy Matney received his Ph.D. in 1993 from the University of Pennsylvania. His research focuses on protohistoric and early historic archaeology, the rise of urbanism, city planning and the spatial analysis of ancient domestic residences. In addition to co-directing the excavations at Titriş, Dr. Matney runs a field project at the Assyrian border capital of Ziyaret Tepe on the Tigris River. His publications include several reports on the excavations at Titriş. He is currently Professor of Cultural Anthropology at the University of Akron.

Weiss, H.

1983 Excavations at Tell Leilan and the Origins of North Mesopotamian Cities in the Third Millennium BC. *Paléorient* 9:39–52.

1986 The Origins of Tell Leilan and the Conquest of Space in the Third Millennium North Mesopotamia. Pp. 71–108 in *The Origins of Cities in Dry-Farming Syria and Mesopotamia in the Third Millennium BC*, edited by H. Weiss. Guilford, CT: Four Quarters Publishing.

1990 Tell Leilan 1989: New Data from Mid Third Millennium Urbanization and State Formation. *Mitteilungen der Deutschen Orient-Gesellschaft* 122:193–218.

Wilkinson, T.

1990 *Town and Country in Early Southeastern Anatolia I: Settlement and Land Use at Kurban Höyük in the Lower Karababa Basin.* Oriental Institute Publications 109. Chicago: The Oriental Institute of the University of Chicago.

1994 The Structure and Dynamics of Dry Farming States in Upper Mesopotamia. *Current Anthropology* 35:483–520.

Zettler, R.

1996 Tell es-Sweyhat 1989–1995. *Expedition* 38:14–29.

Swords, Armor, and Figurines

By K. Aslıhan Yener

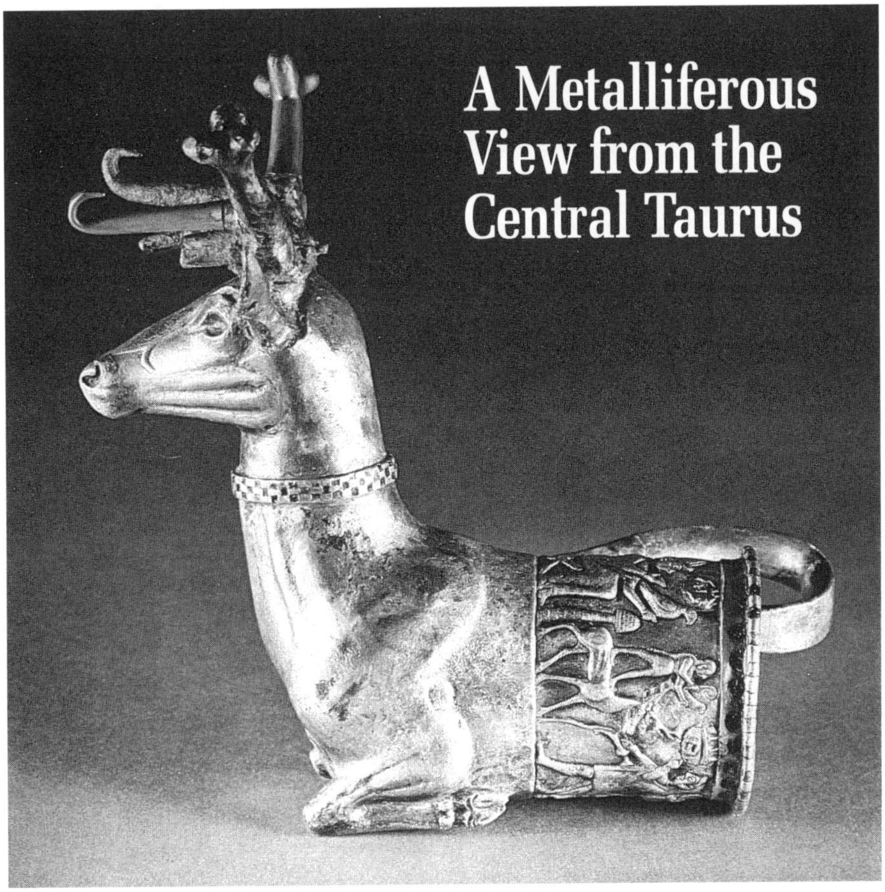
A Metalliferous
View from the
Central Taurus

Silver rhyton, a stag vessel with frieze, exemplifies the highly developed state of metallurgy among the Hittites. Metropolitan Museum of Art. *All photographs courtesy of Aslıhan Yener.*

This article collects observations on the nature of metal industries in Anatolia, with special reference to the Hittites. Along with this, I make some suggestions for sourcing the ores, which were exploited from the Chalcolithic period to the Late Bronze Age in the south-central Taurus mountains. This provides some insights into the resource strategies of the Hittite and earlier cultures by illuminating a highland industry that is often missing in the archaeological record.

One of the more puzzling aspects of Hittite imperial geography has been the location of the Hittite capital, Boğazköy (Ḫattuša), in north central Turkey. A large number of the excavated documents reflect imperial political and economic interests in bellicose southern regions, such as Karkamiš, Aleppo, and Alalakh. Yet the Hittites chose to manage their empire from the mountainous region in the north—an area that was sometimes politically troublesome. Powerful military forays descended into the southern Syro-Anatolian bread basket, a place that had fluctuating allegiances with Egypt. This arena of great conflict between Egypt and Ḫatti had yet another important asset: rich mineral resources and metallurgical technology. Recent archaeometallurgical studies in the Taurus and Amanus ranges make this wealth evident. The same holds true for north central Turkey, which has mineral resources that are easily accessible in the Pontic Mountains. As a result, exceedingly complex relationships emerge between the Hittite imperial center and its resource-rich frontiers.

Of particular interest is the nature and impact of metal manufacture on the producers of metals when urban demands from imperial centers such as Ḫattuša increased. The attempt to control access to needed highland resources was the strategic rationale for a number of third and second millennium Mesopotamian legends involving the military intervention of various lowland armies. The magnitude of that intrusion has been largely unknown since the archaeological history of the highland industries has been understood only recently.

Excavations at Ḫattuša, the capital of the Hittite Empire, revealed a people with considerable engineering skills and distinct organizational strategies. The Hittites were able to integrate the mountainous terrain of their Empire with their building technologies. They were heirs to a metal technology that had unparalleled development in Anatolia since the eighth millennium BCE (Maddin 1988). The Sungurlu area in north central Turkey around the highland capital, Boğazköy, is fertile in agricultural potential, and even more significantly, it has an environment rich in metals, minerals, and wood. These resources abound in the Pontic Mountains to the north and the Taurus range to the south. Thus, Hittite industries had some strategic advantages over the lowland empires by their immediate access to metalliferous deposits, forest supplies, and abundant game. Clearly a large number of areas to the south such as Kizzuwatna, elusive Tarḫuntašša, and the "Silver Mountain" Taurus and Amanus ranges were quickly integrated into the empire. This suggests that resource procurement was important. By commanding priority rights over these resources, the Hittites had an economic risk strategy that provided insurance in times of imperial financial difficulties.

Finally, it is worth reiterating the obvious point that exchange networks tapping into the resource areas were established in the periods prior to Hittite ascendancy (Marfoe 1987). These exchange networks were at least maintained and possibly strengthened during the Hittite period. This paper deals with only a small portion of the Hittite metal industry, sketching the implications of source characterization by lead isotope analysis published earlier (e.g., Yener et al. 1991). Over the last decade this analysis has provided some insight into the nature of metal exploitation patterns.

Some Aspects of Hittite Metallurgy

It has long been acknowledged that the highland regions of Anatolia, rich in natural resources, were among the earliest places where metallurgy developed. In this region, metallurgy advanced in the Near East and from here metallurgical technologies spread to neighboring Mesopotamia and Syria. Styles and traditions of metalworking exhibit great inventiveness and the products of these techniques—the metal objects themselves—display a virtuosity that often outshines other aspects of technology as a whole. The most striking feature of this metallurgical tradition is its precociousness. From the earliest occurrences of metal objects in the aceramic Neolithic (eighth millennium BCE) through the discovery of iron metallurgy, this innovative characteristic never altered. It encompassed the very early recognition of the ductility of copper as well as the late fourth millenium BCE discovery of the strength, range, and colors of functional alloys. This knowledge was put to use in both decorative and utilitarian objects.

Current understanding of Hittite metallurgy comes from metal assemblages excavated from several Late Bronze Age sites such as Boğazköy, Maşat, and Alaca Höyük. A partial list of these assemblages includes metal armor, weapons, pins, tools, wagons, figurines, seals, and treaties. Several examples of bull and deer-shaped rhytons of silver, such as the stag vessel with frieze (Muscarella 1974), and the fist-shaped vessel in Boston's Museum of Fine Arts (Güterbock and Kendall 1995) reflect the developed nature of their craft (Güterbock 1983). A recent hoard found near Kastamonu produced other examples of ritual iconography in metal: plates engraved with hieroglyphic inscriptions and decorated with registers in relief of griffins; trees of life, combat scenes with lions and bulls, lions and lions, and hunting scenes (Emre and Çınaroğlu 1993). Moreover a fragment of an oxhide ingot of copper excavated at Boğazköy (Müller-Karpe 1980) links this seemingly landlocked empire with a circum-Mediterranean maritime commerce. This network moved tons of copper and tin during the Late Bronze Age and was revealed in the spectacular results of the underwater excavations at Uluburun Kaş and Cape Gelidonya (Bass et al. 1989; Maddin 1989).

The quantities of metal objects with ritual significance began early, as the findings at Troy and Alaca Höyük demonstrate. Weapons are prominent members of this grouping. Two examples from the Middle Bronze Age are a bronze spearhead engraved with inscriptions of Anitta the King and a sword dedicated to the god Nergal (Güterbock 1965). Engraving inscriptions onto metal continued into the Hittite period. A sword with an Akkadian inscription celebrates Tutḫaliya II's victory over the western Aššuwa-land (1430 BCE). The inscription dedicated the sword to the Storm God (Ertekin and Ediz 1993; Ünal 1993). Another example of a numinous weapon is a spearhead inscribed "*Walwaziti*, Greatscribe," probably dating to the reign of Ḫattušili III and Queen Puduḫepa (Bilgi and Dinçol 1989). Swords and axes were decorated with humans, animals, and fantastic divine creatures. These weapons have a smooth background from which figures stand out in relief. Their forms are reflected in the Hittite relief depicting the Dagger God at Yazılıkaya, which may have been based on a metal prototype. Its hilt is shaped like a god's head framed by four lions (Bittel et al. 1941). In addition to weapons, treaties were cast in metal. Recent excavations at Boğazköy revealed a bronze tablet inscribed with a treaty between Tutḫaliya IV and Kurunta, King of Tarḫuntašša (Otten 1988; Houwink ten Cate 1992).

Aside from the expected metal tools, weapons, and jewelry, the variety of metal artifacts manifest the tremendous extent to which metal was used in shaping objects (Boehmer 1972, 1979; Waldbaum 1978). A whole range of shaping techniques (Maxwell-Hyslop 1971) exists in the artifacts of non-ferrous fabrication: chasing, cloisonné, filigree, granulation, drawing of wire, and various methods of gilding and repoussé. Tools, weapons, ornaments, figurines, and toilet articles were cast and hammered. Sheet metal was crafted and a number of fittings were cast and riveted (for techniques see Moorey 1985; Moorey and Fleming 1979, 1984).

Texts by the hundreds exacavated at Boğazköy refer often to objects made of metal. A number of the texts mention ceremonial artifacts that are multi-media and polychrome: decorated with tin, gold, silver, rock crystal, ivory, alabaster, and lapis lazuli (Güterbock 1983). A valuable dagger is described as "its front shimmering, its tail and pommel of rock crystal" (Košak 1982), while another text speaks of a votive gold bow (Güterbock 1989). Writing boards are described as equipped with writing implements of gold.

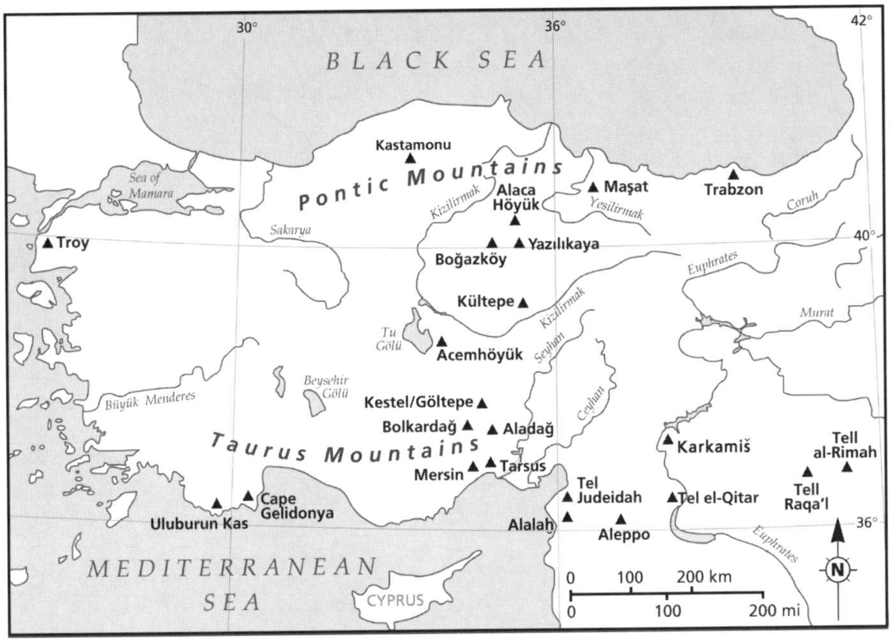

The Pontic and Taurus mountain ranges offered rich mineral resources at the frontiers of the Hittite imperial center. An intricate trade in metals linked highland sources with lowland markets.

There are iron ritual objects such as the animal attributes of the major deities, specifically lions and bulls, as well as animal shaped rhytons and human statues cast of iron or made of wood and inlaid with gold, silver, and tin. Inventory texts enumerate metal chariots, axes, horse bits, arrows, sickles, and maces. Other utilitarian objects such as weapons and tools are described as being made of iron (Košak 1985; Muhly et al. 1985). Textual references conjure up a whole arsenal of metal weapons.

Inventory lists of luxury items bear witness to the extent of moveable and storable wealth in the Hittite Empire. These include silver pyxis, gold and silver necklaces, pins, copper bathtubs, cymbals, and other musical instruments. Garments were lavishly decorated with gold and silver appliqués, gold pendants, and beads. An iron throne was given to the earlier Middle Bronze Age monarch, Anitta the King of Kaneš, while iron blooms, lumps, and iron smelting(?) hearths are mentioned in Hittite texts. A tub, small figurines, and ornamental jewelry are also mentioned as being made of iron. Texts made the distinction between meteoric iron (referred to as black iron of heaven) and terrestrial (smelted) iron; copper and iron can be qualified by "good" or "not good."

The provenance of various metals is sometimes listed. Most relevant to this discussion is the state of Kizzuwatna (Cilicia), which supplied the Hittite center with silver, copper, and tin. The amounts of metal from tribute lists are noteworthy as well: 42 minas; 16 minas 30 shekels; 134 minas. From another text, 56 iron blades for daggers, 8 blades for use in the kitchen, 16 maces of black iron, two thousand blades, and over 2,200 other metal objects are listed as tribute. At times copper is listed as ingots from 2 to 40 minas. Weights in larger scale, talents, are also mentioned. Silver ingots averaged about 1.5 to 2 minas.

Production in the Industrial Highlands

A dramatic economic threshold was crossed in the variety, quality, and quantity of metals manufactured. Metal was a critical high technology in a number of ways. It was the standard of value, medium of exchange, and the raw material of tool and weapon industries. Often metal was a vehicle for complex reciprocal gift exchanges. Yet reconstruction of these processes and economies often neglects the technologically advanced mining and smelting operations that were the backbone of the industry. The dynamics of provisioning metal to lowland centers and the impact of this industry upon different subsystems of Anatolian society are much more complex than the Hittite artifacts found in excavations lead us to believe. Thus, while the metal objects from Late Bronze Age sites highlight sophisticated metallurgical skills, their very existence at this level points to a hidden production technology that operated at industrial strength in the mountain source areas.

What emerges from behind the inventory lists and excavated metal artifacts is the existence of a many-tiered, complex production industry. The first tier was the extraction and smelting sites in the mountains. The manufacture of metal at the mines and smelting sites is the least-studied major aspect of early states. Information from specialized function sites in the resource zones has been comparatively scarce, leading to an understanding of metallurgical techniques skewed toward the end users. Yet the primary industrial phase took place in the mountain zones and consisted of extraction, mining, smelting, and refining. It is this industry that is mostly missing in the archaeological record for the Hittites, though such industrial operations were already in operation in the Early Bronze Age as evidenced by the metal processing site, Göltepe, and the tin mine, Kestel (Yener and Vandiver 1993).

Workshop production centers found at urban lowland sites constitute the second tier of the metal industry. The technological aspects of the urban workshops can be gleaned from the artifacts, as well as from the specialized craft assemblages unearthed at Boğazköy (Neve

1992; Bachmann 1984) and the Assyrian Colony period at Kültepe (Özgüç 1955, 1986). Urban workshops executed alloying, casting, inlaying, shaping, and other refinements. Hittite ritual texts and functionally important objects make clear the strategic and economic ramifications of this multi-faceted industry. Arsenical copper is the majority alloy represented. Nickel, tin, and lead alloys are present in late Hittite artifacts (Bachmann 1984). The diversity of metals and the technologies of their production presuppose some form of relationship with special function industrial sites in the mountains. Whether the Hittites engaged in reciprocal exchange with the polities controlling the mines or whether they directly controlled the production by politically integrating the source areas, hardly alters the impressiveness of the still mute industrial system as a whole.

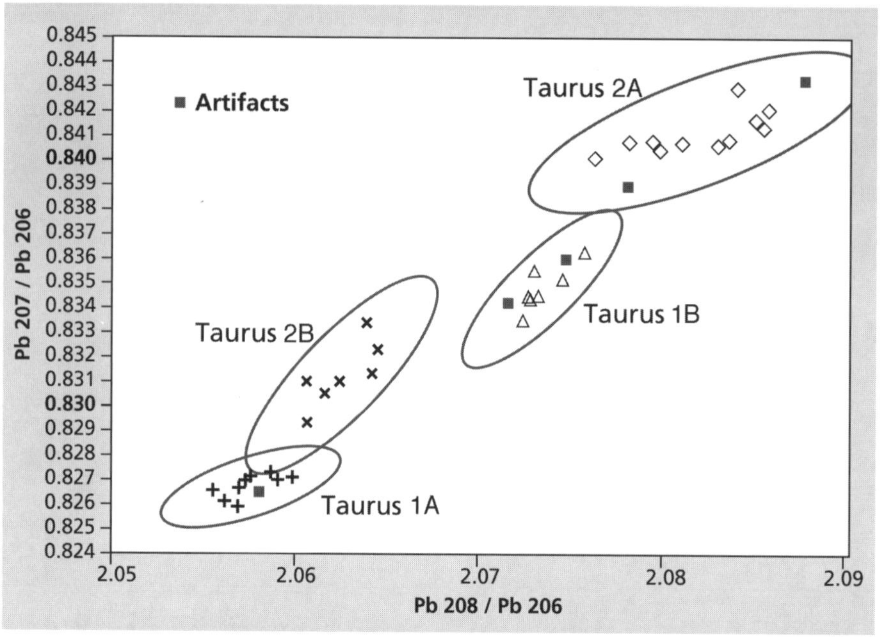

Artifacts of Syrian and Anatolian origin fit well within the ellipses of several Taurus mountain ore fields. Sourcing is based upon the lead isotope fingerprints of the ores, the ratio of the various naturally occurring isotopes of the metal lead. Lead frequently accompanies other metals in ore bearing deposits.

The South-Central Taurus Metal Sources

The identification of exotic materials and products is one of the functions to which archaeology is best suited. Trade between the metal-rich highlands and urban centers held significance as a social force, if only as the link between mining production and consumption of metal commodities. Highland metalliferous zones supplied pre-state societies in Anatolia from the Chalcolithic period or earlier. This dynamic continued for the later Hittite imperial periods as well. Recent anthropological research demonstrates that demands for metal and its trade increased with the emergence of a hierarchy in administration. This traffic in metals may partly be definable by the use of lead isotope analysis.

The use of isotope ratios of lead to characterize sources and objects depends upon the fact that the lead ores occurring in different mining regions differ from one another in their isotopic compositions. These can then be used as "fingerprints" with which to compare isotopic ratios derived from artifact samples (Gale et al. 1985). Isotopic ratios can also be derived for ores containing other metals besides lead; many ore bodies are polymetallic and, therefore, are potentially capable of being analyzed using this technique. The methodology and data handling aspects of the research have been published elsewhere (Yener et al. 1991; Sayre et al. 1992). The implications are given below. Since the selection and processing of ores are directly reflected in the lead isotope ratios, this analysis will help assess the possibility that various Anatolian sources were exploited in the formative years of metallurgy and that some form of local and nonlocal exchange has taken place.

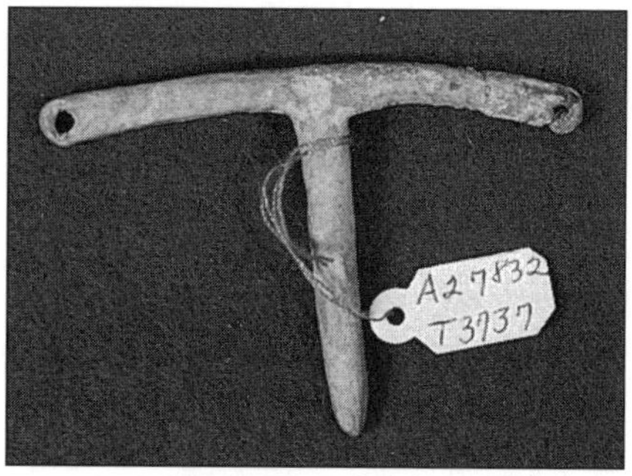

This t-shaped pendant from the second mixed range (Phases I–J) from Tell Tayinat in southern Turkey was probably made from metal extracted from the Taurus ore fields. More than one thousand years before the Hittites established their industrial operations, miners were already at work in these same rich deposits. Early artifacts come from disparate locations—Tarsus, Tell Raqaʿi, and Tell Judaidah—suggesting that a number of sites exploited the same ore.

The central Taurus range in Turkey has been well defined isotopically. A number of Syrian and Anatolian artifacts have isotopic ratios that suggest that they were derived from ores in this region. In addition a number of artifacts from the southern frontier of the Hittites, such as Cilicia and the Amuq, ranging from Chalcolithic to Late Bronze Age, have been analyzed. Their isotopic ratios assign nine of them to recently-defined ore fields. The probability of their best fit is in the Taurus. This suggests that these

Isotopic analysis of a fragment from the silver/gold helmet on this nude male statuette from Tell Judaidah showed that it originated in the same mining sector as the tin of its predominate tin-bronze alloy. At one time holding a club and long spear in his hands, this Chalcolithic/EB I diminutive figurine represents one of the earliest examples of tin alloys.

industrial areas were already in operation for more than a millennia before the Hittites made use of them. The same thing can be said of the Pontic Black Sea sources (Sayre *et al.* 2001).

The Chalcolithic and Early Bronze Age Artifacts

A number of Chalcolithic and Early Bronze Age artifacts from the Amuq in southcentral Turkey correlate well with the ore groups of the Taurus. These include two samples taken from Tell Judaidah, which is situated on a well-traveled east–west route approximately 250 km to the southeast of the mines at Bolkardağ. Dated to late fourth through late third millennium BCE (levels G–J), a copper-nickel blade, a t-shaped pendant, and a copper pin (Braidwood and Braidwood 1960:fig. 185:5; fig. 371:4; fig. 239:7) show strong probability of coming from the Taurus ore fields. Included in this group are a specimen from a Chalcolithic lead object from Tarsus and a lead coil dated to the Early Bronze Age (Goldman 1956:435:no.3). The excavations at Tell Raqaʿi in Syria yielded a copper pin and slag dated to the third millennium BCE which are consistent with Taurus ores.

A matching set of artifacts suggests that a number of sites exploited the same ore source from the Taurus range, at Aladağ (Sayre et al. 1992). The earliest artifact samples come from Tell Judaidah. A fragment from the silver/gold helmet on a nude male statuette holding a club and long spear in his hands derives from level G (Braidwood and Braidwood 1960:315, fig. 241, pl. 58). Another specimen taken from the torque on the female figurine in the same hoard is also consistent with this group. These two objects from Tell Judaidah had previously been analyzed spectrographically (Braidwood and Braidwood 1960: fig. 245, 315) to measure the trace element composition of the metal. Both the helmet and the torque had silver, copper and gold reported as major elements and bismuth, chromium, lead, silica, and tin as minor. The statuettes themselves are tin bronze (Braidwood, Burke, and Nachtrieb 1951). Fragments of other tin bronzes (containing 7.79% and 10% tin respectively) and fragments of slag (5% tin) in crucibles were excavated in secure level G contexts at Judaidah, making these some of the earliest examples of tin alloys (Braidwood and Braidwood 1960:300–15; Braidwood, Burke, and Nachtrieb 1951).

By the mid-third millennium BCE, relatively good tin bronzes are found in most areas of Anatolia and at sites along the Mediterranean coast. Tarsus Early Bronze II levels revealed copper-based artifacts of which 24% are tin bronzes and in Tarsus Early Bronze III, good tin bronzes are present as well. These bronzes have up to 6% tin. There are high grade tin bronzes in the coeval Phases H and I in the Amuq as well. The discovery of an Early Bronze Age tin mine at Kestel (Yener 2000; Moorey 1994:300–301) makes these early alloys all the more important technologically. The isotope ratios indicate that the silver from the statuettes was from the very same mining district from which the tin of the bronze may have come. Kestel Mine, however, went out of production at the end of the third millennium BCE.

Middle Bronze Age and Late Bronze Age Artifacts

More relevant to the Hittites is the exploitation of the Taurus source in the Middle and Late Bronze Age. A silver specimen from a Middle Bronze Age silver hoard at Acemhöyük and a fragment from a Late Bronze Age silver hoard from Tell el-Qitar in Syria correlate strongly with the Taurus ore from Aladağ. The southern Hittite frontier, Kizzuwatna, is represented by the sourcing of a copper pin from Mersin level IXb. A lead pin from Tell al-Rimah in Syria dated to 1500 BCE and a lead block from Aššur in northern Mesopotamia, dated to 1300 BCE, point to Anatolian interaction with urban centers in the southern frontier, an area of great conflict during the Hittite period.

Several specimens of lead net sinkers and a tin flask[1] from the shipwreck at Uluburun Kaş also correlate with the Taurus mountains. Interestingly, an unpublished Late Bronze/Iron Age armor plate (T97) from Tayinat in the Amuq also belongs to the Taurus groups. Larger quantities of similar armor plates were recently found at Boğazköy (Neve 1992:Abb. 65).

The Black Sea sources are also quite active throughout the periods noted above as suggested by new analyses from the Pontic mining districts (Sayre et al. 2001). Correlations with a number of artifacts from Late Bronze Age sites and Trab-

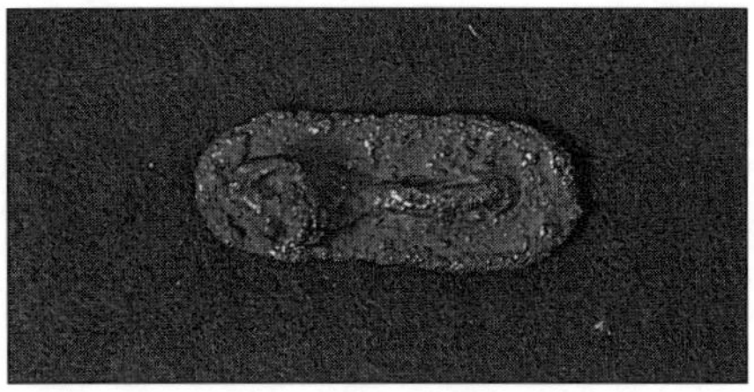

Late Bronze/Iron Age armor plate: Unearthed at Tayinat in the Amuq, this element of warriors' garb also hails from a Taurus mountain source. Similar examples of this armor have recently turned up at Boğazköy.

zon ores suggest that both the Taurus and the Pontic mines were potentially exploited for critical raw materials. This research leads to the conclusion that several contemporary production operations were utilized in the mountainous regions to the north and south of the Hittite capital.

Conclusions

The development of metallurgy in Anatolia was an exceedingly complex process. The results of lead isotope research suggest an intricate traffic of metals—at least for lead, silver, and lead containing copper based artifacts. Isotope ratios of the central Taurus region have shown that many metals were extracted from its resources. A much clearer picture of the history of the resource zones is beginning to emerge than was heretofore possible. It is now evident that neither the development of lowland prestate societies nor the emergence of complex urban centers can be understood in isolation. Rather, throughout most of their history, the lowlands and highlands were interconnected and intertwoven by traders. Recent investigations of the mining districts have revealed that a regional procurement strategy had already developed in the Early Bronze Age and tied together the mountain sources with the lowland markets. A two-tiered production system existed consisting of the sites that extracted ores and did the rough smelting and casting into ingots, and the urban centers that subsequently refined, crafted, and manufactured idiosyncratic metal items in workshops.

Work done on the highland regions has gone a long way towards couching intelligent questions regarding the context and organization of metal production in the region. By closing a significant gap in the understanding of metal production at a site within a strategic metal zone, research in the source zones has become central to future efforts seeking to assemble and interpret the growing corpus of metals from urban centers. These efforts will illuminate the metallurgical development of a little known region that was of fundamental importance to the entire ancient Near East.

Note

[1] Yener et al. 1991. Specimen no. AAN809 is mislabeled and should read "tin flask, excavation number KW 1085, Late Bronze Age."

Bibliography

Bachmann, H. G.
1984 Düsenrohre und Gebläsetöpfe: Keramikfunde aus Metallverarbeitungs-Werkstätten. Pp. 107–15 in *Boğazköy V. Funde aus den Grabungen bis 1979.* Ausgrabungen des Deutschen Archäologischen Institute. Berlin: Gebr. Mann Verlag.

Bass, G. F., Pulak, C., Collon, D., and Weinstein, J.
1989 The Bronze Age Shipwreck at Ulu Burun: 1986 Campaign. *American Journal of Archaeology* 93:1–29.

Bilgi, Ö. and Dinçol, A. M.
1989 A Unique Spearhead from Sadberk Hanım Museum. Pp. 29–31 in *Anatolia and the Ancient Near East: Studies in Honor of Tahsin Özgüç*, edited by Kutlu Emre, Barthel Hrouda, Machteld Mellink, and Nimet Özgüç. Ankara: Türk Tarih Kurumu Basımevi.

Bittel, K., Naumann, R., and Otto, H.
1941 *Yazılıkaya. Architektur, Felsbilder, Inschriften und Kleinfunde.* Leipzig: Wissenschaftliche Veröffentlichungen der Deutschen Orient-Gesellschaft.

Boehmer, R. M.
1972 *Die Kleinfunde von Boğazköy aus den Grabungskampagnen 1931–1939 und 1952–1969.* Wissenschaftliche Veröffentlichungen der Deutschen Orient-Gesellschaft 87: Boğazköy-Ḫattuša Berlin: Gebr. Man Verlag.
1979 *Die Kleinfunde aus der Unterstadt von Boğazköy Grabungskampagnen 1970–1978.* Boğazköy-Ḫattuša 10. Berlin: Gebr. Man Verlag.

Braidwood, R. J. and Braidwood, L. S
1960 *Excavations in the Plain of Antioch.* Oriental Institute Publications 61. Chicago: The Oriental Institute of the University of Chicago.

Braidwood, R. J. Burke, J. E., and Nachtrieb, N. H.
1951 Ancient Syrian Coppers and Bronzes. *Journal of Chemical Education* 28:87–96.

Emre, K. and Çınaroğlu, A.
1993 A Group of Metal Hittite Vessels from Kınık-Kastamonu. Pp. 675–713 in *Aspects of Art and Iconography: Anatolia and its Neighbors. Studies in Honor of Nimet Özgüç*, edited by M. J. Mellink, E. Porada, and T. Özgüç. Ankara: Türk Tarih Kurumu Basımevi.

Ertekin, Ahmet and Ediz, Ismet
1993 The Unique Sword from Boğazköy/Hattusa. Pp. 719–26 in *Aspects of Art and Iconography: Anatolia and its Neighbors. Studies in Honor of Nimet Özgüç*, edited by M. J. Mellink, E. Porada, and T. Özgüç. Ankara: Türk Tarih Kurumu Basımevi.

Gale, N. H., Stos-Gale, Z. A., and Gilmore, G. R.
1985 Alloy Types and Copper Sources of Anatolian Copper Alloy Artifacts. *Anatolian Studies* 35:143–73.

Goldman, H.
1956 *Excavations at Gözlü Kule. Tarsus Vols. I–II.* Princeton: Princeton University Press.

Güterbock, H. G.
1965 A Votive Sword with Old Assyrian Inscription. Pp. 197–98 in *Studies in Honor of Benno Landsberger on his 75th Birthday, April 21, 1965.* Chicago: University of Chicago Press.
1983 Hethitische Götterbilder und Kultobjekte. Pp. 203–17 in *Beiträge zur Altertumskunde Kleinasiens, Festschrift für Kurt Bittel*, edited by R. M. Boehmer and H. Hauptmann. Mainz: Philipp von Zabern.

1989 Hittite Kurša Hunting Bag. Pp.113–19 in *Essays in Ancient Civilization Presented to Helene J. Kantor*, edited by A. Leonard and B. Williams. Studies in Ancient Oriental Civilization 47. Chicago: The Oriental Institute of the University of Chicago.

Güterbock, H. G. and Kendall, T.
1995 A Hittite Silver Vessel in the Form of a Fist. Pp. 45–60 in *The Ages of Homer: A Tribute to Emily Townsend Vermeule*, edited by J. B. Carter and S. P. Morris. Austin: University of Texas Press.

Houwink ten Cate, Philo H. J.
1992 The Bronze Tablet of Tudhaliyas IV and its Geographical and Historical Relations. *Zeitschrift für Assyriologie* 82/2:233–70.

Košak, S.
1982 *Hittite Inventory Texts (CTH 241–50)*. Texte der Hethiter 10. Heidelberg: Carl Winter Verlag.
1985 The Gospel of Iron. Pp.125–35 in *Kaniššuwar: A Tribute to H.G. Güterbock on his 75th Birthday*. Assyriological Studies 23. Chicago: The Oriental Institute of the University of Chicago.

Maddin, R. ed.
1988 *The Beginning of the Use of Metals and Alloys. Papers from the Second International Conference on the Beginning of the Use of Metals and Alloys, Zhengzhou, China, 11–26 October 1986*. Cambridge, MA: MIT Press.
1989 The Copper and Tin Ingots from the Kaş Shipwreck. Pp. 99–106 in *Old World Archaeometallurgy*, edited by A. Hauptmann, E. Pernicka and G. A. Wagner. Bochum: Deutschen Bergbau-Museums.

Marfoe, L.
1987 Cedar Forest to Silver Mountain: Social Change and the Development of Long-distance Trade in Early Near Eastern Societies. Pp. 25–35 in *Centre and Periphery in the Ancient World*, edited by M. Rowlands, M. Larsen, and K. Kristiansen. Cambridge: Cambridge University Press.

Maxwell-Hyslop, R.
1971 *Western Asiatic Jewellery, c. 3000–612 B.C.* London: Methuen.

Moorey, P. R. S.
1985 *Materials and Manufacture in Ancient Mesopotamia: The Evidence of Archaeology and Art, Metals and Metalwork, Glazed Materials and Glass*. BAR International Series 237. Oxford: British Archaeological Reports.
1994 *Ancient Mesopotamian Materials and Industries. The Archaeological Evidence*. Oxford: Clarendon Press.

Moorey, P. R. S. and Fleming, S.
1979 Re-appraisal of a Syro-Palestinian Bronze Female Figurine. *MASCA Journal* 1:73–75.
1984 Problems in the Study of the Anthropomorphic Metal Statuary from Syro-Palestine before 330 B.C. *Levant* 16:57–90.

Muhly, J. D., Maddin, R., Stech, T., and Özgen, E.
1985 Iron in Anatolia and the Nature of the Hittite Iron Industry. *Anatolian Studies* 35:65–84.

Müller-Karpe, M.
1980 Die Funde. *Archäologischer Anzeiger* 3:303–7.

Muscarella, O. W.
1974 *Ancient Art. The Norbert Shimmel Collection*. Mainz: Philipp Von Zabern.

Neve, P.
1992 Ḫattuša—Stadt der Götter und Tempel: Neue Ausgrabungen in der Hauptstadt der Hethiter. *Antike Welt* 23/Sondernummer (Kurt Bittel zum Gedenken):2–88.

Otten, H.
1988 *Die Bronzetafel aus Boğazköy: Ein Staatsvertrag Tudhalijas IV*. Studien zu den Boğazköy Texten, Beiheft 1. Wiesbaden: Otto Harrassowitz.

Özgüç. T.
1955 Report on a Workshop Belonging to the Late Phase of the Colony Period Ib. *Belleten* 73:77–80.
1986 *Kültepe-Kaniş, II. Eski yakındoğu'nun ticaret merkezinde yeni araş tırmalar. New Researches at the Trading Center of the Ancient Near East.* Türk Tarih Kurumu Yayınları, V/41. Ankara: Türk Tarih Kurumu Basımevi.

Sayre, E. V., Yener, K. A., Joel, E. C., Blackman, J. M., and Özbal, H.
2001 Stable Lead Isotope Studies of Black Sea Anatolian Ore Sources and Related Bronze Age and Phrygian Artefacts from Nearby Archaeological Sites. Appendix: New Central Taurus Ore Data. *Archaeometry* 43:77–115.

Sayre, E. V., Yener, K. A., Joel, E. C., and Barnes, I. L.
1992 Statistical Evaluation of the Presently Accumulated Lead Isotope Data from Anatolia and Surrounding Regions. *Archaeometry* 34:73–105.

Ünal, Ahmet.
1993 Boğazköy Kılıcının Üzerindeki Akadca Adak Yazısı Hakkında Yeni Gözlemler. Pp. 727–30 in *Aspects of Art and Iconography: Anatolia and its Neighbors. Studies in Honor of Nimet Özgüç*, edited by M. J. Mellink, E. Porada, and T. Özgüç. Ankara: Türk Tarih Kurumu Basımevi.

Waldbaum, J. C.
1978 *From Bronze to Iron. The Transition from the Bronze Age to the Iron Age in the Eastern Mediterranean*. Studies in Mediterranean Archaeology 54. Göteborg: Paul Åströms Forlag.

Yener, K.A.
2000 *The Domestication of Metals: The Rise of Complex Metal Industries in Anatolia (c. 4500–2000 B.C.)*. Amsterdam: E. J. Brill.

K. Aslıhan Yener is Associate Professor of Anatolian Archaeology at the Oriental Institute of the University of Chicago and is the director of the Göltepe and Kestel mine excavations. She has directed archaeometallurgy surveys as part of a lead isotope analysis characterization project throughout Turkey since 1981. She has excavated at Erbaba, Ikiztepe and Kurban Höyük since 1974. Dr. Yener received her Ph.D. from the Art History and Archaeology Department of Columbia University. She taught archaeology and archaeometry at Boğaziçi University in Istanbul and the Anthropology Department of Hunter College, New York from 1980–1988. She has been a John Paul Getty fellow at the Metropolitan Museum of Art and a visiting scientist and postdoctoral fellow in Materials Science in the Archaeometry Division of the Conservation Analytical Laboratory of the Smithsonian Institution from 1987–1993.

Yener, K. A., Sayre, E. V., Joel, E., Özbal, H., Barnes, I. L., and Brill, R. H.
1991 Stable Lead Isotope Studies of Central Taurus Ore Sources and Related Artifacts from Eastern Mediterranean Chalcolithic and Bronze Age Sites. *Journal of Archaeological Science* 18:541–77.

Yener, K. A. and Vandiver, P. B.
1993 Tin Processing at Göltepe, an Early Bronze Age Site in Anatolia. *American Journal of Archaeology* 97:207–37.

Environment, Archaeology, and History in Hittite Anatolia

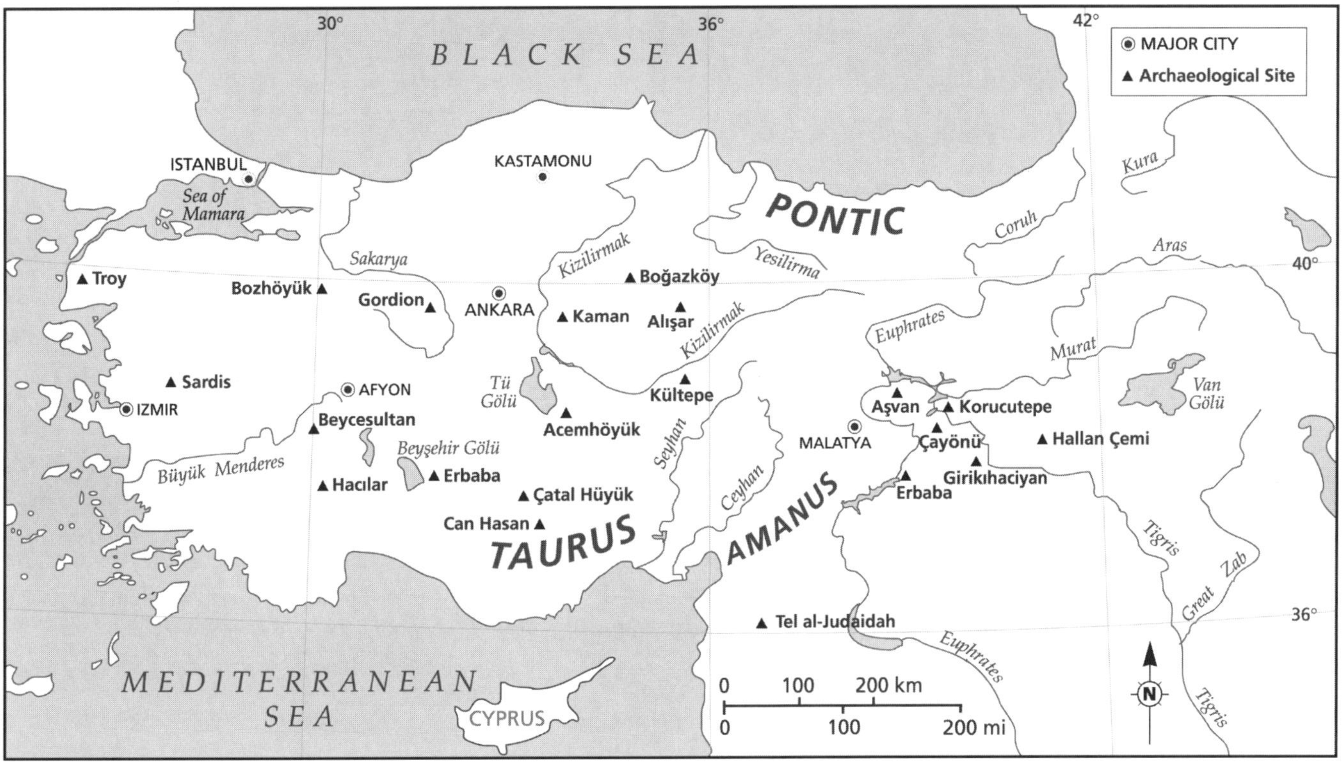

By Ronald L. Gorny

Anatolia is a large geographical unit, much of which is archaeologically unknown.[1] The focus of this article is the central plateau, the portion of Anatolia mostly enclosed by, or in proximity to, the region's primary river, the Kızil Irmak (River Halys). Within the bounds of this catchment area are the remains of several ancient cities that played key roles in the development of Hittite Anatolia.

Kaneš (modern-day Kültepe)[2] was the center of an Assyrian trade network that tapped into the resources of the plateau at the beginning of the second millennium BCE. Ḫattuša (modern Boğazköy/Boğazkale)[3] was the capital of the powerful Hittite Empire until it fell around 1200 BCE. In addition, the mound at Acemhöyük, which lies near the southern shore of the great Salt Lake, was the site of the important city of Purušḫanda (compare Özgüç 1966:29–30; Kempinski and Košak 1982:99–100). Although other cities such as Ḫurma, Zalpa, and Waḫšušana also played important roles during this period, Kaneš, Ḫattuša, and Acemhöyük seem to best epitomize the urban setting of central Anatolia at the beginning of the second millennium.

Anatolia has always been a land dominated by villages and peasants (Tenney 1938:628), an agrarian and pastoral society in which the basic relationship is the one between human beings and the land. This theme is pervasive in the warp and woof of Hittite culture, touching every sphere of life. This subsistence pattern was fraught with difficulties, however, as the plateau experienced the vicissitudes of a fickle climate (Ünal 1977; Mitchell 1993:133, 144). If peasants, pastoralists, and princes were to survive and prosper, they had to acknowledge the primacy of the land and come to grips with its environmental framework.

Although the nomenclature of Anatolian archaeology is still problematic, it is not difficult to identify a common thread woven into its historical fabric. In keeping with the nature of its subject matter, Anatolian archaeology should focus on the villages and farmsteads that have always represented the region's most typical form of settlement. The peasants who inhabited these settlements have long formed the backbone of civilization on the plateau. Unfortunately, only a handful of villages have been excavated.

It has often been suggested that the Hittites may be traced back archaeologically to the people who fashioned the third millennium tombs at Alaca Höyük, such as the rectangular shaft tombs shown here, which date to the Early Bronze III period. Serving as final resting places for several generations of the city's royal house, these tombs contained numerous precious metal grave goods. *Photo by Ronald L. Gorny.*

The few attempted analyses of village life in ancient Anatolia have combined speculation, modern analogies, and what little can be gleaned from textual sources (e.g., Macqueen 1986:74–75, 111–15; Archi 1973). Archaeologists must rely on data from the excavations at major cities in order to understand daily life in Hittite Anatolia. Unfortunately, such excavations provide scholars with an undeniably urban slant (compare Adams 1984:81, 113).

Land and People

Although there are no reliable studies of the demographic situation during the Middle and Late Bronze Ages, it appears that, beginning with Early Bronze III, the number of urban settlements on the plateau declined drastically. Settlements that survived, however, experienced a concurrent increase in size (Mellaart 1971:406–10). This does not mean that the city was an anomaly during this period, but it does lead us to believe that urban ruins present neither a comprehensive nor a necessarily accurate picture of daily life on the plateau.

Characteristically, the two cities from which we possess substantial data, Kaneš and Ḫattuša, are notable for their cosmopolitan and syncretistic natures. Kaneš built an international reputation as an important terminal for long-distance trade. Ḫattuša, on the other hand, developed its unique character in a dual role as the capital of a far-flung empire and the center of an ever-growing cult. The character of these cities, however, was probably atypical of what was to be found throughout the greater part of Anatolia. The "real" Anatolia was to be found in villages and smaller land-holdings scattered through out numerous valleys that characterized the Anatolian landscape.

The ancient Anatolian inhabitants whom we call the Hittites were, above all else, an agrarian people, pastoralists and agriculturalists who depended on a positive interaction with the land (Hoffner 1974; von den Driesch and Boessneck 1981; Klengel 1986; Beckman 1988; Yakar 2000). The plateau's environmental framework had a great deal to do with how these remarkable people sustained themselves, in cities as well as villages, a fact of which we are constantly reminded in both the archaeological and literary records. Unfortunately, archaeologists, anthropologists, and historians have only recently begun to examine seriously the role of environmental research within the framework of Anatolian archaeology (Angel 1972; Archi 1973; Adams 1981; Deighton 1982; Weiss 1982; Zimansky 1985; Neumann and Parpola 1987).

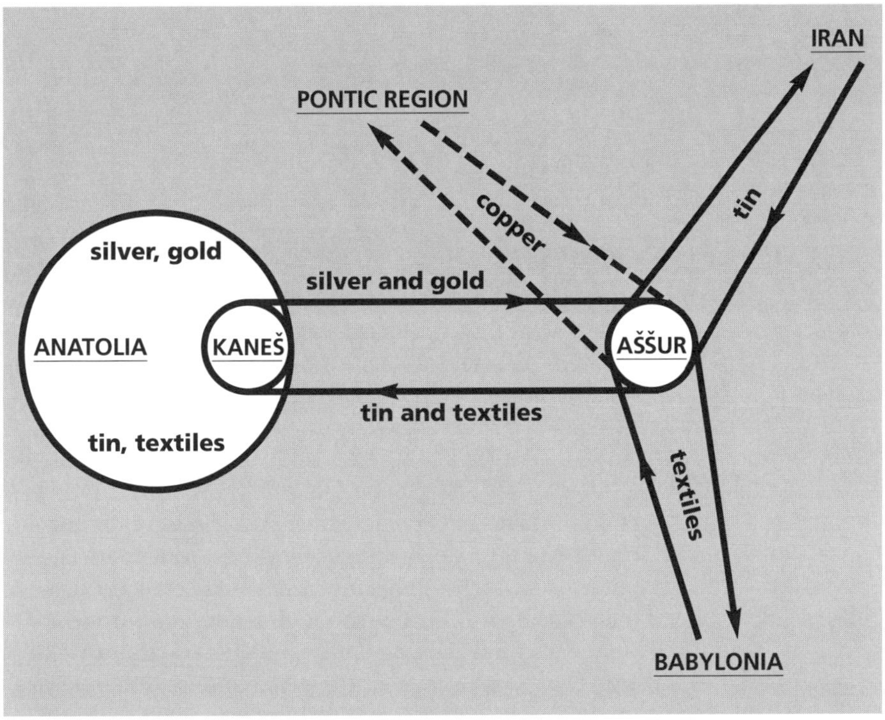

Schematic model of the Old Assyrian trade network that operated during the Colony Age in the early second millennium BCE. This network was made up of mercantile centers, known as *karums*, that were established as suburbs of already existing settlements. Based on Aššur, the Old Assyrian merchants chose Kaneš as the hub of their activities in Anatolia. *Model adapted from Larsen (1987).*

The Proto-Hittite Period

It has often been suggested that the origin of the Hittites may be traced back archaeologically to the people who fashioned the tombs of Alaca Höyük (Frankfort 1954: 212–14; Gimbutas 1963:822–23; but compare Burney and Lang 1972: 49–50; Mellink 1956:39–58). Linguistically, however, scholars link the Hittite-speaking peoples generally with the movement of Indo-European peoples into Anatolia, probably during the second half of the third millennium BCE (Gimbutas 1963; Burney and Lang 1972:86–89; Winn 1974; Yakar 1976, 1981; Mellaart 1981; compare Steiner 1981, 1990). The actual details of population movements during this period remain extremely unclear, and the lack of data allows for widely differing opinions. That various ethnic groups, such as Hattians, Nešites,[4] and Hurrians, all fall under the modern designation "Hittite" further confuses the situation. Whereas the Hattic peoples of the north, to which the Alaca culture must belong, showed strong connections with the east, the Nešites may have been associated with the Indo-European migrations from the west (compare Steiner 1981, 1990). Thus it is quite possible that the archaeologically attested Hittites of the northern part of the plateau may not be the ethnic equivalent of the original linguistically attested, Hittite-speaking peoples who migrated further south (Steiner 1981, 1990). Therefore, our current designation of Hittite represents an artificial categorization of the peoples who lived under the political banner of Ḫattuša. All that can be said about the origins of the Hittites is that they lie hidden, for now, within the fabric of late Anatolian prehistory.

Hittite culture evidently evolved slowly and in relative isolation until the arrival of the Old Assyrian trade merchants spurred its development at the beginning of the second millennium BCE (Mellink 1966:121). These foreign merchants established a widespread network of trading communities in central Anatolia. This network was made up of mercantile centers known as *karums* and *wabartums*. The merchants established them as suburbs of already existing settlements (Orlin 1970: 25–29; Larsen 1976:230–41). They chose Kaneš as the hub of their activities in Anatolia. The peripheral portion of the network consisted of outlying settlements and their trade centers. These were subject to the Assyrian *karum* at Kaneš (Larsen 1976:277–82). Thus, Kaneš assumed a position of leadership in the Old Assyrian trade network. In this regard, it is possible that Kaneš provided an economic prototype for political centralization in Hittite Anatolia. For this reason, Kaneš serves a critical role in our understanding of state formation in early Hittite Anatolia.

It may be suggested, therefore, that the Hittite process of political centralization drew inspiration from, and occurred partly in response to, the emergence of Kaneš as the central focus of the Old Assyrian trade network. This process began an initial phase of widespread integration of local Anatolian polities into a supraregional structure (Orlin 1970: 58, 171, 183). Such a secondary political development finds a parallel in ethnographically and historically documented examples of cultural interaction (Gallagher and Robinson 1953; Robinson 1976; Smith 1976).

In more practical terms, centralization of Assyrian economic activity in Anatolia allowed for the orderly exploitation of resources on the plateau. The advantages and benefits inherent in the position of Kaneš must have become obvious very quickly to many within the community of native Anatolian rulers. While these rulers would doubtless have wanted to emulate the economic success of the Assyrians, they would have had to overcome the

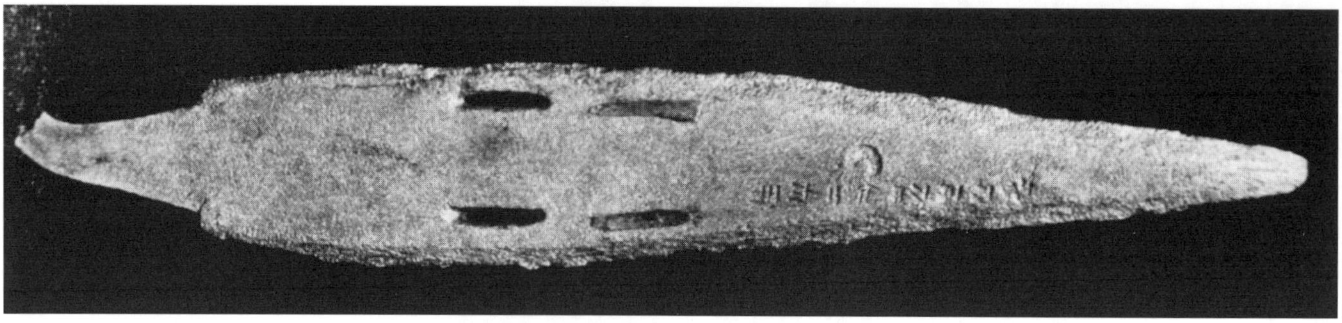

This nine inch dagger, or spearhead, inscribed with "the palace of Anitta the king" was found in the city district of the ancient site of Kaneš. The dagger could indicate that Anitta, a king of Kuššara, actually ruled over Kaneš during the Assyrian Colony Age or, if destruction of the palace is attributed to him, that the dagger was lost there. Note that the original two holes through which the head was attached to the shaft were filled in and remade further down. *Photo courtesy of Tahsin Özgüç.*

disparate character of the Anatolian city-states, each of which was limited to a region that probably extended somewhere between 30 to 60 miles from the chief city. An obvious remedy for this political fragmentation would have been the concentration of power inside central Anatolia itself. Inevitably, these regional states had conflicts that could be resolved only by imposing one city's authority over another. The fact that the king of Purušḫanda seems to have been called "great king" (see Larsen 1976:268–69, n. 56) suggests that the process of centralization was well under way by the end of the Old Assyrian period and that Purušḫanda had achieved an early advantage in the drive for hegemony. Purušḫanda's advantage did not, however, result in long term domination. Perhaps it was the role Kaneš had played within the Old Assyrian network that offset Purušḫanda's quick start, preparing the way for the far-reaching conquests of the early Anatolian king, Anitta.

The Role of Kaneš

Two aspects of Kaneš' strategic location may explain its initial economic primacy in the Old Assyrian trade system. On the one hand, as Itamar Singer has indicated (1981: 119–34), it might be possible to delineate the ethnocultural zones of Anatolia in the second millennium BCE. Extrapolating from Singer's model, it becomes apparent that Kaneš was situated at the intersection of these zones, which placed it on the cutting edge, as it were, of a vigorous ethnocultural exchange taking place between these zones. Having this kind of activity funnel through the gates of the city must have made Kaneš especially influential. Furthermore, its geographic position on the northern terminus of several passes through the Taurus Mountains (Garelli 1963: 96–100; Orlin 1970:39–43) allowed Kaneš to dominate the lines of communication and exchange traveling through those passes. As such it was the ideal center from which to control the redistribution of trade commodities. This fortuitous set of circumstances probably helps explain why Kaneš ultimately became the focal point of the trade between Anatolia and Assyria. As the preeminent marketplace of Anatolia, Kaneš became the gateway through which the hinterland of Anatolia could be reached from the plains of northern Mesopotamia (Burghardt 1971; Hirth 1978; compare Smith 1976:319, 336).

Gateway communities are associated with the formation of dendrite-like market networks that develop in response to the demands of long distance trade or the settlement of sparsely populated areas. A gateway community might develop along important natural routes of travel and communication or at the intersection of passage points between distinct natural or cultural zones. An intersection could develop between zones of agriculture, natural resources, and pastoralism, in the marginal areas that act as borders between regions of dense population, at the interface of zones with differing technologies, or at the point of contact between areas with different sociopolitical organizations. Gateway communities stand at the top of a hierarchical organization with all subsidiary market activity directed toward them. Gateways are linked in linear fashion with far-removed core areas from where the initial economic impulse originated. Their primary function is to facilitate the flow of trade in and out of these contrasting areas, to act as a gateway back and forth between the natural irregularities of the real world (see Johnson 1970; Burghardt 1971; Smith 1976; Hirth 1978).

Kaneš likely played such a role in a similar pattern of long-distance trade already predating the arrival of the Old Assyrian traders (Matthiae 1981:176). New discoveries from the tell of Kaneš now seem to confirm the early date of this pattern (Özgüç 1986) which may have been in place during the last phase of the third millennium, if not earlier (Orlin 1970:88–89; Marfoe 1987; Algaze 1987). By establishing themselves at Kaneš, the Assyrians were only following a time-honored Mesopotamian tradition of trade with the highlands of Anatolia. As such they may have been able to secure a market for their own surplus goods as well as exercise

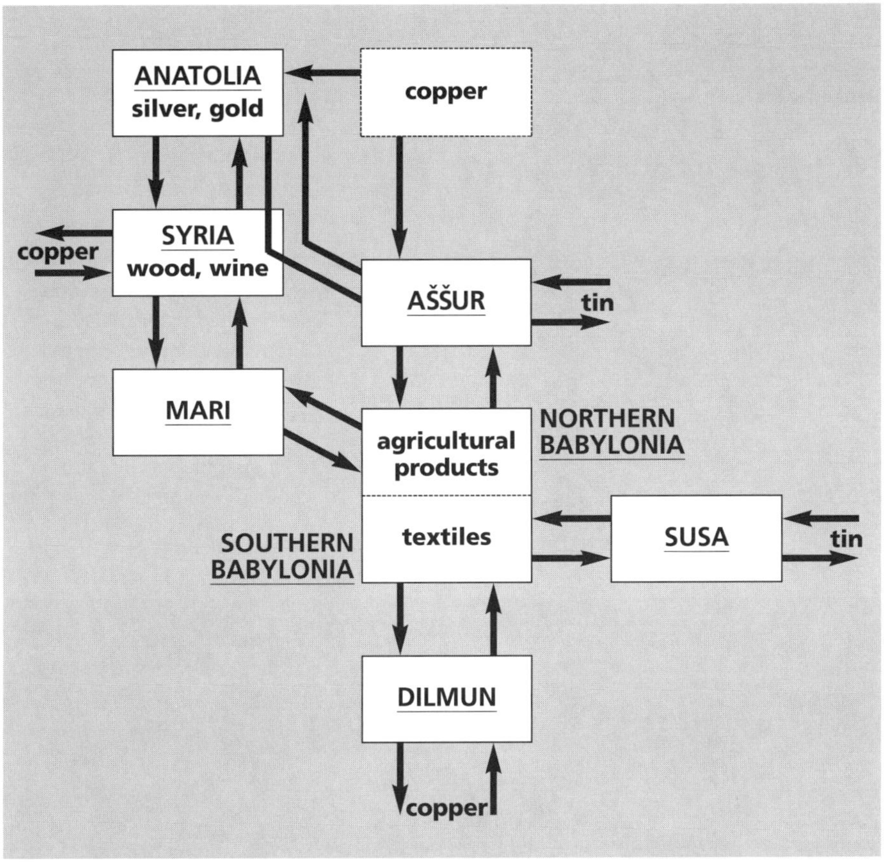

Located on the northern terminus of several passes through the Taurus Mountains, Kaneš was the ideal center from which to control the redistribution of trade commodities such as precious metals, wine, and agricultural products. As the preeminent marketplace of Anatolia, Kaneš became the gateway through which the hinterland of Anatolia could be reached from the plains of northern Mesopotamia. *Schematic model of commodities adapted from Larsen (1987).*

a greater degree of control over the redistribution and, indirectly, the exploitation of Anatolia's highly coveted natural resources.

The exact political relationship between Kaneš and neighboring Anatolian settlements during this period is unclear. On the one hand, textual evidence suggests that, because of its strategic location within the context of the Assyrian trade network, the role of Kaneš was primarily economic. Nevertheless, the promotion of Kaneš to the dominant position in this network must have been prompted not only by its strategic location but by a long tenure of consistent, albeit limited, regional dominance (Orlin 1970:236–41). Only under such conditions could the merchants be assured of having the security and stability necessary for success in long-distance trade.

The establishment of *karums* at cities such as Purušḫanda, Waḫšušana, Ḫurma, and Ḫattuša must have been dictated by many of the same concerns that led to the nomination of Kaneš as the focal point of the system. The hinterlands dominated by these small regional powers were not particularly expansive, but a fortuitous blend of social and environmental factors encouraged the growth of these cities into alternative gateways that pierced the farthest reaches of Anatolia and, as such, became logical locations for the establishment of outlying trade centers. All told, it appears that there was at least some relationship between the establishment of an Assyrian trade center and a pattern of previous regional dominance.

The question then arises as to what happened when one of the *karum* cities went into decline or ceased to exist. The Assyrians may have created a system of zones in which they located their *karums*, one per zone. If a *karum* city was destroyed or abandoned for some reason, the *karum* may have been reinstituted in another city within that zone. This would account for the elevation of several cities that apparently did not have *karums* in period II to *karum* status during the Kültepe Ib period (Larsen 1976:239). Tawiniya, for instance, may have replaced Ḫattuša after the latter's defeat at the hands of Anitta. Wašḫaniya likewise may have replaced either Waḫšušana or Purušḫanda after their political demise. Šamuḫa and Timelkiya are two other cities that may fit into this pattern. Through such a system, the Assyrians maintained a sense of equilibrium throughout the trade system in times of political distress.

Socioeconomic factors notwithstanding, the physical setting in central Anatolia can be viewed as the common denominator around which the culture of the plateau initially coalesced into a distinctively Hittite culture. The physical environment provided the region with a unified subsistence base that must have helped initially to nurture a common bond between the various peoples of the plateau. This perception must have been heightened by the emergent Old Assyrian trade network, which provided the possibility of structured and centralized authority. Such insights may have imbued the region with its first sense of supraregional political power and economic unity. In this respect, the Old Assyrian trade network may have helped lay the groundwork for the political integration process through which the diverse elements of central Anatolia fused into a viable supraregional state (Orlin 1970:58, 183). The only question appears to have been who would finally control the system once the process of political integration was completed.[5]

Typical views of an excavation area in the *karum* at Kaneš. Enormous amounts of pottery were preserved and have been found *in situ*, thus providing valuable information about demographic patterns and ceramic development during the period. *Photos courtesy of Tahsin Özgüç.*

The Political Unification of Central Anatolia

The highly charged activity swirling around Kaneš ultimately brought about a metamorphosis in central Anatolia that probably began as an emerging sense of self-awareness among the inhabitants of the plateau. As previously noted, small city states formed around local centers such as Kaneš, Ḫattuša, Waḫšušana, Zalpa, and Purušḫanda at a very early stage of Anatolian history. The appearance of the Old Assyrian traders may have accentuated an already developing pattern of larger and ever-expanding regional units by providing the inhabitants of the plateau with both a sense of common identity and a central focus. In the short term, the growth of regional kingdoms led to internecine conflicts, as the closely situated states competed for space. In the final analysis, however, such struggles represented only the initial phase of an integration process that ultimately bequeathed the reins of political power in central Anatolia to Ḫattuša.

The emerging states of central Anatolia had also become pockets of dense population in which the stratification of society had greatly accelerated (compare Smith 1976). The rise of urbanization and elitism is probably linked with increased demand for luxury goods and the ability of the elite to manipulate regional trade patterns in their favor as well as to the increasing efficiency of military technology (Adams 1984: 109–14; Hirth 1978:35; Smith 1976). Thus, with a jump in the urban population, increased demand for resources and commodities, the appearance of social elites, and the necessity to control the production and redistribution of trade goods must have become increasingly important factors in interstate competition. Other factors may have been involved, of course, but it is within the context of heightened economic competition that we can best understand the internecine political struggles of the Anatolian states during the early part of the second millennium BCE (Steiner 1981:163–64).

The drama of this period of rivalry is narrated in several Hittite texts, among them the Anitta Text (Neu 1974:10–15), the Telipinu Edict (Hoffmann 1984), and the Annals of Ḫattušili I (Goetze 1962; Imparati and Saporetti 1965; Kempinski and Košak 1982). These texts suggest that the city states had outgrown their roles as regional gateway centers and had developed into politically astute central places that were capable of competing on even terms with Kaneš (Burghardt 1971:284; Hirth 1978:42–43). Thus, the heightened political consciousness of the plateau signaled a significant new role for central Anatolia. Once only peripheral to the major civilizations of Mesopotamia and Syria, this highland area evolved into the core of the nascent Hittite state. Out of this political maelstrom, Ḫattuša eventually emerged as the dominant city in the region.

The Rise of Ḫattuša

Like other sites in central Anatolia, Ḫattuša may originally have been chosen for settlement because of its environmental assets. Water was abundant, and the precipice of Büyükkale offered protection from hostile elements (Bittel 1970:30). In addition, the surrounding valleys offered arable land, and the region appears to have been wooded (Bittel 1970:12–13; compare Brice 1978:141). More important, it was well-positioned to tap into both the east–west and north–south trade routes. As such, Ḫattuša appealed to the Assyrians, who saw in the city's strategic position an ideal secondary gateway to the farthest reaches of northern Anatolia and the thickly populated Bafra region where the important city of Zalpa was located (Haas 1977). Assyrian merchants passed through this gateway to trade their goods and commodities, and their presence must have broadened considerably Ḫattuša's sociopolitical consciousness. As this political consciousness evolved into a complex state ideology, the city began to struggle for control of its own destiny.

The emergence of Ḫattuša as a political power in central Anatolia began at an early period and occurred in several phases. In fact, if we can trust the texts, Ḫattuša, like Kaneš, must have also been a regional power as early as the twenty-third century BCE when a certain "Pamba, king of Ḫatti" is said to have been one of seventeen kings to oppose the incursion of the Akkadian king Naram-Sin into Anatolia (Güterbock 1938). Later, around 1750 BCE, Ḫattuša remains prominent as one of the principal regional powers on the plateau. The Anitta Text mentioned its king, Piyušti, as a principal opponent of the proto-Hittite dynast, Anitta, during his campaigns in central Anatolia (Neu 1974:13). Anitta's subsequent conquest of Ḫattuša seems to have been only a temporary setback, as the city was apparently rebuilt soon after its capture, possibly by one of Anitta's own offspring (Helck 1983:275). The old Hittite texts reflect an expeditious resumption of its vigorous pursuit of power.

Through out its history, Ḫattuša displayed a remarkable resilience. Although it was destroyed on several occasions, other local powers were unable to capitalize permanently on the resultant political vacuum (Haas 1977; Singer 1981:132 and n. 8). Ḫattuša repeatedly rose from the ashes to reassert itself as a leader of Anatolia's north-central region (Bittel 1970). Though literary records are minimal and corroborative archeological evidence exceedingly meager (Bittel 1970:30–47), nevertheless, it seems clear that Ḫattuša had established itself, alongside Kaneš, as one of the dominant regional powers, not only during but prior to the period of the Assyrian traders.

Ḫattuša's rise to prominence was obviously sociopolitical in nature, but its ascendancy only brought to fruition a tendency inherent in the region's environmental unity. This process was prodded along by the centralization of economic authority during the period of commercial contacts with the Assyrians. It was consummated by the establishment of a royal ideology during the Old Hittite Kingdom, an ideology that found its most eloquent expression in the Telipinu Edict (Hoffmann 1984). Whereas the environment provided the foundation upon which the Hittite state was erected, the royal ideology served as the mortar that bonded the political superstructure together.

The Hittite State

The initial period of Hittite dominance on the plateau can be described as a continuation of the intense infighting that characterized the end of the *karum* period. The Telipinu Edict tells us that intrigue and assassination were commonplace in the Old Hittite court. This royal drama may be attributed, in part, to the residual effects of the integration process. Certainly, it illustrates the insecurity felt by the crown during the early stage of state formation. The drama could reflect

These pedestaled vessels, often called "fruitstands" (above), and the red, highly burnished pitchers (opposite) were discovered at the *karum* site at Kaneš. These pieces are characteristic examples of clay pottery dating to the Old Assyrian Colony Age. *Photos courtesy of Tahsin Özgüç.*

the struggle between crown and nobility to determine either the line of succession (Beckman 1986) or the mode of succession (Bryce 1986).

It is amazing that, in the midst of this turbulent period, the Hittites were able to make their first incursions into the world beyond the Anatolian plateau, thus reversing the route of earlier Mesopotamian monarchs and traders. Undoubtedly, the most notable of these campaigns was the conquest of Babylon by Muršili I. This momentary flirtation with greatness was thwarted, however, by the inability of the Hittites to resolve the thorny issue of royal succession (Beckman 1986). The assassination of Muršili I and the ensuing dynastic disputes robbed the state of its leaders and effectively sapped the vitality of the Old Kingdom. As a result, the expansionist tendencies of this period gave way to a modest retrenchment during the following Middle Kingdom (compare Beal 1986).

A second period of dominance began about 1400 BCE with the emergence of strong kings like Tudḫaliya II and Šuppiluliuma I. The expansion of the state took place on both a geographical and an ideological level. Not only did the Empire reach its maximum extent, it came into sustained contact with other major civilizations of the ancient Near East such as Mesopotamia and Egypt. This contact took place on military, diplomatic, and cultural levels and ultimately resulted in the formulation of an imperial ideology that differed somewhat from that of the Old Hittite kings. This new royal ideology was characterized by a greater theocratic sense in which the concepts of divine election and empowerment (*para ḫandandatar*) played significant roles. The concept of divine intervention was not totally unknown in previous periods, but it seems to have found its most extreme expression during the last phase of the Empire (compare Hoffner 1980: 360). Characteristic of this ideology was an increased emphasis on the sacral character of royalty as well as a greater involvement by the divine in the affairs of state. This was especially apparent in warfare; certain kings saw divine intervention as a form of judgment between the contestants (see Hoffner 1980:314–17). As the capital of this theocratically oriented state, Ḫattuša became the focal point and exponent of the royal ideology (see Neve 1987). This is evident not only in the textual materials but also in the sculpted images of Yazılıkaya. These materials suggest that this emphasis was connected to the blossoming Hurrian influences

already known from the Old Hittite period (Güterbock 1954; also see Ünal in this volume).

The earliest settlements at Ḫattuša must have been representative of the essentially indigenous culture of the plateau. The city eventually transcended its regional character, however, and, by the last days of the Empire, had become the showcase of a widespread syncretism that reflected the official ideology of this religiopolitical amalgam through a state cult (Laroche 1975; Gurney 1977). In the process, it came to include much that was not native to Hittite culture. It became fully cosmopolitan, both in the breadth of its international contacts and in the scope of its religiopolitical ideology. This made Ḫattuša unique in central Anatolia. Naturally, because of the nature of a capital city, its material culture may not give us an accurate picture of life among rural inhabitants during this period. Instead, its remains probably depict a mixed culture that many inhabitants of the nearby Hittite countryside probably regarded as somewhat foreign.

In the final analysis, Ḫattuša emerged as a center of power not only because of its positive response to the physical world but also because its kings had both the will and the capacity to rule. This dynamic interplay between human beings and the land ultimately fashions the distinctive character of a civilization, and this brings me back to my original point: Although the superstructure of the Hittite state was political in nature, it must not be forgotten that the kingdom was built on an underlying ecological foundation.

The End of the Hittite Empire

Numerous literary texts outline the last days of the Hittite Empire (Otten 1963, 1983). These narratives tend to focus on events in which human beings played a major role (Liverani 1987; Hoffner 1992). I contend, however, that there were other, less visible events taking place that ultimately helped shape the historical picture of Anatolia. These events were environmental in nature.

Although we lack reliable climatic and chronological data for central Anatolia, the available evidence suggests that the Hittite Empire flourished during a climatically favorable period. In fact, the three centuries between 1500 and 1200 BCE (the Late Bronze Age) appear to have been cooler and moister throughout the whole of the ancient Near East (Bintliff 1982:147; Neumann and Parpola 1987). This era was followed by a somewhat drier period that likely lasted from 1200 to about 900 BCE (Kay and Johnson 1981:258; Neumann and Parpola 1987:163–65, 177; cf. Brice 1978:145). The beginning of this drier period seems to have coincided with a chain of events that greatly influenced the course of history, not only on the Anatolian

Hittite Chronology

Unlike the Mesopotamian and Egyptian scribes who compiled listings of successive rulers, called *king lists*, the Hittites apparently never developed the same sense of chronology and kept no real king lists. They did, however, compile the so-called *offering lists* for dead Hittite kings (Otten 1955; Gurney 1972). These offering lists provide a great deal of information regarding Hittite royalty, including the number and types of offerings left for certain individuals of the royal house as well as the names of some Hittite queens. The lists are problematic, however, not only because of their fragmentary state of preservation but also because they exclude some known kings while including royal princes who, as far as we know, never attained kingship. Consequently, most attempts at determining historical context in Hittite Anatolia have emphasized relative sequences rather than absolute dates.

Efforts to provide absolute dates for Hittite history rest on a few known synchronisms. These are records of events shared between the Hittites and their neighbors in which a Hittite king is linked in the historical documentation to an event, a foreign king, or a personality to whom we can give a relatively secure absolute date. In so doing, it becomes possible to link the relative Hittite sequences to an external absolute sequence (generally Egypt) and to record them in terms of approximate calendar years.

The events that most readily allow us to do this are important astronomical phenomena recorded by ancient scribes. By using current knowledge of these astronomical occurrences, including the time it takes for such events to recur, it is possible to fix these dates with a fair degree of accuracy. These dates then become linchpins around which the blocks of relative dates swing and from which the pieces of Hittite history are fit together into a chronological framework.

In the case of Anatolia, the historical linchpin of early Hittite chronology has always been the sack of Babylon by Muršili I. The date of this event has traditionally been established on the basis of astronomical observations from the so-called Venus tablets, records referring to the sixth year of the king Ammisaduqa, which we know from the Babylonian king lists to have been 46 years before the Hittite raid and collapse of the dynasty of Hammurapi (Astour 1989). In the tablet detailing observations of that year, the scribe noted the occurrence of a conjunction between the moon and Venus, which can theoretically be fixed in time by modern calculations. The fact that this is a relatively frequent occurrence, however, combined with the knowledge of certain textual difficulties, leaves the actual date of this conjunction open to various interpretations (Smith 1951: 67; Reiner and Pingree 1975:25; Huber 1982:120). Based on these calculations, scholars arrive at three different dates for the sack of Babylon: 1651 BCE for the high chronology, 1595 BCE for the middle chronology, and 1531 BCE for the low chronology.

The uncertainty surrounding the historical documentation means that the framework within which the absolute chronology of the Hittite state is to be understood remains a highly conjectural issue. Practically every period of Hittite history remains a matter of intense debate, and there are almost as many viewpoints as there are Hittitologists. Problems start at the very beginning of recorded Hittite history with questions regarding their emergence as a people and their role in the Old Assyrian colonies of central Anatolia. The succeeding Hittite Old Kingdom and the Hittite Middle Kingdom were times of palace intrigue and political

plateau but throughout the ancient Near East (Neumann and Parpola 1987; Carpenter 1966).

As suggested at the beginning of the chapter, patterns of settlement and subsistence in central Anatolia were the direct result of human interaction with the environment. The successful political integration of Anatolian settlements into the Hittite state depended to a degree on the way in which its inhabitants responded to their physical setting. Although the Hittites rose to a position of world prominence, they were never able to escape the constraints of their environment, and because of the specialized nature of urban society, they may have become even more constrained by them. Thus, if we are prepared to accept the idea that the initial integration of the Hittite state was due in part to the inhabitants' positive response to the environmental framework of the central plateau, we should not be surprised to find that the end of the Hittite Empire may have occurred partly as the result of a general disintegration of this association. This breakdown was probably precipitated by a combination of negative forces in the environment—perhaps elicited by higher solar activity (Eddy 1977; but compare Landsberg 1980:182)—that resulted in the warmer and drier climate mentioned previously.

Natural catastrophes were not rare in the land of Hittite Anatolia (Ünal 1977), but the type of warming trend suggested here would have had a much more significant impact on the ecology of the plateau than the disasters commonly experienced in the region. Modern environmental studies indicate that even a small downward variation in the amount of precipitation can adversely affect agricultural production on the plateau as well as vegetation of the steppe upon which the nomads de-

assassinations. The exact sequence of events during these periods is confused in a tangle of kings, princes, and royal retainers. As a result, the precise number and sequence of kings attributable to these periods are not universally agreed upon. The Hittite Empire is somewhat better understood because of the relatively frequent synchronisms with Egypt, but even here debate continues on several issues, not the least of which is the manner and date of the Empire's demise.

While Egyptian evidence provides the best data for correlating events in Hittite history to an established chronological framework, one must also take into account the Mesopotamian evidence, of which the Assyrian evidence is the most important. Connections with the Assyrians are more difficult to assess, however, because neither they nor the Hittites mention each other in their royal annals. The foundation for our understanding of Assyro-Hittite relations is built on an important corpus of correspondence between the royal houses of Hatti and Assyria. Unfortunately, the Assyrian information is not easily correlated with the Egyptian material, and it becomes the role of the Hittites to provide indirect synchronisms between the two. When the names of the correspondents in the Assyro-Hittite correspondence are preserved, they provide an independent means of checking the Egyptian synchronisms. All too often, however, the names of the sender, the recipient, or both, are missing, and the identification of the correspondents becomes a matter of educated guesswork. Nevertheless, a fairly secure system of synchronisms with Assyria can now be postulated to exist between Urḫi-Tešub (Muršili III) and Adad-nirari I, between Ḫattušili II and both Adad-nirari I and Šalmaneser I, and between Tudḫaliya IV and Tukulti-ninurta I. (For a full listing of Hittite and pre-Hittite kings using both low and middle chronology dates, see page 60).

Thus, although the chronology of Hittite Anatolia remains enigmatic, progress has been made. Recent years have witnessed a steady lowering of absolute dates in the ancient Near East. This is especially true of events related to Egypt (see, for example, Beckerath 1964; Hornung 1964; Helck 1972; Wente and van Siclen 1977) where new excavations at Tell el Dabʿa provide strong evidence for the lowering of Egyptian dates, especially during the Middle Bronze Age (Bietak 1984). This trend has produced a kind of ripple effect in Mesopotamia where Egyptian materials provide evidence for a similar lowering of dates there (Redford 1979:277–79). In addition, clear and convincing evidence for the low chronology comes from the north Levantine city of Alalakh (Gates 1987). Because the lack of fixed dates for the reigns of the various Hittite kings forces scholars to build relative chronologies based primarily on synchronisms with the Egyptian system, any lowering of the Egyptian chronology, not to mention those of Mesopotamia and Syro-Palestine, will have a domino effect on Anatolian chronology.

Generally speaking, the low chronology—in one variation or another—has gained an increasing array of adherents (see, for example, Wilhelm and Boese 1987; Boese and Wilhelm 1979; Bietak 1984; Gates 1987; for the ultralow chronology, see Wente and van Siclen 1977). Acceptance of the low chronology is far from universal, but many Hittitologists and students of the ancient Near East (myself included) have accepted it as the standard, believing it provides the best vehicle by which to convey a sense of time to the study of Hittite chronology. The matter is still much in debate, however, and students are left to determine with which system to cast their lots. The one sure thing is that whichever chronology one decides on, he or she is in good company.

pend (Erinç 1950; Fisher 1978: 94; Adams 1981:11; Neumann and Parpola 1987:162). According to recent studies, the overall impact of a drier period could have become manifest by drought (Weiss 1982) and crop failure (Erinç 1978:75–76) as well as famine and malnutrition (Astour 1965:255; Klengel 1974), resulting, one would anticipate, in disease and declining fertility.

The sociopolitical implications of deleterious environmental varation also merit consideration. One result could have been internal dissatisfaction and revolt in the homeland. Similar circumstances on the periphery of the Empire might have set off mass movements of peoples in search of less effected regions (Angel 1972:99; Fisher 1978: 94). We know that during the late thirteenth century BCE, a variety of sociopolitical forces were probing the perimeter of the Hittite state. Foremost among these forces was the large-scale movement of peoples in the form of both migrating nomads (von Schuler 1965: 65–66) and marauding Sea Peoples (Sandars 1978:139–44). If the negative environmental conditions actually prevailed at the end of the Empire, they could have helped undermine the foundations of the Hittite political structure. With the underlying weaknesses of the state exposed, the Empire would have been highly vulnerable to the forces confronting it. Accounts of the Egyptian pharaoh Ramses III detailed the Hittites inability to withstand relentless pressures (Sandars 1978:139–44). Thus, the convergence of various environmental and sociopolitical factors weakened the Hittites and left them unable to maintain their Empire in the face of relentless pressure from without. The Empire came to an end.

Conclusion

Discontinuity of civilization marks the major sites on the plateau after the fall of the Hittite Empire (Bittel 1983:37–38). This gap continued until the appearance of Iron Age settlements during the ninth through eighth centuries BCE (Bittel 1983:37), a resurgence that coincided with the appearance of a moister climate throughout the region (Neumann and Parpola 1987:162). Thus, we are confronted with one of the more serious dilemmas facing Anatolian archaeologists: how to explain the apparent cessation of urban settlements on the plateau after the fall of the Hittites. As mentioned before, the demise of the Late Bronze Age economic structure is generally attributed to the incursions of nomadic peoples (von Schuler 1965:65–66). This assumption is reasonable in light of historical narratives indicating that such a coupling of climatic change and nomadic incursions may not be without parallel in the history of the ancient Near East (Ritter-Kaplan 1984; Ghawanmeh 1985:315; Neumann and Parpola 1987:162, n. 4). Questions remain, however, as to the disposition of the indigenous population after this event.

The answer to this problem is probably multifaceted. Some inhabitants may have been killed by newcomers while others were assimilated. Those who were able may have migrated to other areas of comparative safety. By and large, however, it seems reasonable to assume that many inhabitants of the Hittite heartland simply returned to their pastoral-nomadic roots. Indeed, such a shift may not have been as drastic as is often supposed (Kohl 1978:472). Recent ethnographic studies show that there is no clear-cut line between pastoralism and sedentism and that the two subsistence patterns need not be viewed as mutually exclusive (Adams 1974). Instead, we may find a fluidity that allows movement between the two modes as a means of dealing with an unpredictable environment (Kohl 1978:471; Barth 1962:350; Nissen 1980:285–90). This mode of subsistence leaves little in the way of material remains, however, so it may appear that the plateau was unsettled during this period. The absence of settlements during this period is clear at the major urban sites of the Late Hittite Empire, but we simply do not have enough data to make definitive statements on the overall situation. It may be that a new pattern of settlement emerged apart from that of the Hittite Empire and that this pattern had a new center of focus of which we are not yet aware (Bittel 1983:37) Perhaps data of this kind will emerge from future studies related to the native Iron Age kingdoms of Anatolia, such as Tabal.[6] There is, however, no evidence for such a demographic shift.

Finally, one fact should be kept in mind. Because the nature of the physical evidence makes it very difficult to trace archaeologically the existence of rural inhabitants in any culture, it may be that they are not missing at all. The real missing persons of the post-Hittite era may well be the urban elite and the urban elite alone. Their absence in no way precludes the possibility that the remainder of the population could have continued to exist much as they always had in smaller, more traditional village settlements. Such an option would have presented an alternative strategy more suited to the conditions present in Anatolia after the breakdown of the Late Bronze Age palace economy. In the absence of comprehensive regional surveys, evidence for nonurban types of settlement is unavailable. Evidence for sedentary life in this region may yet come from some of the many small tells around Ḫattuša. If the aristocracy had become somewhat estranged from the native rural population, however, these farmers and shepherds, even if they had the power, may not have had the inclination to restore the cities that had become seats of power for an urban elite. If this were the case, the decline of the Hittite political structure could have been seen as a welcome relief from an artificial system that excluded rural people from the fruits of power, but not from its burdens.

The role of the environment in the collapse of the Hittite state is not well-attested, but I believe future study will show that environmental factors were intimately involved in both the integration of the Hittite state and its eventual demise. My intention has not been to take the side of environmental determinism but to provoke study into an area that has been somewhat neglected in Anatolian studies. Obviously, some of the ideas expressed here need to be tested further in the field. One of the goals of future excavations in Turkey should be to devise strategies by which such hypotheses can be addressed.

Notes

[1] For other overviews of Hittite archaeology, see Goetze (1961), Lloyd (1965), Mellink (1965, 1966), Bittel (1980), and Bryce (1998).

[2] Located about 12 miles northeast of Kayseri, Kaneš consists of a high mound and surrounding lower city where the *karum* was located (Orthmann 1976–1980). Excavation at the ancient city was first carried out by Friedrich Hrozný in 1925 but has been under the direction of Tahsin Özgüç since 1948.

[3] The village has recently been renamed Boğazkale, but for the sake of consistency archaeologists and philologists continue to use Boğazköy.

[4] The toponym Neša is now equated with the city of Kaneš. Thus, the Nešites are to be understood here as the people of Kaneš. The situation is complicated, however, by the fact that the Hittites were also speakers of Nešita (*Nešumnili*), or the language of Neša (Güterbock 1958).

[5] The Hittite records indicate that many cities took part in the struggle for supremacy before Ḫattuša finally won out. Among them were Kaneš, Purušḫanda, Zalpa, and Šanaḫuitta (Haas 1977; Singer 1981: 132, note 8).

[6] For further information on the study of Iron Age Hittite states, see Hawkins (1982) and McMahon, this volume.

Bibliography

Adams, R. M.
1974 Mesopotamian Social Landscape: A View from the Frontier. Pp. 1–20 in *Reconstructing Complex Societies: An Archaeological Colloquium*, edited by C. Moore. Cambridge: Cambridge Archaeological Seminar.
1981 *Heartland of Cities*. Chicago: University of Chicago Press.
1984 Mesopotamian Social Evolution: Old Outlooks, New Goals. Pp. 79–129 in *On the Evolution of Complex Societies: Essays in Honor of Harry Hoijer*, edited by T. Earle. Malibu, CA: Undena.

Algaze, G.
1987 *Mesopotamian Expansion and its Consequences*. Ph.D. dissertation, The University of Chicago.

Alp, S.
1987 *Beiträge zur Erforshung des Hethitischen Temples: Kultlagen im Lichte der Keilschnfttexte*. Türk Tarih Kurumu Yayinlari Series VI, 23. Ankara: Türk Tarih Kurumu Basımevi.

Angel, L.
1972 Ecology and Population in the Eastern Mediterranean. *World Archaeology* 4:101–27.

Archi, A.
1973 Bureaucratie et communautés d'hommes libres dans le système économique hittite. Pp. 17–23 in *Festschrift Heinrich Otten 27. Dez. 1973*, edited by E. Neu and C. Rüster. Wiesbaden: Otto Harrassowitz.
1978 La feste presso gli ittite. *La Parola Del Passato* 179:81–89.

Astour, M.
1965 New Evidence on the Last Days of Ugarit. *American Journal of Archaeology* 69:253–58.
1989 *Hittite History and Absolute Chronology of the Bronze Age*. Partille: Paul Åströms Forlag.

Barth, F.
1962 Nomadism in the Mountain and Plateau Areas of South West Asia. Pp. 341–55 in *The Problems of the Arid Zone, UNESCO, 1960*. Indianapolis: Bobbs-Merrill.

Beal, R.
1983a The Hittites after the Empire's Fall. *Biblical Illustrator* Fall:72–81.
1983b Studies in Hittite History. *Journal of Cuneiform Studies* 35:122–26.
1986 The History of Kizzuwatna and the Date of the Šunaššura Treaty. *Orientalia* 55:424–45.

Beckerath, J. von
1964 *Untersuchungen zur politischen Geschichte der zweiten Zwischenzeit in Ägypten*. Glückstadt: J. J. Augustin.

Beckman, G.
1986 Inheritance and Royal Succession among the Hittites. Pp. 13–31 in *Kaniššuwar: Studies in Honor of Hans Güterbock*. Chicago: The Oriental Institute of the University of Chicago.
1988 Herding and Herdsmen in Hittite Culture. Pp. 33–44 in *Documentum Asiae Minoris Antiquae*, edited by E. Neu and C. Rüster. Wiesbaden: Otto Harrassowitz.

Bietak, M.
1984 Problems of Middle Bronze Age Chronology: New Evidence from Egypt. *American Journal of Archaeology* 88:471–85.

Bintliff, J. L.
1982 Climatic Change, Archaeology, and Quaternary Science in the Eastern Mediterranean Region. Pp. 143–61 in *Climatic Change in Later Prehistory*, edited by A. Harding. Edinburgh: Edinburgh University Press.

Bittel, K.
1969 Bericht über die Ausgrabungen in Boğazköy im Jahre 1968. *Mitteilungen der Deutschen Orientgesellschaft* 101:5–13.
1970 *Hattusha: The Capital of the Hittites*. New York: Oxford University Press.
1976 *Die Hethiter*. Munich: C. H. Beck.
1980 The German Perspective and the German Archaeological Institute. *American Journal of Archaeology* 84:271–77.
1983 Quelques Remarques Archéologiques sur la Topographie de Ḫattuša. Pp. 485–509 in *Comptes rendus de l'académie des inscriptions*. Paris: Diffusion de Boccard.

Boese, J. and Wilhelm, G.
1979 Assur-Dan I: Ninurta-Apil-Ekur und die mittelassyrische Chronologie. *Wiener Zeitschrift für die Kunde des Morgenlandes* 71:19–38.

Börker-Klahn, J.
1969 Zur Datierung von Karum Kanis II und Ib. *Istanbul Mitteilungen* 14: 79–83.

Brice, W. C.
1978 The Desiccation of Anatolia. Pp. 141–47 in *The Environmental History of the Near and Middle East*, edited by W. C. Brice. London: Academic Press.

Brinkman, J. A.
1964 Mesopotamian Chronology of the Historical Period. Pp. 335–52 in *Ancient Mesopotamia: Portrait of a Dead Civilization*, edited by A. L. Oppenheim. Chicago: University of Chicago Press.

Bryce, T.
1986 Review of Inge Hoffmann, *Der Telipinu Erlass*, Heidelberg: Carl Winter, 1984 (=Text der Hethiter 11). *Bibliotheca Orientalis* 43:750–51.
1998 *The Kingdom of the Hittites*. Oxford: Clarendon Press.

Bryson, R. A., Lamb, H. H., and Donley, D.
1974 Drought and the Decline of Mycenae. *Antiquity* 48:46–50.

Burghardt, A. F.
1971 A Hypothesis about Gateway Cities. *Annals of the Association of American Geographers* 61:269–85.

Burney, C., and Lang, D. M.
1972 *Peoples of the Hills: Ancient Ararat and Caucasus*. New York: Praeger.

Canby, J. V.
1975 The Walters Gallery Cappadocian Tablet and the Sphinx in Anatolia in the Second Millennium B.C. *Journal of Near Eastern Studies* 34:225–48.

Carpenter, R.
1966 *Discontinuity in Greek Civilization*. New York: W. W. Norton.

Carruba, O.
1977 Beiträge zur Mittelhethitischen Geschichte I, II. *Studi Micenei ed Egeo-Anatolici* 18:166–77.

Deighton, H. J.
1982 *The "Weather-God" in Hittite Anatolia: An Examination of the Archaeological and Textual Sources*. BAR International Series 143. Oxford: BAR.

Driesch, A. von den and Boessneck, J.
1981 *Reste von Haus- und Jagdtieren aus der Unterstadt von Boğazköy-Ḫattuša*. Berlin: Gebr. Mann.

Eddy, J. A.
1977 Climate and the Changing Sun. *Climatic Change* 1:182.

Edwards, D. R.
1997 Miletus. Pp. 26–28 in *The Oxford Encyclopedia of Archaeology in the Near East*, edited by E.M. Meyers. Oxford: Oxford University Press.

Emre, K.
1963 The Pottery of the Assyrian Colony Period According to the Building Levels of the Kaniš Karum. *Anatolia* 7:87–89.

Erinç, S.
1950 Climatic Types and the Variation of Moisture Regions in Turkey. *Geographical Review* 40:224–35.
1978 Changes in the Physical Environment in Turkey Since the End of the Last Glacial. Pp. 87–110 in *The Environmental History of the Near and Middle East since the Last Ice Age*, edited by W. Brice. London: Academic Press.

Fisher, W. B.
1978 *The Middle East: A Physical, Social, and Regional Geography.* 7th ed. London: Metheun & Co.

Frankfort, H.
1954 *The Art and Architecture of the Ancient Orient.* London: Penguin Books.

Gallagher, J. and Robinson, R.
1953 The Imperialism of Free Trade. *Economic History Review*, Second Series 6:1–15.

Garelli, P.
1963 *Les Assyriens en Cappadoce.* Paris: Librairie Adrien Maisonneuve.

Gates, M.-H.
1987 Alalakh and Chronology Again. Pp. 60–86 in *High, Middle or Low?*, edited by P. Åström. Gothenburg: Paul Åströms Forlag.

Ghawanmeh, Y.
1985 The Effect of Plague and Drought on the Environment of the Southern Levant during the Late Mamluk Period. *Studies in the History and Archaeology of Jordan* 11:315–22.

Gimbutas, M.
1963 The Indo-Europeans: Archaeological Problems. *American Anthropologist* 65:815–36.
1985 The Primary and Secondary Homeland of the Indo-Europeans. *Journal of Indo-European Studies* 13:185–202.

Goetze, A.
1957 *Kulturgeschichte Kleinasien.* Munich: C. H. Beck.
1961 Hittite and Anatolian Studies. Pp. 316–27 in *The Bible and the Ancient Near East: Essays in Honor of William Foxwell Albright*, edited by G. E. Wright. Garden City, NY: Doubleday.
1962 Review of H. G. Güterbock and H. Otten, *Keilschrifttexte aus Boğazköy X: Text aus Gebäude K. 1. Teil. Wissenschaftliche Veröffentlichungen der Deutschen Orient-Gesellschaft* 72:24–30.

Gurney, O. R.
1972 Review of H. Otten, *Die hethitischen historischen Quellen und die altorientalische Chronologie. Orientalische Literaturzeitung* 67:451–54.
1977 *Some Aspects of the Hittite Religion.* The Schweich Lectures 1976. Oxford: Oxford University Press.
1981 *The Hittites.* New York: Penguin Books.

Güterbock, H. G.
1938 Die Historische Tradition bei Babyloniern und Hethitern. *Zeitschrift für Assyriologie* 44:65–80.
1954 The Hurrian Element in the Hittite Empire. *Cahiers d'Histoire Mondiale (Journal of World History)* 2:383–94.
1958 Kaneš and Neša, Two Forms of One Anatolian Name. *Eretz Israel* 5:46–50.

Haas, V.
1977 Zalpa, die Stadt am Schwarzen Meer und das althethitische Königtum. *Mitteilungen der Deutschen Orient-gesellschaft* 109:15–26.

Hauptmann, H.
1997 Nevali Çori. Pp. 131–34 in *The Oxford Encyclopedia of Archaeology in the Near East*, edited by E.M. Meyers. Oxford: Oxford University Press.

Hawkins, J. D.
1982 The Neo-Hittite States in Syria and Anatolia. Pp. 372–441 in *Cambridge Ancient History.* Vol. III/1. Cambridge: Cambridge University Press.

Helck, W.
1972 *Die Beziehungen Ägyptens zu Vorderasien im 3. un 2. Jahrtausend v. Chr.* Wiesbaden: Otto Harrassowitz.
1983 Zur Ältesten Geschichte des Ḫatti-Reiches. Pp. 271–81 in *Beiträge zur Altertumskunde Kleinasiens: Festschrift für Kurt Bittel*, edited by R. M. Boehmer and H. Hauptmann. Mainz: Philipp von Zabern.

Henrickson, R. C. and Voigt, M. M.
1998 The Early Iron Age at Gordion: Evidence from the Yassihoyuk Stratigraphic Sequence. Pp. 79–106 in *Thracians and Phrygians: Problems of Parallelism*, edited by N. Tuna, Z. Aktüre, and M. Lynch. Proceedings of an International Symposium on the Archaeology, History, and Ancient Languages of Thrace and Phrygia, Ankara, 3–4 June 1995. Ankara: METU, Faculty of Architecture Press.

Hirth, K. G.
1978 Interregional Trade and the Formation of Prehistoric Gateway Communities. *American Antiquity* 43:35–45.

Hoffmann, I.
1984 *Der Telipinu Erlass.* Heidelberg: Carl Winter.

Hoffner, H. A.
1974 *Alimenta Hethaeorum: Food Production in Hittite Asia Minor.* American Oriental Series 55. New Haven: American Oriental Society.
1980 Histories and Historians of the Ancient Near East: The Hittites. *Orientalia* 49:283–332.
1992 The Last Days of Khattusha. Pp. 46–52 in *The Crisis Years: The 12th Century B.C. From Beyond the Danube to the Tigris*, edited by W. A. Ward and M. S. Joukowsky. Dubuque: Kendall Hunt Publishers.

Hornung, E.
1964 *Untersuchungen zur Chronologie und Geschichte des neuen Reiches.* Wiesbaden: Harrossowitz.

Houwink ten Cate, P.
1970 *The Records of the Early Hittite Empire (c. 1450–1380).* Istanbul: Nederlands Historische-Archaeologisch Instituut.
1974 The Early and Late Phases of Urhi-Tesub's Career. Pp. 123–50 in *Anatolian Studies Presented to Hans Gustav Güterbock on the Occasion of his 65th Birthday*, edited by K. Bittel et al. Istanbul: Nederlands Historisch-Archaeologisch Instituut.

Huber, P.
1982 *Astronomical Dating of Babylon I and Ur 111.* Occasional Papers on the Near East I/4. Malibu, CA: Undena.

Imparati, F. and Saporetti, C.
1965 L'Autobiografia di Ḫattušili I. *Studi classici e orientali* 14:40–85.

Jewell, E.
1974 *The Archaeology and History of Western Anatolia during the Second Millennium.* Ph.D. dissertation, University of Pennsylvania.

Johnson, E. A. J.
1970 *The Organization of Space in Developing Countries.* Cambridge, MA: Harvard University Press.

Kay, P. A. and Johnson, D. L.
1981 Estimation of Tigris-Euphrates Streamflow from Regional Paleoenvironmental Proxy Data. *Climatic Change* 3:251–63.

Kempinski, A. and Košak, S.
1982 CTH 13: The Extensive Annals of Ḫattušili I (?). *Tel Aviv* 9:87–116.

Klengel, H.
1974 "Hungerjahre" in Hatti. *Altorientalische Forschungen* 1: 165–74.
1986 The Economy of the Hittite Household (É). *Oikumene* 5:23–31.

Kohl, P.
1978 The Balance of Trade in Southwestern Asia in the Mid-Third Millennium B.C. *Current Anthropology* 19:463–92.

Landsberg, H. E.
1980 Variable Solar Emissions, the "Maunder Minimum" and Climatic Temperature Fluctuations. *Archiv für Meteorologie, Geophysik und Bioklimatologie* 28:181–91.

Laroche, E.
1975 La réforme religieuse du roi Tudhaliya IV et sa signification politique. Pp. 87–95 in *Syncrétismes dans les religions de l'antique*, edited by F. Dunand and P. Lévéque. Études préliminaries aux religions orientales dans l'empire Romains 46. Leiden: E. J. Brill.

Larsen, M. T.
1976 *The Old Assyrian City-State and Its Colonies.* Copenhagen: Akademisk Forlag.
1987 Commercial Networks in the Ancient Near East. Pp. 47–56 in *Center and Periphery in the Ancient World,* edited by M. Rowlands, M. Larsen, and K. Kristiansen. Cambridge: Cambridge University Press.

Lebrun, R.
1984 À Propos de quelques Rois Hittites Bâtisseurs. Pp. 157–66 in *Archéologie et Religions de L'Anatolie Ancienne,* edited by R. Donceel and R. Lebrun. Louvain-La-Neuve: Centre D'Histoire des Religions.

Liverani, M.
1987 The Collapse of the Near Eastern Regional System at the End of the Late Bronze Age: The Case of Syria. Pp. 66–73 in *Center and Periphery in the Ancient World,* edited by M. Rowlands, M. Larsen, and K. Kristiansen. Cambridge: Cambridge University Press.

Lloyd, S.
1965 Anatolia: An Archaeological Renaissance. *Bulletin of the Institute of Archaeology* 5:1–14.

Macqueen, J. G.
1986 *The Hittites and Their Contemporaries in Asia Minor,* rev. and enl. ed. London: Thames and Hudson.

Marfoe, L.
1987 Cedar Forest to Silver Mountain: Social Change and the Development of Long-Distance Trade in Early Near Eastern Societies. Pp. 25–35 in *Centre and Periphery in the Ancient World,* edited by M. Rowlands, M. Larsen, and K. Kristiansen. Cambridge: Cambridge University Press.

Matthews, R.
1998 The Kerkenes Dağ Project. Pp. 177–94 in *Ancient Anatolia: Fifty Years' Work by the British Institute of Archaeology at Ankara,* edited by R. Matthews. London: British Institute of Archaeology at Ankara.

Matthiae, P.
1981 *Ebla: An Empire Rediscovered.* Translated by C. Holme. Garden City, NY: Doubleday.

Mellaart, J.
1971 Anatolia, c. 4000–2300 B.C. Pp. 365–415 in *Cambridge Ancient History.* Vol. 1, pt. 2. Cambridge: Cambridge University Press.
1981 Anatolia and the Indo-Europeans. *Journal of Indo-European Studies* 9:135–49.

Mellink, M.
1956 *A Hittite Cemetery at Gordion.* Philadelphia: University Museum of the University of Pennsylvania.
1965 Anatolian Chronology. Pp. 101–31 in *Chronologies in Old World Archaeology,* edited by R. W. Ehrich. Chicago: University of Chicago Press.
1966 Anatolia: Old and New Perspectives. *Proceedings of the American Philosophical Society* 110:111–29.

Mitchell, S.
1993 *Anatolia: Land, Men, and Gods in Asia Minor.* Vol. 1. *The Celts in Anatolia.* Oxford: Clarendon Press.
1999 Kerkenes Dağ. *British School at Athens Archaeological Reports* 45:187–88.

Naumann, R.
1983 *Architektur Kleinasien.* Tübingen: Ernst Wasmuth.

Neimeyer, W.-D.
1998 The Mycenaeans in Western Anatolia and the Problem of the Origins of the Sea Peoples. Pp. 17–65 in *Mediterranean Peoples in Transition: Thirteenth to Early Tenth Centuries BCE*, edited by S. Gitin, A. Mazar, and E. Stern. Jerusalem: Israel Exploration Society.

Neu, E.
1974 *Der Anitta-Text.* Studien zu den Boğazköy-Texten 18. Wiesbaden: Otto Harrassowitz.

Neumann, J. and Parpola, S.
1987 Climatic Change and the Eleventh-Tenth-Century Eclipse of Assyria and Babylon. *Journal of Near Eastern Studies* 46:161–77.

Neve, P.
1982 *Büyükkale: Die Bauwerke.* Berlin: Gebr. Mann.
1984 Ein althethitisches Sammelfund aus der Unterstadt. Pp. 63–89 in *Boğazköy-Ḫattuša VI: Funde aus der Grabungen bis 1979.* Berlin: Gebr. Mann.
1987 Hattuscha, Haupt- und Kultstadt der Hethiter—Ergebnisse der Ausgrabungen in der Oberstadt. *Hethitica* 7:297–318.

Nissen, H. J.
1980 The Mobility between Settled and Non-Settled in Early Babylonia: Theory and Evidence. Pp. 285–90 in *L'Archéologie de L'Iraq,* edited by M. T. Barrelet. Paris: Centre National de la Recherche Scientifique.

Orlin, L.
1970 *Assyrian Colonies in Cappadocia.* Paris: Mouton.

Orthmann, W.
1976–80 Karum Kanis: Archaeologisch. *Realexicon der Assyriologie* V:378–83.

Otten, H.
1955 Die hethitischen Königslisten; und die altorientalische Chronologie. *Mitteilungen der Deutschen Orient-gesellschaft* 83:47–71.
1963 Neue Quellen zum Ausklang des Hethitischen Reiches. *Mitteilungen der Deutschen Orientgesellschaft* 94:1–23.
1983 Zur frühen Stadtgeschichte von Ḫattuša nach den inschriftlichen Quellen. *Istanbuler Mitteilungen* 33:40–52.

Özgüç, N.
1966 Excavations at Acemhöyük. *Anatolia* 10:29–52.

Özgüç, T.
1959 *Kültepe-Kaniš: New Researches at the Center of the Assyrian Trade Colonies.* Türk Tarih Kurumu Yayinlarindan, series 5, no. 19. Ankara: Türk Tarih Kurumu Basımevi.
1963 The Art and Architecture of Ancient Kanish. *Anatolia* 7:27–48.
1986 New Observations on the Relationship of Kültepe with Southeast Anatolia and North Syria during the Third Millenium B.C. Pp. 31–47 in *Ancient Anatolia: Aspects of Change and Cultural Development: Essays in Honor of Machteld J. Mellink*, edited by J. V. Canby. Madison: University of Wisconsin Press.

Redford, D.
1979 A Gate Inscription from Karnak and Egyptian Involvement in Western Asia during the Early 18th Dynasty. *Journal of the American Oriental Society* 99:270–87.

Reiner, E. and Pingree, D.
1975 *Babylonian Planetary Omens. Volume 1: The Venus Tablet of Ammiṣaduqa.* Bibliotheca Mesopotamica 2/1. Malibu, CA: Undena.

Ritter-Kaplan, H.
1984 The Impact of Drought on the Third Millennium B.C. Cultures on the Basis of Excavations in the Tel Aviv Exhibition Grounds. *Zeitschrift der Deutschen Palästina-Vereins* 100:2–8.

Robinson, R.
1976 Non-European Foundations of European Imperialism: Sketch for a Theory of Collaboration. Pp. 128–52 in *Imperialism: The Gallagher and Robinson Controversy,* edited by W. R. Louis. New York: Franklin Watts.

Rosenberg, M.
1992 Hallan Çemi Tepesi: An Early Aceramic Neolithic Site in Eastern Anatolia. *Anatolica* 18:1–17.
1994 Hallan Çemi Tepesi: Some Further Observations Concerning Stratigraphy and Material Culture. *Anatolica* 29:121–40.

Sandars, N. K.
1978 *The Sea Peoples: Warriors of the Ancient Mediterranean, 1250–1150 B.C.* London: Thames and Hudson.

Schirmer, W.
1969 *Die Bebauung am Unteren Büyükkale-Nordwesthang.* Berlin: Gebr. Mann.

Schuler, E. von
1965 *Die Kaskäer: Ein Beitrag zur Ethnographie des Alten Kleinasien.* Berlin: Walter de Gruyter.

Seeher, J.
1997 Die Ausgrabungen in Boğazköy-Ḫattuša 1996. *Archäologischer Anzeiger* 1997:319–41.
1998 The Early Iron Age Settlement on Büyükkaya, Boğazköy: First Impressions. Pp. 71–78 in *Thracians and Phrygians: Problems of Parallelism,* edited by N. Tuna, Z. Aktüre, and M. Lynch. Proceedings of an International Symposium on the Archaeology, History, and Ancient Languages of Thrace and Phrygia, Ankara, 3–4 June 1995. Ankara: METU, Faculty of Architecture Press.
1998b Die Ausgrabungen in Boğazköy-Ḫattuša 1997. *Archäologischer Anzeiger* 1998:215–41.
1999 Die Ausgrabungen in Boğazköy-Ḫattuša 1998. *Archäologischer Anzeiger* 1999:319–27.

Singer, I.
1981 Hittites and Hattians in Anatolia at the Beginning of the Second Millennium B.C. *Journal of Indo-European Studies* 9:119–34.
1987 Dating the End of the Hittite Empire. *Hethitica* 8:413–21.

Smith, C.
1976 Exchange Systems and the Spatial Distribution of Elites: The Organization of Stratification in Agrarian Societies. Pp. 309–74 in *Regional Analysis,* 2nd ed., edited by C. Smith. New York: Academic Press.

Smith, S.
1951 Commentary. P. 67 in *Compte rendu de la seconde Rencontre assyriologique internationale.* Paris: Imprimerie national.

Steiner, G.
1981 The Role of the Hittites in Ancient Anatolia. *Journal of Indo-European Studies* 9:150–73.
1990 The Spread of the First Indo-Europeans in Anatolia Reconsidered. *Journal of Indo-European Studies* 18:185–214.

Summers, G. D., Summers, M. E. F., Bayburtoğlu, N., Harmansah, Ö., and McIntosh, E. R.
1996 The Kerkenes Dağ Survey: An Interim Report. *Anatolian Studies* 46:201–34.

Tenney, F., ed.
1938 *An Economic Survey of Ancient Rome.* Vol. 4. Baltimore: The Johns Hopkins University Press.

Todd, I.
1980 *The Prehistory of Central Anatolia I: The Neolithic Period.* Studies in Mediterranean Archaeology. Gothenburg: Paul Åströms Forlag.

Ünal, A.
1977 Naturkatastrophen in Anatolien im 2. Jahrtausend v Chr. *Belleten* 41:447–72.

Veenhof, K. R.
1980 Karum Kanis: Philologisch. *Reallexicon der Assyriologie* V:369–78.

Weiss, B.
1982 The Decline of Late Bronze Age Civilizations as a Possible Response to Climatic Change. *Climatic Change* 4:172–98.

Wente, E. and Siclen, C. van
1977 A Chronology of the New Kingdom. Pp. 217–61 in *Studies in Honor of George R. Hughes.* Studies in Ancient Oriental Civilization 39. Chicago: The Oriental Institute of the University of Chicago.

Wilhelm, G. and Boese, J.
1987 Absolut Chronologie und die hethitischen Geschichte des 15. und 14. Jahrhunderts v. Chr. Pp. 74–117 in *High, Middle or Low?,* edited by P. Åström. Gothenburg: Paul Åströms Forlag.

Winn, M. M.
1974 Thoughts on the Questions of Indo-European Movements into Anatolia and Iran. *Journal of Indo-European Studies* 2:117–42.

Yakar, J.
1976 Anatolia and the "Great Movement" of Indo-Europeans, ca. 2300 B.C.E.—Another Look. *Tel Aviv* 3:151–57.
1981 The Indo-Europeans and Their Impact on Anatolian Cultural Development. *Journal of Indo-European Studies* 9:94–112.
2000 *Ethnoarchaeology of Anatolia: Rural Socio-Economy in the Bronze and Iron Ages.* Monograph 17. Tel Aviv: Tel Aviv University.

Zimansky, P.
1985 *Ecology and Empire: The Structure of the Urartian State.* Studies in Ancient Oriental Civilization 41. Chicago: The Oriental Institute of the University of Chicago.

Zohary, M.
1973 *Geobotanical Foundations of the Middle East.* Stuttgart: Gustav Fischer.

Ronald L. Gorny is the Director of the Alişar Regional Project and is currently excavating at Çadır Höyük in Yozgat Province, Central Turkey. His primary interests involve Hittite Anatolia and he has written widely on the origins of the state in Hittite Anatolia. His Ph.D. dissertation re-examined materials from the Oriental Institute's 1927–32 excavations at Alişar Höyük and paved the way for his recent work in the Kanak Su Basin of central Turkey. Dr. Gorny's current excavations at Alişar Höyük and Çadır Höyük in central Turkey follow on the heels of work at both Kurban Höyük and Titriş Höyük in southeastern Turkey. He has traveled extensively in Turkey, as well as in Armenia, Israel, and Greece and has excavated at both Tel Dan and Ashkelon in Israel, as well as at Horom in the Republic of Armenia.

The History of the Hittites

At the western entrance to the Upper City of Ḫattuša is the monument known as Lion Gate, named for the two heavy-chested lions that guard it. The lion on the righthand side of the gateway, shown in profile on page 61, is almost intact. Notice how the mane is rendered in a complicated pattern of incised tufts. Carved out of two very large arched blocks, the lions were cut to fit each other exactly. *All photos in this article are by Gregory McMahon.*

By Gregory McMahon

Sometime near the beginning of the second millennium BCE, a group of Indo-Europeans made their way into Anatolia, the area we know today as Asia Minor. These people carved a new face on the peninsula situated between the Black Sea and the eastern Mediterranean. They established a powerful kingdom, built a great empire, and influenced their neighbors in the ancient Near East for several centuries. Vestiges of their great empire can be seen today in huge stone monuments, rock carvings, hundreds of texts, and in several score of biblical passages referring to the Hittites.

Pre-Hittite Anatolia—The Assyrian Colony Age

The earliest writing, and therefore the beginnings of history in Anatolia, can be traced to the Old Assyrian Colony Age, a period lasting from about 1925 to 1650 BCE.[1] During this time Assyrian merchants, based in Aššur, established trading colonies at several Anatolian cites and, through them, did a thriving business in metals and other commodities. The best known of these trading colonies (*karum* in Old Assyrian) is Kaneš, the site of modern-day Kültepe.

Excavation in the upper levels of the *karum* at Kaneš has uncovered cuneiform tablets written in a distinctive script and dialect of Akkadian called Old Assyrian. Most of these documents are commercial in nature—correspondence with the home office in Assur, records of goods transported, and contracts. As exemplified by written trade agreements, the foreign businessmen enjoyed formalized relations with their Anatolian hosts. The local prince granted trading concessions

Lineage and Chronology of Hittite Rulers

KING	ROYAL RELATIONSHIP	MIDDLE CHRONOLOGY[1]	LOW CHRONOLOGY[2]
PRE-HITTITE RULERS			
Pitḫana		early 18th Century	late 18th Century
Anitta	son of Pithana	mid-18th Century	early 17th Century
OLD HITTITE KINGDOM RULERS			
Labarna	first known Hittite king	1680–1650	1600–1570
Ḫattušili I	nephew/adopted son of Labarna	1650–1620	1570–1540
Muršili I(+)[3]	grandson/adopted son of Ḫattušili I[4]	1620–1590	1540–1530
Ḫantili	assassin and brother-in-law of Muršili I	1590–1560	1530–1500
Zidanta I(+)	son-in-law of Ḫantili	1560–1550	1500–1490
Ammuna	son of Ḫantili	1550–1530	1490–1470
Ḫuzziya I(+)	son of Ammuna?	1530–1525	1470–1465
Telipinu	son of Zindanta I?/brother-in-law of Ammuna	1525–1500	1465–1440
Taḫurwaili(*)	?		1440?
Alluwamna	son-in-law of Ḫuzziya I		1440–1430
Ḫantili II	son of Alluwamna[5]	1500–1450	1430–1420
Zidanta II(e)	?		1420–1410[2]
Ḫuzziya II(e, +)	?		1410–1400[2]
Muwatalli I (k,+)	?		1400?[2]
MIDDLE KINGDOM RULERS			
Tudḫaliya II[6]	son of Huzzlya II?[7]	1450–1420	1400–1380
Arnuwanda I[8]	son-in-law of Tudḫaliya II	1420–1400	1370–1360
Tudḫaliya III	son of Arnuwanda I	1400–1380	1360–1343
Tudḫaliya (the younger)(+)	son of Tudḫaliya III[9]	1380?	1343?
Ḫattušili II(e)	?	?	?
HITTITE EMPIRE PERIOD RULERS			
Šuppiluliuma I	son of Tudḫaliya III	1380–1340	1343–1322/18[10]
Arnuwanda II	son of Šuppiluliuma I	1340–1339	1322/18
Muršili II	son of Šuppiluliuma I	1339–1306	1322/18–1296
Muwatalli II[11]	son of Muršili II	1306–1282	1296–1273
Muršili III(d) (=Urḫi-Tešub)	son of Muwatalli II	1282–1275	1273–1266
Ḫattušili III[12]	son of Muršili II	1275–1250	1266–1235
Tudḫaliya IV[13]	son of Ḫattušili III	1250–1220	1235–1215
Kurunta(k)	son of Muwatalli II/cousin of Tudḫaliya IV[14]	?	?
Arnuwanda III	son of Tudḫaliya IV	1220–1215	1215–1210[15]
Šuppiluliuma II	son of Tudḫaliya IV	1215–1200	1210–1200[16]

KEY (+)murdered (*)position unclear (e)existence debated (d)deposed (k)kingship disputed

Note: This table was compiled by Ronald L. Gorny. Except where noted, the dates used here are schematizations based on a few known synchronisms and the use of a time span of twenty years per generation with adjustments made for kings thought to be long-lived and those thought to be short-lived. The lack of accurate chronological or genealogical data for the Hittite kings precludes the possibility of accurate chronological dating at this time.

[1] Middle chronology after framework established by Brinkman (1964). Hittite dates based on approximate dates suggested by Gurney (1990:218).

[2] Low chronology after Wilhelm and Boese (1987).

[3] Sack of Babylon, 1595 BCE middle chronology/1531 BCE low chronology.

[4] See Beal (1983b).

[5] See Otten (1987).

[6] Tudḫaliya I is a shadowy figure whose existence is uncertain. He was originally proposed as the first king of this name because the name Tudḫaliya was found at the beginning of one variant of the sacrificial lists as the father of one PU-šarruma (*KUB* XI 7; compare Otten 1968:122). Consequently, the convention that begins the numbering of the Tudḫaliyas in this fashion was established at an early date. The sequence of that variant, however, has remained enigmatic, and many Hittitologists would dispute the existence of this figure, beginning the sequence of Tudḫaliyas with our present Tudḫaliya II (compare Astour 1989:50–51). The early system is retained here as a means of explaining different numbering systems found in the literature.

[7] See Otten (1987).

[8] For possible coregency of Tudḫaliya II and Arnuwanda I, see Houwink ten Cate (1970:58, n. 2), Carruba (1977:166–69, 177 n. 7), and Gurney (1979:214–15).

[9] Compare Astour (1989: 78).

[10] Compare Wilhelm and Boese (1987)

[11] Battle of Kadesh, fifth year in reign of Ramses II, around 1275 BCE.

[12] Treaty with Ramses II, twenty-first year in reign of Ramses II, around 1259 BCE, marriage of Ḫattušili III's daughter to Ramses II, thirty-fourth year in reign of Ramses II, around 1246 BCE.

[13] For a possible coregency between Ḫattušili III and Tudḫaliya IV, see Mora (1987).

[14] See Neve (1987:402–4), Otten (1988), and van den Hout (1989:87–105).

[15] Compare Singer (1987:417).

[16] Compare Singer (1987:418). Wente and van Siclen (1977) would set this date at 1175 BCE.

At the top of this glacis, along the southern boundary of the Upper City of Ḫattuša, is the monolithic entryway known as the Sphinx Gate. One of the sphinxes that guarded the gate is still visible, but the other two are in the Istanbul and Berlin Museums. The lower portal, or postern gate (Yerkapı in Turkish meaning "ground-gate"), opens into a tunnel that runs underneath the earthworks and enters into the Upper City.

and protection to the merchants and, in return, taxed commerce pursued in his domain. The Old Assyrian records contain some names with Indo-European elements, attesting to the presence of Indo-Europeans who would later create the Hittite kingdom.

From the discovery of tablets written in Old Assyrian in the palace at Kaneš, it is evident that the local Anatolian princes adopted the important new technology of writing. These tablets were presumably written by an Assyrian scribe employed by the prince, but a letter to king, Waršama of Kaneš from the king of Mama, Anum-Ḫirbe, indicates that writing was practiced in other parts of Anatolia as well (Balkan 1957).

In addition to writing, the Assyrians brought with them the cylinder seal, a type of seal developed in Mesopotamia. The cylinder seal is a small cylinder of stone or metal with an incised inscription and/or scene. When rolled across a wet clay tablet, the seal leaves an impression of the legend inscribed on it and thus "signs" the tablet. Many of the Old Assyrian tablets are sealed in this way, as are the clay "envelopes" in which some of the tablets were enclosed. That the local inhabitants adopted the cylinder seal may be inferred from the Anatolian motifs on the seals in addition to the expected Mesopotamian forms.

Development of the Hittite State

We are not certain who put an end to Assyrian commercial activity in Anatolia in the eighteenth century BCE, but we know that the foundation of a Hittite state followed shortly thereafter (Güterbock 1983:24–25, n. 8). Most of our textual evidence for the history of the Hittite kingdom comes from the archives found at the Hittite capital at Ḫattuša, present-day Boğazköy, a village east of Ankara. Other important evidence has come from archaeological sites including Alaca Höyük, Alişar Höyük, and Maşat Höyük.

The term *Hittite* derives from the place-name Ḫatti used for the pre-Indo-European inhabitants of central Anatolia. The Hittites who were Indo-Europeans, referred to themselves as Nešites, or people of Neša (Kaneš), a tradition supported by the evidence of Hittite names in the tablets found at Kaneš. What we call Hittite civilization is a mix of the early Hattic culture with that of the Indo-European newcomers and, later, with the culture of the Hurrians of northern Mesopotamia.

One of the most important and obvious contributions of these newcomers was their language, the language we call Hittite today, the oldest attested Indo-European language. Curiously, the Hittites did not get their script from the merchants based in Aššur; their writing

Overall view of the main chamber of Yazılıkaya, an open-air rock sanctuary located a mile northeast of Ḫattuša. A grand procession of Hittite gods is carved in a long relief frieze that follows the contours of the natural chamber. The male and female sides of the procession meet in the main scene, visible in the middle of the photograph. The sanctuary dates to the reign of Tudḫaliya IV, toward the end of the Hittite Empire.

most closely resembles Old Babylonian and may have been borrowed from the scribes of northern Syria, an area in the orbit of the Old Babylonian dynasty of Hammurapi (Güterbock 1983:24–25; Hoffner 1973:204). By the beginning of the Old Hittite period (sixteenth century BCE), the new state had borrowed the cuneiform writing system and adapted it to the Hittite language, beginning a distinctively Hittite scribal tradition.

The archives at Ḫattuša contain texts written in several different languages, the most predominant of which is the Indo-European Hittite. The other major language of the archive is Akkadian, the Semitic language of Mesopotamia that the Hittites used early, along with Hittite, for state records and, later, for international correspondence and diplomacy. Texts, including bilinguals, were written in Hattic and in two other Indo-European languages, Luwian and Palaic. In addition, many texts dating mostly to the later stages of the kingdom contain, or are written in, Hurrian, the agglutinative language of the people of southern Anatolia and northern Mesopotamia. Sumerian, the Mesopotamian language that was already used exclusively as a scholarly language, is attested at Ḫattuša in the common use of Sumerian logograms as well as in vocabulary lists that give Sumerian, Akkadian, and Hittite equivalents. An Indo-Aryan language related to Sanskrit supplied a few technical terms in horse training texts adopted from the Hurrians.

In tracking noticeable changes that took place in the Hittite language and writing system during the roughly four centuries of the kingdom's scribal tradition, modern scholars use the noted characteristics of the language in a particular period to date texts that cannot be dated by other criteria. Because many of the texts found in the Hittite archives were considered important enough to be copied, Hittitologists are interested in the date of an original composition as well as that of a particular copy. Thus, for example, a clearly Old Hittite text such as the Anitta text (*CTH* 1)[2] may exist in copies

Left: This rock relief of Muwatalli II is located at Sirkeli in southern Anatolia, on an outcropping of rock at a bend in the Ceyhan River. Ruling at the beginning of the thirteenth century BCE, Muwatalli is known for two major events: the Battle of Kadesh around 1275 BCE and his moving the capital to Tarḫuntašša, a city somewhere in southern Anatolia, thus shifting the Empire's center of gravity toward Syria and the troublesome Egyptian frontier.

Right: This elaborate rock relief, which dates to the Empire period, was carved on a giant boulder at Imamkulu in central Anatolia. The center section shows the Storm-God driving a chariot pulled by bulls over bowing mountain gods held up by smaller gods. The figure to the left, perhaps a Hittite prince, carries a bow over this shoulder. The figure to the right is a goddess, possibly Ištar.

written in both Old Script and New Script.

The Old Hittite Kingdom

The Old Hittite Kingdom may be said to begin with Labarna I, the first king of the dynasty that established the kingdom of Ḫattuša. Two earlier kings, Pitḫana and his son Anitta, bear an as yet unclear relationship to the first Hittite dynasty of Labarna (Güterbock 1983:25). Pitḫana and Anitta occur in Old Assyrian texts (Gurney 1990:19), and a dagger or spearhead inscribed with "the palace of Anitta the king" discovered in the city district at Kaneš provides additional documentation (see illustration, page 46). This dagger could indicate that Anitta was king at Kaneš or, if the destruction of this level of the cult can be attributed to him, that the dagger was lost there. According to the Anitta text, the one text from the Hittite state archives attributed to him, Anitta and Pitḫana, based at their home city of Kuššara, created an empire made up of neighboring small kingdoms. Anitta later moved his residence to Kaneš/Neša. Among the kingdoms that he conquered was Hattuš, which had a *karum*. He sowed weeds on the site and cursed—to no avail—any who would rebuild it. In the Hittite form of the name, Ḫattuša, a Hittite stem vowel is added on the older Hattic name, Ḫattuš.

It is uncertain how long it was after Pithana and Anitta before Labarna I established the first Old Hittite dynasty. His son, Labarna II, changed his name to Ḫattušili I, which means "man of Ḫattuša," and may have resettled Ḫattuša and made it his capital. It was during the reign of Ḫattušili I that the Hittite state emerged into the light of history. With the exception of the Anitta text,

Above: Two men, or gods, raise their arms to a seated deity (not visible in photo) on this rock relief located at Gâvur Kelesi, southwest of Ankara. There is no inscription, and the relief has no architectural framework, but its style is characteristic of Hittite imperial art.

Below: This Neo-Hittite relief dating from the eighth century BCE depicts Warpalawa of the kingdom of Tuwanuwa worshipping Tarḫu, a god of vegetation and storms. Located at Ivriz near Konya in southern Anatolia, the sculpture shows Assyrian influence, especially in the treatment of the beards and hair, which are tightly curled and carefully sculpted. Warpalawa's cap and robe also could be Assyrian, but the fibula, or clasp that holds his robe together, appears to be Phrygian.

which was discovered in the city he had sacked, the Hittite state archives begin with Ḫattušili I. By the time of his death, Ḫattušili had not only established the capital that would serve the Hittite kingdom for most of its history, he had created an empire by campaigning beyond the traditional borders, especially south into Syria.

The Political Testament of Ḫattušili I describes the problems encountered by this king in finding a successor to the throne; it also gives insights into the institution of the Hittite assembly, which the king addressed (Beckman 1982:437–39). The document, which is from the state archives, indicates that Hittite procedures for dynastic succession were fairly fluid during the early days of the kingdom. Ḫattušili's adopted successor was Muršili I who, in the mid-sixteenth century BCE, carried on Ḫattušili's tradition of campaigning and extending the Empire. Following the direction of Ḫattušili's campaigns south, Muršili I pushed the Hittite army deep into Mesopotamia and sacked Babylon around 1531 BCE. This raid ended the Old Babylonian dynasty of Hammurapi and is the most important synchronism between Hittite and Mesopotamian history for the early period. Babylon was the deepest into Mesopotamia the Hittites ever penetrated, however. The attack was nothing more than a raid and did not represent a serious attempt to control Mesopotamia as far as Babylon. Unfortunately for Muršili—and for Hittite dynastic stability—his absence during the Babylonian campaign allowed the development of a palace intrigue. Upon his return, Muršili I was murdered, and the Hittite state was beset with dynastic difficulties that led to a succession of weak kings who could not keep up the campaigns necessary to maintain the successes of previous Old Hittite Kings.

The most important king of the final throes of the Old Hittite period is Telipinu, a king known for his Edict (*CTH* 19), a proclamation dealing with the subject of dynastic succession. The text chronicles some of the internal problems and disunity experienced since the death of Muršili I and, in an effort to put an end to the turmoil, sets forth rules to determine legitimate dynastic succession. Problems of succession proved to be disastrous for the Old Hittite state, but the kingdom demonstrated sufficient political resiliency to survive this early period. Five or six ephemeral kings succeeded Telipinu before Tudhaliya II began a new, stronger dynasty that ruled in the Middle Hittite period.

The Middle Hittite Kingdom

Tudḫaliya II's new dynasty drew strength from that king's renewed interest in campaigning as the early Old Hittite kings had done (see Beal 1986 for evidence for Hittite conquest and diplomacy under Tudhaliya II). Later Middle Hittite kings failed to continue the campaigns, however, and it was left to Šuppiluliuma I in the later fourteenth century BCE to renew Hittite conquests abroad and inaugurate the New Hittite, or Empire, period.

The short-lived Middle Hittite period is distinguished partly on linguistic and paleographic grounds based on a characteristic form of the language (Middle Hittite) and a distinctive type of script (Middle Script). Our understanding of the late Old Hittite and Middle Hittite periods suffers from a scarcity of documentation—even the number and proper sequence of kings between Telipinu and Šuppiluliuma I is disputed. Unlike their neighbors in Mesopotamia, the Hittites did not keep a list of rulers as a formal part of their state records. They did keep lists of offerings made to deceased kings—which help in reconstructing the names and sequences of the kings—but not all of the kings are included in these lists, and some of those who are included never became king. Therefore, the only sure way to establish a dynastic sequence is to find records for each king and use the genealogical information contained in them. For some kings of the middle period we do not have such records. Some kings are attested only by seals or seal impressions that give their name and ancestry.

Perhaps the best known Middle Hittite king is Arnuwanda I, who ruled in the mid-fourteenth century BCE. With his queen, Ašmunikal, Arnuwanda wrote a prayer (*CTH* 375) that poignantly reflects the political situation of the Middle Hittite era. In the prayer, the king and queen bemoan the loss of the important cult city of Nerik; at the same time, they remind the gods how well the Hittites had cared for them, in contrast to the Kaška, the barbarian peoples of the north who now held Nerik. The prayer reflects the importance of maintaining cult offerings to all the gods when Arnuwanda and Ašmunikal promise to continue to give the gods of Nerik all their offerings by moving the site of their worship to Hakpiš, a city still under Hittite control.

The Kaška people referred to in the prayer were one of the Hittites' most troublesome neighbors. Situated in north central Anatolia, north of the Hittite homeland, they were a rugged tribal people who had no centralized capital and were therefore difficult to pin down and conquer. In periods of strength, the Hittites were able to keep the Kaška tribes at bay, but they exerted constant pressure on the northern border of the kingdom and were ready to take advantage of any weakness in Hittite military capability. Thus, the Kaška held the cult city of Nerik—in spite of its great religious importance—until Ḫattušili III was able to reestablish Hittite control half a century later.

Above: Ancient Samʿal, located at modern day Zincirli in the area south and east of the Hittite homeland, was the site of a Neo-Hittite (sometimes called Syrian-Hittite) kingdom. Removed in time from the Alaca Höyük sphinxes of the Empire period, this sphinx from Zincirli was manufactured at Yesemek, a Hittite quarry and sculpture workshop. It is currently housed in the garden of the Gaziantep archaeological museum.

Information about the Middle Hittite kings is also available in a series of unusual texts that scholars designate as instructions, texts that set forth the duties of a particular officer or a group of state officials. In addition to Arnuwanda's instructions to his "mayors" (*CTH* 157), which details their duty to maintain security in cities throughout the

Carved into the living rock at a mountain pass at Hanyeri (Gezbel) in central Anatolia is this relief of a late Empire Hittite prince. The prince, who carries a spear and a bow, is accompanied by a hieroglyphic inscription. Birds are also seen flying in the air.

kingdom, there is an extremely interesting series of instructions to the border guards (*CTH* 261), usually denoted by the Hittites with the Akkadian phrase *bel madgalti*, "lord of the watchtower." These texts make clear the priority given to guarding the frontiers and keeping hostile neighboring lands under surveillance during the Middle Hittite kingdom, a period of military weakness.

The Hittite Empire Period

With the accession of Šuppiluliuma I in the mid-fourteenth century BCE, the period of relative Hittite weakness ended, and the final phase of the kingdom, the Empire period, began.

Šuppiluliuma I was an exceedingly vigorous king who, like the first Hittite kings, campaigned every year in order to increase the size of the kingdom and create a true empire encompassing different geographic regions. After reestablishing Hittite power in central Anatolia, Šuppiluliuma directed his energies toward a formidable neighbor to the southeast, the state of Mitanni. This Hurrian kingdom had grown strong during the period of Hittite weakness, becoming one of the major powers of the ancient Near East and establishing equal diplomatic relations with Egypt. After being defeated in his first encounter with the Mitannian king, Tušratta, Šuppiluliuma mounted a second campaign against this powerful enemy, attacking the Mitannian capital, Waššukanni, and sacking it. Tušratta escaped and set up a kind of government-in-exile, but Mitanni's days of power were numbered. Šuppiluliuma, meanwhile, proceeded to correspond with Egyptian pharaohs of the Amarna period just as Tušratta had done before him.

Although the Hurrian state had been vanquished, Hurrian culture, especially literature and cult practice, continued to flourish; taken up by the Hittites, it was preserved in their literary tradition. The Mitannian capital (Waššukanni), with its state archives written in Hurrian, has not yet been discovered. Most Hurrian texts come from Ḫattuša, an indication of the great cultural influence exerted by the Hurrians on the Hittites in the Empire period despite the collapse of their political power base.

It was perhaps as many as thirty years later that Šuppiluliuma returned to Syria (Gurney 1990: 30–31) and, taking advantage of the final collapse of Mitanni, annexed more of northern Syria, including the strategic fortress at Karkamiš. This site became the center of Hittite control in Syria, where a viceroy for Syria, usually a royal prince, was stationed. Šuppiluliuma had eliminated his most powerful southern neighbor and thus opened the road to Syria, an important component of the Hittite Empire. This was to have significant repercussions in Near Eastern politics. Assyria, which had been kept in check by its neighbor Mitanni, was now free to expand its territory, and this expansion

This block monument, made up of individual stones with deities carved in relief, is located at Eflâtun Pınar, a late Empire cult site at a spring in west central Anatolia. The monument, which is about 23 feet long, has a typically Hittite layered composition in which the central deities help support the winged sundisk, symbolic of Hittite royalty.

eventually brought Assyria into conflict with the Hittites near the end of the Empire period (Singer 1985). Hittite expansion into Syria coincided with a revival of Egyptian interests in the same area, leading eventually, around 1275 BCE, to the Battle of Kadesh.

Šuppiluliuma also turned his attention west, toward the land of Arzawa, which, in the Middle Hittite period, had become independent enough to correspond directly with the Egyptian pharaoh. The Hittite king was again able to subdue these neighboring lands and incorporate them into the Empire. However, when Šuppiluliuma died, followed by his son, Arnuwanda, their successor, Muršili II, faced a revolt in the lands of Arzawa.

The campaigns of this Muršili are particularly well-known because of two different series of annals in which the young king describes his campaigns and the peoples he conquered. Many rulers from the surrounding lands—including Arzawa—thought Muršili was too young to rule and, consequently, tried to detach themselves from the Hittite orbit. But Muršili proved them wrong by reconquering much of his father's empire and consolidating it for future kings. Muršili campaigned in other areas as well. He repeatedly journeyed north to subdue the Kaška, and he had to make one major expedition to Syria to replace the viceroy at Karkamiš and force the Syrian provinces to recognize the new imperial deputy.

Two major events make the reign of Muršili II's son, Muwatalli, especially noteworthy. One is the Battle of Kadesh, around 1275 BCE, a direct confrontation between the Egyptians and the Hittites over border disputes in Syro-Palestine (Murnane 1985). Under Muwatalli, the Hittites outmaneuvered the Egyptian army led by Ramses II, who was fortunate to escape with his life. This did not prevent the pharaoh from describing Kadesh as a victory in his representations of it in Egypt. Yet continued Hittite control of the area indicates that the victory belonged to the Hittites. The other noteworthy event of Muwatalli's reign in the early thirteenth century BCE was his moving the capital to Tarḫuntašša, a city somewhere in southern Anatolia. This city has not been definitely located, but Emmanuel Laroche has suggested Meydancik Kalesi as a possible site (Mellink 1974:111). Locating a new capital in southern

A large unfinished stela from the late Empire period still lies in the area where it was found, at Fasılar near Eflâtun Pınar in west central Anatolia. Visible here are the head and figure of the Storm-God who wears a conical cap and who his right hand raised above his head. A copy of this stela is set up in the garden of the Museum of Anatolian Civilizations in Ankara.

Anatolia shifted the Empire's center of gravity toward Syria and the troublesome Egyptian frontier. Muwatalli placed his brother, Ḫattušili III, in charge of the northern portion of the kingdom and gave him the status of a lesser king. When Muwatalli died, his son Urḫi-Tešub succeeded him (as Muršili III) and soon came into conflict with his uncle. Having retaken much of the northern area for the Hittites, including the cult city Nerik, Ḫattušili III responded to Urḫi-Tešub's attempts to exclude him from his share of the rule by deposing his nephew and usurping the throne. This incident gave rise to one of the most unusual documents in the Hittite archives, the Apology of Ḫattušili III (*CTH* 81). In it the king tells his version of the story, justifying his actions by noting the great wrongs done to him by Urḫi-Tešub and the special patronage shown to him by the goddess Ištar.

Ḫattušili III, ruling in the mid-thirteenth century BCE, proved to be an excellent king. He inherited a smoothly operating empire and kept it that way. During his reign, relations with Egypt, strained since the battle at Kadesh, were normalized. The treaty that was drawn up between these two great powers around 1259 BCE is unique in the ancient Near East; it is extant in the languages of both parties. The Egyptian version was inscribed on the walls of a temple of Ramses. Archaeologists discovered the other version—written in Hittite on a clay tablet—very early in the excavations at Ḫattuša.

Ḫattušili's wife, Puduḫepa, the daughter of a priest of Kizzuwatna (Cilicia), was an exceedingly active queen. On his way home from helping his brother, Muwatalli, at the Battle of Kadesh, Ḫattušili was instructed by Ištar to stop in Kizzuwatna and wed Puduḫepa. Puduḫepa brought Hurrian culture with her from her Hurro-Luwian homeland, which, when she later became queen, had a great impact on Hittite culture. She also proved to be a very vigorous monarch in her own right, conducting royal correspondence in her own name and remaining active in affairs of state after her husband died (Singer 1987: 415; Otten 1975).

With the death of Ḫattušili III, his son Tudḫaliya, the fourth king of that name, took the throne. Ruling at the end of the thirteenth century BCE, Tudḫaliya enjoyed the peace won by his father and his predecessors and turned his efforts toward religious reform. The Hittites tended toward a religious eclecticism in which every god, no matter what its origin, was to be propitiated with the appropriate ceremonies. The cult inventories of Tudḫaliya beautifully exemplify this orientation. These texts are lists compiled by special deputies commissioned by the king to visit cult sites throughout Anatolia and inventory all the religious accoutrements in the area. Cultic equipment, personnel, and traditional cult ceremonies are all listed as cult paraphernalia. Tudḫaliya IV also tried to make sure that traditional local cults continued to perform the required ritual ceremonies, and he brought some local cults to the capital as well.

The potential for conflict along the Hittite-Assyrian border was finally realized during this monarch's reign. Tudḫaliya IV and an Assyrian ruler, probably Tukulti-Ninurta, fought a major battle (Singer 1985). Tudḫaliya also corresponded both with the Assyrian court and with the Egyptian pharaoh.

Two of Tudḫaliya's sons succeeded him on the throne. Arnuwanda III ruled for only about five years, and we have little material from his reign. His brother, Šuppiluliuma II, was almost certainly the last king of the Hittite Empire, although the recent discovery of a tomb intended for him (Bayburtluoğlu 1989) has cast doubt on this long-held idea. If Šuppiluliuma was buried in a tomb, there must have been at least one king to follow him. In any case, correspondence from Ugarit dating to his reign indicates that disaster was on the way. In the correspondence, the ruler of Ugarit, responding to the pressure of invaders, appeals to the great Hittite king for help. Apparently, however, the Hittites were themselves in need of help. The Egyptian pharaoh Merneptah sent aid to the Hittites—grain to alleviate the effect of famine—near the end of the Empire (Singer 1987:415–16).

The actual end of the Hittite Empire can only be guessed at, for the obvious reason that no one was left to chronicle the event after the capital was taken around 1200 BCE (see Singer 1985 and 1987 for problems in dating the fall of the Empire). With the sacking of Ḫattuša, the centralized Hittite polity came to an end forever. Likewise, the Hittite cuneiform scribal tradition ceased. No Hittite cuneiform tablets that post-date the fall of Ḫattuša have been discovered in either Anatolia or Syria. The capitol city itself was later occupied by the Phrygians and later still by the Byzantines. After the fall of the Empire, many cities in Anatolia retained their Hittite character but eventually developed a distinctive culture characterized by a mixture of Anatolian and Syrian elements.

The Hittites and the Bible

Several different Hebrew words or phrases in the Hebrew Bible are usually translated as Hittite or Hittites.[3] One is "sons of Heth," which occurs only in Genesis. (See Gen 10:15 for a listing of Heth as one of the sons of Canaan.) The "daughters of Heth,"translated as "Hittite women" in the Revised Standard Version and the New International Version, occurs in Gen 27:46. In that passage, Rebekah voices fear of the local non-Hebrews because she does not want Jacob to take a foreign wife. Thus the patriarchs perceived the Hittites as early inhabitants of Canaan, or, in the broadest sense of the term, *Canaanites*.

The more common Hebrew word used to denote the Hittites, *hittî*, is

A king of the Neo-Hittite kingdom of Milid, located at Arslantepe close to present-day Malatya, is depicted in this 10-foot-tall limestone statue dating from the eighth century BCE and currently housed in the Museum of Anatolian Civilizations, Ankara. The king's wavy hair and curled beard are evidence of an Assyrian influence as are the pose, full robe, and sandled feet. The king holds a scepter in his right hand and clutches a cloak in his left. Sculpture in the round, as opposed to relief sculpture, was rare in Hittite times but was commonly produced by the Assyrians.

also based on the name Heth. This form may be used to designate the ethnicity of an individual, for instance, "Ephron the Hittite" in Gen 23:10. Ephron's appearance in Gen 23 along with many occurrences of the sons of Heth confirms their identification with the Hittites. This word, *hittî*, is also used in lists of peoples living in the promised land. In modern versions of the Hebrew Bible, the singular form is used in a generic sense and usually translated in the plural, "the Hittites." In this way, the Hittites are included in what is considered to be the standard list of the seven major peoples of Palestine: the Hittites, the Girgashites, the Amorites, the Canaanites, the Perizzites, the Hivites, and the Jebusites—as, for example, in Deut 7:1. The one attested example of a plural feminine form occurs in a list of the foreign (non-Israelite) women admired by Solomon (l Kgs 11:1), again indicating that the Hittites were a recognizable local ethnic group.

The five occurrences of the term Hittite in the masculine plural form deserve special mention. Unlike most other forms of the word, which have a narrowly defined usage, the masculine plural form appears in widely varying contexts. In Josh 1:4, the phrase "land of the Hittites" occurs as part of God's description of the land promised to Moses. The same phrase crops up in Judg 1:26, which tells the story of the man who betrayed Bethel to the Israelites and escaped to the land of the Hittites. In 1 Kgs 10:29, and its parallel in 2 Chr 1:17, the phrase "kings of the Hittites" refers to some of the rulers who imported chariots and horses from Solomon. Finally, in 2 Kgs 7:6, the very rumor of the kings of the Hittites and the kings of Egypt is sufficiently alarming to cause the Syrians to flee while be sieging Samaria.

References to the Hittites in the patriarchal narrative indicate that Abraham encountered them as a settled people of Palestine. Indeed, the Hittites were included in another description, in Gen 15:20, of the land promised to Abraham. The concern felt by Isaac and Rebekah about the foreign wives their sons might take turned out to be justified when Esau married Judith and Basemath (Gen

Karkamiš was a major independent kingdom in the Old Testament period and the greatest center of Neo-Hittite sculpture. It had a distinctive style that influenced surrounding cities. These orthostats, large stone slabs decorated with relief carving and used as architectural ornamentation, are from Karkamiš and date from the ninth century BCE. The war scene relief shown here was carved on alternating black (basalt) and white stones, average height about 5 1/2 feet. The basalt stones have apparently weathered the years better than the white stones. These orthostats are currently housed in the Museum of Anatolian Civilizations, Ankara.

26:34), two Hittite women. Rebekah worried that Jacob would also choose a bride from among the local non-Hebrew inhabitants of Canaan, including the Hittites.

When the Hebrews returned from Egypt under Moses and Joshua, they again encountered the Hittites, along with many other Canaanite peoples. When Moses' spies returned after forty days and made their report at Kadesh Barnea (Num 13:29), they located the Hittites, Jebusites, and Amorites in the hill country and other groups on the coast or in the Negeb. Josh 11:3 cites the same three peoples, plus the Perizzites, as inhabitants of the hill country. References to the Hittites also appear in God's cataloging of the peoples the Israelites must fight in order to conquer the promised land. In Deut 20:16–18, the Israelites are told that they must utterly destroy the Hittites (among others), indicating that Hittite territory was in the heart of the region that the Israelites were to take over. Some kind of political organization is indicated by the reference to the kings of the Hittites, Amorites, Canaanites, and other peoples in Josh 9:1–2.

The patriarchs also encountered the Hittites around Hebron (Gen 23) and Beer-sheba (Gen 26:24; 27:46), and most of the literary evidence we have relating to their location at the time of the conquest is consistent with those locations. The exception to this is Josh 1:4, which refers to the area around the Euphrates as "the land of the Hittites." This contradicts the other references to the Hittites as one of the local peoples of southern Palestine; it probably refers to the Neo-Hittite principalities of northern Syria of this period.

According to the biblical account, from the conquest on, the Hebrews struggled with the problem of Canaanite influence, partly because they did not completely eradicate the local inhabitants of Palestine. One of the Canaanite peoples whom the Israelites continued to encounter in the period of the judges was the Hittites. Judg 3:5–6 note the failure of the Hebrews to eradicate the Hittites and, consequently, the resulting intermingling of the peoples, including intermarriage and the assimilation of "Canaanite" religious influences.

Those Hittites who survived the Israelite conquest of the promised land continued to interact with the Hebrews during the period of the monarchy. One of King David's comrades while he was being pursued by Saul was Ahimelech the Hittite, whom David asked to accompany him into Saul's camp at night (1 Sam 26:6). Ahimelech's Hebrew name indicates that he had been integrated into Hebrew society. Chapters 11 and 12 of 2 Sam tell the story of Uriah the Hittite, who lived in Jerusalem, served in the Hebrew army, had a Hebrew wife, and a Yahwistic name.

Hittites were among the Canaanite peoples ruled by King Solomon. As mentioned previously, 1 Kgs 2 mentions Hittite women as some of the foreign women in Solomon's court. Solomon also forced the Hittites, along with other Canaanite peoples who had survived the conquest, to work on his building projects (1 Kgs 9:20–21 and their parallel in 2 Chr 8:7–8).

It is understandable that references to the Hittites of Solomon's time would describe them as local Canaanite people who were left over from the pre-conquest days, but 1 Kgs 10:29 (and its parallel in 2 Chr 1:17) details a relationship with Solomon that does not fit into this context. This passage describes Solomon's exportation of horses and chariots to the kings of the Hittites and the Arameans. These Hittites cannot be the same group Solomon was using for forced labor. The pairing of Hittite and Aramean kings indicates that these monarchs should be located in the city-states of northern Syria, states that were of Neo-Hittite and/or Aramean background.

In the years after Solomon, during the period of the divided monarchy, the mere reputation of the kings of the Hittites, coupled with the kings of the Egyptians, helped out the kings of the northern monarchy, and this alliance also raises the question of which Hittites are being cited. During the Syrian siege of Samaria described in 2 Kgs 7:6, the attackers fled their camp when they heard the sound of a great army that they convinced themselves was made up of the kings of the Hittites and the Egyptians hired by Israel. It is extremely unlikely that the local Palestinian Hittites who had earlier worked as forced labor under Solomon would now be a vital military force in the same region as Israel. Again, this must be a reference to the kings of Neo-Hittite principalities in Syria.

In the Exilic and Second Temple periods, Jews continued to come into contact with, or recall previous contact with, the Hittites in Palestine. One of Ezekiel's prophecies refers to the ancestry of Jerusalem: "your mother was a Hittite and your father an Amorite" (Ezek 16:45; 16:3 similar). When, in the late sixth century BCE, Jews returned from exile in Babylon, Ezra was faced with the same crisis of intermarriage that had caused problems for Isaac and Rebekah and for Solomon. In Ezra 9:1–3, he is horrified by information that the Hebrews have taken wives from all the local tribes of Palestine, including the Hittites. This represents a serious breach of Israelite purity from idolatry, no less grave a matter than it was at the time of the conquest. The patriarchal description of the promised land as the land of the Canaanites, the Hittites, the Amorites, and so on is again recalled in Neh 9:8.

This Neo-Hittite relief of a "mixed being," a sphinx with a lion and man's head, is also on an orthostat from Karkamiš and dates from the ninth century BCE. The relief is carved on basalt in the distinctive Karkamiš style. Notice that the tail has a bird's head. A little more than 4 feet tall, the sculpture is housed in the Museum of Anatolian Civilizations, Ankara. A modern three-dimensional copy sits at a traffic signal outside the train station there.

References to the Hittites in the Hebrew Bible seem to refer to two distinct groups. One group, described as the descendants of Canaan through the eponymous ancestor Heth, interacted with Abraham around Hebron. Because these sons of Heth resided in the heart of the land that had been promised to the Israelites, God commanded the Hebrews, upon their return from Egypt, to destroy the Hittites utterly. That the Hittites were not completely eradicated but continued to inhabit southern Palestine, including the area around Jerusalem, can be seen in the references to them in the Hebrew army, as forced labor conscripts, and as possible wives for the Hebrews—all the way until the return from exile in Babylon. Most Hebrew Bible references to the Hittites make sense when

The Hurrians and the Horites

The Hurrians were a neighboring people whose culture greatly influenced that of the Hittites after they were conquered by Šuppiluliuma I early in the Empire period. Probably originating from the mountains of eastern Anatolia, the Hurrians in the mid-second millennium BCE formed the state of Mitanni and became a major power along with the Babylonians, Egyptians, and Hittites. The Hurrians spread out over a large part of the ancient Near East, through northern Mesopotamia and Syria and south into Palestine (Bright 1981:63). Evidence that they migrated all the way through Palestine and down into Egypt may be found in the occurrence of Hurrian names among those of the Hyksos, foreign rulers of Egypt during the second millennium (Hoffner 1973:224–25). When the Hyksos were finally expelled from Egypt in the middle of the second millennium, some of these Hurrians settled in Palestine (Hoffner 1973:225).

E. A. Speiser (1962:664–66) identified the Hurrians with the Horites, Hivites, and Jebusites of the Old Testament. He tempered this identification, however, by alluding briefly (1962:665) to an indigenous group, located around Seir, called Horites. This situation is perhaps analogous to confusion over the term Hittite for indigenous and foreign groups with similar names. The identification of Hurrians with Horites and other Canaanites peoples has been contested by Roland de Vaux (1967). Hoffner (1973:225) agreed with Speiser that the Jebusites, some of whom had identifiably Hurrian names, could be Hurrian. It is very likely that Hurrians had settled in Palestine before the conquest, and therefore, we would expect that the Israelites encountered them during their conquest of the promised land. In this period, the Egyptian name for Palestine was Huru, presumably because there was a sizable population of Hurrians in the region (Bright 1981:116; Speiser 1962:664).

R. K. Harrison (1983:245) followed Speiser's suggestion that Jebusite and Horite were local terms for people known elsewhere as Hurrians, citing the archaeological evidence for Hurrians in Palestine during the fifteenth and fourteenth centuries BCE. K. A. Kitchen (1983:242) has been more cautious, preferring to keep the Hurrians distinct from the Hivites until we have more evidence regarding their identity. Edwin Yamauchi (1983:256), while noting de Vaux's objections to locating the Hurrians in mid-second-millennium Palestine, has accepted evidence of Hurrian names for Jebusite rulers as an indication that they may indeed have been Hurrians. Thus, it is at least possible that Hurrians can be found in the Old Testament as the Horites, Hivites, and Jebusites.

they are pictured as a local Canaanite people who were never quite exterminated during the Hebrew conquest of Canaan.

Five references in the Hebrew Bible, however, do not fit this picture (Gelb 1962:613–14). The reference in Josh 1:4, for example, which describes the area around the Euphrates as being Hittite territory, refers not to the Hittites of Hebron but rather to the Neo-Hittite kingdoms of northern Syria (see Boling and Wright 1982: 122–23 for a different view). In Judg 1:26, the reference to the man who, after betraying Bethel, goes to the "land of the Hittites" could refer to either southern Palestine or northern Syria, but in view of the use of the phrase *ereṣ haḫittîm* ("land of the Hittites")—Josh 1:4 being the only other occurrence of this phrase—it is quite possible that it, too, refers to the Neo-Hittite area. Boling (1975:59) has indirectly implied that he understands this phrase as referring to the area of the Anatolian Syrian Hittites. Also, references to the "kings of the Hittites" who imported horses and chariots from Solomon (1 Kgs 10:29 and 2 Chr 1:17) must indicate a powerful and wealthy group of kings, not a local Canaanite people who had been enslaved by Solomon. The same can be said for "the kings of the Hittites" whose reputation alone caused the Syrian army to flee (2 Kgs 7:6). By contrast, the Neo-Hittite kingdoms fit quite well in terms of chronology and geography. They were in the same area as the Syrians, and thus were known to them. The plural "kings" fits very well with the nature of these states, which were not unified into one polity but consisted of several small kingdoms.

It is noteworthy that these five references to the Hittites, which, on the basis of context, should be understood as referring to the Neo-Hittites of north Syria, are also the only five occurrences of the plural form *ḫittîm* in the Hebrew Bible. This may not be significant, but it could be some indication of a distinction made in the text between the Hittites of Palestine, descendants of Heth, and the Hittites of Anatolia and north Syria, the men of Ḫatti. We should distinguish, then, between the "sons of Heth" of Palestine and the "men of Ḫatti" of Anatolia and northern Syria (see Gelb 1962:614; Hoffner 1973:213–14; Speiser 1983: 169–70). The use of *hittî* to refer to both may reflect nothing more than the similarity of the names Heth and Ḫatti (Hoffner 1973:214). This does not imply that the two groups called Hittites in the Hebrew Bible may not be related ancestrally from some period antedating our earliest records or that the Canaanite Hittites were never confused with the Hittites of the Anatolian or north Syrian kingdoms who may have migrated into Palestine and settled there. Aharon Kempinski (1979) has argued convincingly for extensive penetration of the Hittites into Palestine after the fall of Ḫattuša, and certainly there is archaeological evidence of Hittite cultural influence in Palestine during the Late Bronze Age (Shanks 1973:

234–35, plate 63c; Callaway and Cooley 1971:15–19). For the period covered by the Hebrew Bible, however, the terms usually translated as Hittites referred to two distinct groups of people.

Syria in the Hebrew Bible Period

The history of northern Syria (and southern Anatolia) in the period between the Hebrew conquest of Canaan and the fall of the northern kingdom of Israel is basically that of the Aramean and Neo-Hittite kingdoms, sometimes called the Syro-Hittite kingdoms. Assyrian documents dating to the first millennium BCE refer to northern Syria as the land of Ḫatti, reflecting the continued presence of small Hittite states in the southern part of the former Hittite Empire in spite of the collapse of the Hittite polity in central Anatolia.

Although the collapse of the capital at Ḫattuša signaled the end of the Hittite Empire, many cities through out the Empire retained their Hittite character for centuries after the imperial structure had vanished. These Neo-Hittite cities show a cultural mix of Hittite and Aramean elements in a period of increasingly strong Aramean presence in Syria. The annals of the Assyrian kings, who eventually incorporated all of these cities into their Empire, provide one of the available sources for the political history of these states. The archaeological record from this period includes architectural remains and many examples of Neo-Hittite sculpture. Local documentation consists basically of inscriptions in hieroglyphic Luwian and Aramaic; there is no corpus of nonmonumental documentation analogous to the Hittite archives at Ḫattuša.

As has been mentioned, the city of Karkamiš, located on the modern day Syria-Turkey border, was a provincial capital during the Hittite Empire. After the Empire fell, it became the center of an independent kingdom. Excavations at the site have uncovered a wonderful series of orthostats, stone slabs carved in low relief and used to decorate public buildings. Much of this sculpture, which dates to the first millennium BCE, is on display in the Museum of Anatolian Civilizations in Ankara. The art of the surrounding states reflects the influence of the Karkamiš school, a style that may have indirectly influenced the Greeks via the Phrygians.

One of the most spectacular of all the Neo-Hittite sites was Karatepe. Because the orthostats have been preserved *in situ*, the modern visitor can walk through the city and get a sense of what it looked like in antiquity. The reliefs and long bilingual inscription of king Azitawanda, written in hieroglyphic Luwian and Phoenician, illustrate the blending of Hittite and Phoenician culture at this site.

The Neo-Hittite states were quite definitely heirs to Hittite civilization, but they developed a distinctive culture by synthesizing Anatolian and Syrian traditions. As indicated by references to them in the Hebrew Bible, these principalities had some contact with the kingdom(s) of the Israelites and Judaites further south in Palestine. They never unified to create a polity on the scale of the Hittite Empire, and this fragmented political situation made them easy targets for Assyrian expansion during the early first millennium BCE. As Assyria absorbed each state, culturally as well as politically it lost its distinctive Hittite-Aramean character. Thus, for southern Anatolia and northern Syria, the period immediately following the Neo-Hittite states was one of Assyrian domination, a domination that eventually extended down to the northern kingdom of Israel.

Notes

[1] This date, and all dates cited in this article, are based on the low chronology dating system. Under the middle chronology dating system the Colony Age lasted from around 1925 to 1725 BCE. For a larger discussion of issues related to an absolute Hittite chronology, see p. 52.

[2] Hittitologists identify individual Hittite texts by their number in the comprehensive (when compiled) *Catalogue des textes hittites* by Emmanuel Laroche (Paris: Editions Klincksieck, 1971), which is abbreviated *CTH*.

[3] Biblical passages used in this article are from the Revised Standard Version or the New International Version.

Bibliography

Alkım, U. B.
1968 *Anatolia I (From the Beginnings to the End of the 2nd Millennium B.C.)*. Cleveland: World Publishing Company.

Astour, M.
1989 *Hittite History and Absolute Chronology of the Bronze Age*. Gothenburg: Paul Åströms Förlag.

Balkan, K.
1957 *Letter of King Anum-Hirbi of Mama to King Warshama of Kanish*. Ankara: Türk Tarih Kurumu Basımevi.

Bayburtluoğlu, I.
1989 The Most Interesting Finding of Boğazköy in 1988 Campaign: The Remains of a Royal Tomb (Interview with Dr. Peter Neve). *Museum (Müze)* 1:59–61.

Beal, R.
1983a Studies in Hittite History. *Journal of Cuneiform Studies* 35:115–26.
1983b The Hittites After the Empire's Fall. *Biblical Illustrator* Fall: 72–81.
1986 The History of Kizzuwatna and the Date of the Šunaššura Treaty. *Orientalia* 55:424–45.

Beckman, G.
1982 The Hittite Assembly. *Journal of the American Oriental Society* 102:435–42.
1986 Inheritance and Royal Succession among the Hittites. Pp. 12–31 in *Kaniššuwar: Studies in Honor of Hans Güterbock*. Chicago: The Oriental Institute of the University of Chicago.

Bittel, K.
1970 *Hattusha: The Capital of the Hittites*. New York: Oxford University Press.

Boling, R. G.
1975 *Judges*. The Anchor Bible, vol. 6A. Garden City, NY: Doubleday.

Boling, R. G. and Wright, G. E.
1982 *Joshua.* The Anchor Bible, vol. 6. Garden City, NY: Doubleday.

Bright, J.
1981 *A History of Israel.* 3rd ed. Philadelphia: Westminster Press.

Brinkman, J. A.
1964 Mesopotamian Chronology of the Historical Period. Pp. 335–52 in *Ancient Mesopotamia: Portrait of a Dead Civilization,* edited by A. L. Oppenheim. Chicago: University of Chicago Press.

Callaway, J. A. and Cooley, R. E.
1971 A Salvage Excavation at Raddana, in Bireh. *Bulletin of the American Schools of Oriental Research* 201:9–19.

Carruba, O.
1977 Beiträge zur Mittelhethitischen Geschichte I, II. *Studi Micenei ed Egeo-Anatolici* 18:166–77.

Gelb, I. J.
1962 Hittites. Pp. 612–15 in *The Interpreters Dictionary of the Bible,* edited by G. A. Buttrick. New York: Abingdon Press.

Gurney, O. R.
1973a Anatolia c. 1750–1600 B.C. Pp. 228–55 in *The Cambridge Ancient History,* II/1, 3rd ed., edited by I. E. S. Edwards et al. Cambridge: Cambridge University Press.
1973b Anatolia c. 1600–1380 B.C. Pp. 659–85 in *The Cambridge Ancient History,* Vol. II/1, 3rd ed., edited by I. E. S. Edwards et al. Cambridge: Cambridge University Press.
1977 *Some Aspects of Hittite Religion.* The Schweich Lectures 1976. Oxford: Oxford University Press.
1979 *The Anointing of Tudḫaliya.* Studia Mediterranea 1. Pavia.
1990 *The Hittites.* 4th edition. New York: Penguin Books.

Güterbock, H. G.
1957 Toward a Definition of the Term Hittite. *Oriens* 10:233–39.
1958 Kaneš and Neša, Two Forms of One Anatolian Name. *Eretz Israel* 5:46–50.
1983 Hittite Historiography: A Survey. Pp. 21–35 in *History, Historiography, and Interpretation,* edited by H. Tadmor and M. Weinfeld. Jerusalem: Magnes Press.

Harrison, R. K.
1983 Hurrians. P. 245 in *The New International Dictionary of Biblical Archaeology,* edited by E. M. Blaiklock and R. K. Harrison. Grand Rapids, MI: Regency Reference Library.

Hawkins, J. D.
1982 The Neo-Hittite States in Syria and Anatolia. Pp. 372–441 in *The Cambridge Ancient History,* III/1, 2nd ed., edited by I. E. S. Edwards et al. Cambridge: Cambridge University Press.
1988 Kuzi-Tešub and the "Great Kings" of Karkamiš. *Anatolian Studies* 38:99–108.

Hoffner, H. A.
1969 Some Contributions of Hittitology to Old Testament Study. *Tyndale Bulletin* 20:27–55.
1973 The Hittites and Hurrians. Pp. 197–228 in *Peoples of Old Testament Times,* edited by D. J. Wiseman. London: Oxford University Press.
1980 Histories and Historians of the Ancient Near East: The Hittites. *Orientalia* 49:283–332.

Hout, T. P. J. van den
1989 Studien zum Spätjunghethitischen Texte der Zeit Tudhalijas IV: KBo IV 10 + (CTH 106). Ph.D. dissertation, University of Amsterdam.

Houwink ten Cate, P.
1970 *The Records of the Early Hittite Empire (c. 1450–1380 B.C.).* Istanbul: Nederlands Historisch-Archaeologisch Instituut.
1974 The Early and Late Phases of Urhi Tesub's Career. Pp. 123–50 in *Anatolian Studies Presented to Hans Gustav Guterbock on the Occasion of his 65th Birthday,* edited by K. Bittel et al. Istanbul: Nederlands Historisch-Archaeologisch Instituut.

Kempinski, A.
1979 Hittites in the Bible: What Does Archaeology Say? *Biblical Archaeology Review* 5.4:21–45.

Kitchen, K. A.
1983 Hivites. P. 242 in *The New International Dictionary of Biblical Archaeology,* edited by E. M. Blaiklock and R. K. Harrison. Grand Rapids, MI: Regency Reference Library.

Košak, S.
1986 The Gospel of Iron. Pp. 125–35 in *Kaniššuwar, Studies in Honor of Hans Güterbock.* Chicago: The Oriental Institute of the University of Chicago.

Mellink, M.
1974 Archaeology in Asia Minor. *American Journal of Archaeology* 78:105–30.

Metzger, H.
1969 *Anatolia 11. First millennium B.C. To the End of the Roman Period.* London: Barrie and Jenkins.

Mora, C.
1987 Una Probabile Testimonianza di Coreggenza tra due Sovranti Ittiti. *Istituto Lombardo* 121:97–108.

Murnane, W.
1985 *The Road to Kadesh.* Chicago: The Oriental Institute.

Neve, P.
1987 Die Ausgrabungen in Boğazköy-Ḫattuša 1986. *Archäologischer Anzeiger* 1987:381–410.

Otten, H.
1968 *Die hethitischen historischen Quellen und die altorientalische Chronologie.* Wiesbaden: Franz Steiner.
1975 *Puduhepa: Eine hethitische Königin in ihren Textzeugnissen.* Mainz: Akademie de Wissenschaften und der Literatur.
1987 *Das hethitische Königshaus im 15. Jahrhundert v. Chr.: Zum Neufund einiger Landschenkurkunden in Boğazköy.* Wien: Verlag Der Osterreichischen Akademie der Wissenschaften.
1988 *Die Bronzetafel aus Boğazköy.* Wiesbaden: Otto Harrassowitz.

Gregory McMahon is a professor in the Department of History at the University of New Hampshire, where he has taught courses on ancient Near Eastern, Greek and Roman history. He received his Ph.D. from The Oriental Institute of The University of Chicago in 1988. Dr. McMahon has received numerous fellowships, including a Fulbright Fellowship for research in Turkey (1984¡85) and has published a book entitled *The Hittite State Cult of the Tutelary Deities* (Chicago 1991).

Shanks, H.
1973 An Incised Handle from Hazor Depicting a Syro-Hittite Deity. *Israel Exploration Journal* 23:234–35.

Singer, I.
1977 A Hittite Hieroglyphic Seal Impression from Tel Aphek. *Tel Aviv* 4:178–90.
1985 The Battle of Nihriya and the End of the Hittite Empire. *Zeitschrift für Assyriologie und Vorderasiatische Archäologie* 75:100–23.
1987 Dating the End of the Hittite Empire. *Hethitica* 8:413–21.

Speiser, E. A.
1962 Hurrians. Pp. 664–66 in *The Interpreter's Dictionary of the Bible,* edited by G. A. Buttrick. New York: Abingdon.
1983 *Genesis.* The Anchor Bible, vol. 1. Garden City, NY: Doubleday.

Sürenhagen, D.
1986 Ein Königssiegel aus Kargamiš. *Mitteilungen der Deutschen Orientgesellschaft* 118:183–90.

Wente, E. and Siclen, C. van
1977 A Chronology of the New Kingdom. Pp. 217–61 in *Studies in Honor of George R. Hughes*. Studies in Ancient Oriental Civilization 39. Chicago: The Oriental Institute of the University of Chicago.

de Vaux, R.
1967 Les Hurrites de l'histoire et les Horites de la Bible. *Revue Biblique* 74: 481–503.

Wilhelm, G. and Boese, J.
1987 Absolut Chronologie und die hethitischen Geschicht des 15. und 14. Jahrhunderts v. Chr. Pp. 74–117 in *High, Middle or Low?*, edited by P. Åström. Gothenburg: Paul Åströms Forlag.

Yamauchi, E.
1983 Jebusites. Pp. 256–57 in *The International Dictionary of Biblical Archaeology,* edited by E. M. Blaiklock and R. K. Harrison. Grand Rapid MI: Regina Reference Library.

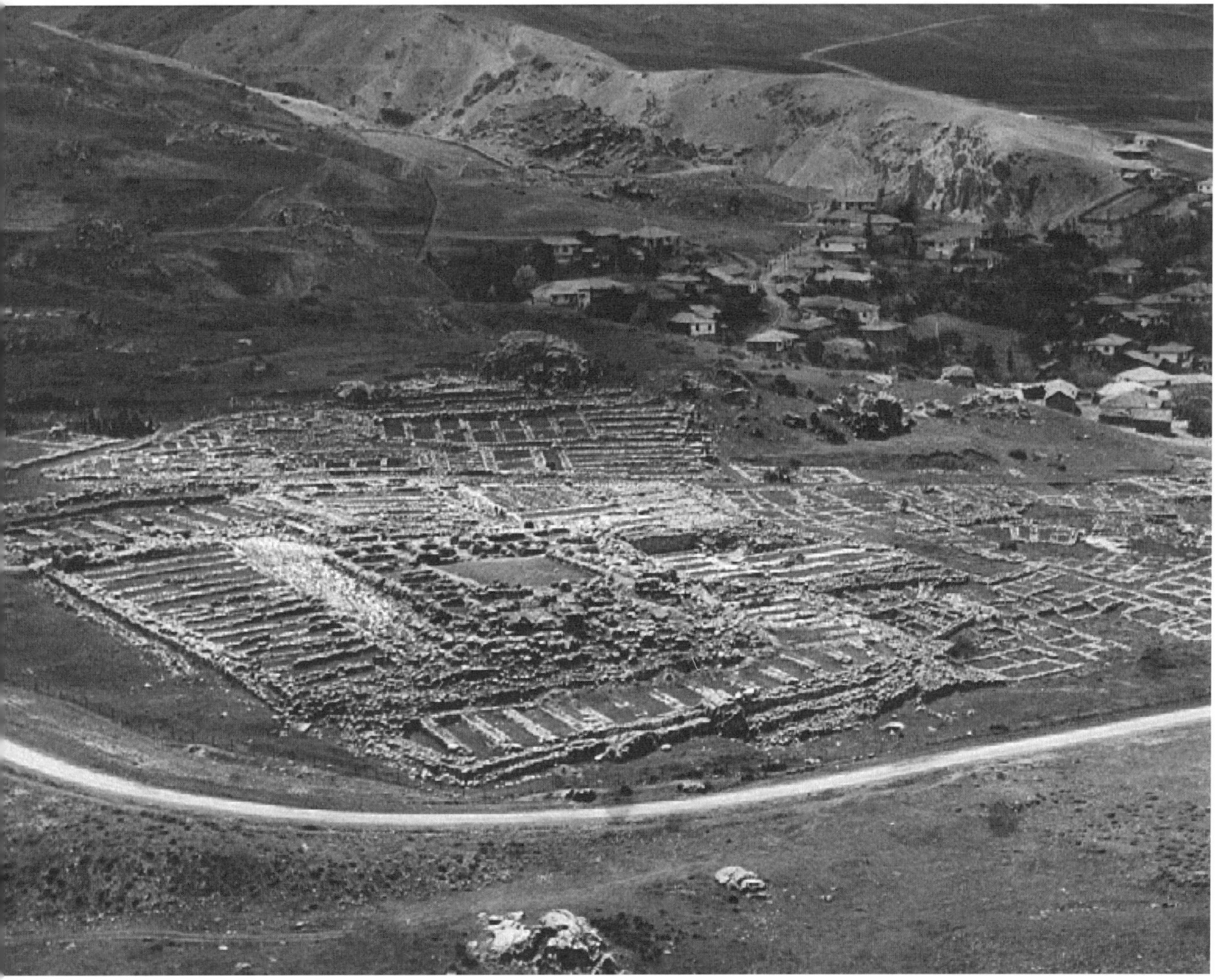

Temple 1 after its final exposure, 1968. The Temple Platform covered an area of 2.6 hectares.

The Great Temple in Boğazköy-Ḫattuša

By Peter Neve

No structure better represents Hittite architecture than the Great Temple (Temple I) at Ḫattuša. Beyond its stupendous size and superior structural quality, the Temple is a unique document and expression of a time that was the Hittite Empire's golden age of greatest power and highest prestige.

Especially noteworthy are the years of Emperor Ḫattušili III's reign (ca. 1265–1235 BCE). Without a doubt, his most meaningful foreign policy achievement was the treaty with Ramses II of Egypt. The compact ended the belligerence between the two powerful rulers and laid the cornerstone for decades of friendly relations that lasted until the end of the Empire. This diplomatic success was crowned with the marriage of one of Ḫattušili's daughters to the Pharaoh. Both contributed decisively to the consolidation of the Hittite Empire.

Ḫattušili may also have been the builder of the Great Temple, which—as far as can be determined through historical documents, but is supported also through archaeological discoveries—he presumably built as a double temple for the highest god of the Empire, the Storm God of Ḫatti, and his divine spouse, the Sun Goddess of Arinna. He succeeded at this achievement in no small measure because of the support of his highly active and ambitious wife, the Great Queen Puduḫepa, a priest's daughter from Kizzuwatna in southeastern Anatolia.

Ḫattušili should also be considered the initiator of the extensive building activities in the course of which, with the subsequent founding of the temple quarter in the so-called Upper City under his son Tutḫaliya IV, the capital Ḫattuša attained its greatest expansion. At the same time, as the excavation results of the last twenty years suggest, the capital experienced a fundamental structural change that apparently moved the city towards a purely palatial and cultic metropolis. As sometimes happens with such large-scale plans, this too never reached its completion. The demise of the Empire and the destruction of Ḫattuša (ca. 1200 BCE) brought it to an abrupt, premature end.

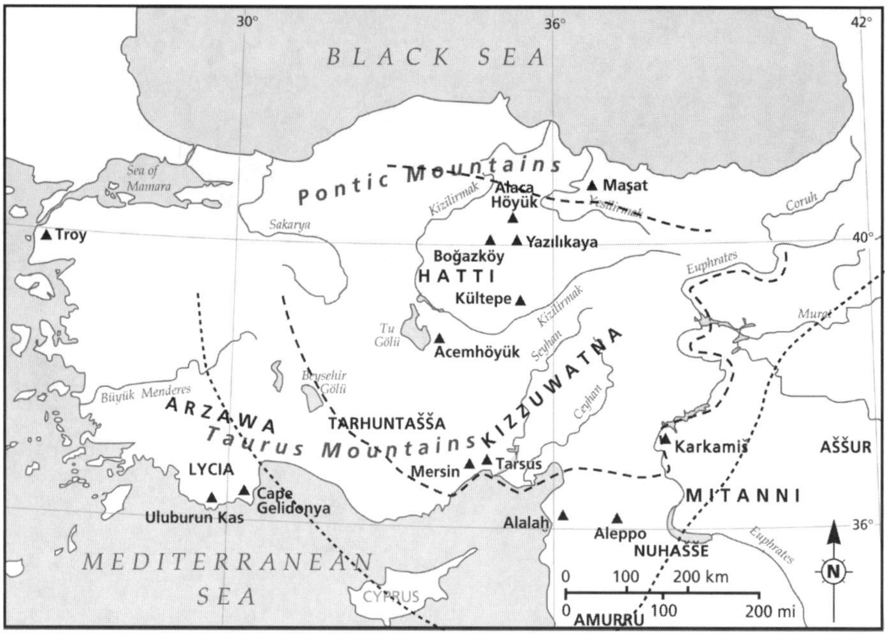

The Hittite Empire at the time of its greatest expansion, the middle of the thirteenth century BCE. *Redrawn on the basis of K. Bittel (1976:ill. 344).*

The History of Discovery and Archaeological Research

Charles Texier who discovered Ḫattuša's ruins, provided the first information about the Temple site on his plan of the visible wall remains (1939). Texier already identified therein the ruins of a temple.

The architect, Daniel Krencker, and the archaeologist, Ludwig Curtius, undertook the first comprehensive archaeological investigation of the area a good seventy years later—in the early summer of 1907—resulting in its definitive identification as a temple. Earlier, in the spring of the same year, during a sounding, Theodor Makridi of the Ottoman Museum of Constantinople had already succeeded in finding the second voluminous cuneiform tablet archive of the Hittite capital. (Makridi and the Assyriologist, Hugo Winckler, had found the first of these one year earlier in the palace on Büyükkale.) In the course of Krencker and Curtius' project, they completely uncovered the temple and partially uncovered the surrounding storerooms. Otto Puchstein, then the director and coordinator of the expedition, presented the results of the project in his publication of the edifices of Ḫattuša (1912).

After the renewal of excavations in 1931 under the leadership of Kurt Bittel, Rudolf Naumann unearthed the southern section of the Temple storerooms along with the main entrance of the Temple precinct in 1937. Thirty years later (in the campaigns of 1967/68), the final and complete exposure of the Temple precinct took place with myself as field director. This included the so-called South Area, which had only previously been explored by probes. In addition, we instituted the first conservation and stabilization measures intended to keep the original ruins intact and free from further decay.

Building Description

Site overview

The Temple Complex, which occupies the center of the Old City/Lower City of Ḫattuša, lies in an extensive temenos that originally remained free of buildings in the north and the south. A double wall enclosed it in the north. Its eastern border may have been the so-called "House on the Slope." Obviously an official building, this "house" stood across from the entrance to the Temple site on the way up to the king's palace and, therefore, must have served the Temple in a functional relationship.

The temenos extended in the south up to the so-called Postern Wall and westward to the so-called Sectional Wall of the Lower Town. In that way, other sacred buildings were included such as a spring sanctuary, an as yet unexplored Temple site in the area of Yarıkkaya (i.e., "split cliff") hill in the south, and an old city district in the west. In the final phase of the Empire, the latter was supplemented with new edifices and extended into the northern part of the temenos, serving now apparently as living and working quarters for Temple personnel.

Two gates in the Sectional Wall—the south gate and the later north gate—connected the temenos with the Lower City terrace. This terrace may have been associated with the Temple area as a special quarter.

The Temple precinct occupied a platform measuring a maximum of 200 m on its northeast–southwest

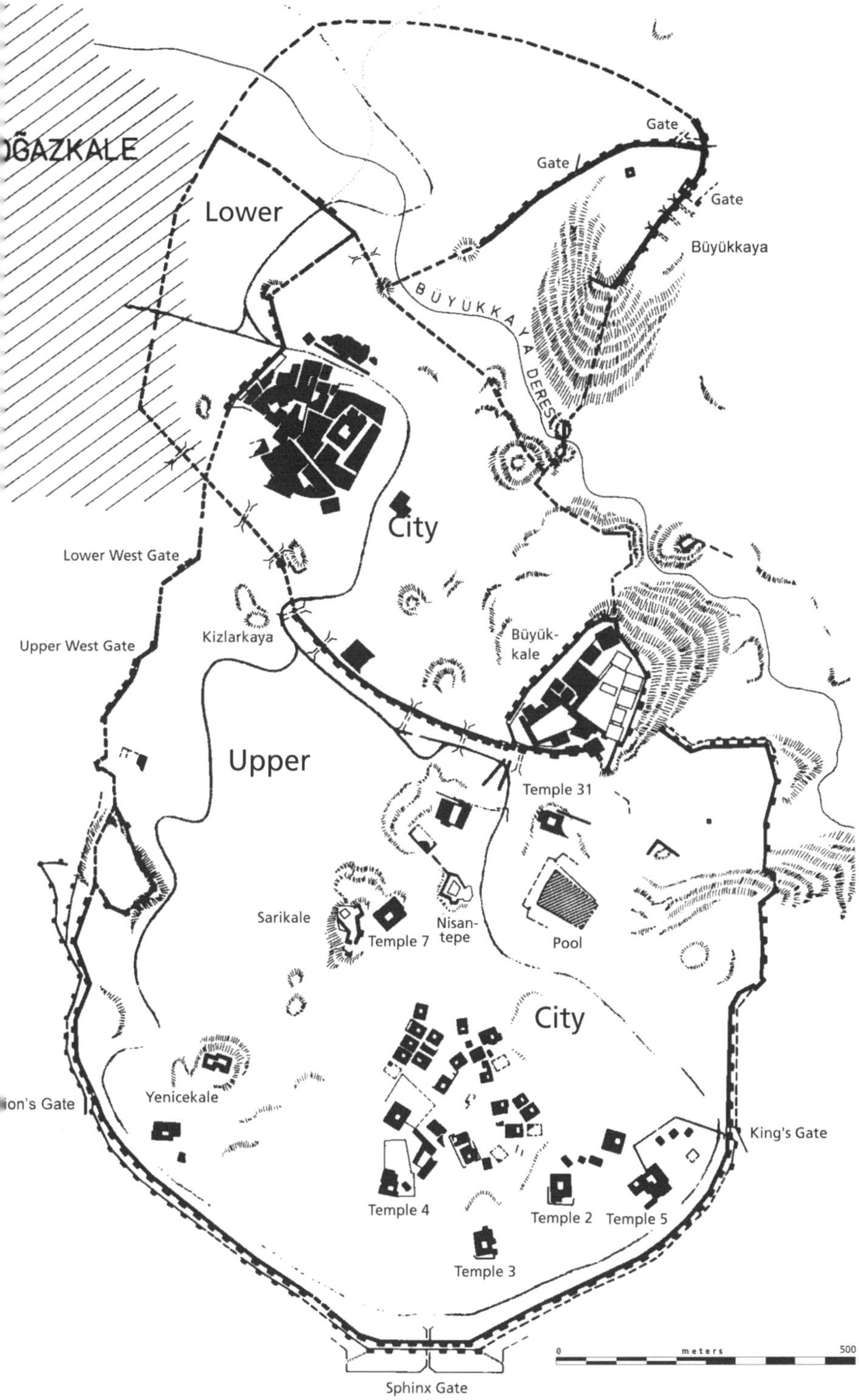

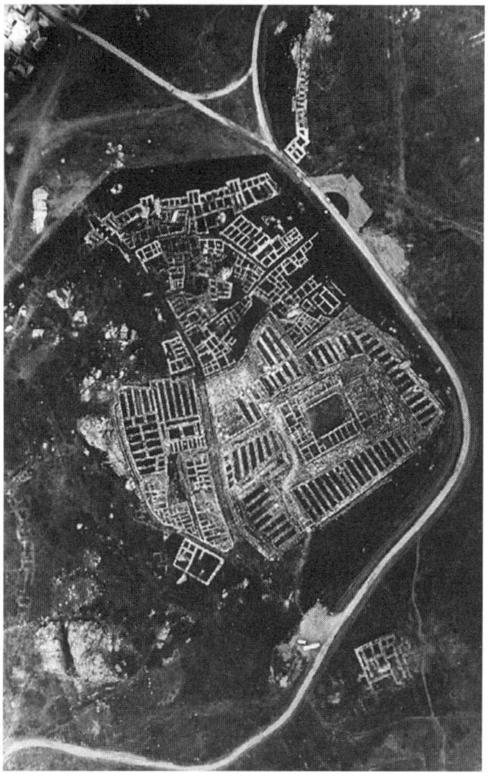

Temple 1 and Lower City (aerial shot, 1988).

This plan of the Hittite capital at Ḫattuša shows its proximity to the rock shrine Yazılıkaya as well as the modern day village of Boğazköy. Also visible, at points along the outer city walls, are the monumental gateways leading into and out of the city. Note the location of the Great Temple of the Storm-God (Temple I) in the Lower City and, on the acropolis to the east, the fortress of Büyükkale, the seat of the great kings. Many cuneiform tablets have been found there. *Plan courtesy of the German Archaeological Institute.*

side and of 130 m on its northwest–southeast side. It had straight borders on the north and east in connection with the undeveloped temenos. In the south and the west, on the other hand, following the existing structures and street network, it adopted a partly curved and partly jagged contour.

An eight meter wide paved street divided the precinct into a larger North Area and a smaller South Area. The actual Temple building stood in the north surrounded by storage buildings. In the South Area, additional room clusters and storerooms form a complex.

Both parts were erected on expanses of stone terraces. Thanks to these solid substructures, substantial segments of the building walls still exist, if they have not been eroded over time or been robbed out. In each case, the remains include the nearly two-meter wide foundations, most base courses and door openings recognizable through their stone thresholds, as well as—in the deeply buried depressions—the remains of the floors heavily black-

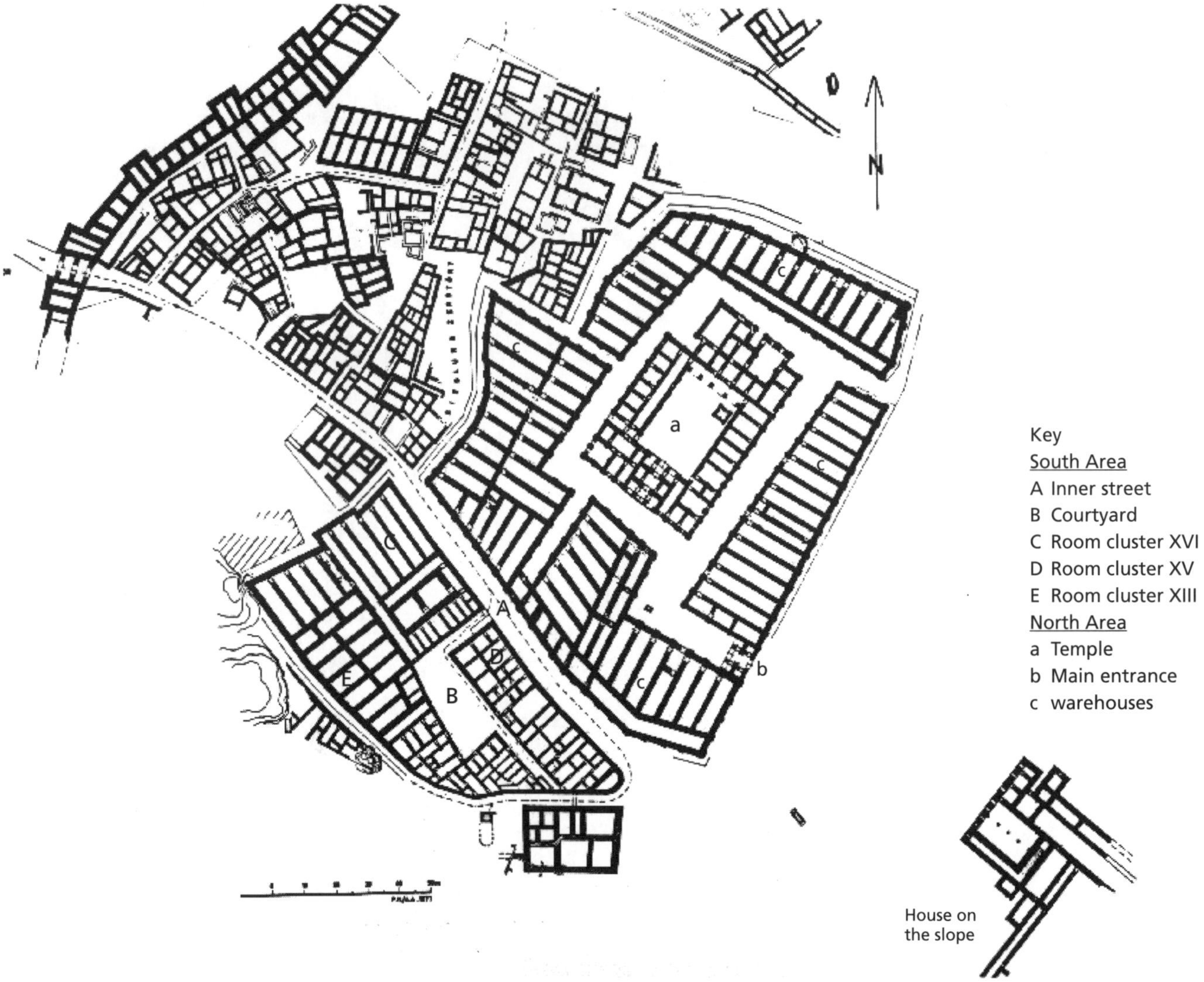

Top plan of the Great Temple, including north and south areas.

ened by the burnt walls that once ran over them and by the carbonized wood of the collapsed roof. All told, the remnants provide a vivid witness that the Temple, like all the other official and sacred buildings of the capital, was destroyed in a conflagration.

Because of this state of preservation, we were able to reconstruct the floor plan almost perfectly. In addition, we have been able to gather essential information about the details of construction, the building plan, and organization, as well as insight into the building process of the entire site.

The North Area

Enclosure

Four passages permitted access to the North Area. The main entrance stood on the east side facing the palace on Büyükkale. It was flanked by human-height base courses and outfitted with massive door thresholds. The entrance was constructed as a multi-room gate building, consisting of a gate chamber with guard rooms on the sides and a colonnade extending to the inside. This entrance to the North Area occupied at the same time the point at which the road from Büyükkale forked into northern and southern routes. At the fork, and before the road reached the Temple district, it came to a five-meter long water basin. The massive basin was decorated with the relief of crouching lions.

The northern path led towards the main portal, as the correspondingly positioned water basin showed, while the southern path advanced in the direction of the lower city terrace through the broad paved street between the north and south area. This path probably also marked the beginning of the processional street leading to Yazılıkaya (the rock sanctuary) in the northeast outside of the city, which, as supplement to the City Temple, constituted in a sense the country seat of the Divine Couple. Known in texts as the "House of the Weathergod," it clearly served a special religious festival, namely, the AN.TAḪ.ŠUM festival.

On the same street and opposite the entrance to the South Area, between the south and west storehouses, stood a second simple gate structure.

In addition, two open passages existed on the northwest side and near the east corner of the North Area. One reached them by way of long ramps built in front of the terrace with the storage buildings. They could have served as side entrances for Temple personnel and for delivery of goods to the Temple.

Main and side entrances led towards a wide street paved with large stone tiles and provided with canalization. This street circled around the Temple and, along with making the building accessible, it was surely also intended for festival processions. On the way from the main entrance to the Temple, one passed by a second similarly massive, but undecorated water basin, which, like the lion basin before the outer entrance, could have contained purifying water used for ceremonial cleaning. The basin was sunk into the cobblestone pavement. Today it has been moved from its original position.

Paved street between the North and South areas of the Temple 1 complex.

The Temple

The Temple covered an area of 42 m in width and 65 m in length[2], with its long axis running from the southwest to the northeast. It was laid out as a large building complex consisting of the entrance wing, the inner court, and connecting clusters of rooms along the sides. The complex possessed a continuous rectangular enclosure, together with a smaller and narrower wing attached in the northeast that harbored the "holy of holies," and presented a sharply segmented profile through its projecting exterior face. Its base-course stones were hewn from dark green gabbro (basalt-like rock) in unmistakable color contrast to the gray limestone otherwise employed.

One entered the southern and narrow side of the Temple through a gate house which, like the outer gate, consisted of a symmetrical structure with guard rooms along its sides. Besides the inner colonnade that faced the Temple court, an additional outer one pointed towards the Temple street. Low balustrades once adorned the lateral transoms. In addition, there was an entrance on the northwest side that was equipped with a drainage ditch in order to drain the water out of the yard.

Originally paved with stone slabs, the inner courtyard measured 20 m in width and 27 m in length. On its long side, it was enclosed by a continuous wall, only interrupted on the south end by door openings. On the narrow side, towards the northeast across from the main entrance, there was a hall supported by three columns on gabbro bases. This portico facilitated access to the holy of holies. In front of it and off to the side, in the east corner of the yard, there lay blocks similarly hewn from gabbro that belonged to a smaller structure with an inner space barely two to three meters in size. Based on its material, but also because one can still see the thresholds of door openings leading toward the colonnade,

Main gate entrance to the Temple. Note basin in back center. North Area.

this smaller structure must have had a functional connection with the sanctuary. Depictions on Hittite seals as well as ceramic models of pre-Hittite origin could suggest that this structure had the form of an accessible altar tower with a raised platform for sacrifices.

The sanctuary consisted of a number of interconnected rooms among which the actual cult room stood out because of its exposed position, size, and decorations. It could be approached from the colonnade through two antechambers with staggered and apparently unsealable passages and entered through a narrow and also doorless opening on its west corner. Four window openings distinguished the 7.9 x 10.4 m wide cult room. The windows were a good 1 m wide and scarcely 10 cm above the floor. They were distributed in both corners of the room's protruding northeastern part.

In between, i.e., in front of the mid-point of the outer wall, stood the stone pedestal of the cult-image which, consequently, was in position to receive bright daylight. Across from this, in the middle of the southwest wall and in the middle of the long walls, one can still recognize the graduated protrusions of wide pilasters. Apparently, these manifested majesty and emphasized the sacred significance of the room.

A second almost equally large cult room appears to have occupied the north corner of the sanctuary as the extant foundation walls and thresholds indicate. This room was connected with the antechambers by means of a room, the south half of which was occupied by a single, massive gabbro block weighing in excess of forty tons that was partly integrated into the surrounding walls and partly worked into a low pedestal.

Apart from two single rooms near the side entrance and at the west end of the portico, the rest of the rooms surrounding the courtyard were all joined as apartments, three on the east, two on the west. Four of these apartments contained a larger room that, like the cult room, had window openings on the narrow wall toward the outside as well as pilasters in the middle of the wall. Labeled by Puchstein as "staterooms," these rooms may have provided further cult rooms, perhaps—as the central relief at Yazılıkaya demonstrates—for the next in line to the supreme divine couple, i.e., for the members of the divine family.

The apartments to the east were reached directly from the courtyard, from the main portal, and the colonnade respectively. The ones to the west were entered from the side entrance by means of a long corridor, which also served as an internal access to the sanctuary.

The Storerooms

The storerooms around the Temple consisted of four separate wings divided by the external entrances: the east gate, the south gate, and the two open passages. They could be accessed through corridors and staircases that had been combined into individual traffic zones. Thereby, the individual rooms were directly connected with one another as suggested by the remaining thresholds positioned throughout alongside the outer walls.

All of the wings were obviously built with multiple floors, two stories high to the south and east and three stories high to the north and west. This conclusion follows in part from their deep foundation courses, as well as from the partly intact stair

North Area Temple

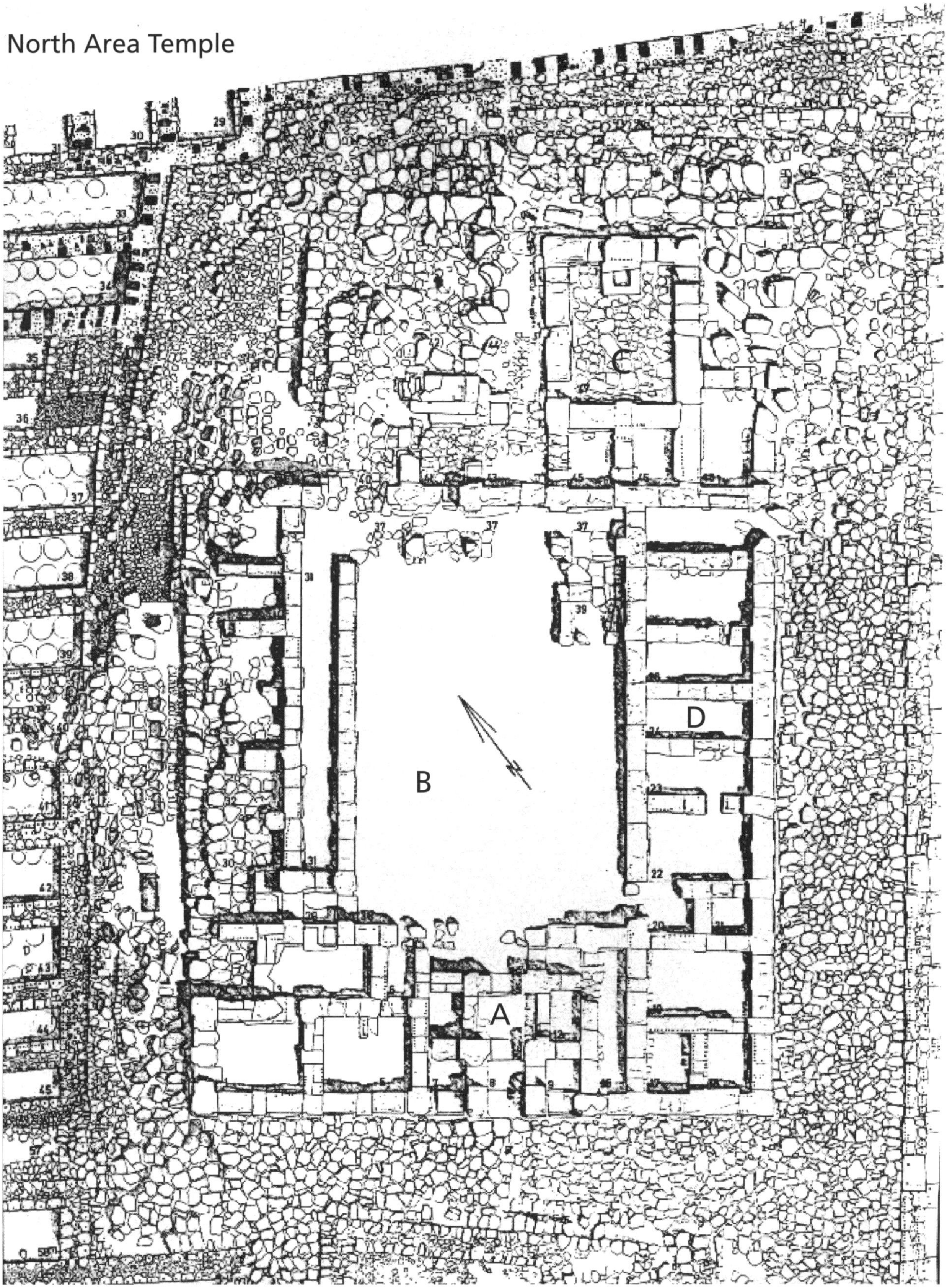

Key
A Main entrance
B Inner courtyard
C Cult room
D Apartment

Temple building. Main entrance with inner courtyard, entrance hall, cult roomwings.

Temple building. View into the cult room.

connections, particularly their substructures. Each story stood about 3.8 m high from the upper surface to the upper edge of each floor. This design means that an estimate of the original number of storerooms would have to reach at least two hundred.

The length of each room varied greatly, falling anywhere between 5 and 25 meters because of the irregular ground plan of the wings. The width of each measured uniformly 4 meters with the exception of the more narrow corridors and staircases. Altogether the storage rooms of the north area comprised 12,000 m^2 of usable space.

The storerooms were used as depots, as demonstrated by the furnishings recovered partially *in situ*. The lower stories of the spaces in the northwest, west, and south tracts served for the storage of big pithoi, that held up to 2,000 liters. Unfortunately, neither references in the inscriptions nor the materials retrieved through excavation offer any insight regarding the nature of

Temple building. Apartment in the south corner.

their contents. All of the vessels had apparently been systematically plundered before the conflagration of the Temple.

Most of the storerooms on the ground floor as well as the upper stories were apparently equipped with wooden shelves. This can be deduced from support bases that were found *in situ* in front of the long walls or in the building destruction debris. Moreover, metal locks and clay seals, which lay in the burnt rubble of the north storerooms, point to the existence of containers composed of perishable material—presumably transport vessels in the form of cases and baskets. Nothing is left of the goods that were stored on the shelves and in the containers. The same thing probably happened as with the pithoi, that is, they were plundered before the destruction of the rooms.

The east rooms survived in better shape in this regard. This is where, in 1907, Makridi discovered the Temple's archives, which consisted of several thousand inscribed tablets, now just fragments, which apparently did not interest the plunderers.

Many of the rooms could well have served as offices and workshops, which were indispensable for the administration and maintenance of the Temple goods alone. The numerous scribal names that were found chiseled into the outer walls of the south storerooms and into the street pavement in front, for example, hint that offices were housed in the adjacent rooms

South Area

Access

The South Area, situated on the opposite side of the paved street, formed an enclosed district with access by means of a wide path across from the south gate of the main Temple complex. The path led into a trapezoid-shaped courtyard, then narrowed and continued to the south side of the area where it ended in a cul-de-sac.

Through the internal, paved, and channeled traffic system, it was possible to access up to 100 rooms, from the smallest to the hall-sized spaces. They formed sixteen uniquely designed groups, combining two to sixteen rooms. Large-scale, spacious complexes could be found in preferred locations near the entrance as well as the courtyard. Smaller groups of rooms consisting of the tiniest chambers that occasionally enclosed one another were concentrated especially in the southeast tip of the area.

The Room Clusters

Only the basement story of the room cluster XV, southeast of the entrance, survived. It consisted of fourteen directly connected rooms, which were used in an unfinished state as their partially incomplete door thresholds show.

Across from this and northwest of the entrance lay the similarly preserved room cluster group XIV. Its basement rooms were distributed over three adjacent wings. The floor plan clearly adopted a symmetrical concept. In this way, the wing closest to the entrance contained, besides a staircase on the east end, a row of rooms that was made up of a wide room with axially ordered stone

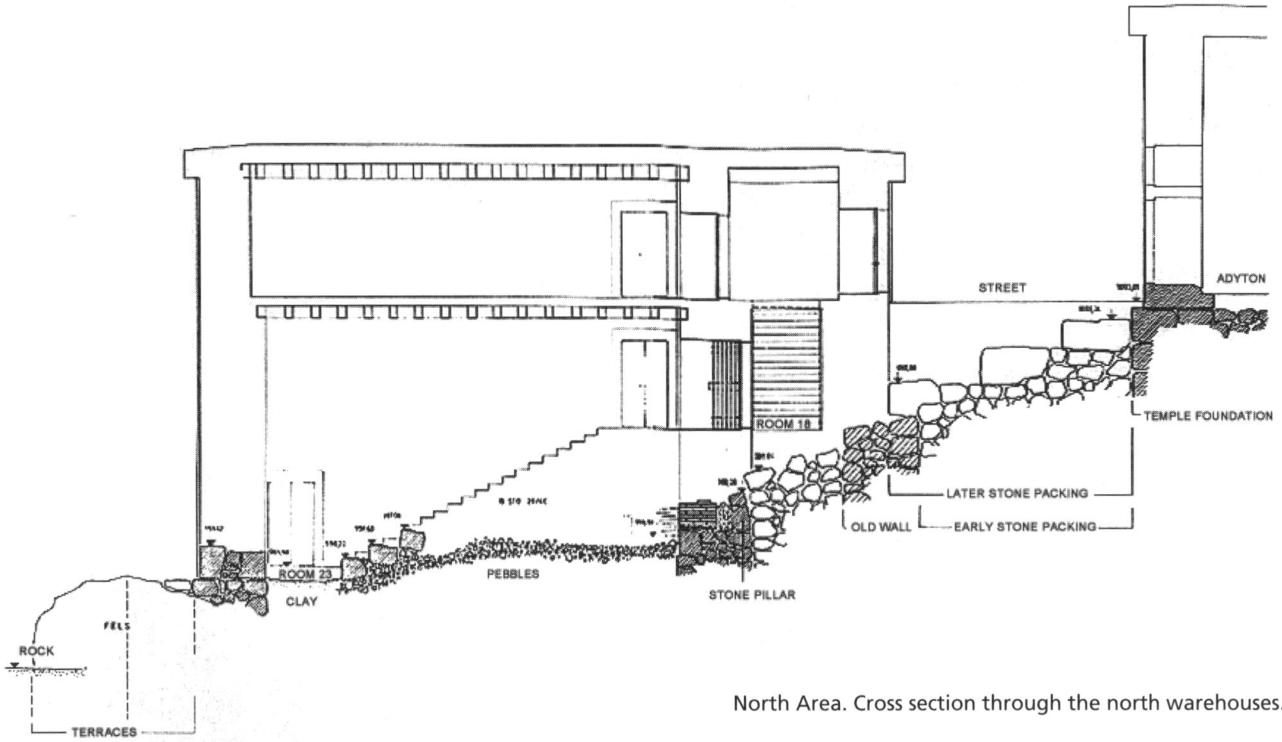

North Area. Cross section through the north warehouses.

North Area. Northwest warehouses. Room 37, with pithoi *in situ.*

posts and wall pillars in the middle, as well as three equally sized smaller chambers to each of its sides.

Next a wide wing with noticeably thick walls spanned the full length of the cluster: apparently the central divider of the room cluster. It contained two hall-sized square rooms whose dividing wall corresponded visibly to the symmetry of the axis of the neighboring wing. The northern wing of the group took the shape of a long narrow repository in which excavators discovered a great number of terracotta vessels.

Room cluster XVI in the northwest wing of the area consisted solely of storage rooms that one could reach from the courtyard by way of a long corridor. Clay containers filled the northernmost rooms (1–5), while the rooms to the south (7–11), since not fully completed, remained unused. The bigger, neighboring group of rooms of cluster XIII should also be considered incomplete. Only the upper edge of the foundation remained and was also covered with earthen berms, indicating that the construction of the building had

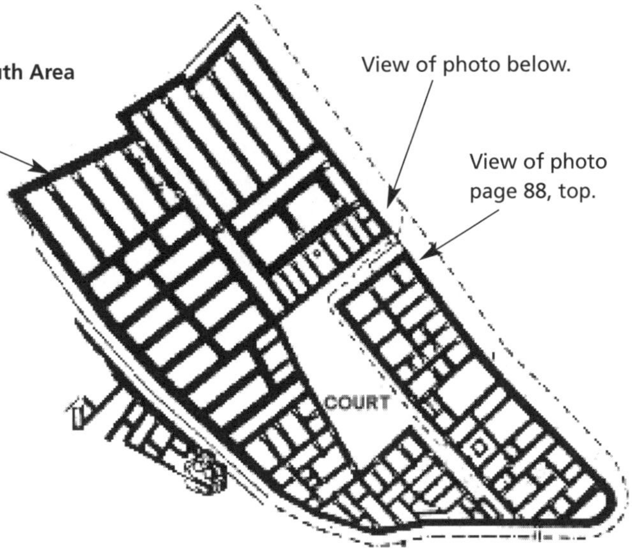

South Area. Room group XIV, Rooms 1–8.

been aborted prematurely. Judging from the layout of the foundations, a great pillared hall structure had been planned with a gate house in front towards the courtyard and a double nave entrance hall.

In regard to the smaller room clusters (I–XIII), we can determine that all better preserved units had one (in the case of of cluster IV, two) room that distinguished itself with a pilaster in a way comparable to the basement room at the entrance. Apparently, two rooms were also equipped with stone pedestals, as the preserved foundations show, and one also had a centrally located fireplace. A third pillar room had a square bordered by yellow sandstone in its middle instead. Another room (1 of room cluster I) was—like the side room in the cult wing in the Temple—half taken up by a monolithic stone block that here was chiseled into a flat basin and connected to the drainage system.

The many votive and libation vessels that were found on the floors and in the rubble of the building stand out in the artifactual inventory. All in all, this leads one to attribute a cultic function to these rooms, perhaps as auxiliary small side temples, just as is assumed for the "state room" of the Temple.

The economic role of the southern areas finds confirmation not only in the storerooms, but by virtue of the fragment of a clay tablet found in its rubble. The tablet contains a list of temple personnel belonging to a guild, É.GIŠ*kinti*, namely a "house of labor."

Construction

Builders founded the North as well as the South Area of the Temple district on human-made stone terraces, into which they incorporated projecting spurs of bedrock. Following the incline from northwest to southeast, the terraces rose in several steps, which determined the size as well as outline of the individual room complexes.

South Area of the Temple Complex. Room group XV.

South Area of the Temple Complex. View looking southeast toward Room groups XIII, XIV, and XVI.

The Temple terrace itself proved to be the most elaborate. It consisted of uniform rows of intricately fitted, colossal stone blocks that rose as a homogeneous platform more than twelve meters above the city terrain to the north.

Masons fashioned the up to 1.6 m high stone base of the Temple walls out of enormous squared stone blocks, up to ca. 6 m long. Their width corresponded to the thickness of their respective walls. For the cult rooms, the base measured 1.7 to 1.8 m, otherwise 1.2 to 1.4 m for the inner and 1.5 to 1.6 m for the outer walls. On the other hand, the nearly 2 m wide storeroom walls possessed only a low, leveling layer bordered by worked-stones on either side. Builders constructed the storeroom walls on deep-reaching foundations to accommodate the huge pithoi that had to be stored in the lower story. Only the base courses of the outer walls stood considerably higher there. The walls in the southern area were of lesser quality, but were principally built in the same way.

The wall structures above the base courses consisted of a skeleton of vertical and horizontal wooden beams as a static framework that was fastened with dowels to the foundation walls, as the drill holes along the outer edge of the bases still show. The compartments between the beams were filled by air-dried mudbricks. Clay and small stones served as filling around the wooden posts. The walls were plastered and probably painted in color (as we know from other Hittite buildings at Boğazköy and elsewhere) and, with the exception of the cultic rooms and "state-rooms," articulated with sculpted pilasters on the outer and courtyard façades.

Builders equipped the door openings with monolithic thresholds—grouped in pairs in the storerooms—and, but for a few exceptions, provided with carved bottom and side recesses in the shape of shallow depressions as sockets for door pivots. The doors of the Temple and the room clusters in the South Area were one-winged with a width of 1.0 to 1.1 m, but those of the storerooms were double paneled with a width of 1.5 but occasionally up to 1.9 m. The even wider main gates called for special hinge stones on their rear sides.

Excavators found several unfinished threshold stones, in different stages of completion, in the western storerooms of the North as well as South Area. One can assume that they reached the building site fresh from the quarry or as half-finished products, and masons finalized their shape on site. Apparently, workers first used templates to determine the hole spaces for the pivots of the door casings. Then, step by step, the door recesses were completed with these.

North Area. North warehouse , Room 26. Burnt wall structures.

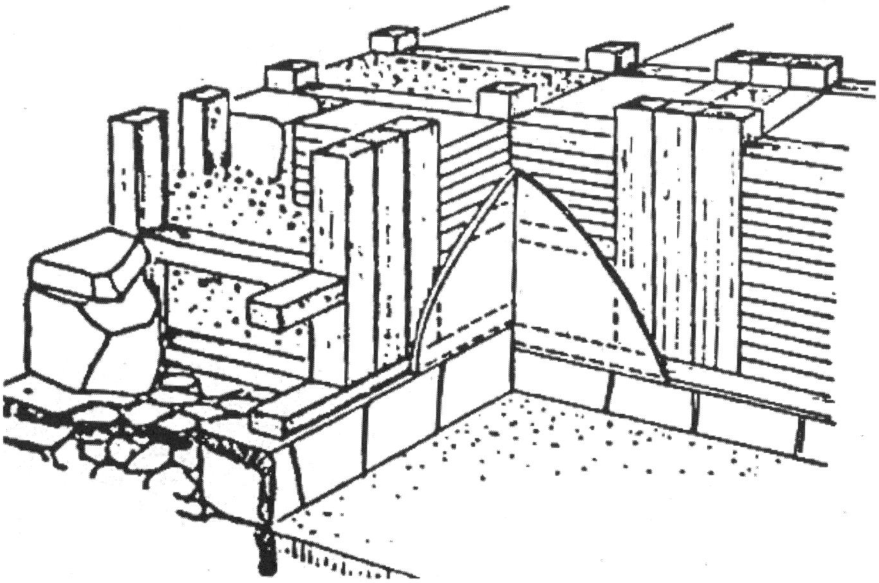

North Area. North warehouse, Room 26. Reconstruction of the wall structures.

Corresponding with the doors, masons also provided the windows with bottom and side recesses, to judge merely from the documented examples in the Temple. In addition, stone-carvers chiseled in one corner a socket for the hinge of the window shutters. The width of these windows in the sacred room and in the so-called "state rooms" was ca. 1.0 m. There they reached down almost to the ground, otherwise as far as can be ascertained, they occurred elsewhere in the normal banister height of 90 cm and had a width of 80 cm which made them also considerably narrower. The almost 2 m wide "arcade" by the main portal once had low wooden banisters that were

Temple Complex, North Area. Door threshold in the Temple (Room 18/19).

Temple Complex, North Area. Door thresholds in the South Warehouses (Room 76–79).

anchored to the base wall by dowels in the ground behind the edge of the window sills as well as by the end supports on the side. We can infer from the architectural details of the Hittite domestic house models how the windows and banisters once looked.

The floors consisted of beaten earth, which was applied to a stone underlayment in the lower story and a beamed ceiling in the upper stories. The floors of the Temple as well as those of the gate chambers were additionally plastered with lime,

Ḫattuša, Upper City. Fragments of a Hittite domestic building model with window openings.

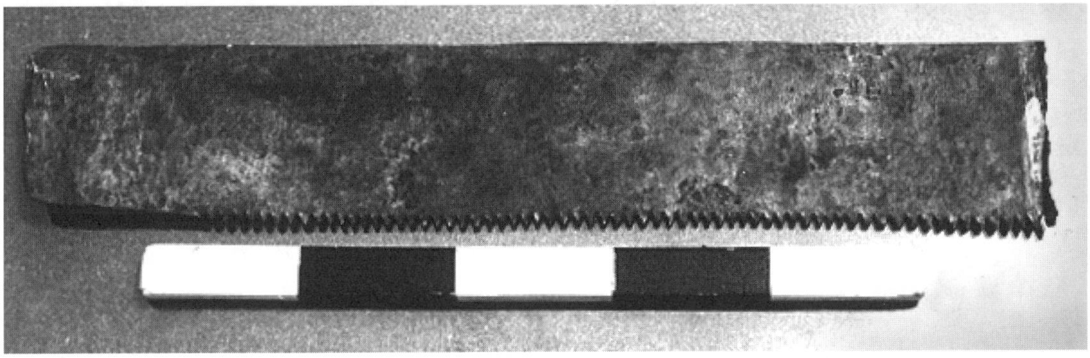

Lower City. Hittite Bronze saw.

Below: Upper City. Egyptian adze. Length 13 cm.

remains of which the 1907 excavation was still able to observe. Only grooved junctures in the door thresholds reveal this floor treatment today.

Building Process

Prerequisites

The indispensable prerequisite for the realization of such an extensive undertaking was then—as it is today—a well-thought out organization totally congruent with an architectural plan. This plan—insofar as it concerns the Temple enclave—must have established something like a blueprint design of true proportions, if only to have been able to determine the measurements and forms of the stone blocks from the quarries that were to be used as the material for the foundations. Moreover drawings were necessary for the rest of the room complexes so that the engineers could execute the layout on site, as well as make an estimate for the quantity of the necessary materials. Contemporary documents of Mesopotamia and Egypt verify this scenario. Therefore, it was necessary to have a team of experienced professionals—something similar to the medieval construction guilds—under the leadership of a master builder and chief planner who was primarily responsible for the overall undertaking. Naturally, the execution of the project demanded a large work crew.

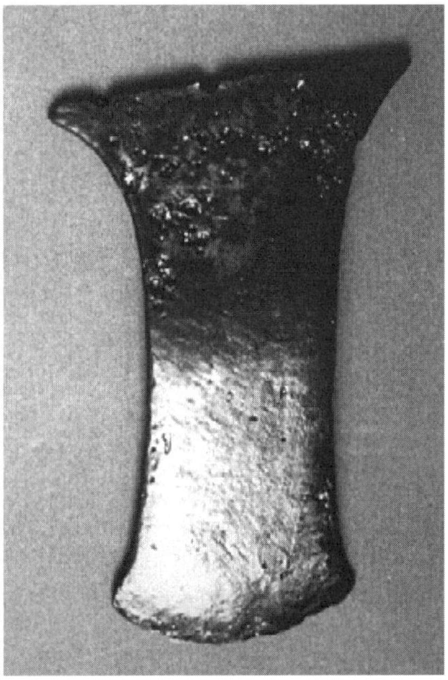

Boğazköy. Hittite stone quarry near Ciradere.

Temple Building. Foundation stones of the cult room with cut marks made by a pendulum saw.

Building material was readily available on site and in the neighboring areas. The majority of the wall stones apparently derived from the rocks at the building site itself as well as nearby rock outcrops. Material of superior quality, like the gabbro blocks of the sanctuary, had to be imported from farther away. In regard to this, a few years ago we discovered a discarded block that apparently had been broken during its transport to the site. This led to an as yet unexplored quarry, situated by a brook 5 km away from the city and covered by debris and shrubbery. This creek bed probably served as a path for transportation, especially in the winter when it was frozen and covered with snow. It leads us to consider the use of sleds for transportation, as, for example, depictions on Egyptian and Assyrian reliefs show. Such sleds are still used in the impassable forests of the Pontic and Taurus Mountain Ranges.

The mountainous land on the east, south, and west of the city, once covered with thick alpine forests, undoubtedly supplied the necessary wood for construction. The workers surely manufactured mudbricks at the edge of the nearby Büyükkaya creek.

Apparently, only a limited selection of tools was available. The setting of the great base quadrants took place on site, through the help of levers, judging by the bosses left on the stones or by the deep hollows therein. In light of the fact that the stones weighed tons and considering that their butt joints were extremely complicated and at the same time fitted together with accuracy to the last millimeter, a reel or lifting jack must also have been used in the process. The stone work was carved out predominantly with tools made of tough basalt or gabbro, unworked but for a hole for the shaft. They were relatively simple, that is, swung with two hands like a sledge hammer, and they left dot-like blow marks, typical for Hittite wall stones. By virtue of similar, but decidedly finer marks, for example, on the door and window rabbets, as well as on the basis of a tool fragment, it is clear that bronze pick hammers were also in use.

Temple Building. North wall of the cult room. Exterior side of foundation stone.

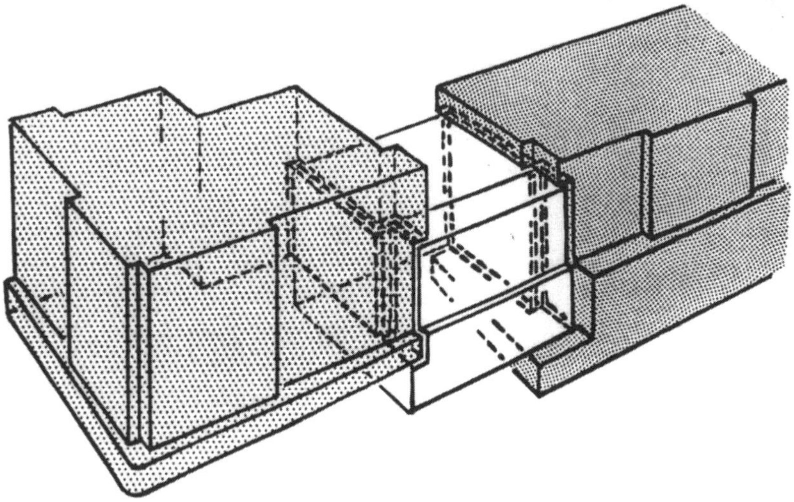

Temple Building. North wall of the cult room. Reconstruction of the foundation stone connections.

Only cut marks—rather than finds of tools—demonstrate the use of drills and saws in the stone work. For drills, metal pipes with a diameter of ca. four to six centimeters must have been used as is evident from not only drill marks in the dowel holes, but also numerous drill cores found at the building site. They were probably mechanically operated in combination with water and fine sand as a grinding substance. This allowed for a more efficient process utilizing a smaller expenditure of personnel than with the chisels normally used for this purpose.

For the same reason, it appears that the construction employed saws. As was the case with the drills, workers sawed blocks, especially those of particularly hard stone. Based on the cut marks, sawing utilized two different models: one that leaves a straight track and one that leaves curved cuts, i.e. a saw that must have been operated in a pendulum-like way.

Tools used for woodwork are documented through the preservation of several tool types. These include remains—about half—of a ca. 140 cm long bronze saw which was found in the immediate proximity of the Temple; as well as through "adzes" and flat axes of varying sizes. Especially noteworthy is the example of an "adze" of apparently Egyptian origin. While this did not come from the Temple district, but

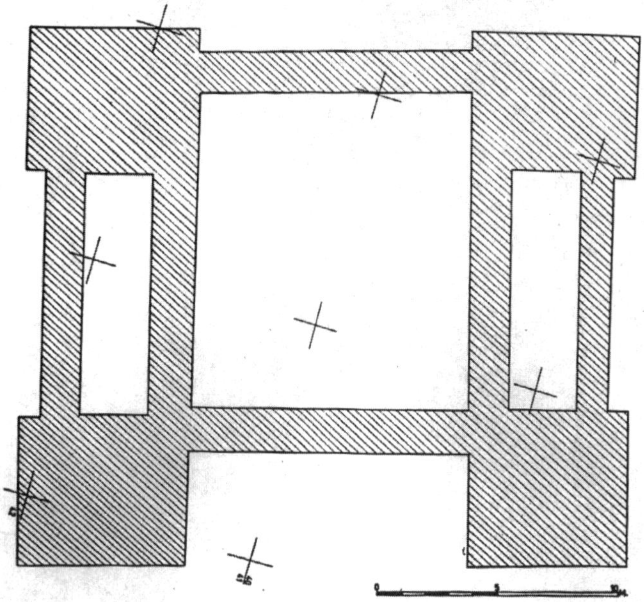

Temple site of Kültepe, period Ib (eighteenth century BCE). *(After Özgüç 1993:167, ill. 2. 4).*

from the Upper City, it indicates nonetheless the use of foreign specialists in Ḫattuša. In this case, they came from Egypt or more likely out of the Syrian-Egyptian region, which bordered the Hittite Empire at this time.

The drills permit the supposition that specialists were employed from the very same region that was already in the first half of the second millennium characterized by highly developed masonry techniques. Drills left similar marks of identical measurements in the palace of Alalakh at Tell ʿAṭchana in north Syria (eighteenth century BCE). Drill holes of a similar nature were also found on Crete and in the palace of Tiryns. Moreover, this palace—like Mycenaean stone architecture in general—corresponds in many technical details to Hittite stone architecture and is nearly contemporaneous with Boğazköy's Temple. The use of pendulum saws in Tiryns offers a further indication of an interrelationship.

But it is more probable that northern Syria actually developed and disseminated advanced building techniques and know-how to Ḫattuša. This follows from the aforementioned examples—to which numerous others could be added—and also makes sense in light of the geopolitical situation.

The bronze saw represents another possible indicator of foreign workers: a single comparable example has not yet appeared in all of the ancient Near East. On the other hand, Crete—which presents us, like Syria, with highly developed building techniques from which the Mycenaeans profited—boasts several such saws, including nearly identical fragments that are apparently all of an earlier date, i.e., late Minoan (end of the seventeenth to the beginning of the fifteenth century BCE).

Building Process

The building execution apparently took place in stages and in separate locations, as each structure had its own building crew. As far as can be determined, the building sections in the north area consisted of the Temple, the individual storeroom tracts, and the Temple's streets. The south area seems to have been divided into four sections, the borders of which were defined by the internal transportation routes. Besides the individual building crews, which will have consisted of a relatively small group of craftsmen and helpers on site and a much larger one for the provision of the materials, there also appear to have been groups of specialists who, for example, assuredly operated the drills and saws.

The beginning of the construction project, naturally, fashioned the Temple itself, followed by the storerooms. The last building activity in the North Area—apparently only in connection with subsequent renovations—was the completion of the main gate of the outer wall following the model of the Temple entrance. Overall, the building process followed the terrain up the slope from the north or northwest to the east and south. The North Area represented the first, and the incomplete South Area the second building phase. Parallel to that, a significant decline in quality manifests itself.

The foundation of the Temple, especially that of the cult room, displays the highest quality construction, as well as a method of building that was planned down to the finest detail. Builders fit every stone individually to the substratum and to its neighboring stone and proceeded in a carefully determined order. The foundation ashlar in the north wall, positioned behind the pedestal for the cult image, evidently determined the place where the building began. It not only lies the deepest, but is also laid in such a way that its upper surface extends under the subsequent window foundations both right and left. These again are covered in the same way by the connecting corner blocks. The bottom edge of the stones therefore has three different levels in accordance to the building process. Aside from this, the blocks are dove-tailed in the connecting surfaces by less than 2 cm deep cuts and ledges. The fit was so exact that it was impossible to move the foundation ashlars in any direction, and this remains so today. Even now they are in exactly the same location and position they were placed in originally.

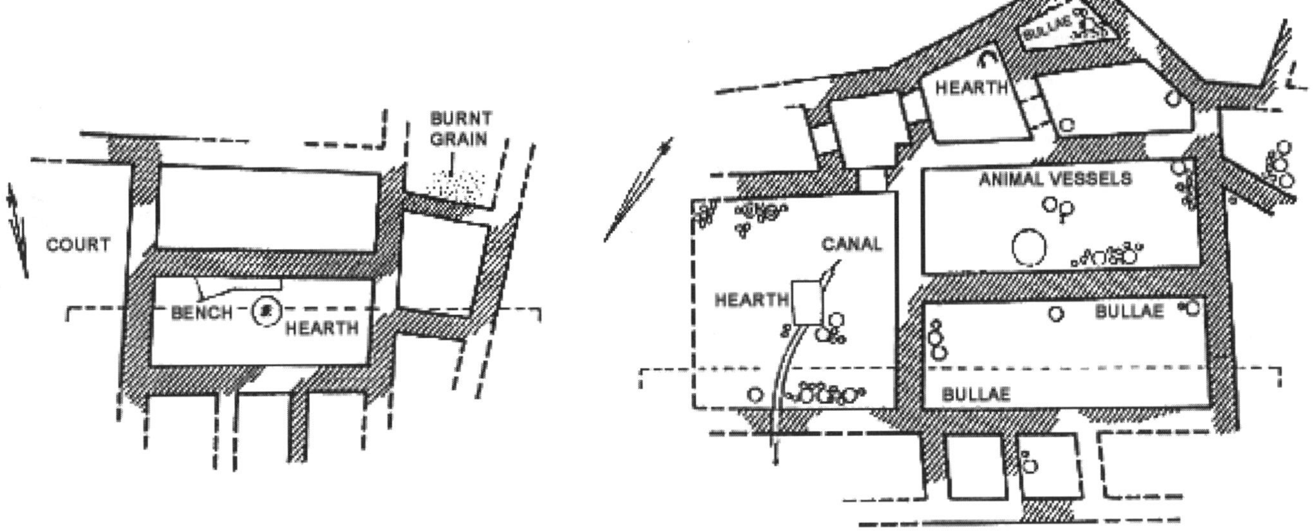

Pre-Hittite (sacred?) buildings of Büyükkale. *Left:* Period BK Vc (20th–19th century BCE). *Right:* Period BK IVd (18th century BCE).

It is noteworthy that masons employed this unusual way of joining the blocks only for the north wall of the sanctuary, the actual area where construction began. This must have had not only architectural, but also ceremonial reasons. Perhaps it indicates a distinct foundation ritual, if not the key to a foundation deposit, which would have been expected under the deepest central foundation stone, i.e., the first stone laid, or under the statue base to the front of it.

A pair of "cup marks" may bear witness to some foundation ritual. They were engraved into the surface of the foundation slab in the form of two closely adjoining, small circular depressions in front of the north corner of the Adyton. The pair must have served as the receptacle for liquid offerings which, if we follow the textual sources, formed an important part of the obligatory construction rituals for sacred structures.

The Temple in the Hittite Written Sources

Finally, in the small number of written documents that have come down to us, there are only a few general references to the Temple design or even to its appearance. They occur mostly in connection with descriptions of festivals and ritual acts, as well as instructions for Temple personnel, and permit at least some deductions regarding the character of the Temple.

Accordingly, courtyard, portico, and the cult room constituted its canonical components. Details of the building, windows and doors, as well as roofs on which sacred acts were performed, also found notice. Instructions concerning the protection of the Temple against fire point towards the generous use of wood.

The main arena for sacred acts was the courtyard, while access to the holy of holies was permitted only for the chosen few, above all, naturally, for the great king—as the chief priest—and his closest entourage.

The Building History of the Hittite Temple

In regard to the architectural-historical position of the Temple, it must be pointed out that until now our knowledge of Hittite sacred architecture has been limited to only the examples from Ḫattuša. To that we can add a temple recently discovered by A. Müller-Karpe, at Hittite Šarišša, far from the capital in the east in the "upper land" of the Hittite Empire at Kuşaklı Höyük. It is dated to the second half of the thirteenth century BCE, and altogether covers only a relatively brief segment of the four-hundred-year duration of the Hittite Empire.

Temple I, presumably built by Ḫattušili III, may represent the oldest construction site. Certain findings suggest its relatively early date: above all, the absence of an entrance hall, which usually stretches out directly in front of the narrow side of the cult room. This combination exists in all later temples of Ḫattuša, including Yazılıkaya, and also at Kuşaklı. It may be, however, that the absence of the entrance hall has to do with the special function of the Great Temple as a double shrine.

It is striking that there are no figurines connected with the building despite its relatively good preservation and exceeding importance as the state sanctuary. This contrasts with Temples 2 and 3 in the Upper City just as in Yazılıkaya, where the existence of figurines has been verified, as well as further installations—among them Temples 4 and 7—where their existence can be presumed.

Despite these differences, all the sacred buildings at Ḫattuša undoubt-

Hittite Temples of Ḫattuša

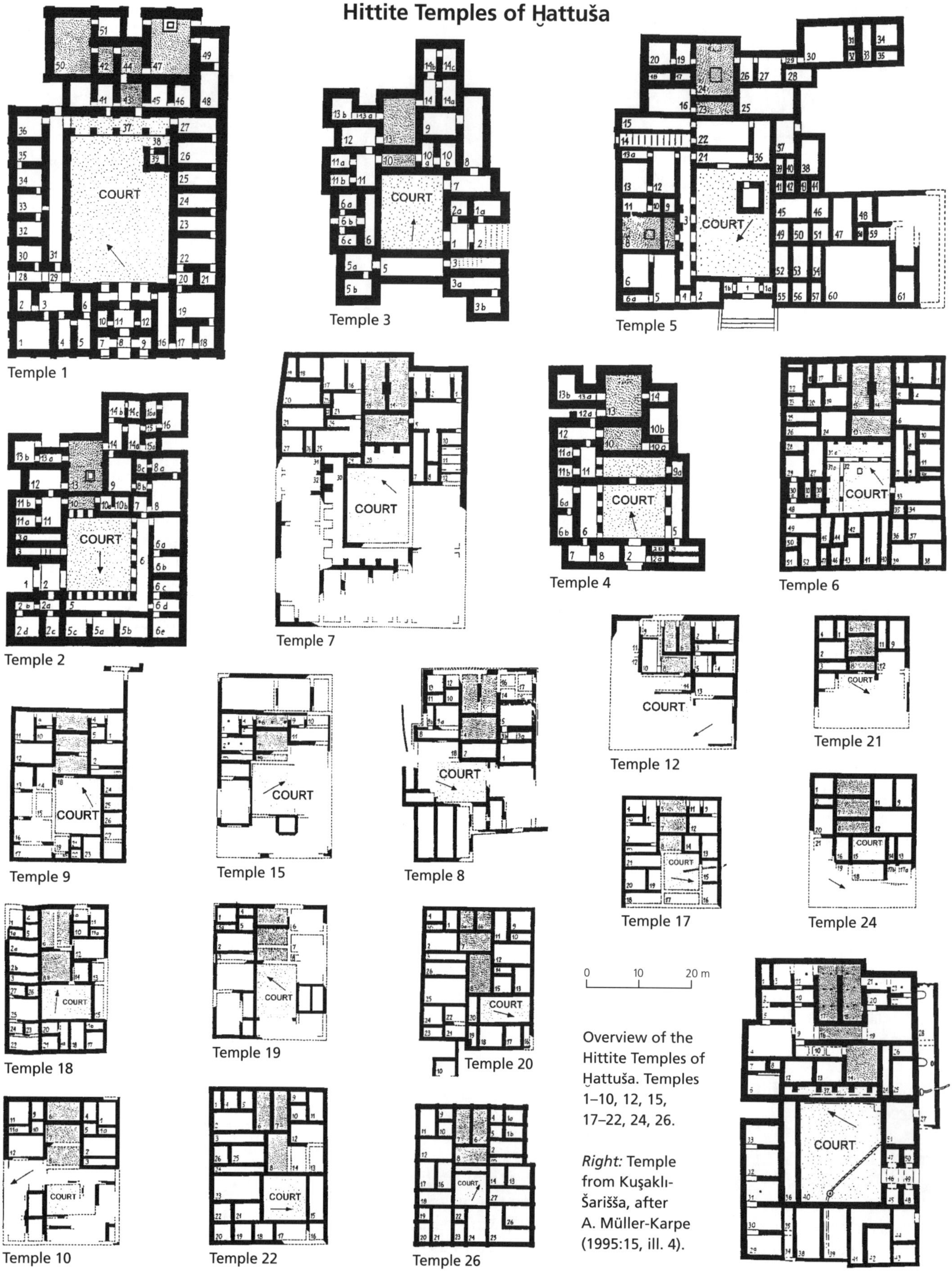

Overview of the Hittite Temples of Ḫattuša. Temples 1–10, 12, 15, 17–22, 24, 26.

Right: Temple from Kuşaklı-Šariššа, after A. Müller-Karpe (1995:15, ill. 4).

edly represented one and the same type, which are to be distinguished from two temples well over 500 years older in Kültepe near Kayseri (Hittite Neša) from the time of the *karums*. Therefore, they cannot be viewed as the formal precursors of the Boğazköy temples.

Contemporary sacred architecture outside Anatolia also offers no direct parallels. With regard to the two-space cult room group, consisting of ante and main chambers, one might imagine influences out of the Syrian-Hurrian area, which is represented by contemporary as well as much older sacred buildings showing a similar concept. Models from Egypt may have served as examples for the layout of the Temple storerooms. In western Thebes, the Temple of Ramses II, Ḫattušili's new ally and son-in-law, presents a comparable arrangement.

Basically, however, the Hittite Temple type appears to have been a local creation, the roots of which lie in the old Anatolian-Hattic "tribal house," which also provided the foundation of the Hittite palatial architecture.

Two designs from the pre-Hittite period, i.e., the twentieth to eighteenth centuries BCE, on Bükükkale where the one temple lies nearly on top of the other, could indeed be forerunners. Not only similar in design, they also possibly represent sacred buildings, to judge by their inventory, which consists for the most part of cultic vessels, especially in the younger building.

It will be necessary to continue basic research into earlier Hittite sacred architecture, as the missing link in the chain of development, in order to prove this theory.

Bibliography

Bittel, K.
1970 *Hattusha: Capital of the Hittites*. New York: Oxford University Press.

Naumann, R.
1971 *Architektur Kleinasiens von ihren Anfängen bis zum Ende der hethitischen Zeit*. 2nd enlarged ed. Tübingen: E. Wasmuth.

Neve, P.
1975 Der Grosse Tempel in Boğazköy-Ḫattuša. Pp. 73–79 in *Le temple et le cult: compte de la vingtième Rencontre Assyriologique International*, edited by E. van Donzel et al. Uitgaven Van Het Nederlands Historisch Archeologisch Inst Te Instanbul 37. Uitgaven: Nederlands Historich Archeologisch Institute Instanbul.
1989 Boğazköy-Hattusha: New Results of the Excavations in the Upper City. *Anatolica* 16:7–20.
1993a Hattusha, City of Gods and Temples: Results of the Excavations in the Upper City. *Proceedings of the British Academy* (1991 Lectures and Memoirs) 80:105–32.
1993b *Ḫattuš a-Stadt der Götter und Tempel: Neue Ausgrabungen in der Hauptstadt der Hethiter*. Mainz am Rhein: Verlag P. Von Zabern.

Puchstein, O.
1912 *Boghasköi, Die Bauwerke*. Wissenschaftliche Veröffentlichung der Deutschen Orient-Gesellschaft 19. Leipzig: J. C. Hinrichs.

Texier, C.
1839 *Description de l'Asie Mineure*. Vol. 1. Paris: Typ. De Firmin Didot frères.

Peter Neve was Director of the German excavations at Boğazköy from 1963 to 1994, having arrived at the site as a student in 1954. His extensive publications of the archaeology and architecture of Hattuša include *Büyükkale: Die Bauwerke* (1982) and *Hattuša: Hauptstadt der Hethiter* (2000).

The Power of Narrative in Hittite Literature

Tablets may have once resided in specially established tablet houses, but it is possible that some might have been moved to secondary locations during the rebuilding and reorganization of Ḫattuša in the final phase of the Empire. The discovery of land grants dating to the pre-Empire period, like the two pictured here, may illustrate this possibility. The cuneiform seal in the center of the clay tablet to the left identifies it as belonging to Zidanta, an Old Kingdom ruler, whereas the land grant to the right is identified by its center cuneiform seal as belonging to Arnuwanda I, a Middle Kingdom ruler. Both tablets were discovered at the site of ancient Ḫattuša. *Photos courtesy of Peter Neve and the German Archaeological Institute.*

By Ahmet Ünal

Even though the connection may not seem obvious at first sight, written sources represent an indispensable component of the archaeological record. In addition to being the cornerstone of any hermeneutical process, they are the sole tools in helping us understand all sorts of archaeological remains, which are principally mute in nature. Written sources are even more critical in the study of Hittite Anatolia not only because they provide straightforward historical accounts of the Hittites, but also because they illustrate the literary values and abstract thought processes that pervaded every aspect of Hittite life. The study of Hittite literature illustrates that archaeology and philology are indeed complementary disciplines and that their relationship must be carefully cultivated if we are to unravel the puzzles of the past (Ünal 1994b). In short, as opposed to the silence of the archaeological remains, the texts are immediate intellectual products of humans and as such they speak directly to us from a distant past. In the following pages, I will discuss the underlying elements of the Hittite literary tradition and present several selective and illustrative text passages from various text genres to show both the development of that tradition and the power of its prose.

The Hittite Archives

The obvious place to begin any discussion of Hittite literature is the archives at the Hittite capital of Ḫattuša near the modern-day district town of Boğazköy and some 110 miles east of Turkey's capital Ankara; additional archives in provincial towns with a limited number of texts have been discovered at Maşat (Alp 1991), Emar (Arnaud 1985; Beckman 1996a), Ortaköy (Süel 1998; Ünal 1998a), and Kuşaklı (Wilhelm 1997; Erkut 1997 gives a compact list of tablet yielding sites). Although little has been written about the archives (Laroche 1949; Otten 1955, 1984, 1986), it is from these written sources that we get our initial impressions of the role literature played in the Hittite state and society.

We must be cautious, however, when speaking of the Hittite archives. The word *archive* connotes a building or several other structures and implies the notion of a library or the like. This is certainly not the correct impression because, in fact, the Hittites built no institution that approached the functioning of a library. We cannot even be sure that the structures in which tablets have been found were actually tablet houses, or archives, in the physical sense of the word. Therefore, in this article, the word "archive" denotes the collections of tablets that have been found throughout the Hittite capital and elsewhere.

The tablets unearthed at Ḫattuša were scattered in buildings throughout the urban area and sometimes outside the settlement, too. In the Lower City, tablets were found in several rooms of Temple 1, the great temple of the Storm-God (Otten 1955:72; Bittel 1970:13–14; Naumann 1971:430; Akurgal 1978:302). On the acropolis, site of the great fortress of Büyükkale, tablets were found in three structures—Buildings A, E, and K (Bittel 1970:84–85, 163). Many tablets were also found in the so-called House on the Slope (Schirmer 1969:20), perhaps the main scribal school (Macqueen 1986:116, n. 71). In recent years, more tablets have been unearthed in Ağaçdenizi, in the Upper City with its numerous temples (Otten 1984:50, 1987:21; Neve 1985:334, 344; 1987a:405; 1987b:311; 1992). The sensational tablet of a state treaty made of bronze was found underneath paving stones alongside the inner city walls near Yerkapı (Neve 1987a:405; Otten 1988, 1989).

The exact functions of the physical structures in which the Hittites kept and stored their tablets also remain obscure. So far, tablets have been found collected in temples, houses, magazines, and perhaps special tablet houses. Otherwise they have been discovered in widely scattered areas and dumps. Recent excavations at Ḫattuša's Büyükkaya, lying beyond the Budaközü across the acropolis and integrated into the urban area by means of fortification walls during the late Empire period, also yielded some ten pieces of tablets (Seeher 1997:325). However, not all of these were *in situ* and seem therefore to have been transported inadvertently from the main city area in loads of earth, perhaps as fill for

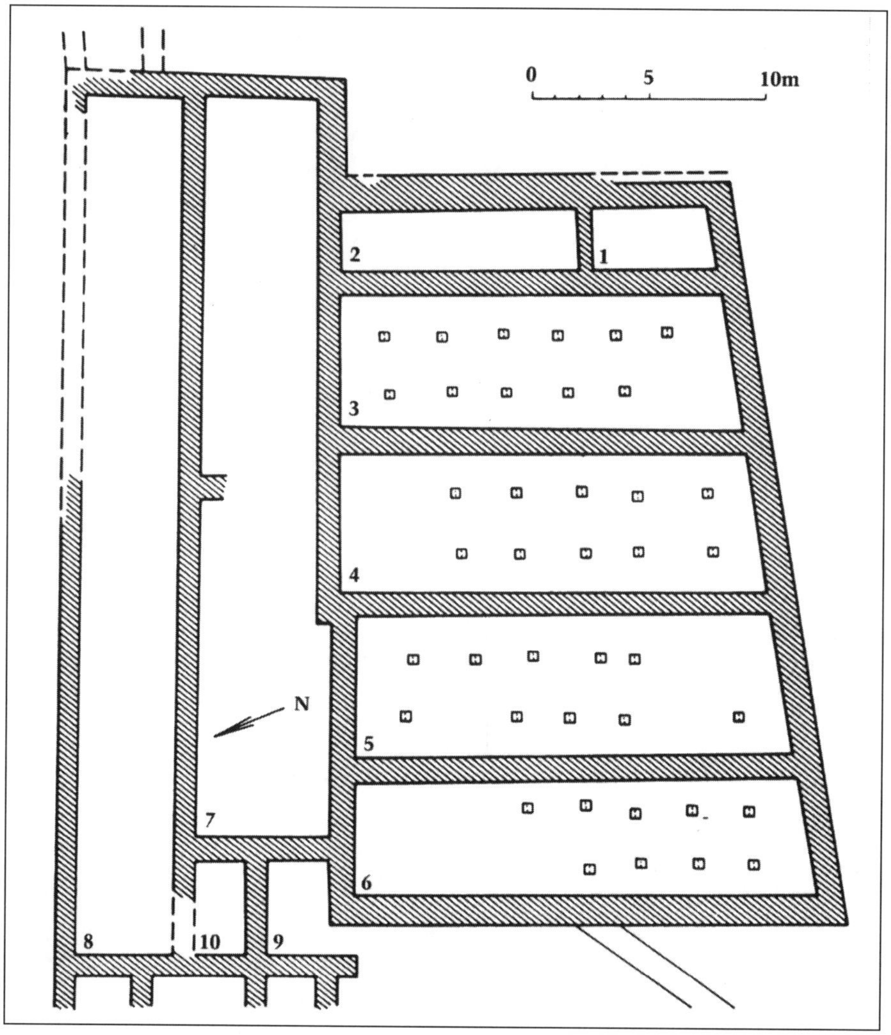

Most of the best preserved clay tablets in the Hittite archives were found in this structure, Building A on Büyükkale, the fortress located southeast of the great temple at Ḫattuša. About 105 feet long, Building A consisted of four storerooms and a long lateral corridor. Pictured in the storerooms are the remaining rectangular limestone bases that once supported parallel rows of pillars, which might have supported wooden racks or shelves for the tablets rather than a second story of the building. Stone bases were not found in the long, outer room to the east of the storerooms. *Courtesy of Peter Neve and the German Archaeological Institute.*

Tablets have been found scattered throughout the Hittite capital of Ḫattuša, including the Great Temple of the Storm-God, shown here, located in the Lower City. The entire complex, including the central courtyard and surrounding storerooms, is described by its excavator in the previous chapter. *Photo by Ronald L. Gorny.*

construction. In Ortaköy, most of the tablets have been found in a bulky masonry building called "Building A," the function of which is still to be determined (Süel and Süel 1995:265–69), though at first sight it reminds one the Great Temple of Ḫattuša. There does not seem to have been a particular system of distribution of the text genres at all. (An overview of find spots according to *CTH* numbers can be found in Cornil 1987.)

We can only approximately determine how the tablets once were organized from the structures in which they were housed as well as from the so-called shelf lists (Laroche 1971:154; Karasu 1996). It is presumed that these shelf lists were placed as indices in front of the tablets for quick reference. Some of the structures, especially Buildings A and K on Büyükkale, had rooms with parallel rows of stone pillars that might have supported wooden racks or shelves for the tablets (rather than a second story; see Neve 1982: 106, 108, and plans 41, 45). At one time the tablets may have resided in a few specially established tablet houses, but it is possible that some tablets were moved to secondary locations during the rebuilding and reorganization of the city in the final phase of the Empire (Laroche 1975: 57; Bittel 1970:85). This may be illustrated by the discovery of Old and Middle Hittite land grants dating to the sixteenth and fifteenth centuries BCE in the newly excavated temples in the Upper City (Otten 1987), which date to the thirteenth century BCE.

Other types of tablets have also been found in the Upper City. In addition to the land grants, Hurro-Hittite bilingual literary texts, rituals, letters, and divination texts have been found as well as the previously mentioned bronze tablet that details the treaty between

Ḫattušili III and his nephew, Kurunta, the vassal king of Tarḫuntašša (Otten in Neve 1987a: 405; Otten 1988, 1989).

Hittite Scribes and the Pursuit of Writing

For all we possess of written documents, we are bound in gratitude to the resourcefulness and diligence of the scribes. Unfortunately, we know very little about their education. The Hittite chancellory under Ḫattušili III employed special scribes for correspondence with Assyria. They were either educated in Assyria, or they were imitating straightforward Assyrian writing and grammatical rules (Goetze 1942:32). It seems, however, as a rule, that scribes mostly were of foreign origin (Babylonian or Hurrian; Beckman 1983; Mascheroni 1984; Wilhelm 1990), and they received a very strong education before they were promoted to their illustrious offices of scribes and chief-scribes. They may have been reared in corporate schools, and the period of education and apprenticeship may have lasted for a long time. As a rule, the career of the scribes was hereditary. Mitannamuwa, for instance, the chief scribe under the great kings Muwatalli II and Ḫattušili III, offers a distinctive example for the versatility and prodigiousness of the scribes. Besides being a proficient scribe in correct sense of the word, acquainted with all sorts of writing systems and foreign languages, he was an excellent politician and statesman as well, and possessed the credentials of a physician (Ünal 1974). To illustrate the skill of the scribes, it is worth noting that Walwaziti, another scribe nearly Mitannamuwa's contemporary, and his associates were able to finish at least ten long tablets on a single day (*KBo* 15.52 rev. 39ff. and duplicates).

This twice-impressed envelope of an Old Assyrian tablet was found in Level 1b at Kültepe, site of ancient Kanes. In the scene, worshippers are guided by a God-King. Above the wide guilloche are two sphinxes with an *ankh* sign between them; below them is a bull scratching the ground and an eagle seated upright. Most tablets from Kültepe 1b have this type of impression. *Photo courtesy of Tahsin Özgüç.*

Writing was first introduced to Anatolia by the Old Assyrian merchants who established trading centers in important cities across the central plateau during the early part of the second millennium BCE. The Assyrians brought their own system of writing, called Old Assyrian script, the use of which had died out with the demise of the *karum* trading system around 1750 BCE. The Old Babylonian script, on which Hittite was based, is generally thought to have been first used somewhat later by Old Babylonian scribes who are said to have been brought among the artists and prisoners of war (NAM.RA) to Ḫatti during the campaigns of the first Hittite kings into northern Syria (Beckman 1983:100, n. 17).

It has always been thought that the use of these two scripts was mutually exclusive because they pertained to different eras separated by several hundred years. Such a scenario would leave a literary gap of between one and two centuries in central Anatolia. But according to Hans Güterbock (1983a:24–25), it is possible that the princes of the early city-states employed Assyrian-trained scribes to document their dealings with the Assyrian merchants and Babylonian- or Syrian-trained scribes for documents written in Hittite. Examples to support this excellent idea, however, have not turned up in any excavation. We can state without any hesitation that the Hittite language

Found at Level 1b at Kültepe (ancient Kaneš) is this Old Assyrian tablet with a seal impression of a double-headed eagle within a guilloche border with a star on each side between the tail and wings. *Photo courtesy of Tahsin Özgüç.*

was clearly not a literary language at that time (see in general Beckman 1996b; on the origin of Hittite cuneiform writing, see Hecker 1990).

The Anitta Text (*CTH* 1), which is one of the oldest Hittite texts and came down to us in old and late copies, may be the translation of a text originally written in Old Assyrian, then the only literary language in central Anatolia. Some scholars suggest, however, that the piece displays none of the qualities generally found in a translation (Neu 1974:132; see overview in Ünal 1983b) and that it may have been originally written in Hittite by Anitta's Babylonian-trained scribes (Güterbock 1983a:24–25). This view leaves too many uncertainties, however, and seems impossible to me (Ünal 1983b). The bullae from Acemhöyük, written in Old Babylonian ductus (letter forms), would only suggest that non-Assyrian scribes could (not must!) have been plying their trade in some local royal courts in the central Anatolian highlands long before the alleged importation of the Old Babylonian script during the reign of Ḫattušili I (N. Özgüç 1986:48). But their overall employment remains uncertain. For a final decision we must look forward to new excavations in new sites from the Old Assyrian Trading period.

Commercial and cultural contacts between central Anatolia and northern Syria are known to have taken place already in the last half of the third millennium BCE (T. Özgüç 1986:31). The city of Kaneš was probably a principal partner in this trade, so it is not unreasonable to think that the cradle of Anatolian literary development could be found there. The fact that the language of the Hittites is called *neš umnili*—"in the language of the city of Neša"—and the particular role attributed to Kaneš in early Hittite history lend credibility to this suggestion. That the Hittites were already developing the rudiments of a written language during the period of the Assyrian merchants seems at present improbable; but some day excavations in the non-Assyrian parts of Kültepe-Kaneš may eventually produce some evidence. Nonetheless we should not forget that the heyday of Kaneš was already over and the city was forlorn and lying in ruins as the Hittite state started to emerge (Ünal 1995).

In sum, the heyday of the Babylonian scribes in Anatolia seems not to have occurred until after the period of the Assyrian trade settlements. There is well-documented evidence for their presence in the late fourteenth and the thirteenth centuries BCE, but the tradition probably dates even earlier. A Babylonian scribal school had apparently been established at Ḫattuša by the late fifteenth or early fourteenth century (Beckman 1983:106). It is important to add that the Hurrian scribal tradition was having an immense impact at the time (Mascheroni 1984), and many of the Mesopotamian influences noted in later Ḫattuša may have originally been transmitted through this medium. The overall presence of Hurrian cultural impact during the Middle Hittite period makes now an old theory possible that the Middle Hittite dynasty was of Hurrian origin (Güterbock 1954); this is visible mostly in the Hurro-Hittite bilinguals from Boğazköy and the great number of Hurrian texts in Ortaköy-Šapinuwa (Ünal 1998a).

One type of Hittite scribe was called the scribe of the wooden tablets. This may be a reference to scribes who wrote daily notices and receipts on folding wooden tablets constructed with a recessed area to hold a wax substance. No traces of this highly perishable material have been found in Anatolia, but one example was recently excavated about 150 feet underwater at the site of an ancient shipwreck at Ulu Burun near Kaş off the southwestern coast of Turkey. The tablet has been called the world's oldest known "book" (Bass 1987:730; Payton 1991).

Another writing system practiced by the Hittites are the so-called Luwian hieroglyphs. Since this pictographic writing was more easily handled the scribes who recorded day-to-day records on wooden tablets might have used this style of writing instead of somewhat cumbersome cuneiform. It is possible that the

Some Hittite scribes wrote on folding wooden tablets constructed with a recessed area to hold a wax substance on which daily notices and receipts were written. No traces of this highly perishable material have been found in Anatolia, but this wooden tablet shown vertically was recently found about 150 feet underwater in an ancient shipwreck excavated off the coast of Turkey at Ulu Burun, near Kaş. The tablet, or diptych, has been called the world's oldest known "book." *Photo courtesy of George F. Bass and the Institute of Nautical Archaeology, Texas A & M University.*

bullae, the majority of which derive from Nişantepe, were attached to such wooden tablets (Houwink ten Cate 1994:236). Otherwise the employment of this writing was limited to seals, lapidary inscriptions, and metal or earthenware utensils and vessels. Although Luwian hieroglyphs seem to have been unpopular before the fourteenth century BCE, some attempts have been made to push the origins of this writing system back as far as the third or the first half of the second millennium—but without convincing proof (overview by Alp 1968:281).

The Earliest Literary Sources

Hittite literature appeared on the scene in an already well-established style soon after the foundation of the Old Kingdom (around 1635 BCE) and the adoption of the Old Babylonian writing system. It seems clear that some sort of developmental stage must have transpired prior to the literary medium's full-blown appearance in central Anatolia. Whether this medium was the result of an earlier development in the so-called Dark Age, the consequence of Syro-Babylonian involvement during the reign of Ḫattušili I, or even the product of Hurrian scribes remains debatable. Certainly, future research will increasingly reveal a Hurrian impact on Hittite literacy. The discovery of the Ortaköy archive offers remarkable support for this prediction, which I made one year before the archive's discovery in the first edition of this article in 1989. Additional data is expected to come from Ḫattuša itself as well as central and southeastern Anatolia and north Syrian sites, and these texts will enlighten us about the origins of the Hittite script and emergence of primal literary forms.

The fact remains, however, that we at present see no obvious preliminary or experimental stage of development. This situation is a commonplace with regard to many aspects of Hittite culture. It is especially striking, however, in the literature that displays a complex narration of events and procedures, examples of which are found in the earliest written sources.

The Political Testament of Ḫattušili I (abridged as HAB; *CTH* 6), for instance, gives a verbatim record of a speech given by the king to an assembled court to dismiss his own son from succession to the throne for some sentimental reasons. He adopts instead the young boy Muršili, his nephew or grandchild, as his son. However, since Muršili had not yet verged upon manhood, he was put under the custody of Pimpira, a respectable person from the royal family. To the young boy, the recommendations and admonitions of his stepfather must have been powerful incentives; he exceeded expectation when, in his exaggerated ardor, he conquered Babylon. As a rule Ḫattušili's behest to his fellow men and members of his clan is to exercise moderation and modesty, when he exhorts them "to eat (only) bread and to drink (only) water." A similar proverbial saying is attested in the instruction text *KBo* 16.24 (+) i 35 which can be rendered roughly: "Eat your ration bread and fulfill your duty!" Especially poignant are the following passages of the "Testament:"

> I, the king, called him my son, embraced him, exalted him, and cared for him continually. But he showed himself a youth not fit to be seen. He shed no tears, he showed no pity, he was cold and heartless.

The force of the narrative leads one to anticipate the conclusion: "Enough! He is my son no more!"

Throughout the text there is no trace of scribal alteration; although the tablet is a recent hand-copy, it seems to have been recorded directly from the king's mouth.

The so-called "Palace Chronicle" (*CTH* 8; the full edition is now in Dardano 1997, but for some good reasons Hardy 1941 is still to be taken as basic), a series of anecdotal admonitions, illustrates a distinct genre that seems to have emerged during the Old Hittite kingdom. This collection, which has been preserved on many tablets dating to different periods of Hittite history, is not simply part of an oral tradition. As reflections of real events, these stories played a propagandistic role in the Hittite subjugation of the Anatolian population, revealing a way of life that was vital and dynamic on the one hand and harsh and brutal on the other. The persons mentioned in these stories seem to be partly historical, partly fictional. The collection can be considered a literary achievement because of its unique style of narration. The language is cryptic and remarkably terse, but the author's effort is keenly felt as he tries to accentuate his message with words calculated to instill fear in wrongdoers. Taken from different aspects of daily life, the anecdotes apparently encourage loyalty and good conduct by illustrating that evil will be punished and that good will be rewarded:

> (Once there was) a high functionary named Pappa. He was found to be fraudulently distributing army-bread and *marnuwan*-drink (among the people) in the city of [Tameni]nka.[1] (The authorities) [squashed] the bread (to a sticky mash) and smeared the upper part of his body (with it). (Further) they poured out salt into a [*marnuwan*-] cup and forced him to drink it. They broke the cup on his head. (Because) he (also) was distributing in Ḫattuša (illegally) *walḫi*-drink to the soldiers, they took a wine jar (*šagga*-) and broke it (too) on his head (*KBo* 3.34 i 5–10, treated by Dardano 1997:30).

Other Old Hittite authors also engaged the power of narrative to make their points. In contrast to later literature with its emphasis on divine inspiration and empowerment, this power was often rooted in the omnipotence and wisdom of the ruler. Thus, we should not be surprised to find examples where the king is always presented as making wise pronouncements that imply an unrestricted royal authority. In the "Benediction for Labarna," for example, the king commands:

> Let the whole country be inclined toward Ḫattuša behind his back. The king himself is vigorous. He is (also) able to keep the country vigorous. The king's house is (full) of jocundity and grandchildren. It is set up on (solid) ground (*KUB* 36.110 rev. 9′–16′).

And an immediate simile in the form of a proverb follows:

> The fool's house is b[uilt] within the reach of flood (in a dry riverbed); the flood will flow, wash it away, and [carry] it to the sea (rev. 17ff.; *KUB* 36.110 rev. 9′–16′).

Similarly, in the aforementioned text involving Pimpira there are royal admonitions directing the custodian to "give him (that is, a sick person) bread and water. If somebody is struck by heat, let him be taken to a cool place; if the cold chills somebody, let him be taken to a warm place. Let the king's subjects not be oppressed!" (Archi 1979:37). The benevolent nature of these exhortions may convey to us the deceptive impression that the Hittite state was a welfare state, and that it was among the main duties of the king to care for his subjects. But the fact is that we have to do here with the well-known topos of "Instructions for a Prince."

These passages have been compared with a story detailed in a Hurro-Hittite bilingual from Ḫattuša in which the Storm-God Tešub has gotten into debt (*KBo* 32.15 i–ii; Neu 1988a:16, 1988b, 1988c, 1988d; Haas 1992:30). While Tešub tries to extricate himself from the situation, other gods declare their commitment to assist him as a token of solidarity, supplying him with silver, gold, food, garments, and refined oil, all of which he direly needs. Such acts symbolize liberation or releasing (Hittite *para tarnumar*; Hurrian *kirenzi*), which is the main theme of the Hurro-Hittite bilingual stories (Neu 1996; Haas-Wegner 1997). In light of Hittite interaction with nearby Hurrian principalities, we should ask to what extent these genres are to be considered strictly Hittite. There is strong evidence that many typically Hittite ideas were actually borrowed from the Hurrians and the Babylonians. One of our first examples of Ḫattušili I's involvement in military affairs is the Akkadian text describing the Siege of Uršu, an important Hurrian city in southeastern Anatolia (Kempinski 1983:33; Marazzi 1986; Beckman 2000). The text describes the toils and frustrations felt by the king during this bitter siege in which Hittite forces were evidently inferior to the Hurrians in manpower, strategy, weaponry, and technical equipment. In addition, the account depicts the Hittite military commanders (in a surprisingly frank manner) as weak, slack, anxious, and ineffective. Thus, it is left to the tireless and courageous efforts of the Hittite king himself to overcome the Hurrian forces who are propping up the city of Uršu. The king's frustration is evident in his animated response to discovering that the battering ram has been broken:

> The king waxed wrath, and his face was grim (as he yelled), "They constantly bring me evil tidings; may the Weather-God carry you away in flood! Be not idle! Make a battering ram in the Hurrian manner, and let it be brought into place. Make a mountain (that is, siege machine), and let it (also) be set in its (proper) place. Hew a great battering ram from the mountains of Haššu, and let it be brought into (proper) place. Begin to heap up earth. When you have finished, let every one take post" (*KBo* 1.10 obv.! 13′–17′, translated by Gurney 1990:180–81).

It is almost as if the king were saying, "Do I have to tell you how to do everything?"

These descriptions are as much literary devices as historical narrations of the facts. They set the stage for a statement of the king's wise and courageous decisions, the purpose of which is to emphasize his role and to lead the reader to the obvious conclusion that without the king all would be lost. Unfortunately, the end of the story is missing (but compare the "Annals of Ḫattušili I" in *KBo* 10.1 i 15ff.).

Fortunately, the Old Hittite culmination of this literary pattern is found in the "Telipinu Edict" (*CTH* 19). The powerful narration of the tragic events leading up to this decree presents the reader with what amounts to an apologetic discourse. In contrast to the passionate pronouncement of Ḫattušili I, this decree is formulated in a very unemotional way and with an objectivity peculiar to legal texts. It is, however, a very idealized account of the remote past presented in a schematized form that leaves one with a strong impression of the force of law. Like the "Political Testament of Ḫattušili I," the "Telipinu Edict" has a sense of growing anticipation and fulfilled expectation, which inevitably arise with the final stipulations of the decree. Telipinu thus succeeds in presenting his reforms, not as mere stipulations, but as a well-structured literary composition (Sturtevant and Bechtel 1935:175; Hardy 1941:190; Liverani 1977:105; Hoffmann 1984:13).

The Development of an Emphasis on the Divine

The literature of the Old Hittite Kingdom presents us with a basic outline in which the Hittites couched much of their later literature. Basic to this style is an attempt to involve the reader in the events being described so that the conclusion is seen as inevitable. The wise actions of the king on one hand and the guided actions of the leading heroes on the other help to achieve this end.

Other genres borrowed heavily from this style, for example, the annalistic tradition. Although the most fully developed example of this very Hittite genre dates to the reign of Muršili II (mid-fourteenth century BCE), forerunners can be found in texts dating to both the Old and the Early New Kingdoms, such as the annals of Ḫattušili I, Tudḫaliya II, and Arnuwanda I. These texts are not merely records of events; they are realistic narratives of campaign strategy that attempt to involve the reader in the development of various ideas to their expected conclusions (Cancik 1976). Preceding events and simultaneous actions and circumstances are described perfectly, and the underlying reasons for the decisions are aptly given. In most cases, the historical events were dictated to the scribes by the Great Kings who, principally, as commander-in-chiefs, were involved in all sorts of actions in the battlefield. As stereotyped and mostly reiterated simple war reports, written in a terse and barren style, the annals may lack certain qualities of fine literature altogether; but in regard to their historicity, it is important that they are neither refined nor falsified by means of literary gimmicks. Thus, students as well as historians will more highly appreciate their true historical context than their plain literary style.

In the "Annals of Muršili II," for example, we read:

> (Because the whole enemy population fled to Mount Arinnanda) I, my majesty, went (also) to Mount Arinnanda. Now this Mount Arinnanda is very steep and extends into the sea (that is, it is on a peninsula). It is also very high, difficult of access, rocky, and impossible for chariots to drive up.... Since it was impossible to drive with chariots, I, my majesty, went guiding my army in front on foot and clambered up Mount Arinnanda on foot (Goetze 1933:54).

Another distinctive mark of the annals is that the facts are clearly organized, but the presentation is, in spite of all claims on the part of numerous scholars with regard to objectivity of Hittite historiography, far from being impartial. The description is constructed to make the "reader" sympathize with the king

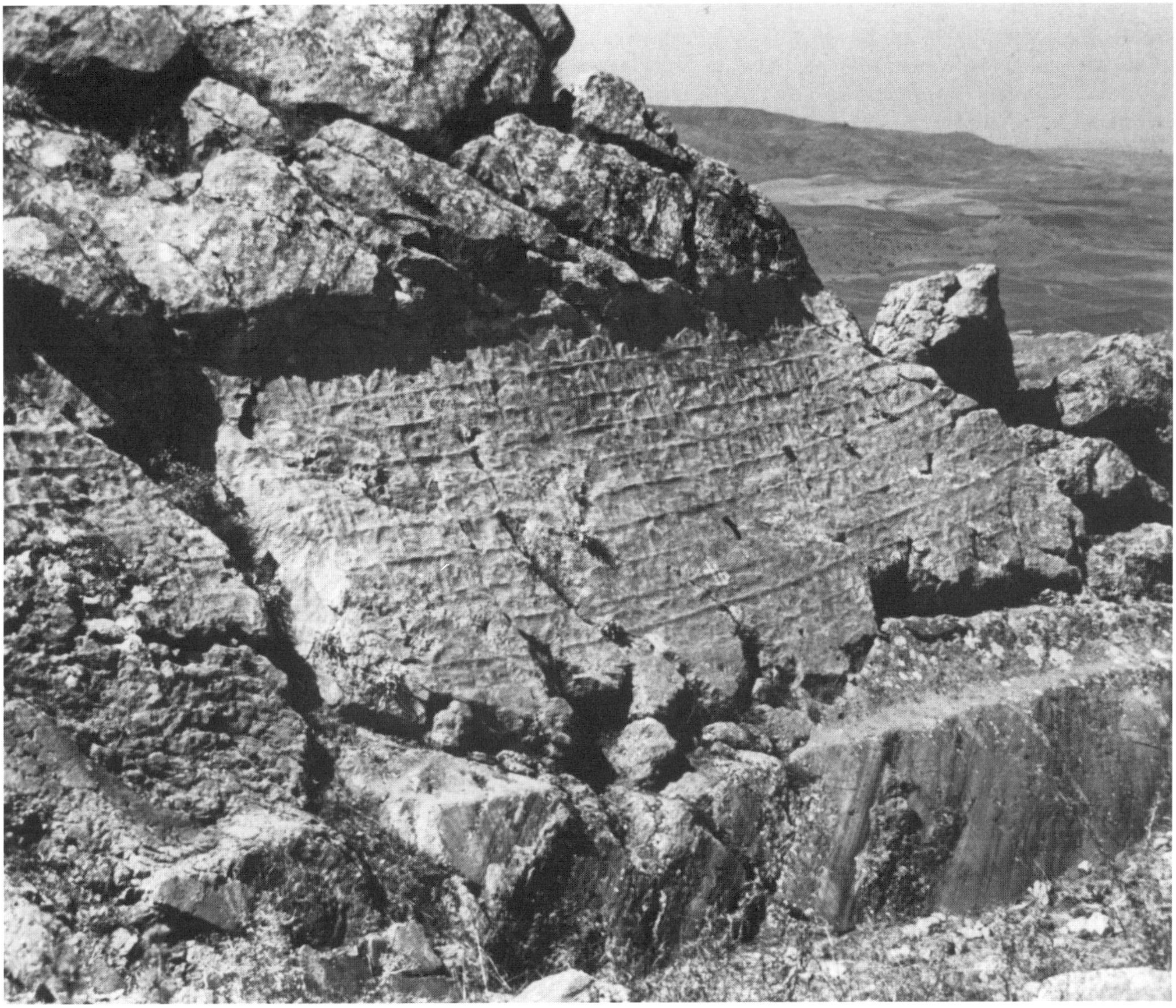

The longest hieroglyphic monument dating to the Hittite Empire period is this weathered eleven-line inscription located on a sloping hill at Nişantepe in the Upper City at Ḫattuša. About 9 m long, the inscription apparently dates to the reign of Šuppiluliuma II. *Photo by Ronald L. Gorny.*

and his difficulties at the same time commending his courage and wisdom in making tactical and strategic decisions. It is also notable for the gratitude that the king accords his patron deity whom he believes supports him throughout his lifetime. In fact, this deity may have been thought to be the sole reader of the text. The king presents an account of his reign to his divine overlord for whom he governs the Ḫatti lands as a proxy. This may be the precursor of depicting kingship in terms related not so much to wisdom and courage as to divine providence and empowerment. It foreshadows the "orientalizing" of Hittite kingship, which came to fruition under the last kings of the Empire.

The best example of this new trend can be seen in the "Apology of Ḫattušili III" (*CTH* 81), a highly sophisticated and unique composition whose purpose was to justify his seizing the throne. Ḫattušili tells first about his childhood, describing how he was dedicated to the goddess Ištar and how he, always an innocent babe—and always sick to the degree of hypochondria, too—was surrounded by jealous enemies. Except for the deity, almost everybody is presented as envious of this child prodigy. The story goes on to tell how Ištar enabled Ḫattušili to prevail against the incessantly evil deeds and plots concocted by these enemies. This document, which so far has no parallels in pre-Classical antiquity, suggests a highly developed political consciousness that relies on reasoned argumentation to make a point (Goetze 1925; Sturtevant and Bechtel 1935:64; Wolf 1967; Ünal 1974:29; Hoffner 1975b; Otten 1981). As with its predecessors, this trend is dependent on the reader's involvement. Its success relies on the power of the narrative to lead the reader subconsciously to a desired conclusion, in this case, that Ḫattušili had done no wrong but sat on the throne only as a result of his natural right of succession and divine selection.

It is remarkable how clemently the omnipotent Hittite rulers tolerated criticism brought against them by common citizens. The Middle Hittite king Tutḫaliya II dedicated almost all of his life to military expeditions that covered every nook of the Anatolian peninsula, but he was neglecting civil, juridical, and administrative affairs at Ḫattuša. It is for this reason that on his return to Ḫattuša from a victorious expedition in the west Anatolian region of Aššuwa the denizens of Ḫattuša reprimanded him as follows:

> His majesty, our lord, you are an (excellent) warrior, however, you are not able to administer a lawsuit. Just look, [how] evil-doers destroyed [the service of feudal obligations] altogether (*KUB* 13.9+ obv. i 6ff.; Ünal 1998b:112).

As a result of this criticism, the king made an edict regarding law. One is almost tempted to see the roots of a primitive democracy in such passages.

Narration in Prayers and Hymns

Seneca observes correctly that the mortals are in the habit of telling to their gods what they would keep strictly secret from their fellow humans. Such are the Hittites when they report in their prayers and oracle texts almost every intimacy to their gods—a practice that seems to come very close to the confession in Christianity (Ünal 1978). In Hittite belief, the gods were held responsible for all kind of maladies and catastrophes. But they are at the same time the ones who are expected to help to rescue from evil. Encouraging such rescue demands reasoning and persuasion. The gods must be convinced in a logical way that they must help the human beings, and this aspect alone lends prayers literary value. This is evident in the plague prayer of Muršili II:

> What is it that you (i.e. gods) have done? A plague you have let into the land. The Hatti land has been cruelly afflicted by the plague. For twenty years now men have been dying in my father's days, in my brother's days, and in mine own since I have become the priest of the gods. ... The few people who were left to give sacrificial loaves and libations were dying too. ... Hattian Storm-God, my lord (and) you (other) gods, my lords! It is only too true that man is sinful. My father has sinned and transgressed against the word of the Hattian Storm-God, my lord (Goetze 1969b:394).

Prince Kantuzili, who was suffering from a terrible, lunatic-like disease, pleads with his personal deity:

> O god, ever since my mother gave birth to me, you, my god, have reared me. You, my god, (are) my [refuge] and my anchor. You, [my god], brought me together with good men. You, my god, did show me what to do in time of distress. ... Life is bound up with death, and death is bound up with life. Man cannot live for ever; the days of his life are numbered. ... (Because of sickness) at night sweet slumber does not overtake me on my bed. While I lie there, good tidings do not come to me. ... Now I cry for mercy in the presence of my god. Hearken to me, my god! (Goetze 1969b:400).

Narration in Myths, Epics, Legends and Tales

The main concern of the myths is to offer a logical explanation for the human and divine order in the universe. Their protagonists are, as a rule, the gods; the most common themes are creation, food, theogony and struggle between the gods for suzerainty. Epics are characterized by their style, i.e. they are written or told in general in verse. Their topics can be myths, as well as the heroic deeds of the mortals. Normally, they are of no great artistic merit. The narrative is couched in the simplest and baldest prose, and there is no attempt at verse or metre (except the "Song of Ullikummi and Kumarbi;" Macqueen 1986:149; see Eichner 1993; Carruba 1995). There are, with only one dubious exception, no poems. This unusual and unique example, the so-called soldier's song, comes from an Old Hittite legendary text, and it has been frequently taken as poetry (Güterbock 1964:110; 1978:243; Gamkrelidze-Ivanov 1995:LXI, 738). It has also often been treated to fantastic interpretations (see, for instance, Melchert 1986:102). The decipherer of the Hittite language designated it once as "le plus vieux chant indo-Européen" (Hrozný 1929:297). It runs as follows:

> *Neš aš [waš peš] Neš aš waš peš*
> *tiyamu tiya*
> *numu annaš maš katta arnut*
> *tiyamu tiya*
> *numu uwaš maš katta arnut*
> *tiyamu tiya*

> [The cloths] of Neša, the cloths of Neša. Come to me, come! My mother has brought (them) for me. My fate(?) (*uwaš*) has brought (them) for me. Come to me, come! (*KBo* 3.40 rev. 12–16).

Among all other text genres, the myths expose most evidently the power of narration. The multilayered deposition of literature is also most clearly visible in the study of myths. Most elaborate compositions belong strictly to Hurrian and Hattic religion, and genuine Hittite myths relating to Hittite deities are poorly attested.

Legends based on early Hittite history have some literary value as well, and Hittite versions of Babylonian legends and epics have come to us in a great number. The various kind of short tales seem again to be of Hurrian origin. This is explained by the political and cultural dominance of the Hurrians during the period between the Old and New kingdoms; even the Babylonian legends probably found their way into Hittite archives by way of the Hurrians.

The Hittite, Hurrian and Hattic myths fall into two main groups: "The Myth of the Slaying of the Dragon" and "The Myth of the Missing God." Though fragments of many types of myths have been preserved, these two myths exist in several different versions.

The Slaying of the Dragon

The slaying of the dragon Illuyanka (the serpent) is a typical new-year myth of the kind represented by many people, regions, and religions. It is embedded in the Hattic *purulli* festival—originally a festival celebrated for the sake of the fertility of the earth—and recited in the course of these celebrations. Its essence is a ritual combat between two protagonists, a god, uniting in his person the Good and Benevolence, and his opponent, the dragon Illuyanka, in the shape of a snake who represents the forces of evil. There are two versions: one from the Empire period and one older. In both, the dragon soundly defeats the Storm-God. According to the older version, the Storm-God appeals to other gods for help. Of these, only the goddess Inara has wit enough to plan a simple trap. She prepares a great banquet with various kinds of concoction in abundance. Then she engages a mortal agent named Ḫupašiya to assist her. Ḫupašiya agrees to assist on the condition that he may sleep with the goddess, which she does. She dresses herself up and invites the dragon to come up from his pit and to partake of the amenities of the feast, (saying):

> "I am preparing a feast; come eat and drink!" Then the serpent came up together with [his children]; and they ate (and) drank-they dra[nk] up every vessel and were sated. They were no longer able to go back down into (their) hole, (so that) Ḫupašiya came up and tied up the serpent with a cord. The Storm-God came and slew the serpent. The (other) gods were at his side.

Here follows a strange episode concerning the fate of the human agent Ḫupašiya:

> Inara built a house on a rock (outcropping) in (the town of) Tarukka and settled Ḫupašiya in the house. Inara instructed him: "When I go into the countryside, you must not look out of the window! If you look out you will see your wife (and) your children!" When (Inara went away and) the twentieth day had passed, he looked out of win[dow] and [saw] his wife (and) children. When Inara returned from countryside, he began to whine, "Let me (go) back home!"

From this point on the details of the myth are lost, but it seems that Ḫupašiya has been destroyed as punishment for his disobedience (for reconstruction of the destroyed part, see Götze 1957:139).

The more recent version of the story goes one step further and makes the story more exciting. Moreover, according to one scholar, it represents higher ethical values (Goetze 1957:140). Here the serpent not only defeats the Storm-God, but gets possession of his heart and eyes. In order to recover them the Storm-God uses a trick. He marries the daughter of a poor man and sires from her a son. When this son grows up, he marries him to the daughter of the serpent. The Storm-God instructs him saying: "When you go to the house of your wife, then demand from them (my) heart and eyes." This he fulfills and carries them back to his father. So, the Storm-God regains his heart and his eyes. Once his body has thus been restored to its former state he is emboldened to take up a third encounter against the serpent. To do this, he goes off to the coast. In the subsequent battle

This orthostat relief from Malatya is usually taken as an illustration of the mythological combat between the Storm-God and the Dragon. *Photo courtesy of Billie Jean Collins.*

he finally succeeds in defeating the serpent and wreaks vengeance (Beckman 1982:18). By this time a member of the house of his father-in-law, the Storm-God's son provoked his father: "Smite me too! Do not spare me!" Thereupon, the Storm-God also killed his own son. It is possible that his son learned through the intermediation of the serpent that he was a foster-child of the Storm-God sired only to this target and was misused for his intrigues. This realization might have disgusted him and caused him to take sides with the serpent. Another possibility is the motif of the punishment of human agents, Ḫupašiya as well as the foster child of the Storm-God, for their "stupidity and gluttony" (Gaster 1950).

The orthostat relief from Malatya is usually taken as an illustration of this mythological combat (Akurgal 1962: pl. 104).

The Myth of the Missing Deity

"The Myth of the Missing Deity" goes back in its origin to the Hattic tradition (Asan 1988; Bernabé 1989). Recently, it has been compared with a Caucasian folktale (Girbal 1990). Once invented obviously only for the Storm-God, it became more and more popular among the Hattians and newly arrived Hittites and Palaians so that the motif of the disappearing god—with the ensuing paralysis of nature and the divine order, and reinvigoration of fertility after his reappearance—has been attributed to almost all major deities of the pantheon such as the Storm-God of the city of Kuliwišna, Sun-God, Telipinu, Inar(a), the Mother Goddess, Hannahanna, the Palaic Storm-God Zaparwa, and the personal deities of historical personalities such as the queens Ašmunikal and Ḫarapšili and the scribe Pirwa (Laroche 1971, *CTH* nos. 322–335). The original myth might reflect a vague memory of a historical reality, namely a natural disaster like drought and the resulting hunger in prehistoric central Anatolia (Ünal 1977:461).

It is significant that in most cases these myths are connected with magical rituals, i.e., they are part of these magical rituals. They have been conducted as preventive measures against drought and, had drought nevertheless occurred, to restore fertility during the disaster. Its popularity is also evident from the continued discovery of new texts: one recently in the temple area in the upper city (Otten 1984:53) and a fragment of the same genre in the provincial town of Maşat (Güterbock 1986:205).

We have a very characteristic example for the usage of myth as a *belle chant* in curing a sick person in a medical ritual. In it, the liberation of the Fire from the vicious and crude violence of a demon Gulzanzipa, representing cruelty, is set in relation to the victory of the patient over his bad fate, i.e. his sickness:

> (Once) the Fire (god) be[came] sullen. (It is) the son of the sun god (who) happened to go into the darkness and concealed himself in the darkness. (There) he curled like a snake, [(yes) he is huddled li]ke a *kunkuliyati*-animal. (The bee) pruned itself (getting itself ready for the voyage); it darted away. (Dashing) like an eagle [it brought] to the eagle (the bad) tidings. On its way it does not (feel) how cold (it is) (*KUB* 43.62 ii 5).

After a gap the tragic story continues:

> But the lower part of the trunk (of the tree) is taken by the snake; its middle part is taken by the bee. At its top the eagle stood; around the lower part of its trunk the snake twisted; the bee swarmed around its middle part. The god Gulzanzipa drags relentlessly at [the coat] of the storm god. They dig the clay (and make a hole) behind him. (It is on this spot that) the dark ea[rth crack]ed and released it (the Fire to the surface). (Thus) [it] could defeat Gulpanzipa. Mankind [has witnessed this event] (Ünal 1992).

Luckily we have another good example illustrating how mythological passages are imbedded in magic rituals. Here the magical practitioner performs an incantation in the form of a dialogue with the Sun-God. The Storm-God is giving a party, attended by not only deities and mortals, but also by the ailing patient himself. Thus we have to do here with an apotheosis. The gods allegedly show on their part great interest in the well-being of the patient and initiate an arduous discussion. They reproach the Sun-God for not inviting the patient to his party:

> Now the ritual expert [utters the words of conjuration] to the Sun-God as f[ollows: You, the Sun-God, have given a party.You have] invited all the gods. You have invited [all the mortals.] The patient, however, [(was not invited), he (just) walked into] it. The gods have eaten and drunk. You, the Su[n-God], have entrusted [these words] to the heart (of the gods); you, the Sun-God, have spoken (to them namely): "What [did I do?] I ha[ve] invited all the gods. [I have invited] all the mortals (as well). [But the patient] has got lost. [The practitioner has concealed] him." [The gods in their entirety walked out (and) [spoke] to the Sun-God: "[Why] did you [not] invite the patient?" The Sun-God responded: "[He has been concealed(?) somewhere; it is why I] could not in[vite] him. (But) now, because [he (just) walked in]to the [party, let him be here?]." The gods spoke as follows: "[You, the Sun-God, he has made his] chief god! Let him (please) participate in the party. Let him eat, [let him drin]k! [Let him] g[o (again)] to

you, to (his) chief(?) (deity). Let the patient come in, [let him eat and drink (with us)! Let him recover his health again!] Let him come [and be a true servant to you,] the Sun-God, (his) [chief god. Let him bring you sacrifices again!"] (*KUB* 58.94 obv. i 3 with its dupl. *KUB* 57.79 obv. i 4; Ünal 1996:51, 95)

The best known version of the missing deity myths is concerned with the Hattic god of vegetation, Telipinu (on the nature of the myth see Gaster 1950 and Kapelrud 1959; further translations can be found in Ünal 1994a; Beckman 1997:151–53; Hoffner 1998:#2). In the lost beginning of the story, there might have been a description of the prevailing divine harmony on earth before the blight struck. Then, suddenly, conspicuously on account of cultic negligences, the god goes crazy and goes off in a hurry in a bad mood "putting his right boot on his left foot and his left boot on his right foot," a sign of confusion and haste. The ensuing blight is described as follows:

> Dust(?)-clouds beset the window, smoke(?) besets the house, the embers on the hearth were choked(?), the gods stifled [in the temple], the sheep stifled in the fold, the oxen stifled in the stall, the ewe spurned her lamb, the cow spurned her calf. … Barley and emmer wheat throve no more, oxen, sheep and humans ceased to conceive, and those who were pregnant could not bear. …
>
> The great Sun-God gave a feast and invited the thousand gods; they ate, but they were not satisfied; they drank, but they did not quench their thirst. Then the Storm-God remembered his son Telipinu (saying): "Telipinu is not in the land; he was angry and has gone away and taken all good things with him." The gods great and small set out to search for Telipinu. The Sun-God sent out the swift eagle, saying: "Go, search the high mountains, search the hollow valleys, search the dark-blue waters." The eagle went forth; but he found him not, and reported to the Sun-God, saying: "I have not found him, Telipinu, the mighty god." Then the Storm-God spoke to the goddess Hannahanna: "What shall we do? Shall we die of starvation?" The goddess in reply urged the Storm-God to go himself and look for Telipinu, and accordingly he set out. He knocked at the gate in his town, but he could not get it opened and (merely) broke his mallet (and) wedge. So the Storm-God … gave up and sat down (to rest).

Hannahanna proposed to send a bee to look for the missing god. The Storm-God protested: "The gods great and small sought him but have not found him. Shall this bee now search and find him? His wings are small and he himself also is too tiny." But the goddess dismissed these objections and sent forth the bee, ordering it to sting Telipinu, when it found him, in his hands and feet and make him wake up, then to smear him with wax and bring him back home. The bee went forth, searched the mountains, the rivers, and the springs, and found finally Telipinu: according to one text he was discovered sleeping on a meadow near the town of Liẖzina. On being stung by the bee the god awoke, but broke out into a fresh storm of anger.

> Then said Telipinu: "I am furious! Why when I am sleeping and nursing a temper do you force me to make conversation?" … Then came Telipinu hastening. There was lightning and thunder. Below the dark earth was in turmoil. Kamrušepas saw him. The eagle's wing brought him from afar. She stilled his anger, she stilled his wrath, she stilled his rage, she stilled his fury. … Telipinu returned to his temple. He took thought for the land. He released the dust(?)-cloud from the window, he released the smoke from the house. The altars of the god were made ready. He released the embers in the hearth, he released the sheep in the fold, he released the oxen in the stall. The mother attended to her child, the ewe attended to her lamb, the cow attended to her calf. Telipinu (took thought for) the king and queen, he took thought for them to grant them life and vigor for the future. (Yea) Telipinu took thought for the king. Then before Telipinu an evergreen was set up. On the evergreen the skin of a sheep was hung. In it was put mutton fat, in it were put corn, cattle(?) and wine(?), in it were put oxen and sheep, in it were put length of days and progeny, in it was put the soft bleating(?) of lambs and abundance(?), in it were put …"

Here the text breaks off (Gurney 1980; Beckman 1997:151–53).

In one of the tales, it is the Sun-God who vanishes. As a result, Ḫaẖẖimaš, the personified Jack Frost, paralyzes nature. The Storm-God asks his sister to help. Since she is not able to help, he later asks his brother the wind: "[Breathe on] the waters of the mountains, the gardens, and the meadows, let thy soothing breath go forth and let him cease to paralyze them." But the efforts of the wind seems to have produced no fruit.

The Storm-God sends different deities such as Wurunkatti and the Protective Genius, to bring the Sun back. But the vicious Ḫaẖẖimaš seizes them all. At last the Storm-God relies upon his son Telipinu: "That son of mine is mighty; he harrows, ploughs, irrigates the field; and makes the crops grow." But him too Ḫaẖẖimaš seized. The dispatching of Gulšeš and Ḫannaḫanna also gets no results. At this point the text breaks; in this lost section the fear of the Storm-God that Ḫaḫḫimaš could be demanding his own surrender might have been described (Gaster 1950:343). After a colophon, the text continues; here there is no trace of the myth. Rather, the text proceeds to describe a ritual, the purpose of which is to attract these deities back into their temples. Clearly, this myth was imbedded in a magical ritual (*CTH* 323; Daddi and Polvani 1990; Ünal 1994a; Hoffner 1998).

Among the disappearing god legends, the one concerning the goddess Inara deserves special attention here, although the textual material is badly damaged (*KUB* 33.57 and 59). As Inar obviously threatens to disappear, Ḫannaḫanna promises to give her land and a man, if she does not abandon the country. The offer of a man is very significant, because in the myth of Illuyanka, she has a human lover, Ḫupašiya. She seems also to have had nymphomaniacal tendencies. Nonetheless, she gets mad and disappears. The Storm-God, her father, misses her. As in the other myths, the bee is charged with the mission to look for her.[2] She, meanwhile, in her outrage seems to have hidden all livestock in a leather bag, called *kurša-*. The consequence of this is that the hunters are unable to find any game. However, the bee is able to bring this magic bag back. Meanwhile, Ḫannaḫanna has built three "springs" or "wells" (*wattaru-*). In one of them she placed an *ippiya*-tree, in the other a *ḫuppara*-tree. In the third one fire was burning. The bee placed the bag in the spring with *ḫuppara-* in it. Miyadanzipa, the genius of fertility, came and sat under the *ippiya*-tree. Although the text is broken, it seems that he was able to break open the magic bag with the animals in it and to make the magic ineffective. At the end, the animals are able to conceive again.

The mythical stories about the disappearance and recovery of various deities have clear similarities with the mythological literature associated with Adonis, Attis, Baal, Osiris, and Tammuz.

Divine Kingship in Heaven

One of the most important literary compositions of Hurrian origin is the famous cycle of myths concerned with the divine kingship in heaven (Güterbock 1961:155; *RlA* s.v. Kumarbi). In this myth, Kumarbi, the father of the gods, is the leading and victorious figure.

The major deities Alalu, Anu, and Kumarbi reigned in heaven for nine years each. One of them was always the servant of the preceding one. In a hierarchical sequence, they dethroned each other, and at last Kumarbi held sway over heaven. According to another myth his authority was endangered when his own son, Tešub, started to conspire against him (see below). The striking resemblance of this divine struggle over the supremacy in heaven with the *Theogony* of the Greek poet Hesiod has been pointed out (Güterbock 1948; Meriggi 1953; Heubeck 1955; Harmatta 1968); there the sequence of Olympic gods is Uranos, Kronos, and Zeus.

In the "Song of Ullikummi," Kumarbi has again a leading role. Unfortunately, this myth is only preserved on fragmentary tablets, and, thus, the consequence of the narratives and the order of the events are uncertain. In fact, the "Song" takes up the legend of kingship in the heaven at the fourth generation. This time, it is Kumarbi's turn to be dethroned by his son Tešub, the Storm-God. Kumarbi created and deployed against him the mighty monster Ullikummi. In his battle against Tešub, Kumarbi is supported by Sea. According to another version he marries the daughter of Sea. From this marriage, his son Ullikummi was born, whose name may mean "the destroyer of Kummiya," the cult city of Tešub. This child was unusual in his physical appearance, since he was made of diorite stone. Kumarbi let the child be carried down to the sea and left him on the shoulders of Upelluri, an Atlas-like figure. Ullikummi grows up so fast that the sea reached to the middle of his body. The Sun-God was the first to notice this growing and intimidating monster and to report about him to Storm-God. When he heard of Ullikummi, Tešub escaped together with his sister Ištar and climbed to the top of Mount Hazzi (Mons Cassius). Full of fear, they could watch from there the monstrous Ullikummi rising out of the sea. The Storm-God started to weep bitterly. His sister tried to encourage him for another battle. Accompanied by his minister Tašmišu, his bulls Šerišu and Tella, and equipped with the thunder and rain, his powerful weapons, he dared a final battle against Ullikummi; however, he lost. The victorious Ullikummi arrived at Kummiya and obliged the Storm-God to surrender. As the Storm-God's wife Ḫebat heard this bad news and herself witnessed the tragic combat from a tower, she almost lost control of herself and nearly fell off the roof in horror: "If she had made a single step, she would have fallen from the roof, but her attendants held her and did not let her fall." Tašmišu advised the Storm-God to go to Ea, the god of wisdom, and to ask him for help. Ea goes to Upelluri, who laments,

> "When heaven and earth were built upon me I knew nothing of it, and when they came and cut heaven and earth asunder with a copper tool, that also I knew not. Now something is hurting my right shoulder, but I know not who that god is." When Ea heard this, he turned Upelluri's right shoulder round and there stood the Diorite Stone [Ullikummi] on Upelluri's right shoulder like a post(?).

Finally Ea brings the huge saw from the ancient store-houses with which heaven and earth were once cut apart. It was with this saw that he cut off Ullikummi at its feet and destroyed its power (Güterbock 1952:12).

The "Song of Ullikummi" contains numerous satyrical threads by means of which Telipinu pokes fun at and mocks the chief deities of the pantheon. They are seen to be very much selfishly concerned with their own comfortable and luxurious life and are too eager not to lose this constellation of power. In terms of this observation, the rebellion and threat of Telipinu are not to be taken seriously, but as an amusement. He amazes himself to the point of breaking out laughing when he observes how distressed the gods are as soon as they envisage the loss of their sovereignty.

The scope of the "Song's" story is uncommonly vast. The parallel running actions as well as subsidiary details are narrated most skillfully in accordance with their role and meaning. In term of details and style, it also shares a great number of threads with adventure romans and criminal stories. It is a first-class literary work. If it were preserved completely and had undergone the revision and compilation of a poem like Homer, it would doubtless count among the highly valued literary achievements of the ancient world (Ünal 1994a).

A myth about another serpentine monster named Hedammu preserved only in fragments belongs again to the cycle of Kumarbi. The character of Hedammu, a giant living in the ocean and in love with the goddess Ištar, closely resembles that of Ullikummi. The story tells in detail how he endangered the life of the gods and how the gods tried to ward him off. At the end, he obviously has been lured by Ištar from his home in the middle of the ocean and has been slaughtered.

Babylonian Texts

Literary works of Babylonian origin also deserve a brief mention. Scientific works of Babylonian origin—such as handbooks on the interpretation of omens of various kinds, horoscopes, models of livers, and medical texts—vocabularies, hemerologies, hymns and prayers, and proverbs have also been found in considerable number at Boğazköy, with new material coming from Ortaköy. Among them there are monolingual, bilingual, or trilingual hymns (such as Laroche 1971 nos. 312, 313, 315), lyrics (no. 315), and wisdom literature (no. 316; Beckman 1983:97).

Many legends originating in Babylonia found their way to Ḫattuša. They are represented in Hittite translation, in Hurrian, or in Akkadian. We have many fragments of the well known Epic of Gilgamiš in Hittite and Hurrian, some sections of which have been "re-edited" for the Hurro-Hittite readers. The episode of Huwawa, for example, with its geographical scenery in Syria and the Lebanon, has been enlarged for the needs of the Anatolian "readers" (Otten 1958:93). The labor of Hittite scribes can be observed in translating highly sophisticated ideas into Hittite, e.g., a trilingual poem (Sumerian, Akkadian, and Hittite) from Ugarit (Puhvel 1996).

The "Epic of Gurparanzaḫu" is a story of foreign origin about a hero, Gurparanzaḫu, who is invincible in archery: "The arrow flies from his bow like a bird. In shooting he defeated sixty kings and seventy young men" (Güterbock 1938:84).

The Hurrian tale of Kešši, the hunter, is another example of how human beings are subject to divine punishment on account of their misdeeds and imprudence at the end. Kešši and his mother subsist by his hunting. One day, he starts a strong infatuation to Sintalimeni, whose beauty enchanted him. Since he does not want to leave the lap of his sweetheart, he neglects the rites and hunting. He also disregards the wise advice of his mother. Once he returns to hunting, it is too late, for the gods, angry because of his dereliction of him, conceal all the game. Kešši is ashamed to return empty handed to his village; so he is condemned to stroll in vain in the mountains (Xella 1977; Ünal 1994a; Hoffner 1998).

Appu and his two sons, Bad and Just, are characters in a story about a man who is apparently impotent. Appu was a rich man in the city of Sudul, possessing cattle, sheep, silver, gold, and lapis lazuli in abundance. He lacks only one thing: children. While all the people in Sudul enjoy their children, pampering them with bread, fat and drinks, Appu is all alone; he does not have anybody to express his tenderness. One day, he came home and lay down on his bed to sleep, however, with his boots on. His wife was complaining and mocking him, showing him to her house maids. She complains that he can never make love to her. Obviously, Appu is aware of his impotence. Thereupon he takes a white lamb and sacrifices it to Sun-God so that he may help him in siring children. The Sun-God responded and suggested he go home, drink a lot, and sleep with his wife. After doing this, his wife conceived and gave birth to a son whom Appu called "Bad." The second son they sired, they called "Just." Once they grew up they started a struggle over the inheritance of paternal goods. Obviously "Bad" tries to cheat his brother. Since the tablet is unfinished we do not know the point of the story (Siegelová 1971; Grottanelli 1978; Daddi and Polvani 1990; Ünal 1994a; Hoffner 1997, 1998).

A recently reconstructed and interesting story about personified Silver pertains again to the Kumarbi cycles. The friends of silver mock him because he is a child out of wedlock. One day, he comes home and threatens to beat his mother if she does not tell him who his father is and where he lives. She tells him that the father is Kumarbi and he lives in Urkiš. Thereupon Silver sets out to find his father (Hoffner 1988a).

A legend about the cannibals can be mentioned here under the category of private literature. Its literary motive, rather than its language is noteworthy: "Whoever arrives among them they eat him. As soon as they see a fat man they kill him and gobble him up." The storyteller takes pains to appear to offer us a real story since he mentions the name of the mother of a man who has been sacrificed by these barbaric cannibals (*KBo* 3.60; Güterbock 1938; Kempinski 1983:41; Bayun 1995).

There is an interesting story of unknown origin on the realm of dead. In it, the netherworld is described in a pessimistic way: "one does not recognize the other. Sisters of the same mother don't recognize (each other). Brothers do not recognize (each other). A mother does not recognize her own child. A child does not recognize his own mother. They do not eat from a fine table. ... they do not eat fine food. They do not drink good drink. They eat bits of mud. They drink waste waters(?)" (*KBo* 22.178 (+) *KUB* 48.109; Hoffner 1988b; Ünal 1994a).

Narration in Legal Texts

Narration was just as powerful in the legal sphere, especially in putting forward specific juridical cases. Hittite legal process used oratory and complex reasoning in the pleading of cases. Among the official documents we have found are depositions, that is, testimonies from the proceedings of legal inquests. There are, for example, speeches made in self-defense by men accused of having stolen or lost items for which they had been given responsibility. These testimonies, which are preserved in the records of Hittite court clerks, deserve special treatment here because they are the literary forerunners of pre-Socratic apologetics that use oratory and rhetoric as a means of self-defense (see Mascheroni 1987).

The best example of these testimonies is the case of a culprit named Ištarziti, who was apparently indicted for a scandalous affair of unknown nature—probably for misappropriating some possessions of palace or temple. In his defense, Ištarziti uses metaphors such as "I am cast down like a reed on the dark earth" and "as a living person I am dead in the eyes of my siblings." A few more of his well-turned phrases help illustrate this style:

> Have I not always been a (true) servant of that deity? ... Once when I was taken ill, I prayed to the gods, saying: "Do not you see, o gods, who has ruined me like this (as I am right now)?" Instead you have weighed on me! (Is it because) you do not want to harm (literally defeat) the king, his majesty? If you always appreciate the absolute truth, why is it that matters are still concealed? ... When something evil happened to the royal heir in the city of Kummanna, Ališarrumma revealed to me that they intended to kill me (because they thought I was guilty in that matter). (On my way to Mount Šaḫḫupidda) the queen intended to have someone lie in ambush behind the road and kill me! ... (From my eyes) the tears flow [like water in the mountains]. These tears I will give to the priest of the Sun-God and he shall pour them out secretly for the Sun-God. ... One day in the city of Šulama I was honoring the god Tarupšani. (A man by the name of) Muti walked in and started to gossip about my person. I seized him by the collar (and) brought him to [the sacred place]. I made him take an oath (there) and warned him (at the same time), saying: "(Behold!) Whoever takes a (false) oath in the presence of this deity, he does not survive anymore!" (*KUB* 54.1; my translation differs in many cases from that of Archi and Klengel 1985).

It is interesting to note that this rhetorical style was employed not only in self-defense; the Hittites used it also in their pleadings to the gods in case of emergencies such as prayers, in vows (which are organized in accordance with the Roman religious principle "do ut des;" Ünal 1996:8, n. 26; 54: n. 144), and even magical rituals. In the case of the latter, a passage in a magical ritual delivers a good example how the Hittites were concerned to persuade the gods by all means:

> Moreover, the conjurer takes oil, honey, thick bread (and) wine jug (and) goes to the mountains. He appeals (to the mountains) as follows: "O great mountains, plentiful children of the awe inspiring dales, on what purpose did I come (to you)? It is because I am worn out, (since) mankind is pent up simply in a corral like a cow. I am in dire need of your help now, o mountains!"
>
> The mountains respond as follows:
>
> Do not be anxious! Surely we will help you. Does a tree breaks off its spadix at all? Does the brushwood obstruct its own growth? Does a deer kill a fawn, i.e., its own progeny at all?

Thus the mountains promulgate their solidarity with human beings and promise, in the fragmentary continuation of the text passage, to help the human agent in dispelling the evil into the dark earth. The same oratory means are repeated also in connection with the springs and sea (*KUB* 30.36 ii 1–18 with duplicates; my translation differs in some significant points from other translations, see *CHD N*:366).

In the category of private literature, the letters deserve a special mention (de Martino and Imparati 1995). However, as compared to classical times, very few of them have any literary value, simply because they were not edited for publication. Only in particular cases do a few people bring their feelings to expression by means of literary sayings. Thus, a Hittite commander reports to the great king: "My friends honor me no more; they refuse me constantly" (*KUB* 40.1). The letters of the royal couple Ḫattušili and Puduḫepa to Egyptian Pharaoh Ramses II in the Akkadian language stand out by virtue of their literary value (Edel 1994).

The Role of the Hurrians

The intermediary role of the Hurrians is one of the most important circumstances in Hittite history. It brought about the incorporation of Hurrian customs and beliefs into the indigenous Hittite culture.

Hurrians first appear in the old Hittite historical texts as fervent enemies of the Hittites. Convincing evidence is lacking, but direct influence may already have begun in the Old Kingdom. Visible influences are more readily observed from the early Empire under Tudḫaliya II and Arnuwanda I who, together with their wives, were in all probability of Hurrian origin. By the time of Ḫattušili III and his Hurrian wife Puduḫepa, the Hurrian cultural invasion was well under way. From the Early Empire period on, Hurrian influence began to be felt so very strongly that some scholars believe the dynasty to be of Hurrian origin. Indeed much evidence points to this conclusion. A case in point is the large number of Hurrian texts or their translations found at Ḫattuša. These include the "Kingship in Heaven" story and the "Song of Ullikummi." Of special interest are the newly discovered Hurro-Hittite bilinguals from the Upper City, which are certainly changing our views of Hittite intellectual life during the last two centuries before the downfall of the Empire. It would be appropriate, therefore, to take a closer look at the contents of these recently discovered texts.

The Hurro-Hittite bilinguals (Otten 1986; Neu 1988a, 1988b, 1988c, 1996; Haas and Wegner 1991:384; Ünal 1994a:860; Hoffner 1998:65–77) are rare examples of what in Mesopotamia was called *wisdom literature* in which good and bad, represented as humans, animals, and various objects, appear as active figures opposing each other. Animals and inanimate objects are depicted in the form of a clerihew (a light verse of four lines rhyming *aabb*) as imbecilic beings, short of wit, and lacking the ability to reason; accordingly they behave in a stupid way. Because of their limited capacity, they can only use their instinct, whereas humans are endowed with sagacity and insight (Hittite, *ḫattatar*; Hurrian, *madi-*). A greedy deer, for example, is compared to an ambitious and capricious governor. The literary theme in these pieces is, again, liberation, release from evil (*para tarnumar*, Hurrian *kirenzi*; Neu 1988a:10), and perhaps the reestablishment of primary divine order on earth. Whether these bilinguals played a part in magical rituals or festivals (perhaps not unlike *Illuyanka* in the *purulli*-festival) is not clear.

Both Hittite and Hurrian versions reveal meticulous efforts to structure the composition, which indicates that they are not mere scribal exercises but first-class literary exemplars. We may surmise that they enjoyed, orally narrated, great popularity of the denizens of the Hittite capital. They are designated as "song, poetry" (SÌR), and both contain traces of well-organized verse, which can be observed in Hattic texts as well (*KUB* 38 p. iv, "Gruppe II;" Haas and Thiel 1978:66–90). Groups of stories all seem to have a single author, as the narrator introduces successive stories with the words, "I will put aside this story (literally, words) and will tell you another." This is important in regard to the individual authorship of literary works, although, unfortunately, in general the authors did not sign their names (see Güterbock 1978:213).

Otherwise, authorship of the texts are solely known from the magical rituals (see Ünal 1996:13), which do not have, generally speaking, any literary value. Nonetheless, this achievement in creating individuality is an enormous "step forward in the intellectual history of [mankind] before the beginning of Greek philosophy in Western Anatolia (Ionia) and must be taken into consideration" (Ünal 1996:13). As concerns other literary genres, evidently, as with the later Homeric epics, the literary devices used by these authors were not of their own invention but were taken from the vast resources of an ever-growing folklore tradition in Anatolia itself and then in North Syria, Mesopotamia, Egypt, and, probably, the Aegean world. These were narrated after having been composed, compiled, and elaborated freely according to the tastes of the time. A multilayered depository of literature does exist in Anatolia. It is often strenuous to discern precisely, as in other fields of cultural life, what is genuine "Hittite" and what is borrowed. In the field of comparative study of Hittite literature there is still much work to do.

Meticulous structural analysis can result in surprises. To give here one example and to illustrate what seems at first sight to be too far-fetched, compare the Hittite saying, taken up to now as genuine Hittite: "My head turns like a potter's wheel" (*KUB* 33.103 ii? 5–6) with the Egyptian saying: "The land spins round like a potter's wheel" (cited in *National Geographic*, January 1995:42).

As is the case with many other branches of culture the Hittites seem not to have brought any profound literary tradition from their original homeland.

The following passage, in which an analogy is made between an ungrateful copper cup, obsessed by a deep iniquity, and a man's son, who scornfully taunts his father, his very own progenitor, will illustrate this point:

> (Once) a coppersmith cast a splendid cup. By casting it he gave it a (graceful) shape. He embossed it with plates and engraved it. He made it iridescent in every detail. However, the simple(-minded) copper began to curse its creator, saying: "Whoever has cast me, may his hand break, may the sinew of his right arm be paralyzed!" As the coppersmith heard this he was grieved in his heart. The coppersmith began to speak to himself: "I formed that copper (into a beautiful cup). Why does it (now) curse me?" The coppersmith uttered (in turn) a curse over the cup: "May the Storm-God smite it, the cup, may he remove its plates. May the cup fall down the water drainage ditch, may (its) plates fall down into the river!"

The analogous story runs as follows:

> (This time it is) not a cup, but a human. It is a son who after growing up became an adversary to his own father; what is worst is that the boy had vindictiveness against quips and quirks of the customs and thus pays neither attention nor obedience to his father. As a result he deserves the curse of the paternal deities!

Perhaps also connected to Hurrian influence is the common motif of child exposure found in three texts from ancient Anatolia that tell the stories of children from humble beginnings who end up achieving astonishing power and success. These stories are the oldest examples of a motif that can be seen in such famous later examples as Sargon of Akkad (Westenholz 1997:41), Moses, Romulus and Remus, and Darius. It seems that this literary motif found its way into Hittite Anatolia through Hurrian intermediaries. Its origin is probably to be found in the Hurrian regions of the upper Tigris and Euphrates rivers where water exposure is given naturally by the abundance of rivers (Ehelolf 1926; Ünal 1985:135).

One of the Hittite stories that falls into this category is the "Queen of Kaneš" (Thirty Sons and Daughters, also called Zalpa Text, *CTH* 3; Otten 1973; Bayun 1994). This text has been evaluated in terms of a pre-Hittite matriarchal structure evident in the Hattic-Hittite world that completely rejected incest. Because of the role of the river and the dismissal of the male progeny, some outside of academic circles have connected this text to the legendary Amazons of Greek mythology who would meet men in the river valleys for orgiastic ceremonies. This view may not be as farfetched as it once seemed in light of festival records that describe a northern Anatolian custom in which young girls were taken from their towns, stripped in the river valley, and evidently raped (*KUB* 57.84; Forlanini 1984:256). The story of the "Queen of Kaneš" may also indicate a process of political integration in central Anatolia (but not an amphictyonic league; Dieterle 1987).

Perhaps the best example of the motif of child exposure is the story of Anum-Ḫirbe, a prince of the city of Mama and Zarwar who seems to have established a relatively large kingdom somewhere on the periphery of the realm of Kaneš. Numerious inscribed spear heads from the region of Gaziantep support now the historicity of this person (Donbaz 1998). Anum-Ḫirbe's prominence gave rise to the story of a legendary birth and childhood: Apparently born out of wedlock, he was carried off by the people of Mama and probably thrown into a river. A shepherd or a sheep found him and carried him to a meadow where he was suckled by animals. The remainder of the story has been lost, but we can imagine the gist of it; Anum-Ḫirbe overcame all odds and returned to Mama as its king (Ünal 1985:132–35). Once again, the reader is captivated by the incredible e vents and can only conclude that it was divinely ordained that Anum-Ḫirbe rise to such heights.

Literature as a Conveyor of Hittite Thought

Contacts with the rest of the ancient Near East and the continued development of Hittite culture led to more complex ideas concerning the afterlife. A preoccupation with these ideas elicited deep feelings and intangible, abstract ideas; it also brought about the stoic recognition that "life is bound up with death, and death is bound up with life" (Goetze 1969b:400). These feelings must have tested the capability of Hittite literature to convey complex ideas. Whereas the earlier literature used vivid accounts and tense narrative to convey its message, this later literature emphasized content over style, often attempting to give a theological reason for events and expressing a new understanding of the relationship between the king and the world. This development, mirrored in the work of Hittite artists from the same period, expressed itself in an overall artistic style calculated to enhance the position of the king. We find something similar in the Hurro-Hittite bilinguals and their attempt to interpret wisdom as well as in the attempt to define a religious hierarchy in the "Kingship in Heaven" story (*CTH* 344). The fact that so much of this literature can be attributed to Hurrian influence suggests that this philosophical development occurred partly as a result of Anatolia's interaction with the more advanced civilizations to the southeast, that is, Mesopotamia.

Conclusion

The development of highly complex literary forms in Anatolia was a slow and tedious process which required millennia to achieve. Yet, it never came to full fruition. Drawing upon the accumulated literary forms of the past and a multilayered folkloristic backbone in Anatolia, Mesopotamia, and Hurriland, the Hittites readily adopted earlier Anatolian cultural traditions and patterns of life to form a composite literary psychology. During the thirteenth century BCE, Ḫattuša was an important crossroads and, consequently, was open to a variety of influences. In it resided an elite composed of aristocrats, bureaucrats, scribes, and artisans, many of whom represented different ethnic backgrounds. This complex demographic mix led to the development of new trends, concepts, and ideas. Simple literary forms no longer satisfied this urban caste. As a result, in this period there was an increasing influx of new literary materials from the south, materials that were more sophisticated and abstract in style. We can only speculate how far this development would have gone if the Hittites had not met an unfortunate end shortly after 1200 BCE.

Notes

[1] Dardano's restoration after the collation of Neu as ^{NINDA}*tuninki*, does not convince (1997:28 with n. 168).

[2] The episode of the mission of the bee is of considerable interest. The ideas that honey is a purifying agent capable of expelling evil spirits and that the sting of a bee can cure paralysis of the limbs are widespread in folklore. According to Lactantius, the priestesses of Cybele, the "Great Mother," were called *melissai*, "bees" (Gurney 1990:157; Collins 2002).

Bibliography

Akurgal, E.
1978 *Ancient Civilizations and Ruins of Turkey from Prehistoric Times until the End of the Roman Empire,* translated by J. Whybrow and M. Emre. Istanbul: Haşet Kitabevi.

Akurgal E. and Hirmer, M.
1962 *The Art of the Hittites.* London: Thames and Hudson.

Alp, S.
1968 *Zylinder-und Stempelsiegel aus Karahöyük bei Konya.* Türk Tarih Kurumu Yayinlarindan 5:26. Ankara.
1991 *Hethitische Briefe aus Maşat-Höyük.* Ankara: Türk Tarih Kurumu Basımevi.

Archi, A.
1968 La storiografia ittita. *Athenaeum* 47:7–20.
1979 L'humanité des hittites. Pp. 37–48 in *Florilegium Anatolicum: Mélanges offerts à Emmanuel Laroche.* Paris: E. de Boccard.
1995 Hittite and Hurrian Literatures: An Overview. Pp. 2367–2377 in *Civilizations of the Ancient Near East*, edited by J. Sasson. Vol. 4. New York: Charles Scribner's Sons.

Archi, A. and Klengel, H.
1985 The Selbstrechtfertigung eines hethitischen Beamten. *Archiv für Orientforschung* 12:52–64.

Arnaud, D.
1985 *Recherches au Pays d'Aštata: Emar.* Paris: Editions Recherches sur les civilisations.

Asan, A. N.
1988 *Der Mythos vom erzürnten Gott. Ein philologischer Beitrag zum religionshistorischen Verständnis des Telipinu-Mythos und verwandter Texte.* PhD. dissertation, Würzburg.

Bass, G. F.
1987 Oldest Known Shipwreck Reveals Splendors of the Bronze Age. *National Geographic* 172/6:693–732.

Bayun, L.
1994 The Legend About the Queen of Kaniš: A Historical Source? *Journal of Ancient Civilizations* 9:1–13.
1995 Remarks on Hittite "Traditional Literature" (Cannibals in Northern Syria). *Journal of Ancient Civilizations* 10:21–32.

Beckman, G.
1982 The Anatolian Myth of Illuyanka. *Journal of the Ancient Near Eastern Society* 14:11–25.
1983 Mesopotamians and Mesopotamian Learning at Ḫattuša. *Journal of Cuneiform Studies* 35:97–114.
1986 Proverbs and Proverbial Allusions in Hittite. *Journal of Near Eastern Studies* 45:19–30.
1996a Emar and its Archives. Pp. 1–12 in *Emar: The History, Religion, and Culture of a Syrian Town in the Late Bronze Age,* edited by M. Chavalas. Bethesda, MD: CDL Press.
1996b The Hittite Language and its Decipherment. *Bulletin of the Canadian Society for Mesopotamian Studies* 31:23–30.
1997 The Wrath of Telipinu. Pp. 151–53 in *The Context of Scripture*, Vol. 1, edited by W. Hallo and K. Younger. Leiden: Brill.
1995 The Siege of Uršu Text (*CTH* 7) and Old Hittite Historiography. *Journal of Cuneiform Studies* 47:23–34.

Bernabé, A.
1987 *Textos literarios hetitas.* Madrid: Alianza Editorial.
1989 Generaciones de dioses y sucesion interrumpida. El mito hittita de Kumarbi, la "Teogonia" de Hesio y la del "Papiro de Derveni." *Aula Orientalis* 7:159–79.

Bittel, K.
1970 *Hattusha: The Capital of the Hittites.* New York: Oxford University Press.

Bryce, T. R.
1982 *The Major Historical Texts of Early Hittite History. Historical and Social Documents of the Hittite World.* Queensland: University of Queensland.

Cancik, C.
1976 *Grundzüge der hethitischen und alttestamentlichen Geschichtsschreibung.* Wiesbaden: Otto Harrassowitz.

Carruba, O.
1995 Poesia e metrica in Anatolia prima dei Greci. Pp. 567–602 in *Studia Classica Iohanni Tarditi oblata* I, edited by L. Belloni, G. Milanese, and A. Porro. Milan: Vita e Pensiero.

CHD = Güterbock, H.G., and Hoffner, H.A., Jr.
1989– *The Hittite Dictionary of the Oriental Institute of the University of Chicago.* Chicago: The Oriental Institute of the University of Chicago.

Collins, B. J.
2002 Necromancy, Fertility and the Dark Earth. The Use of Ritual Pits in Hittite Cult. Pp. 224–41 in *Magic and Ritual in the Ancient World*, edited by P. Mirecki and M. Meyer. Leiden: Brill.

Cornil, P.
1987 Textes de Boğhazköy. Liste des lieux de trouvaille. *Hethitica* 7:5–72.

Dardano, P.
1997 *L'aneddoto e il racconto in età antico-hittita: la cosiddetta "cronaca di palazzo."* Rome: Il Calamo.

Dieterle, R. L.
1987 The Thirty Brothers. *Journal of Indo-European Studies* 15:169–214.

Donbaz, V.
1998 Inscribed Spear Heads and Some Tablets at the Gaziantep Archaeological Museum. *Altorientalische Forschungen* 25:173–85.

Edel, E.
1952 Die Rolle der Königinnen in der Ägyptisch-hethitischen Korrespondenz aus Boğazköy. *Indogermanische Forschungen* 60:72–85.
1953 Weitere Briefe aus der Heiratskorrespondenz Ramses' II: KUB III 37 + KBo I 17 und KUB III 57. Pp. 31–63 in *Geschichte und Altes Testament.* Tübingen: Mohr Siebeck.
1976 *Ägyptische Ärtze und ägyptische Medizin am hethitischen Konigshof: Neue Funde von Keilschriftbriefen Ramses' II aus Boğazköy.* Opladen: Westdeutscher Verlag.
1994 *Die ägyptisch-hethitische Korrespondenz aus Boghazköi in babylonischer und hethitischer Sprache.* Opladen: Westdeutscher Verlag.

Eichner, H.
1993 Probleme von Vers und Metrum in epichorischer Dichtung Altkleinasiens. Pp. 97–169 in *Die Epigraphische und Altertunskundliche Erforschung Kleinasiens: Hundert Jahre Kleinasiatische Kommission der Österreichischen Akademie der Wissenschaften: Akten des Symposiums von 23. bis 25. Oktober 1990*, edited by G. Dobesch and G. Rehrenböck. Ergänzungsbände zu den Tutili Asiae Minoris Nr. 14. Vienna: Verlag der Österreichischen Akademie der Wissenschaften.

Ehelolf, H.
1926 Das Motiv der Kinderunterschiebung in einer hethitischen Erzählung. *Orientalische Literaturzeitung* 766–69.

Erkut, S.
1997 Çiviyazılı Hittit Tabletleri. *Belleten* 61/232:495–98.

Forlanini, M.
1984 Die "Götter von Zalpa." Hethitische Götter und Städte am Schwarzen Meer. *Zeitschrift für Assyriologie und Vorderasiatische Archäaologie* 74:245–66.

Friedrich, F.
1926 *Staatsverträge des Ḫatti-Reiches in hethitischer Sprache I.* Mitteilungen der Vorderasiatisch-Ägyptischen Gesellschaft 31:1. Leipzig: J. C. Hinrichs.
1930 *Staatsverträge des Ḫatti-Reiches in hethitischer Sprache II.* Mitteilungen der Vorderasiatisch-Ägyptischen Gesellschaft 34:1. Leipzig: J. C. Hinrichs.

Gamkrelidze, T. V. and Ivanov, V. V.
1995 *Indo-European and the Indo-Europeans.* Berlin and New York: Mouton de Gruyter.

Gaster, T. H.
1950 *Thespis: Ritual, Myth and Drama in the Ancient Near East.* New York: Schuman.
1959 *The Oldest Stories in the World.* Boston: Beacon Press.

Gates, M. H.
1996 Ortaköy-Çorum, Archaeology in Turkey. *American Journal of Archaeology* 100:297–98.

Girbal, C.
1990 Weiterleben des Telepinu-Mythus bei einem Sudkaukasischen Volk. *Studi Micenei ed Egeo-Anatolici* 22:69–70.

Glassner, J. J.
1985 Sargon "roi du combat." *Revue d'Assyriologie et d'archéologie orientale* 79:115–26.

Goetze, A.
1925 *Ḫattušiliš, der Bericht uber seine Thronbesteigung nebst den Paralleltexten.* Mitteilungen der Vorderasiatisch-Agyptischen Gesellschaft 38. Leipzig: J. C. Hinrichs.
1928 *Madduwattaš.* Mitteilungen der Vorderasiatisch-Agyptischen Gesellschaft 32:1. Leipzig: J. C. Hinrichs.
1930 Die Pestgebete des Muršiliš. *Kleinasiatische Forschungen* 1:161–251.
1933 *Die Annalen des Muršiliš.* Mitteilungen der Vorderasiatisch-Agyptischen Gesellschaft 38. Leipzig: J. C. Hinrichs.

1957 *Kleinasien.* Handbuch der Orientalistik III. 1.3.3.1, 2nd. ed. Munich: Beck.
1969a Hittite Myths, Epics and Legends. Pp. 120–26 in *Ancient Near Eastern Texts Relating to the Old Testament*, edited by J. B. Pritchard. 3rd. ed. Princeton: Princeton University Press.
1969b Hittite Prayers. Pp. 393–400 in *Ancient Near Eastern Texts Relating to the Old Testament*, edited by J. B. Pritchard. 3rd. ed. Princeton: Princeton University Press.

Goetze, A. and Pedersen, H.
1934 *Muršili's Sprachlähmung.* Det Kgl. Danske Videnskabernes Selskab, Historisk-filologiske Meddehelser 21:2. Copenhagen.

Grottanelli, C.
1978 Observations sur l'histoire d'Appou. *Revue Hittite et Asianique* 36:49–57.

Gurney, O. R.
1940 Hittite Prayers of Mursili II. *Annals of Archaeology and Anthropology* 27:3–163.
1977 *Some Aspects of Hittite Religion.* The Schweich Lectures 1976. Oxford: Oxford University Press.
1990 *The Hittites.* 4th edition. New York: Penguin Books.

Güterbock, H. G.
1938 Die historische Tradition und ihre literarische Gestaltung bei Babyloniern und Hethitern bis 1200. *Zeitschrift fur Assyriologie (New Series)* 10:45–149.
1948 The Hittite Version of the Hurrian Kumarbi Myths: Oriental Forerunners of Hesiod. *American Journal of Archaeology* 52:123–34.
1952 *The Song of Ullikumini: Revised Text of the Hittite Version of a Hurrian Myth.* New Haven, CT: American Schools of Oriental Research.
1954 The Hurrian Element in the Hittite Empire. *Cahiers d'histoire Mondiale* 2:383–94.
1956 The Deeds of Šuppiluliuma as Told by His Son Muršiliš II. *Journal of Cuneiform Studies* 10:41–130.
1961 Hittite Mythology. Pp. 139–79 in *Mythologies of the Ancient World*, edited by S. N. Kramer. Garden City, NY: Doubleday.
1964 A View of Hittite Literature. *Journal of the American Oriental Society* 84:107–15.
1969 Sargon, König der Schlacht. *Mitteilungen der Deutschen Orientgesellschaft* 101:14–26.
1978 Hethitische Literatur. Pp. 211–53 in *Altorientalische Literaturen*, Vol. 1, edited by W. Röllig. Neues Handbuch der Literaturwissenschaft. Wiesbaden: Akademische Verlagsgesellschaft Athenion.
1983a Hittite Historiography: A Survey. Pp. 21–35 in *History, Historiography, and Interpretation*, edited by H. Tadmor and M. Weinfeld. Jerusalem: Magnes Press.
1983b A Hurro-Hittite Hymn to Ishtar. *Journal of the American Oriental Society* 103:155–64.
1986 A Religious Text from Masat. *Jahrbuch fur Kleinasiatische Forschungen* 10:205–14.

Güterbock, H. G. and Civil, M., eds.
1985 Erim-ḫuš Boğazköy. Pp. 97–128 in *Materials for the Sumerian Lexicon*, Vol. 17, edited by B. Landsberger, M. Civil, and E. Reiner. Rome: Pontificum Institutum Biblicum.

Haas, V.
1980 Betrachtungen zum ursprünglichen
Schauplatz der Mythen vom Gott
Kumarbi. *Studi Micenei ed Egeo-Anatolici*
22:97–105.

Haas, V. and Thiel, H. J.
1978 *Die Beschwörungsrituale der Allaituraḫ(ḫ)i
und verwandte Texte.* Alter Orient und
Altes Testament 31. Neukirchen:
Neukirchener Verlag.

1992 Soziale Randgruppen und Außen-
seiter altorientalischer
Gesellschaften. *Xenia* 32:29–51.

Haas, V. and Wegner, I.
1991 Review of KBo 32. *Orientalistische
Literaturzeitung* 86:384–91.
1997 Literarische und grammatikalische
Betrachtungen zu einer hurritischen
Dichtung. *Orientalistische
Literaturzeitung* 92:438–55.

Hardy, R. S.
1941 The Old Hittite Kingdom: A Political
History. *American Journal of Semitic
Languages and Literature* 58:177–216.

Harmatta, J.
1968 Zu den kleinasiatischen Beziehungen
der griechischen Mytologie. *Acta
Antiqua* 16:57–76.

Hecker, K.
1990 Zur Herkunft der hethitischen
Keilschrift. *In Uluslararasi 1. Birinci
Hititoloji Kongresi Bildirileri (19–21
Temmuz 1990).* Çorum: Uluslararasi
Çorum Hitit Festivali: Komatesi
Baskanligi.

Heubeck, A.
1955 Mythologische Vorstellungen des
Alten Orients im archäischen
Griechentum. *Gymnasium* 62:508–25.

Hoffmann, I.
1984 *Der Erlass Telipinus.* Texte der Hethiter
11. Heidelberg: Carl Winter.

Hoffner, H. A.
1968 A Hittite Text in Epic Style about
Merchants. *Journal of Cuneiform Studies*
22:34–45.
1975a Hittite Mythological Texts: A Survey.
Pp. 136–45 in *Unity and Diversity: Essays
in the History, Literature and Religion of the
Ancient Near East,* edited by H.
Goedicke and J. Roberts. Baltimore:
Johns Hopkins University Press.
1975b Propaganda and Political Justifica-
tion in Hittite Historiography. Pp.
49–62 in *Unity and Diversity: Essays in
the History, Literature and Religion of the
Ancient Near East,* edited by H.
Goedicke and J. Roberts. Baltimore:
Johns Hopkins University Press.

1980 Histories and Historians of the
Ancient Near East: The Hittites.
Orientalia 49:283–332.
1981 The Hurrian Story of the Sungod, the
Cow and the Fisherman. Pp. 189–94
in *Studies on the Civilization and Culture
of Nuzi and the Hurrians in Honor of E. R.
Lacheman,* edited by M. A. Morrison
and D. I. Owen. Winona Lake, IN;
Eisenbrauns.
1987 Hittite Religion. Pp. 408–14 in *The
Encyclopedia of Religion,* edited by M.
Eliade. New York: Macmillan.
1988a The Song of Silver. A Member of the
Kumarbi Cycle of "Songs." Pp.
143–65 in *Documentum Asiae Minoris
Antiquae: Festschrift fur Heinrich Otten
zum 75. Geburtstag,* edited by H. Otten,
E. Neu, and C. Rüster. Wiesbaden:
Otto Harrassowitz.
1988b A Scene in the Realm of the Dead.
Pp. 191–99 in *A Scientific Humanist:
Studies in Honor of Abraham Sachs,*
edited by E. Leichty, M. de Jong
Ellis and P. Gerardi. Philadelphia:
University Museum.
1997 Appu and His Two Sons. Pp. 153–55
in *The Context of Scripture,* Vol. 1,
edited by W. Hallo and K. Younger.
Leiden: Brill.
1998 *Hittite Myths.* 2nd edition. Atlanta: SBL.

Houwink ten Cate, Ph.
1994 Uri-Teššub Revisited. *Bibliotheca
Orientalis* 51:233–59.

Hrozny, B.
1929 L'Invasion des Indo-Europeens en
Asie Mineure verse 2000 av. J.-C.
Archiv Orientálni 1:273–99.

Imparati, E and Saporetti, C.
1965 L'Autobiografia di Hattusili I. *Studi
classici e orientali* 14:40–85.

Kammenhuber, A.
1955 Die hethitische Geschichtsschreibung. *Saeculum* 9:135–55.
1967 Hethitische Gebete, Hethitische
Geschichtsschreibung, Hethitische
Gesetze, Hethitische Mythen, Hethitische Pferdetexte, Hethitische Rituale,
Hurritische Mythen. Pp. 1731–752,
2267–274 in *Kindlers Literaturlexikon,*
Vol. 3. Zürich: Kindler Verlag.

Kapelrud, A. S.
1959 The Interrelation between Religion
and Magic in Hittite Religion. *Numen*
6:32–50. (Reprinted on pp. 165–83 in
God and His Friends in the Old Testament,
Oslo: Universitets Forlaget, 1979).

Karasu, C.
1996 Some Remarks on Archive-Library
Systems of Ḫattuša-Boğazköy,
Archivum Anatolicum 2:39–59.

KBo
1916– *Keilschrifttexte aus Boghazkoi.*
Wissenschaftliche Veröffentlichun-
gender Deutschen Orient-
Gesellschaft. Leipzig: J. C. Hinrichs.

Kempinski, A.
1983 *Syrien und Palastina (Kanaan) in der
letzten Phase der Mittelbronze IIB-Zeit
(1650–1570).* Ägypten und Altes
Testament 4. Wiesleaden: Otto
Arrassowitz.

KUB
1921– *Keilschrifturkunden aus Boghazköi.*
Staatlich Muuseen zu Berlin,
Vorderasiatische Abteilung. Berlin:
Akademie Verlag.

Kuhne, C.
1978 Hittite Texts. Pp. 146–84 in *Near
Eastern Religious Texts Relating to the Old
Testament,* edited by W. Beyerlin.
Philadelphia: Westminster Press.

Laroche, E.
1949 La bibliotheque de Ḫattuša. *Archiv
Orientálni* 17:7–23.
1969 *Textes mythologiques hittite en transcrip-
tion.* Paris: Klincksieck.
1971 *Catalogue des textes hittites.* Paris: Editions Klincksieck. (Supplement in
Revue Hittite et Asianique 30:94–133)
1975 Les écritures d'Asie Mineure: etat
des déchiffrements. Pp. 57–60 in *Le
Déchiffrement des écritures et des langues.*
Paris: l'Asiatheque.
1977 Litterature hittite; litterature hourrite
et ourarteenne. Pp. 119–36 in *Histoire
des littératures,* Vol. 2. Encyclopédie de la
Pléiade. Paris: Gallimard.

Lebrun, R.
1980 *Hymnes et prieres hittites.* Homo Religiosus 4. Louvain-la-neuve: Centre
d'histoire des Religions.

Liverani, M.
1977 Storiografia politica hittita-II Telipinu, ovvero: della solidarita. *Oriens
antiquus* 16:105–31.

Macqueen, J. G.
1986 *The Hittites and their Contemporaries in
Asia Minor,* rev. and enlg. ed. London:
Thames and Hudson.

Marazzi, M.
1986 *Beiträge zu den akkadischen Texten aus
Boğazköy in althethitischer Zeit.* Rome:
Dipartimento di studi glottoantropo-
logici, Universita "La Sapienza."

de Martino, S. and Imparati, F.
1995 Aspects of Hittite Correspondence: Problems of Form and Content. Pp. 103–15 in *Atti del II Congresso internazionale di Hittitologia*, edited by O. Carruba, M. Giorgiere, and C. Mora. Pavia: Gianni luculano Editore.

Mascheroni, L. M.
1984 Scribi hurriti a Boğazküy: una verifica prosografica. *Studi Micenei ed Egeo-Anatolici* 24:151–73.
1987 Per un approccio retorico alla leterature etea: un esempio. Pp. 3–10 in *Studi offerti ad Anna Maria Quartiroli e Domenico Magnino*. Pavia: New Press.

McMahon, G.
1992 Hittite Texts and Literature. Pp. 228–31 in *The Anchor Bible Dictionary*, Vol. 2, edited by D.N. Freedman. New York: Doubleday.

Melchert, H. C.
1986 Hittite uwas and Congeners. *Indogermanische Forschungen* 91:102–15.

McNeill, L.
1963 The Metre of Hittie Epic. *Anatolian Studies* 13:237–42.

Meriggi, P.
1953 I miti di Kumarpi, il Kronos currico. *Athenaeum* 31:101–57.

Naumann, R.
1971 *Architektur Kleinasiens von Ihren Anfangen bis zum Ende de Hethitischen Zeit*. Tübingen: Ernst Wasmuth.

Neu, E.
1974 *Der Anitta-Text*. Studien zu den Bogazköy-Texten 18. Wiesbaden: Otto Harrassowitz.
1988a *Das Hurritische: Eine altorientalische Sprache in neuem Licht*. Mainz: Akademie der Wissenschaften und der Literatur. Stuttgart: Franz Steiner.
1988b Zur Grammatik des Hurritischen auf der grundlage der hurritisch-hethitischen Bilingue aus der Boğazköygrabungskampagne 1983. Pp. 95–115 in *Xenia, Hurriter und Hurritisch. Konstanzer Althistorische Vorträge und Forschungen*, edited by V. Haas. Konstanz: Universitätsverlag Konstanz.
1988c Varia Hurritica. Sprachliche Beobachtungen an der hurritisch-hethitischen Bilingue aus Ḫattuša. Pp. 235–54 in *Documentum Asiae Minoris Antiquae: Festschrift für Heinrich Otten zum 75. Geburtstag*, edited by H. Otten, E. Neu, and C. Ruster. Wiesbaden: Otto Harrassowitz.
1988d Zum hurritischen 'Essiv' in der hurritische-hethitischen Bilingue aus Ḫattuša. *Hethitica* 9:157–70.
1996 *Das hurritische Epos der Freilassung I. Untersuchungen zu einem hurritisch-hethitischen Textensamble aus attuša*. Studien zu den Boğazköy-Texten 32. Weisbaden: Otto Harrassowitz.

Neve, P.
1982 *Büyükkale: Die Bauwerke*. Berlin: Gebr. Mann.
1985 Die Ausgrabungen in Boğazköy-Ḫattuša 1984. *Archäologischer Anzeiger*: 323–52.
1987a Die Ausgrabungen in Boğazköy-Ḫattuša 1986. *Archäologischer Anzeiger*: 381–410.
1987b Hattuscha, Haupt- und Kultstadt der Hethiter—Ergebnisse der Ausgrabungen in der Oberstadt. *Hethitica* 8:297–318.
1993 *Ḫattuša - Stadt der Götter und Tempel. Neue Ausgrabungen in der Hauptstadt der Hethiter*. Mainz: Von Zabern.

Nougayrol, J.
1960 Une fable hittite. *Revue Hittite et Asianique* 67:117–19.

Oppenheim, H. L.
1956 *The Interpretation of Dreams in the Ancient Near East*. Philadelphia: American Philosophical Society.

Otten, H.
1955 Bibliotheken im Alten Orient. *Das Altertum* 1:67–81.
1956 Hethitische Schreiber in ihren Briefen. *Mitteilungen des Instituts für Orientforschung* 4:179–89.
1958 Die erste Tafel des hethitischen Gilgamesch-Epos. *Istanbul Mitteilungen* 8:93–125.
1961 Das Hethiterreich. In *Kulturgeschichte des Alten Orient*, edited by H. Schmökel. Stuttgart: A. Kröhner.
1963 Aitiologische Erzählung von der Überquerung des Taurus. *Zeitschrift fur Assyriologie (New Series)* 21:156–68.
1964 Schrift, Sprache und Literatur der Hethiter. Pp. 11–22 in *Neuere Hethiterforschung*, edited by G. Walser. Historia; Einzelschriften 7. Wiesbaden: Franz Steiner.
1973 *Eine althethitische Erzahlung um die Stadt Zalpa*. Studien zu den Boğazköy-Texten 17. Wiesbaden: Otto Harrassowitz.
1981 *Die Apologie Ḫattušiliš III: Das Bild der Uberlieferung*. Studien zu den Boğazköy-Texten 24. Wiesbaden: Otto Harrassowitz.
1984 Blick in die altorientalische Geisteswelt: Neufund einer hethitischen Tempelbibliothek. *Jahrbuch der Akademie der Wissenschaften in Göttingen 1984*:50–60.
1986 Archive und Bibliotheken in Ḫattuša. Pp. 184–90 in *Cuneiform Archives and Libraries*, edited by K. R. Veenhof. Leiden: Nederlands Historisch-Archaeologisch Instituut te Istanbul.
1987 Das hethitische Königshaus im 15. Jahrhundert v. Chr. *Anzeiger der phil.-hist. Klasse der Österreichischen Akademie der Wisseinschaften* 123:21–34.
1988 *Die Bronzetafel aus Boğazköy*. Wiesbaden: Otto Harrassowitz.
1989 Die 1986 in Boğazköy gefundene Bronzetafel Zwei Vortrage. 1. Ein hethitischen Staatsvertrag des 13. Jahrhundert v. Chr. *Innsbrucker Beiträge zur Sprachwissenschaft. Vorträge und Kleine Schriftein* 42:7–20.

Özgüç, N.
1986 Seals of the Old Assyrian Colony Period and Some Observations on the Seal Impressions. Pp. 48–53 in *Ancient Anatolia: Aspects of Change and Cultural Development: Essays in Honor of Machteld J. Mellink*, edited by J. V. Canby et al. Madison, WI: University of Wisconsin Press.

Özgüç, T.
1978 *Excavations at Maşat Höyük and Investigations in its Vicinity*. Ankara: Türk Tarih Kurumu Basimevi.
1986 New Observations on the Relationship of Kültepe with Southeast Anatolia and North Syria During the Third Millennium B.C. Pp. 31–47 in *Ancient Anatolia: Aspects of Change and Cultural Development: Essays in Honor of Machteld J. Mellink*, edited by J. V Canby et al. Madison, WI: University of Wisconsin Press.

Payton, R.
1991 The Ulu Burun Writing-Board Set. *Anatolian Studies* 41:99–106.

Pecchioli Daddi, F. and Polvani, A. M.
1990 *La mitologia ittita*. Brescia: Paideia.

Puhvel, J.
1996 Signet of Steel. *Archivum Anatolicum* 2:61–69.

Salvini, M.
1977 Sui testi mitologici in lingua hurrica. *Studi Micenei ed Egeo-Anatolici* 18:73–91.

Schirmer, W.
1969 *Die Bebauung am unteren Büyükkale-Nordwesthang in Boğazköy*. Berlin: Gebr. Mann.

Schuler, E. von
1987 Literatur bei den Hethitern. *Reallexikon der Assyriologie und vorderasiatischen Archäologie* 7:66–75.

Seeher, J.
1997 Boğazköy-Ḫattuša 1995 Yılı Kazı ve Onarım Çalişmaları, 18. *Kazi Sonuçları Toplantısı* 18(1):323–38.

Seters, J. van
1983 *In Search of History.* New Haven, CT: Yale University Press.

Siegelová, J.
1971 *Appu-Märchen und Hedammu-Mythus.* Studien zu den Boğazköy-Texten 14. Wiesbaden: Otto Harrassowitz.

Soysal, O.
1987 KUB XXXI 4 + KBo III 41 und 40 (Die Puhanu-Chronik). Zum Thronstreit Ḫattušiliš. *Hethitica* 7:173–253.

Steiner, G.
1984 Struktur und Bedeutung des sog. Anitta-Textes. *Oriens antiquus* 23:53–73.

Sturtevant E. H. and Bechtel, B.
1935 *A Hittite Chrestomathy.* Philadelphia: Linguistic Society of America, University of Pennsylvania.

Süel, A.
1998 Ortaköy-Šapinuwa: Bir Hitit Merkezi, TUBA-AR 1: 37–47.

Süel, A. and Süel, M.
1995 Yılı Çorum-Ortaköy Kazı Çalişmaları. *Kazı Sonuçları Toplantisi* 17(1) 263–82.

Ünal, A.
1974 *Ḫattušili III.* Texte der Hethiter 3. Heidelberg: Carl Winter.
1977 Naturkatastrophen in Anatolien im 2. Jahrtausend v. Chr. *Belleten* 163:447–72.
1978 *Ein Wahrsagetext über die Intrigen am hethitischen Hof.* Texte der Hethiter 6. Heidelberg: Carl Winter.
1980 Keššši. *Reallexikon der Assyriologie* 5:578.
1983a Untersuchungen zur Terminologie der hethitischen Kriegsführung I: "Verbrennen, in Brand stecken" als Kriegstechnik. *Orientalia* 52:164–80.
1983b Kuššara. *Reallexikon der Assyriologie* 6:379–82.
1985 Das Motiv der Kindesaussetzung in den altanatolischen Literaturen. Pp. 129–36 in *Keilschriftliche Literaturen: Ausgewählte Vorträge der XXXII. Rencontre Assyriologique Internationale,* edited by H. Hecker and W. Sommerfeld. Berlin: Dietrich Reimer.
1988 The Role of Magic in the Ancient Anatolian Religions According to the Cuneiform Texts from Boğazköy-Ḫattuša. Pp. 52–85 in *Essays on Anatolian Studies in the Second Millennium B.C.,* edited by Prince T. Mikasa. Wiesbaden: Otto Harrassowitz.
1992 Parts of Trees in Hittite According to a Medical Incantation Text (*KUB* 43.62). Pp. 493–500 in *Hittite and Other Anatolian and Near Eastern Studies in Honour of Sedat Alp,* edited by H. Otten et al. Ankara:Türk Tarih Kurumu Basımevi.
1994a Hethitische Mythen und Epen. *Texte aus der Umwelt des alten Testaments* 3/4:802–65.
1994b The Textual Illustration of the "Jester Scene" on the Sculptures of Alaca Höyük. *Anatolian Studies* 44:207–18.
1995 Reminiszenzen an die Zeit der altassyrischen Handelskolonien in hethitischen Texten. *Altorientalische Forschungen* 22:269–76.
1996 *The Hittite Ritual of Hantitaššu from the City of Hurma Against Troublesome Years.* Ankara: Turkish Historical Society Printing House.
1998a *Hittite and Hurrian Cuneiform Tablets from Ortaköy (Çorum), Central Turkey with Two Excursuses on the "Man of the Storm God" and a Full Edition of KBo 23.27.* Istanbul: Simurg.
1998b Ein Vogelorakel aus Boğazköy mit pseudo-rechtlichen Bemerkungen über Familienrecht (KUB 43.22 + = Bo 854 mit Dupl. KBo 13.71). *Altorientalische Forschungen* 25:112–18.
1999 *The Hittites and Anatolian Civilizations.* Istanbul: Iletisim Sanatları. (In Turkish.)

de Vries, B.
1967 *The Style of Hittite Epic and Mythology.* Ph.D. dissertation, Brandeis University.

Weidner, E. F.
1923 *Politische Dokuzmente aus Kleinasien: die Staatsverträge in akkadischer Sprache aus dem Archiv von Boğhazköi.* Leipzig: J. C. Hinrichs.

Wemer, R.
1967 *Hethitische Gerichtsprotokolle.* Studien zu den Boğazköy-Texten 4. Wiesbaden: Otto Harrassowitz.

Westenholz, J. G.
1997 *Legends of the Kings of Akkade.* Winona Lake, IN: Eisenbrauns.

Wilhelm, G.
1990 Zur babylonisch-assyrischen Schultradition in Ḫattuša. In *Uluslararası 1. Birince Hititoloji Kongresi Bildirileri (19–21 Temmuz 1990).* Çorum: Uluslararası Çorum Hitit Festivali Komatesi Baskanligi.

A native of Uşak in western Turkey, Ahmet Ünal has been Professor of ancient Anatolian languages and Hittitology at the University of Munich since 1988. He studied at the Universities of Ankara and Munich, where he received his Ph.D. in 1972. Dr. Ünal has participated in difference excavations in the Hittite homeland, in particular Alaca Höyük, and has conducted his own excavations at Çengeltepe near Yozgat. He has authored books and numerous articles on Hittite history, religion, language, archaeology and culture.

1997 Keilschrifttexte aus Gebäude A. *Kušaklı-Šarišša I,* edited by A. Müller-Kerpe. Rahden/Westfallen: Verlag Marie Leidorf.

Wolf, H. H.
1967 *The Apology of Hattusili Compared with Other Political Self-Justifications of the Ancient Near East.* Ph.D. dissertation, Brandeis University.

Xella, R.
1978 Remarques comparatives sur le "roman de Keššši." *Revue Hittite et Asianique* 36:215–24.

Hittite Pottery and Potters:

The View from Late Bronze Age Gordion

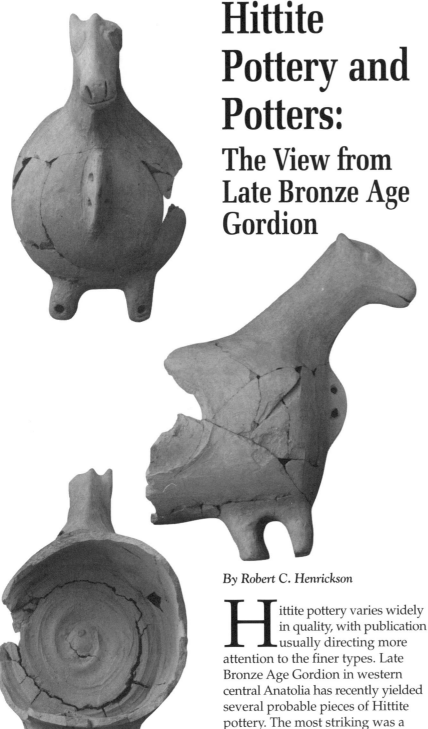

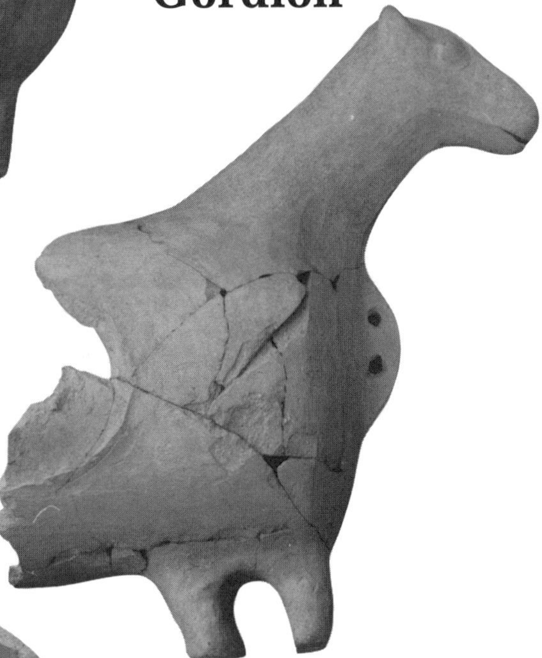

Side, front, and interior views of zoomorphic vessel from Late Bronze Age (YHSS 8) Gordion (Field number [Fn] YH88-153). Both temper, finish, and form mark this rhyton as an import to the small settlement. *All photographs by Laura Foos.*

By Robert C. Henrickson

Hittite pottery varies widely in quality, with publication usually directing more attention to the finer types. Late Bronze Age Gordion in western central Anatolia has recently yielded several probable pieces of Hittite pottery. The most striking was a zoomorphic vessel, a barrel rhyton, found on the floor of a Late Bronze Age structure. Its distinctive micaceous reddish color and well-burnished finish suggest that it was probably an import. Other possible imports included a jar rim and jar shoulders with stamp seal impressions, although the recovery of a clay stamp seal indicates some local use. The great majority of Hittite pottery, however, is plain ware with simple, standardized shapes, cursory finishes, and no decoration.[1] Study of vessel and rim shapes and stylistic analysis of finer pieces document links among sites, thus delineating the broad distribution of Hittite Late Bronze Age pottery, including Gordion.

Pottery, either as vessels or more commonly as innumerable sherds, is probably the most common artifact recovered in excavations. Pottery vessels are not just objects; they are the end-product of the interactions of raw materials, culture, and technology. Shape, size, forming and finishing methods, organization of production, and properties of the raw materials are all interrelated. A technological approach to the seemingly unpromising plain ware pottery can yield a wide range of information that the much rarer fine ceramics may not. Much of the ancient potter's craft can be reconstructed, even without recovering actual workshops or tools, thus providing information on the ancient economy.

The long-term German excavations at the Hittite capital at Ḫattuša-Boğazköy have provided copious data from the Hittite heartland and shed light on many aspects of the Hittite material culture. Excavations at other sites in central Anatolia, such as Maşat Höyük and Alaca Höyük, have further documented the ceramic assemblage.[2] Stylistic analysis of the shapes has shown that the pottery tradition extends over a remarkably broad area in the Late Bronze Age, including such sites in western central Anatolia as Gordion (Mellink 1956; Gunter 1991; Henrickson 1993, 1994) and Yanarlar (Emre 1978), Porsuk in the south (Dupré 1983), and Korucutepe (Van Loon 1980) and Norşuntepe (Korbel 1985) to the southeast.

Here I would like to take a hinterland perspective on this widespread ceramic tradition, examining the Hittite impact on the Late Bronze Age (ca. 1400–1200 BCE) ceramic assemblage at Gordion, then a small settlement on the edge of the Empire. My approach will emphasize technology, since reconstructing the ancient potter's craft not only provides insight into the local economy but also better defines the strength of the Hittite impact on the local material culture.

Stamp seal impression with a hieroglyphic Hittite inscription on the rim of a large jar or vat from Late Bronze Age (YHSS 8) Gordion (Fn YH88–157). The large container was probably made locally—as its ware and neutron activation analysis suggest—and thus, locally stamped as well. By whom is not known: the seal's personal name is unintelligible.

Sherds, Vessels, and the Ancient Potter's Craft

Pottery sherds and vessels retain many residual traces that permit reconstruction of the ancient potter's craft, including the forming and finishing sequences for individual vessel types and sizes. Each forming and finishing method leaves characteristic residual traces, both within the fabric and on the surfaces.[3] Studies of traditional potters and replication experiments have established correlations between such residual traces and original forming and finishing methods. Combined with technical approaches from materials science, forming and finishing sequences for individual types and sizes of vessels can be reconstructed.[4]

Although each stage of manufacture may obscure or obliterate evidence left by previous ones, this does not always happen. In addition, each stage tends to have somewhat more superficial effects than the previous one. Secondary forming may add, alter, or replace traces left by primary forming both in the fabric and on the surfaces. Finishing, such as smoothing, tends to leave marks on surfaces. Thus, although residual traces may result from any stage of production, most on surfaces will come from later, finishing rather than forming stages, while those within the fabric will tend to derive more from primary forming, perhaps later altered by secondary working.

Choice of forming methods is dependent on both vessel form and size, as well as materials and local technology. Making any vessel usually involves combinations of various forming and finishing methods.[5]

How a vessel breaks provides evidence for how it was made, since the characteristics of the breaks themselves, and their overall patterning on the entire vessel, are related to specific forming methods. For example, *throwing on a potter's wheel* leaves a spiraling internal ridge ("wheelmarks" or "throwing marks") and consistent diagonal orientations of inclusions ("temper") within the clay fabric. Breaks tend to spiral upward and outward from the base. *Multi-piece construction methods*, such as coil or slab building, leave weaknesses where separate pieces of clay joined. Breaks therefore tend to follow construction joins, since these are not as strong as the clay body itself. A periodic spacing of *horizontal* breaks suggests coiling. Indeed, surfaces of the individual coils are often recognizable in the horizontal and vertical cross-sections left by breaks. In the clay fabric itself, patterning of texture (such as orientation of tempering particles) provides information as to specific forming techniques used. For example, repetitive circular patterning within vertical section of the vessel wall indicates coiling (Rye 1981; Vandiver 1987:App. III; Henrickson 1991).

Basic Terms of Pottery Production

Primary forming involves the creation of the basic vessel shape. *Secondary forming* modifies a basic form produced by primary forming. *Finishing* subsumes the final modifications to details of shape or surface treatment (smoothing and decoration). A *potter's wheel* is used to *throw* pottery, using the centrifugal force generated by rotation of the wheel to help raise the walls of the vessel. *Wheelmade* refers to pottery that is *thrown on a potter's wheel*. In contrast, a *turntable or tournette*, often called a "slow wheel," is a support on which the vessel being formed may be turned *slowly* to regularize shape and to finish. Using the slow rotation of a turntable for shape modification or finishing yields a *wheel-finished* vessel. Surface traces left by wheel-finishing may be mistaken as evidence for throwing on a potter's wheel (Henrickson 1991). *Coiling* involves using strips or "snakes" of clay to build the vessel; *slabs* of clay may be used instead of coils. *Molding* involves shaping clay either into or over a form (*female* vs. *male* mold; Shepard 1968; Rye 1981).

Gordion Late Bronze Age remains: YHSS 8 "basement" and pits dug into YHSS 9 wash and trash strata (view to south). Though its overall extent and nature have not yet been discovered, Gordion appears to be a village or small town site. While its few imported wares and administrative artifacts suggest Hittite connections, analysis of the forming techniques of its plain ware speaks more unequivocally about the extent of Hittite influence as well as the nature of the local economy.

The complexity of production organization varies widely. Characteristics of the assemblage—the number of types of vessels, their variability or standardization, and methods of forming and finishing—offer clues to the organization of production. Specialist potters tend to use potter's wheels, among other tools, producing large numbers of relatively standardized simple shapes and sizes; common wares tend to have simple finishes (Peacock 1982:12–51; Van der Leeuw 1977; Rice 1991; Costin 1991).

Technological analysis of pottery, focusing on methods of production, thus opens new areas of study: reconstruction of an ancient craft, recognition of culturally distinctive "technologies," assessment of technological sophistication, and nature and degree of technological transfer or acculturation between ceramic traditions. These afford insights into the ancient economy and society, such as identification of organization of production and specialist craftspeople.

Late Bronze Age Gordion

R. Young dug small soundings into the Bronze Age levels on Gordion's main mound, and Mellink excavated part of a Hittite cemetery (Young 1966; Mellink 1956; see also Gunter 1991). Building on these earlier excavations, the recent Yassıhöyük Stratigraphic Sequence (YHSS) excavations, directed by M. M. Voigt in 1988–89, have enhanced our understanding of Late Bronze Age Gordion. The Late Bronze Age strata (phases YHSS 9–8) consisted of trash strata covered with a meter thick layer of clay derived from decayed mudbrick (YHSS 9) into which large storage pits and a cellar more than a meter deep were cut (YHSS 8). On the soft ashy floor were masses of broken pottery (Voigt 1994). Parallels to Boğazköy and other Hittite sites (see below) indicate that YHSS 9–8 date to ca. 1400–1200 BCE (Henrickson 1993, 1994; Voigt 1994; Gunter 1991). Although its size and nature are unknown, Gordion was likely a rather small settlement—a village or small town—as were all other known Late Bronze Age sites in the region (Voigt 1994; Sams and Voigt 1989).

Gordion Late Bronze Age (YHSS 9–8) Pottery Industry

The Gordion Late Bronze Age assemblage is notable for its standardization and overall simplicity. Standardization is pronounced in the distinctive repetition of production sequences for individual vessel types and sizes and in the clustering of vessel sizes. The simplicity and limited number of vessel forms, rim profiles, and generally rather cursory finishing all suggest that ease and speed of production were important considerations.

Three broad ware (fabric) categories may be distinguished. Variation among them primarily involves differences in clay preparation and methods of manufacture and finishing. Color ranges from creamy-white through tan or buff to reddish-orange to brown. *Common ware* (87–90% of all sherds recovered) has a rather dense paste with variable amounts of medium grit temper (usually <0.2 mm in diameter). *Fine ware* (1–5%) has no visible temper. *Cooking ware* (5%) has a less dense paste with large amounts of medium grit and voids from burnt-out chaff temper. Red slip or paint is found on 3–4% of the common and fine wares.

The Late Bronze Age potters used the potter's wheel, turntable, and a variety of hand-forming methods, in varied combinations. Production sequences for individual vessel types varied with vessel size. Most vessels thrown on a potter's wheel, aside from shallow rounded bowls, tended to be small, with a maximum diameter 20 cm. Forming larger vessels usually involved various combinations of handbuilding techniques, often coiling.

Secondary forming, mostly on a turntable, was common. The bodies of medium and large vessels were altered, such as by scraping, then regularized and smoothed on a turntable. Rim forming and finishing were simple. Bowl rims were usually simply rounded and smoothed. Jar and pot rims were formed either by everting and folding down the lip or by adding some clay to thicken and strengthen it. The base of most small and medium bowls and jars was rounded by trimming, probably on a turntable.

Overall finishing usually consisted of simple smoothing; few true slips are identifiable. Most of the "slips" are actually "self-slips" resulting from wet-smoothing, which concentrates fine clay particles on the surface. Decoration usually consists of red slip or painted bands. Some jars have rather inconspicuous, isolated vertical burnish strokes.

The common and fine ware pottery was well-fired, yielding a hard fabric that tends to fracture along sharp linear breaks. Experimental refiring of YHSS 8 sherds indicate that the common and fine buff wares were fired at 800–1000°C, a temperature high enough to imply use of kilns. Cooking ware was fired at a lower temperature (<700°C), perhaps in the open (Rye 1981:96–122).

Forming Sequences for Individual Vessel Types[6]

Let us now turn to how some of the common vessel types were made and what this information has to offer. Although no complete examples of the medium to large types were recovered, pieces were adequate to determine methods of manufacture. All have parallels at Hittite sites.

Small fine ware bowls

In YHSS 8, small shallow bowls with a rounded bottom and slightly carinated or rounded profile were thrown on a potter's wheel using a fine paste. When leather-hard, the exterior of the base was shaved and smoothed to yield a rounded bottom and uniform wall thickness. Sagging or flexing due to thin walls often resulted in slightly irregular shapes. Many have a rim diameter of 17±1 cm, standard within the margin of error for measuring diameters from sherds. Parallels, which seem to have been thrown but may not be as fine in ware, are found at Maşat Höyük and Boğazköy.

Small fine ware "Welt Bowls"

In YHSS 9, fragments of at least several small rounded bowls embodied a unique method of decoration. Small cylindrical pellets (diameter 2–3 mm) of clay were forced into the sides of the bowl from the exterior. On the interior, these pellets produced bumps or welts, while on the exterior their flat ends were concealed by smoothing.

Small conical bowls

Small, shallow conical bowls with flat bases were thrown using a common ware paste. The base retains marks left by the string used to free the bowl from the potter's wheel.

Medium bowls with rounded base

The forming sequence for medium-sized shallow, rounded bowls (diameter 26–32 cm, with diameters tending to cluster at 26 and 32 cm) is similar to that for fine ware. Each was thrown, dried to leather-hardness, inverted, and the base trimmed on a turntable to yield a rounded exterior profile. Careful examination of the exterior surface usually identifies residual scraping scars in the basal area, although final smoothing has usually removed most; near the rim ridges left by throwing survive. Breaks tend to spiral outward from the center to the rim, suggesting throwing on the potter's wheel. Rim forms tend to become even simpler from YHSS 8 to YHSS 9.

Cache of Gordion Late Bronze Age (YHSS 8) pottery. Clockwise from the front left: Small shallow fine ware bowl (Fn YH88-103); Medium bowl with flat base (Fn YH88-102); Beaker (Fn YH88-108); Small deep bowl with rim pinched to oval outline (Fn YH88-152); Medium shallow bowl (Fn YH88-151).

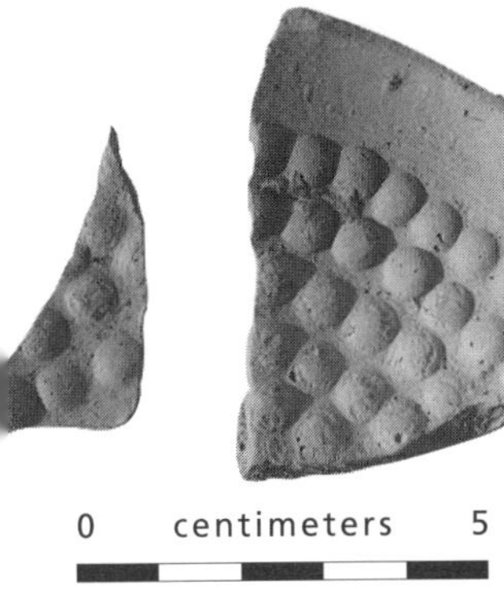

Small Fine Ware bowl with "welt decoration" (Fn YH89-62; YHSS 9). Potters accomplished this unique method of decoration by inserting small pellets into the external sides of the bowl. They then concealed the pellets, smoothing over their ends and creating "welts" on the inside of the bowl.

Alternative forming methods were occasionally used. Distinctively different patterns of breakage indicate that one rounded base bowl made with a slightly coarser fabric than usual was molded and the rim finished by the addition of a single strip or coil of clay around its perimeter.

Medium conical bowls with flat bases

Although the same general size and only slightly deeper than the previous type, medium sized conical bowls (diameter 26–32 cm) were handbuilt rather than thrown. Relatively thick sides were butted onto a heavy slab base; adding coils or strips of clay, which were drawn upward and outward, completed the sides. The rim, entire interior, and upper exterior were smoothed, probably on a turntable. The base exterior remained poorly finished, sometimes retaining grit or chaff impressions from the surface on which it had rested. These flat-base bowls were thus *not* simply rounded profile bowls whose bases had not been trimmed, but rather the product of an entirely different forming approach.

Jars

Jars have narrow necks, heavy rounded or slightly triangular folded rims, rounded sloping shoulders, and handles attached at the neck and shoulder. Two types are common at Gordion: 1) thin-walled jars of small to moderate size and 2) larger jars with tapered cylindrical bodies and pointed bases.

The small to medium size thin-walled jars were probably thrown on a potter's wheel, judging from the thin walls, throwing ridges on the interior of the shoulder, and sometimes diagonal compression ridges on the interior of the neck resulting from constricting the shoulder to form the neck. Their overall thinness yields relatively small pieces, with lower bodies and rounded bases difficult to identify and reconstruct.

The large tapered cylindrical jars with pointed base, usually have strong "throwing marks" on their interior. They were, however, built from at least three separate components: 1) rim/neck/upper shoulder; 2) main body; and 3) lower body and base. The general forming sequence is reasonably clear. Patterns of breaks and texture variations and voids in the fabric demonstrate the use of coiling or piecemeal construction, on a turntable, for primary forming

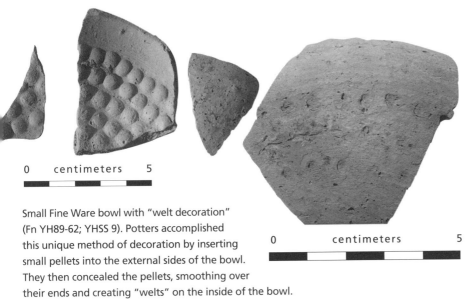

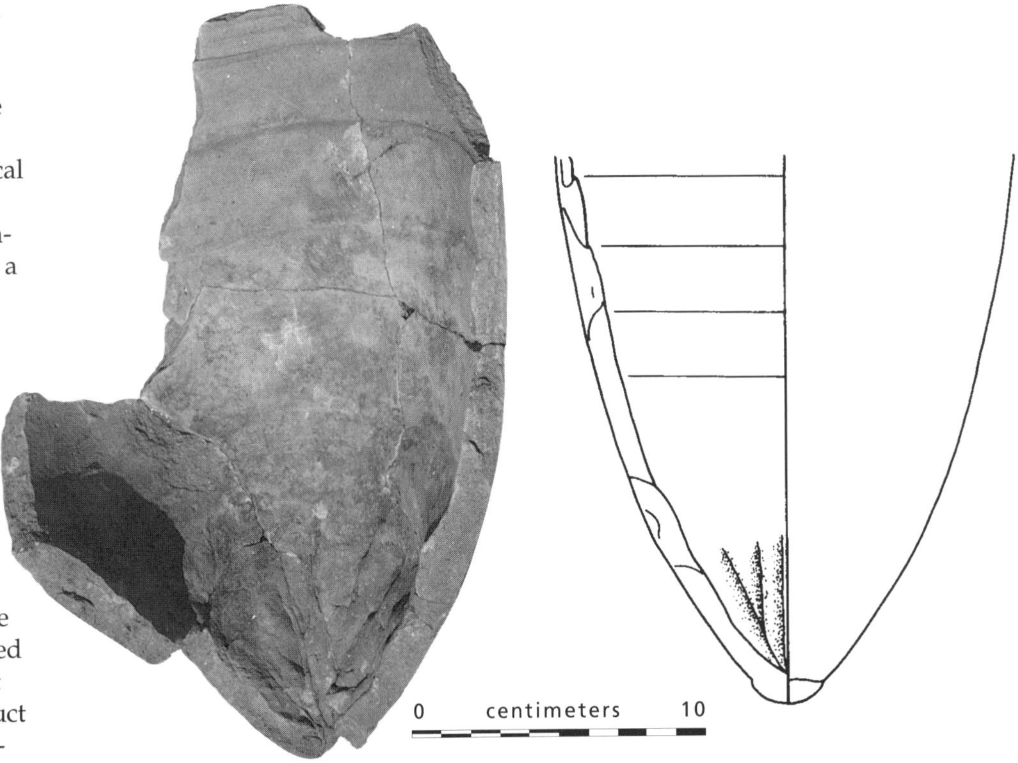

Gordion potters assembled large cylindrical ("torpedo") jars as three distinct components: rim/neck/upper shoulder; main body; and lower body and base. They employed coiling techniques on a turntable to form the main and lower bodies. Patterns of fracture show this clearly. The parallel breaks in the lower body of this vessel (YHSS 8; Fn YH 23834.1) correspond to joins between clay elements in the wall. *Drawing by Robert Henrickson.*

of the walls of the main and lower body. Parallel breaks correspond to joins between clay elements in the wall. The upper shoulder/neck piece was perhaps formed separately and attached to the main body, or built onto the upper edge of body. The shoulder was consolidated and the neck diameter reduced on a turntable, leaving "wheelmarks" inside the shoulder and compression ridges inside the neck, and the handle added finally.

Bringing the base to a point must have been one of the very last steps in the entire vessel production sequence. Two techniques seem to have been used. Vertical ridges left by compression indicate that squeezing or "choking" brought the bottom of the jar to a point. The absence of any evidence for smoothing over the interior compression ridges indicates pointing the base was a very late stage in production. A second forming technique, also used for somewhat more rounded bases, involved successive additions of small strips or coils of clay to close the open base gradually.

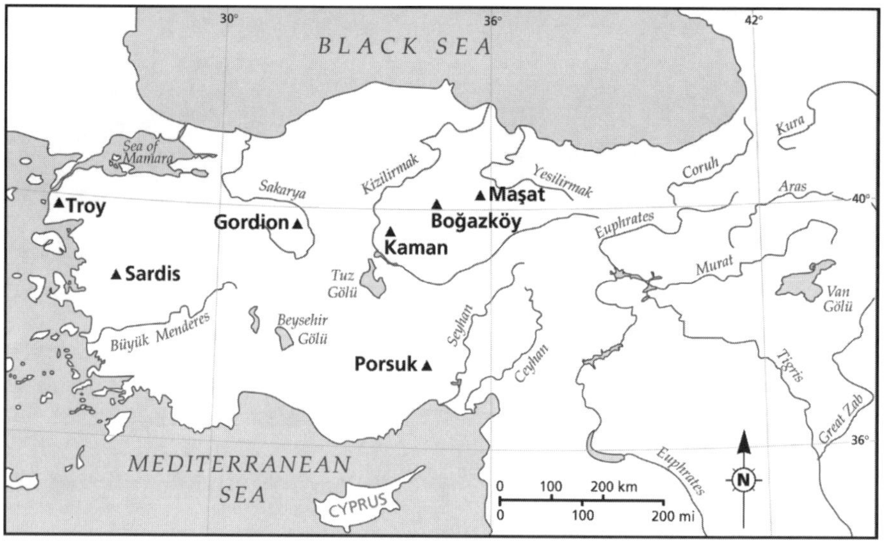

Gordion lies at the western periphery of the Hittite Empire, yet its ceramic traditions felt the decided impact of its powerful, though distant, neighbor.

Cooking pots

Cooking pots were rather baggy wide-mouthed handmade vessels with rounded bases, slightly enlarged rounded rims, and vertical loop handles. The fabric was noticeably coarser and somewhat more friable than for other vessels, due to use of much greater amounts of chaff temper. The lower body may be been formed in a mold, but the sides were built by coiling. As might be expected with a cooking pot, the interior surface is better smoothed than the outer, probably on a turntable.

"Vats" and large storage vessels

Given the relatively small size of sherds recovered relative to vessel size, the overall shapes remain uncertain. The long, parallel, horizontal breaks, and joins visible in broken edges of sherds, demonstrate that coiling was the primary forming method. Surface marks again suggest secondary forming and finishing on a turntable. The base of a large jar clearly shows the construction method using layers or slabs of clay.

The Potter's Craft at Gordion

Although the limited area of Late Bronze Age architecture excavated is modest, the pottery assemblage does suggest some economic complexity at Gordion. Simple profiles, limited number of vessel types, tight clustering of sizes, cursory finish, and general simplicity of most attributes—in short, its standardization—all suggest large-scale production by specialist potters. Two jars had "potter's marks" incised on their shoulders before firing, although their meaning remains unclear (cf. Gunter 1991:pl. 26.493, 28.517–21).

Neutron activation analysis of both Gordion Late Bronze Age pottery samples and clays from the Sakarya River banks adjacent to the site has demonstrated that most have very similar chemical compositions. Therefore, much of the Late Bronze Age pottery must have been made at or near Gordion; it clearly is not imported from another area. Since the nature of the assemblage suggests professional potters and relatively large-scale production, output would have far exceeded the modest needs of the small Late Bronze Age settlement at Gordion. Contemporary settlements in the area were also small, so the potters must have been supplying at least several of them as well. Pottery thus provides the best evidence for some regional economic complexity at present; the limited area of Late Bronze Age strata excavated at Gordion have yet to yield much other evidence for local economic complexity (Voigt 1994). The pottery suggests the presence of at least one group of specialist craftspeople. In such an economy, other specialists might be expected. Pottery provides information we otherwise lack, or have yet to recognize. Closer study of other types of data may well yield similar results.

Gordion and the Hittites

The Hittites dominated central Anatolia; Gordion lay on or near the imperial periphery. The basic types of vessels in the Late Bronze Age assemblage at Gordion are well-known from imperial Hittite sites (see above; Henrickson 1993, 1994; Gunter 1991). Gordion's assemblage seems to be a simplified

Two additional Late Bronze Age (YHSS 9) stamped impressions on jar shoulders (Fn's YH89-530 [star] and 531 ["signe royale"] and a baked clay stamp seal (Fn YH89-563) point to local stamping. While these artifacts suggest official local administrative activities (e.g., stamping of containers), further research is needed to establish the probability of a Hittite official at Gordion.

version of the basic Hittite assemblage. All major vessel types found at Gordion are known at Ḫattuša, but Ḫattuša has others not found at Gordion. More important, the production sequences at Gordion are similar, if not identical, to those at the Hittite capital of Ḫattuša (Müller-Karpe 1988:Abb. 2–6). This is noteworthy since all of the vessel shapes involved could easily be produced using other combinations of methods.

The replication of not only shapes but also forming methods demonstrates that Gordion had strong connections to the Hittite ceramic tradition, since a potter's craft methods are less likely to change under outside influence than the vessel shapes produced. For example, during the Persian and Hellenistic periods at Gordion, local potters very carefully copied the shape and all of the details of imported Greek Black Glazed vessels but used their own, distinctly different *local* forming and finishing methods to do so (Henrickson 1993, 1994).

The broad stylistic and technological connections between Gordion common ware pottery and Hittite heartland assemblages traced above find further support in the several probable Hittite imports. Alaca Höyük provides the best parallel for the zoomorphic rhyton, but fragments from Boğazköy provide further parallels, as do Late Bronze Age Porsuk and Ilıca.[7] The stamp seal impression with an unintelligible personal name in hieroglyphic Hittite on a storage vessel rim implies at least contact.[8] The two jar shoulders with stamp seal impressions, particularly the one with the "signe royale," also have parallels at Boğazköy. The clay stamp seal with the "signe royale" motif allows for local stamping, but it is not enough to establish the presence of a Hittite official at Gordion. Further investigation is needed.

Concluding Remarks

Gordion was apparently a small settlement near the periphery of the Hittite Empire in the Late Bronze Age. Even there, however, the Hittites had a dramatic impact on pottery, a basic local industry. The methods and probable scale of pottery production suggest a regional distribution network for pottery. Looking at the plain pottery and its underlying technology has both clarified Gordion's Hittite connections and shown that the rhyton and stamp sealings on jars are one aspect of a much more pervasive phenomenon.

Vessel shapes and rim forms have long provided stylistic evidence for a connection between Gordion and the Hittites. The technological similarities in production methods and sequences imply a stronger, more fundamental craft relationship. The technological approach to the pottery assemblage has yielded both a reconstruction of the Late Bronze Age potter's craft at Gordion and shed light on the nature of the local economy.

Acknowledgments

The Gordion Excavation Project is sponsored by the University of Pennsylvania Museum. During 1988–1991, the project received a grant from the National Endowment for the Humanities. The National Geographic Society supported the 1988 season. In 1988–89, my work at Gordion was funded by the Committee for Field Archaeology of the Royal Ontario Museum (Toronto). Comments from M. M. Voigt, M. J. Mellink, E. F. Henrickson, and R. Gorny have improved the text.

Notes

[1] See in particular Müller-Karpe (1988) but also Fischer (1963), Orthmann (1963, 1984), Özgüç (1978, 1982).

[2] For Ḫattuša/Boğazköy see Fischer (1963), Müller-Karpe (1988), Orthmann 1963; Seidl 1972. For Maşat Hüyük see Özgüç (1978, 1982) and for Alaca Höyük see Koşay and Akok (1944, 1951, 1973).

[3] Noble 1965; Shepard 1968; Rye 1981; Vandiver 1987:App. III; Van As 1984, 1989; Henrickson 1991.

[4] For studies of traditional potters and replication experiments see Hampe and Winter (1962, 1965), Matson (1974), Rye and Evans (1976), Rye (1981), Kramer (1985), see Longacre (1991) for bibliography. For technical approaches from materials science see Matson (1974), Kingery (1981), Kingery and Vandiver (1988), Kramer (1985), Vandiver (1988).

[5] E.g., Güner 1988; Hampe and Winter 1962, 1965; Rye and Evans 1976; Reina and Hill 1978; Kramer 1985; Longacre 1991; Henrickson 1991.

[6] Additional material on the forming sequences for individual vessel types can be found in the following sources. For *small fineware bowls* see Gunter (1991:fig. 12.212, 17.352), Mellink (1956:pl. 15d-l, 30a-b). For Maşat Höyük see Özgüç (1982:pl. 46.1, 6) and for Boğazköy see Müller-Karpe (1988:Taf. 40), Fischer (1963:Taf. 102. 802, 803, 823–828, 835). For *small fineware "Welt Bowls"* cf. Gunter (1991:pl. 25.414). For *small conical bowls* see Müller-Karpe (1988:96, Abb. 6). Boğazköy provides parallels, see Müller-Karpe (1988:Taf. 41.N1a). For *medium bowls with rounded base* cf. Müller-Karpe (1988:Taf. 32–36), Fischer (1963:Taf. 95–96), Özgüç (1978:pl. 45.1, 3, 4), Özgüç (1982:pl. 46.2–4; fig. A.1–4, 37–42). For *medium conical bowls with flat bases* cf. Müller-Karpe (1988:Taf 29.S1d). For *jars* cf. Müller-Karpe (1988:Taf. 5–7), for forming methods of jars, cf. Müller-Karpe (1988: 32, Abb. 3; for parallels ibid. taf. 3), for pointing of bases cf. Müller-Karpe (1988:32, Abb. 3). For forming of *cooking pots*, cf. Müller-Karpe (1988:51, Abb. 4; for parallels Taf. 9–11); Özgüç (1982:fig. D.25, E.1–2). For *vats* cf. Müller-Karpe (1988:Taf. 12–17, 27; 63 Abb.5).

[7] For Alaca Hüyük see Koşay and Akok (1973:80; pl. XXXIX, Al n. 102; cf. also pl. XXXVIII, Al n. 90). For Boğazköy see Fischer (1963:Taf. 133.1278, 138.1335). For Porsuk see Abadie-Reynal et al. (1989:Resim 8). For Ilıca see Orthmann (1967:pl. 16).

[8] Güterbock personal communication to M. Voigt; cf. Güterbock (1980: fig. 4) and Gunter (1991:pl. 24.381 and 29.532). Seals are also found on jar shoulders. Cf. Seidl (1972).

Bibliography

Abadie-Reynal, C., Pelon, O. and Tibet, A.
1989 Porsuk Çalışmarı. *Kazı Sonuçları Toplantısı* 12(1):443–54.

Bittel, K. et al.
1958 *Die Hethitischen Grabfunde von Osmankayasi.* WVDOG 71. Berlin: G. Mann.
1969 *Boğazköy IV: Funde aus Grabungen 1967 un 1968.* Berlin: G. Mann.

Costin, C. L.
1991 Craft Specialization: Issues in Defining, Documenting, and Explaining the Organization of Production. Pp. 1–56. in *Archaeological Method and Theory* 3, edited by M. B. Schiffer. Tucson: University of Arizona Press.

Dupré, S.
1983 *Porsuk I: La Céramique de l'Age de Bronze et de l'Age du Fer.* Paris: Editions Recherches sur les Civilisations.

Emre, K.
1978 *Yanarlar: Afyon Yöresinde Bir Hitit Mezarligi / A Hittite Cemetery Near Afyon.* Türk Tarih Kurumu Yayınları VI. Dizi–Sa. 22. Ankara: Türk Tarih Kurumu Basımevi.

Fischer, F.
1963 *Die Hethitische Keramik von Boğazköy.* (WVDOG 75) Berlin: Gelor. Mann.

Hampe, R. and Winter, A.
1962 *Bei Töpfern und Töpferinnen in Kreta, Messenien, und Zypern.* Römisch-Germanisches Zentralmuseum, Mainz. Bonn: Rudolf Habelt.
1965 *Bei Töpfern und Zieglern in Süditalien Sizilien und Griechenland.* Römisch-Germanisches Zentralmuseum zu Mainz. Bonn: Rudolf Habelt.

Güner, Gungor
1988 *Anadolu'da Yaşamakta Olan Ilkel Çomlekçilik.* Istanbul: Akbank'n Bir Kultur Hizmeti.

Gunter, A. C.
1991 *The Bronze Age.* The Gordion Excavations Final Reports III. University Museum Monograph 73. Philadelphia: University Museum.

Güterbock, H. G.
1980 Seals and Sealings in Hittite Lands. Pp. 51–63 in *From Athens to Gordion*, edited by K. DeVries. University Museum Papers, 1. Philadelphia: University Museum.

Hampe, R. and Winter, A.
1962 *Bei Töpfern und Töpferinnen in Kreta, Messenien, und Zypern.* Römisch-Germanisches Zentralmuseum, Mainz. Bonn: Rudolf Habelt.
1965 *Bei Töpfern und Zieglern in Süditalien Sizilien und Griechenland.* Römisch-Germanisches Zentralmuseum zu Mainz. Bonn: Rudolf Habelt.

Henrickson, Robert C.
1991 Wheelmade or Wheel-Finished? Interpretation of "Wheelmarks" on Pottery. Pp. 523–41 in *Materials Issues in Art and Archaeology II*, edited by P. B. Vandiver, J. R. Druzik, and G. Wheeler. Materials Research Society Symposium Proceedings 185. Pittsburgh: Materials Research Society.
1993 Politics, Economics, and Ceramic Continuity at Gordion in the Late Second and First Millennia B.C. Pp. 89–176 in *Social and Cultural Contexts of New Ceramic Technologies*, edited by W. D. Kingery. Ceramics and Civilization VI. Westerville, OH: American Ceramic Society.
1994 Continuity and Discontinuity in the Ceramic Tradition at Gordion during the Iron Age. Pp. 95–129 in *Anatolian Iron Ages 3. Proceedings of the Third International Anatolian Iron Age Symposium in Van, Turkey 6–12 August 1990*, edited by D. French and A. Çilingiroğlu. Monograph 16. London: British Institute of Archaeology at Ankara.

Kingery, W. D.
1981 Plausible Inferences from Ceramic Artifacts. *Journal of Field Archaeology* 8:457–468.

Kingery, W. D. and Vandiver, P. B.
1988 *Ceramic Masterpieces.* New York: Free Press.

Korbel, G.
1985 *Die Spätbronzezeitliche Keramik von Norşuntepe.* Institut für Bauen und Planen in Entwicklungsländern, Mitteilungen Nr. 4. Hannover.

Koşay, H. Z. and Akok, M.
1944 *Ausgrabungen von Alaca Höyük, Vorbericht ... 1936.* Türk Tarih Kurumu Yayinlarindan V. Seri Sa. 2A. Ankara: Türk Tarih Kurumu Basımevi.
1951 *Les Fouilles d'Alaca Höyük: Rapport Préliminaire 1937–1939.* Türk Tarih Kurumu Yayinlarindan V. Seri Sa. 5. Ankara: Türk Tarih Kurumu Basımevi.

1973 *Alaca Höyük Kazisi: 1963–1967 Çaliş malari ve Keşiflere ait ilk Rapor / Alaca Höyük Excavations: Preliminary Report on Research and Discoveries 1963–1967*. Türk Tarih Kurumu Yayinlarindan V. Seri Sa. 28. Ankara: Türk Tarih Kurumu Basımevi.

Kramer, C.
1985 Ceramic Ethnoarchaeology. *Annual Review of Anthropology* 14:77–102.

Longacre, W. A.
1991 *Ceramic Ethnoarchaeology*. Tucson: University of Arizona.

Matson, F. R.
1974 The Archaeological Present: Near Eastern Village Potters at Work. *American Journal of Archaeology* 78:345–47.

Mellink, M. J.
1956 *A Hittite Cemetery at Gordion*. University Museum Monograph. Philadelphia: University Museum.

Müller-Karpe, A.
1988 *Hethitische Töpferei der Oberstadt von Hattusa: Ein Beitrag zur Kenntnis spätgrossreichzeitlicher Keramik und Töpferbetreibe*. Marburger Studien zur Vor- und Frühgeschichte, 10. Marburg: Hitzeroth Verlag.

Noble, J. V.
1965 *The Techniques of Attic Painted Pottery*. New York: Watson-Guptill.

Orthmann, W.
1963 *Frühe Keramik aus Boğazköy*. WVDOG 74. Berlin: G. Mann.
1967 *Das Graberfeld bei Ilica*. Wiesbaden: F. Steiner.
1984 Keramik aus den altesten Schichten von Büyükkale. Pp. 9–62 in *Boğazköy VI*, edited by K. Bittel et al. Berlin: G. Mann.

Özgüç, T.
1978 *Maş at Höyük Kazılarıve Çevresindeki Araştırmalar / Excavations at Maş at Höyük and Investigations in Its Vicinity*. Türk Tarih Kurumu Yayınları V. Dizi, Sa. 38. Ankara: Türk Tarih Kurumu Basımevi.
1982 *Maş at Höyük II: Boğazköy'ün Kuzeydoğusunda Bir Hitit Merkezi / A Hittite Center Northeast of Boğazköy*. Türk Tarih Kurumu Yayınları V. Dizi, Sa. 38a. Ankara: Türk Tarih Kurumu Basımevi.
1988 *Inandıktepe: Eski Hitit Çağında Önemli Bir Kült Merkezi (An Important Cult Center in the Old Hittite Period)*. Türk Tarih Kurumu Yayınları V. Dizi, Sa. 43. Ankara: Türk Tarih Kurumu Basımevi.

Peacock, D. P. S.
1982 *Pottery in the Roman World: An Ethnoarchaeological Approach*. London: Longman.

Reina, Reuben E., and Hill, Robert M., II
1978 *The Traditional Pottery of Guatemala*. Austin: University of Texas.

Rice, P. M.
1991 Specialization, Standardization, and Diversity: A Retrospective. Pp. 257–79 in *The Ceramic Legacy of Anna O. Shepard*, edited by Bishop, R. L., and Lange, F. L. Niwot CO: University Press of Colorado.

Rye, O. S.
1981 *Pottery Technology: Principles and Reconstruction*. Washington: Taraxacum.

Rye, O. S. and Evans, C.
1976 *Traditional Pottery Techniques of Pakistan: Field and Laboratory Studies*. Smithsonian Contributions to Anthropology 21. Washington: Smithsonian Institution.

Sams, G. K. and Voigt, M. M.
1989 Work at Gordion in 1988. *Kazı Sonuçları Toplantısı* XI(2):77–105.

Seidl, U.
1972 *Gefässmarken von Bogazköy*. WVDOG 88. Berlin: G. Mann.

Shepard, A. O.
1968 *Ceramics for the Archaeologist*. Publication 609. Washington: Carnegie Institution of Washington.

Van As, A.
1984 Reconstructing the Potter's Craft. Pp. 129–60 in *The Many Dimensions of Pottery: Ceramics in Archaeology and Anthropology*, edited by S. E. van der Leeuw and A. C. Pritchard. Cingvla VII. Albert Egges van Giffen Instituut voor Praeen Protohistorie. Amsterdam: Universiteit van Amsterdam.
1989 Some Techniques Used by the Potters of Tell Hadidi during the Second Millennium B.C. Pp. 41–79 in *Pottery Technology: Ideas and Approaches*, edited by G. Bronitsky. Boulder: Westview Press.

Robert C. Henrickson is currently Senior Archaeologist in charge of the ceramics, Gordion Excavations Project (1988–present), working on Late Bronze through Roman pottery from recent and ongoing excavation. His recent research has concentrated on various approaches to reconstructing ancient pottery craft and technology in the Near East in the Bronze and Iron Ages, including work at the Conservation Analytical Laboratory at the Smithsonian Institution. His previous field work has been in Iran, Iraq, Turkey, and Greece. Dr. Henrickson received his B.A. in Latin from Vanderbilt University (1973), and his M.A. (1976) and Ph.D. (1984) in West Asian Archaeology from the Department of Near Eastern Studies at the University of Toronto.

Van der Leeuw, S. E.
1977 Towards a Study of the Economics of Pottery Making. Pp 68–76 in *Ex Horreo*, edited by B. L. van Beek, R. W. Brandt and , W. Groenman-van Wateringe. Cingula IV. Albert Egges van Giffen Instituut voor Parae-en Protohistorie, Universiteit van Amsterdam.

Van Loon, M. N., ed.
1980 *Korucutepe III: Final Report on the Excavations of the Universities of Chicago, California (Los Angeles), and Amsterdam in the Keban Reservoir, Eastern Anatolia 1968–1970*. Amsterdam: North Holland.

Vandiver, P. B.
1987 Sequential Slab Construction: A Conservative Southwest Asiatic Ceramic Tradition ca. 7000–3000 B.C. *Paléorient* 13(2):9–35.

1988 Reconstructing and Interpreting the Technologies of Ancient Ceramics. Pp. 89–102 in *Materials Issues in Art and Archaeology*, edited by E. V. Sayre, P. B. Vandiver, J. Druzik and C. Stevenson. Materials Research Society Symposium Proceedings 123. Pittsburgh.

Voigt, M. M.
1994 Excavations at Gordion 1988–89: The Yassıhöyük Stratigraphic Sequence. Pp. 265–93 in *Anatolian Iron Ages 3. Proceedings of the Third International Anatolian Iron Age Symposium in Van, Turkey 6–12 August 1990*, edited by D. French and A. Çilingiroğlu. British Institute of Archaeology at Ankara, Monograph 16.

Young, R. S.
1966 The Gordion Campaign of 1965. *American Journal of Archaeology* 70:267–78.

The Religion of the Hittites

In this relief from the main chamber of the rock sanctuary Yazılıkaya, located just outside the city of Ḫattuša, a procession of male gods (to the left) led by the Storm-God greets a procession of goddesses led by the Sun-Goddess of Arinna, here given her Hurrian name Ḫebat. This grand procession, which wraps itself around the contours of the rock, presumably represents the divine court attendant during the celebration of the new year's festival. The Storm-God wears a tall horned cap, characteristic of his divinity and rank. He stands on two bending Mountain-Gods and greets the Sun-Goddess, who wears a flattened cone-shaped hat and stands on a feline. *Photo by Jeanny Vorys Canby.*

By Gary Beckman

The recovery of Hittite religion is difficult because the creators of the available textual sources did not intend to convey a coherent picture to outsiders. The knowledge we have depends chiefly on the thousands of cuneiform tablets discovered in the ruins of the royal city of Ḫattuša, modern day Boğazköy. Among these tablets, however, there are no canonical scriptures, no theological disquistions or discourses, no aids to private devotion (Laroche 1971; Bittel 1970: ch. 1). Rather, the scribes employed by the Hittite kings compiled their archives in the service of the royal administration. These records aided the bureaucracy in the organization and maintenance of all areas of royal responsibility, many of which the modern observer would consider to be religious.

The study of Hittite religion must therefore be based on various types of practical documents: temple regulations and records of cultic administration, prescriptions for the proper performance of ceremonies, reports of diviners, religious compositions used in scribal education, and so on. Most of the tablets that we have date to the last fifty years or so of the Hittite Empire, although some earlier compositions are available, either as original tablets or in later copies.

To the textual evidence may be added the testimony of other archaeological discoveries, including a few small divine images and other cult objects (Güterbock 1983), the iconography displayed on seals (Beran 1967; Mora 1987) and rock reliefs (Kohlmeyer 1983; Alexander 1986),

The many faceted Semitic goddess Ištar, whose realm included sexuality and armed combat, appears frequently in texts dating to the Middle Kingdom as well as the Empire period of Hittite history. The goddess is shown here as part of the long procession of gods in the main chamber of Yazılıkaya. The accompanying hieroglyphic label gives the Hurrian form of her name, Šaušga. *Photo by Ronald L. Gorny.*

and ground plans of temples (Bittel 1970:55–59; Neve 1987).

General Character of Hittite Religion

At its base, Hittite religion was concerned with the central preoccupation of peasant life on the central plateau: the fertility of crops, domestic animals, and people. An excerpt from a prayer clearly expressed this interest:

> To the king, queen, princes, and to (all) the land of Ḫatti give life, health, strength, long years, and joy (in?) the future! And to them give future thriving of grain, vines, fruit, cattle, sheep, goats, pigs, mules, asses—together with wild animals—and of human beings! (*KUB* 24.2 rev. 12′–16′)

The world of the primitive farmer and herder is reflected throughout Hittite religion. The chief deity retained the unmistakable features of a growth-sustaining Storm-God, even while presiding over the political structure of the Hittite Empire (Goetze 1957:138–42; Deighton 1982). Geographic elements such as springs and mountains, both conceived as sources of fructifying water, played an important role, and the cultivation of grain and the increase of herds were each represented by a deity (Hoffner 1974:82–85; Beckman 1983:55–56). The Hittites naturally endeavored to understand the numinous through imagery drawn from the daily experience of peasant life. Thus the character and majesty of many deities were made manifest through an association with some animal, wild or domestic. Gods were frequently depicted as standing on their associated beasts; some were even represented in animal form (Lebrun 1985).

The Pantheon

The most prominent figures in the state cult were a Storm-God, who was brought into Anatolia by the Indo-European newcomers, and a kind of Sun-Goddess borrowed from the indigenous Hattic people. In spite of her designation, the latter deity was chthonic, or infernal, in character and was a member of the long line of Anatolian fertility gods reaching from the so-called Mother Goddess of Çatal Höyük in the sixth millennium all the way to Cybele and Artemis of the Hellenistic period. This divine couple was presumably worshiped in the twin cellas of Ḫattuša's largest temple.

The number of individual deities mentioned in the Hittite texts is staggering (Laroche 1947; Gurney 1977:4–23). The Hittites themselves referred to their "thousand gods," but many of these figures are cited infrequently in the texts and remain little more than names to us today. This multiplicity is due in part to a resistance to syncretization. For example, many Hittite towns maintained individual storm-gods, declining to identify the local deities as manifestations of a single national figure.

As the Hittite state expanded from its core in central Anatolia, the range of gods mentioned in the royal archives came to include deities that were worshiped in the urban centers of Syria and Mesopotamia as well as those of Indo-European and Hattic origin. In the earliest period, the Hattic deities of cult centers such as Nerik (Haas 1970) and Ḫattuša predominated, later to be joined by increasing numbers of newcomers at home in regions to the south and east. The Luwian deities of Ḫupešna, Ištanuwa, and Lallupiya, and particularly the Hurrian gods of Šamuḫa (Lebrun 1976), Kummanni, Karkamiš, and Aleppo well represent this process. Lists of divine witnesses to treaties present the imperial pantheon most clearly (Kestemont 1976), although it is puzzling that these groupings omit several otherwise prominent deities.

In the thirteenth century BCE, the court made some efforts at systemization, and grouped many divinities into *kaluti*, or "circles" of males and females, as depicted visually in the bas-relief processions of Yazılıkaya. It is significant that, although their iconography makes most of these deities immediately recognizable as long-standing members of the Hittite pantheon, their hieroglyphic labels give their names in Hurrian (Laroche 1948, 1952). That is, syncretization had finally been carried out. This process is also reflected by an invocation from a prayer of queen Puduḫepa:

> Sun-Goddess of Arinna, my lady, you are the queen of all lands! In the land of Ḫatti you have assumed the name Sun-Goddess of Arinna, but in respect to the land which you have made (the land) of cedars (that is, Syria), you have assumed the name Ḫebat (*KUB* 21.27 i 3–6).

This modern impression of the seal of Eḫli-kuša illustrates the iconography of two important Hittite deities. On the left stands the Storm-God, holding his mace and the "W" hieroglyph representing his name. The figure on the right wears the robes and skull-cap common to the Sun-God and the human king, but the sun disc above his head assures us that it is the deity who is intended here. *Photo courtesy of the Yale Babylonian Collection (YBC 16576).*

This systematizing approach reflected the opinion of only a small group at the Hittite court, however, and at no time was a single unitary hierarchy of gods established.

The Place of the King

To the Hittites, the universe was a continuum. There was no strict separation between gods and humans. The two classes of beings were interdependent and existed alongside the world of plants and animals, from which both ultimately drew their sustenance. The gods were literally dependent on the offerings presented by humans, who, conversely, could thrive only when the deities who controlled the basic processes of nature were well disposed toward the agriculturalists and stock-breeders. This situation is well illustrated by a complaint of king Muršili II:

> All of the land of Ḫatti is dying, so that no one prepares the sacrificial loaf and libation for you [the gods]. The plowmen who used to work the fields of the gods have died, so that no one works or reaps the fields of the gods any longer. The miller-women who used to prepare sacrificial loaves of the gods have died, so that they no longer make the sacrificial loaves. As for the corral and the sheepfold from which one used to cull the offerings of sheep and cattle—the cowherds and the shepherds have died, and the corral and sheepfold are empty. So it happens that the sacrificial loaves, libation(s), and animal sacrifices are cut off. And you come to us, o gods, and hold us culpable in this matter! (*KUB* 24.3 ii 4′–17′).

The monarch occupied a central position in Hittite theology (Güterbock 1954; Gurney 1958). He was the linchpin of the universe, the point at which the sphere of the gods met that of human beings. As chief priest of the Sun-Goddess of Arinna, the king was responsible for the proper service of the gods by humankind and, in turn, represented human society before the awesome power of the gods. In a ritual dating to the Old Hittite period, the monarch speaks of his charge: "the gods, the Sun-God and the Storm-God, have entrusted to me, the king, the land and my household, so that I, the king, should protect my land and

In Hittite ideology there was no strict separation between gods and humans. Gods depended on humans for offerings and humans depended on gods for good harvests. The king occupied a central position in this interdependent relationship, representing the point at which the sphere of the gods met that of human beings. As chief priest, he was responsible for the proper service of the gods by humankind and, in turn, acted as the representative of human society before the awesome power of the gods. The relationship between a king and his personal god is seen in this rock relief, from Yazılıkaya, which shows Tudḫaliya IV in the embrace of his personal god Šarruma. Notice the tall horned cap worn by Šarruma and the king's cartouche in the upper right-hand corner. *Photo by Jeanny Vorys Canby.*

my household for myself" (*KUB* 29.1 i 17–19).

Although to a certain extent the king was identified with the male Sun-God, as shown by his costume and his title "My Sun" (Kellerman 1978), he was not deified until after his death, at which time he was said "to become a god" and began to receive cultic observances (Otten 1958). Indeed, archaeologists suggest that a section of Yazılıkaya served as the mortuary temple of King Tudḫaliya IV (Bittel 1970:ch. 4).

The queen, in turn, had a special relationship with the Sun-Goddess (Bin-Nun 1975:197–202), and all defunct members of the royal family received occasional offerings (Otten 1951). All households were responsible for the service of their ancestors (Archi 1979b), however, so the afterlife of Hittite royalty was probably just a grander version of that awaiting the ordinary person.

The State Cult

The Hittites considered needs and desires of their gods as similar to those of humans of high rank. The temple of a god was simply his house, and strict regulations governed the service and behavior of priests within its precincts (Korošec 1974). Temples housing the most important divinities were large establishments containing many storerooms and workshops where artisans manufactured products necessary for divine service (Güterbock 1975). Outside the city, extensive tracts of agricultural land were devoted to the support of these divine households, and, consequently, the temples were an important part of the Hittite economy (Klengel 1975).

The primary religious functions of the state were carried out in the numerous temples of the capital (McMahon 1995), but the king and his government were also ultimately responsible for the more modest shrines that served minor deities throughout Ḫatti. We are indebted to a census made of local cults during the late thirteenth century BCE for information about the worship and iconography of many Hittite deities (von Brandenstein 1943; Carter 1962). The following report on the cult of a small village is typical:

> The town Lapana, (chief deity) Iyaya: the divine image is a female statuette of wood, seated and veiled, one cubit (in height).

In the small chamber of Yazılıkaya, twelve gods carrying scimitars over their shoulders are shown running in unison, their bodies overlapping. These gods, who are also shown at the end of the long procession in the main chamber, were apparently part of the divine court attendant at the new year's festival performed in honor of the Storm-God. *Photo by Ronald L. Gorny.*

> Her head is plated with gold, but the body and throne are plated with tin. Two wooden mountain sheep, plated with tin, sit beneath the deity to the right and left. One eagle plated with tin, two copper staves, and two bronze goblets are on hand as the deity's cultic implements. She has a new temple. Her priest, a male, is a holdover (*KUB* 38.1 iv 1–7).

Regardless of whether his temple was large or small, a deity's priesthood cared for him—fed and clothed him—within his cella. Because these activities were performed routinely, our sources rarely discuss them, but the texts do give information about the special divine festivals or parties that were held in honor of these deities (Güterbock 1969–70). The schedule of worship varied for each deity; some festivals were held monthly or yearly, whereas others marked particular moments in the agricultural calendar, such as the reaping of a harvest or the cutting of grapes. In general, fall festivals featured the filling of storage vessels with the bounty of the harvest, while spring festivals centered around the opening of these vessels. It seems that a new year's festival was performed in honor of the Storm-God of Ḫattuša in the main galleries of Yazılıkaya (Otten 1956); the reliefs executed there depict the divine court attendant upon this occasion.

The celebration of important festivals for the most prominent deities throughout central Anatolia required the presence of the king. To facilitate this, these festivals were organized into a spring and a fall series, known collectively (and respectively) as the *festival of the crocus* (Güterbock 1960) and the *festival of haste* (Košak 1976). The spring tour required the king to travel for at least thirty-eight days, although in some instances, the queen, a prince, or even a symbolic hunting bag (Güterbock 1989) could substitute for the monarch.

Hittite festivals generally consisted of food offerings, often in the form of a communal meal uniting god and worshipers (Archi 1979a), toasts to the deities (Kammenhuber 1971), and entertainment. The gods were amused in various ways: through athletic competitions, such as foot races, horse races, and the throwing of heavy stones, through mock battles, and through the antics of jesters. Various musicians also treated the gods to music performed on a wide variety of instruments (Gurney 1977:34–35). Unfortunately, we know very little about the character of Hittite music or the lyrics sung, for specific information was usually not recorded (Kümmel 1973).

If the requisite worship was performed on time and according to its stringent requirements, the deities were pleased with and favored the king, granting him personal longevity and numerous offspring and running before him in battle. In turn, the Hittite state and its inhabitants prospered. Most important, Hittite armies were victorious, and Hittite farmers raised bumper crops. But if

Myth of Illuyanka

Few of the mythological texts from the Hittite archives have attracted as much attention as this one (*CTH* 321), which narrates the combat of the Storm-God with a foe designated simply by the Hittite common noun for snake or serpent, *illuyanka-*. Although all of the preserved tablets whose size is sufficient to allow dating belong to the Empire period, there can be little doubt that this text itself is an Old Hittite composition. Many archaic grammatical features support this judgment.

Other commentators have discussed many aspects of this text, for example, its reflection of Anatolian marriage customs, its use of widely attested folkloristic motifs, and its relationship to Greek mythology. For my part, I would stress that the two mythological narratives of *CTH* 321, like all known examples of what Hans Güterbock has termed *Anatolian mythology*, are contained within a ritual context. §§ 1 and 2 make this explicit—the *purulli*-festival is performed both when, and in order that, the land should thrive, and the myths are the texts of this festival. These tales clearly present several religious etiologies, the most important of which is the establishment of a royal cult in the town of Kiškilušša, but more significant is the provision of a mythological paradigm for a human situation. Hittite society had to cope with and understand the alternation of periods of growth and stagnation. The obvious symbolizing in *CTH* 321 of the former by the Storm-God and of the latter by the serpent has led to the interpretation of the entire myth as basically an example of the Frazerian Dying God myth, but I feel that the resolution of the crisis of the seasons through the combined efforts of humans and deities is the most significant element here.

In the first version of the myth, only the help of Ḫupašiya enables the Storm-God to avenge himself upon his enemy, although one might have

§1 (This is) the text of the *purulli* (festival) for the [...] of the Storm-God of Heaven, according to Kella, [the "anointed priest"] of the Storm-God of Nerik: When they speak thus—

§2 "Let the land grow (and) thrive, and let the land be secure (literally 'protected')!"—and when it (indeed) grows (and) thrives, then they perform the festival of *purulli.*

§3 When the Storm-God and the serpent came to grips in (the town of) Kiškilušša, the serpent smote the Storm-God.

§4 (Thereafter) the Storm-God summoned all the gods (saying): "Come in! Inara has prepared a feast!"

§5 She prepared everything in great quantity—vessels of wine, vessels of (the drink) *marnuwan* (and) vessels of (the drink) [*wa*]*lḫi*. In the vessels she ma[de] an abundance.

§6 Then [Inara] went [to] (the town of) Ziggaratta and encountered Ḫupašiya, a mortal.

§7 Inara spoke as follows to Ḫupašiya: "I am about to do such-and-such a thing—you join with me!"

§8 Ḫupašiya replied as follows to Inara: "If I may sleep with you, then I will come and perform your heart's desire!" [And] he slept with her.

§9 Then Inara transported Ḫupašiya and concealed him. Inara dressed herself up and invited the serpent up from his hole (saying): "I'm preparing a feast—come eat and drink!"

§10 Then the serpent came up together with [his children], and they ate (and) drank—they dra[nk] up every vessel and were sated.

§11 They were no longer able to go back down into (their) hole, (so that) Ḫupašiya came and tied up the serpent with a cord.

§12 The Storm-God came and slew the serpent. The (other) gods were at his side.

§13 Then Inara built a house on a rock (outcropping) in (the town of) Tarukka and settled Ḫupašiya in the house. Inara instructed him: "When I go out into the countryside, you must not look out the window! If you look out, you will see your wife (and) your children!"

§14 When (Inara went away and) the twentieth day had passed, he looked out the win[dow] and [saw] his wife (and) [his] children.

§15 When Inara returned from the countryside, he began to whine: "Let me (go) back home!"

§16 Ina[ra sp]oke as follows [to Ḫupašiya: "...] away [...] ... [..."] with anger [...] the meadow of the Storm-God [...] she [...killed[?]] him.

§17 Inara [went] to (the town of) Kiškil[ušša] (and) set her[?] house and [the river[?]] of the watery abyss[?] [into] the hand of the king—because (in commemoration thereof) we are (re-)performing the first *purulli*-festival—the hand [of the king will hold[?] the house[?]] of Inara and the riv[er[?]] of the watery abyss[?].

§18 (The divine mountain) Zaliyanu is fir[st] (in rank) among all (the gods). When he has alloted rain in (the town of) Nerik, then the herald brings forth a loaf of *ḫarši*-bread from Nerik.

§19 He had asked Zaliyanu for rain, and he brings it to him [on account of[?]] the bread...

§20′ This [...]

§21′ That which [Kella, the "anointed priest,"] spoke. The ser[pent] defeated the Storm-God and took (his) h[eart and eyes]. And him the Storm-God [. . .]

§22′ And he took as his wife the daughter of a poor man, and he sired a son. When he grew up, he took as his wife the daughter of the serpent.

§23′ The Storm-God instructed (his) son: "When you go to the house of your wife, then demand from them (my) heart and eyes!"

§24′ When he went, then he demanded from them the heart, and they gave it to him. Afterwards he demanded from them the eyes, and they gave these to him. And he carried them to the Storm-God, his father, and the Storm-God (thereby) took back his heart and his eyes.

§25′ When he was again sound in body as of old, then he went once more to the sea for battle. When he gave battle to him and was beginning to smite the serpent, then the son of the Storm-God was with the serpent and shouted up to heaven, to his father:

§26′ "Include me—do not show me any mercy!" Then the Storm-God killed the serpe[nt] and his (own) son. And now this one, the Storm-God [. . .]

§27′ Thus says Kella, [the "anointed priest" of the Storm-God of Nerik: " ...] when the gods [...]

(gap of about 40 lines—insert §§27′a–27′c?)

§27′a [...] and to him to ea[t...] back to Ner[ik...] he releases.

§27′b [. . .] (the god) Zašḫapuna [. . .] (s)he [. . .]ed, and the Storm-God of Nerik [and ...] went. And Zali[yanu ...] gave back [. . .]

§27′c [. . .] then he trans[ported?? . . . t]o? Ne[rik?...]

§28″ [Then f]or the "anointed priest" they made the [fore]most gods the [humb]lest, and the [hum]blest they made the foremost gods.

§29″ The cultic tax of Zali(ya)nu is great. Zašḫapuna the wife of Zali(ya)nu is greater than the Storm-God of Nerik.

§30″ The gods speak as follows to the "anointed priest" Taḫpurili: "When we go to the Storm-God of Nerik, where shall we sit?"

§31″ The "anointed priest" Taḫpurili speaks as follows: "When you sit on a diorite stool, and when the 'anointed priests' cast the lot, then the 'anointed priest' who holds (the image of) Zaliyanu—a diorite stool shall be set above the spring, and he shall be seated there."

§32″ "All the gods will arrive, and they will cast the lot. Of all the gods of (the town of) Kaštama, Zašḫapuna will be the greatest.

§33″ "Because she is the wife of Zali(ya)nu, (and) Tazzuwašši is his concubine, these three persons will remain in (the town of) Tanipiya."

§34″ And thereafter in Tanipiya a field will be handed over from the royal (property)—

§35″ Six *kapunu*-measures of field, one *kapunu*-measure of garden, a house together with a threshing-floor, three buildings for the household personnel—it is (recorded) [on?] a tablet. I am respectful of the m[atte]r, and I have spoken these things (truly).

§36″ One tablet, complete, of the word of Kella, the "anointed priest."

(colophon)

Piḫawaziti, [the scribe], wrote it under the supervision of Walwaziti, the chief scribe.

supposed that his divine assistant, Inara, could have tied up the serpent and his brood. An essential factor in the second version is the participation of a human female as mother, by the Storm-God, of a son who is seemingly entirely human in nature. The joint effort of human and deity is the common element in the two versions of a myth that otherwise differ greatly in plot. A similar relationship of human and divine is found in the Myth of the Vanishing God (*CTH* 322–27) where ritual performances on the part of the divine healer Kamrušepa and of a mortal ritual practitioner are both required to placate the absent deity. Indeed, within this latter text, it is not clear exactly where the activities of the goddess leave off and those of the human begin.

In *CTH* 321, both Ḫupašiya and the mortal offspring of the Storm-God come to grief. Although the direct causes of their destruction are different—the jealousy of Inara in the first instance and the logic of Anatolian family structure in the second—both mortal protagonists are punished for a too intimate relationship with the deities whom they aid, an intimacy symbolized by sexual intercourse. While Ḫupašiya clearly demonstrates hubris by his demand for the favors of Inara, and the anonymous son of the Storm-God is a blameless tragic figure trapped by his social obligations, both have nonetheless crossed the line separating mortals from deities.

The Myth of Illuyanka gives expression to an important facet of the Hittites' conception of the universe. The activity of everyone contributes to the proper functioning of the cosmos, but each individual must remain in his or her proper place. As the god is to the mortal, so in a sense is the king to the subject.

For a complete edition of the text, accompanied by philological notes, see my previous article (1982). This sidebar is adapted from that article.

—*Gary Beckman*

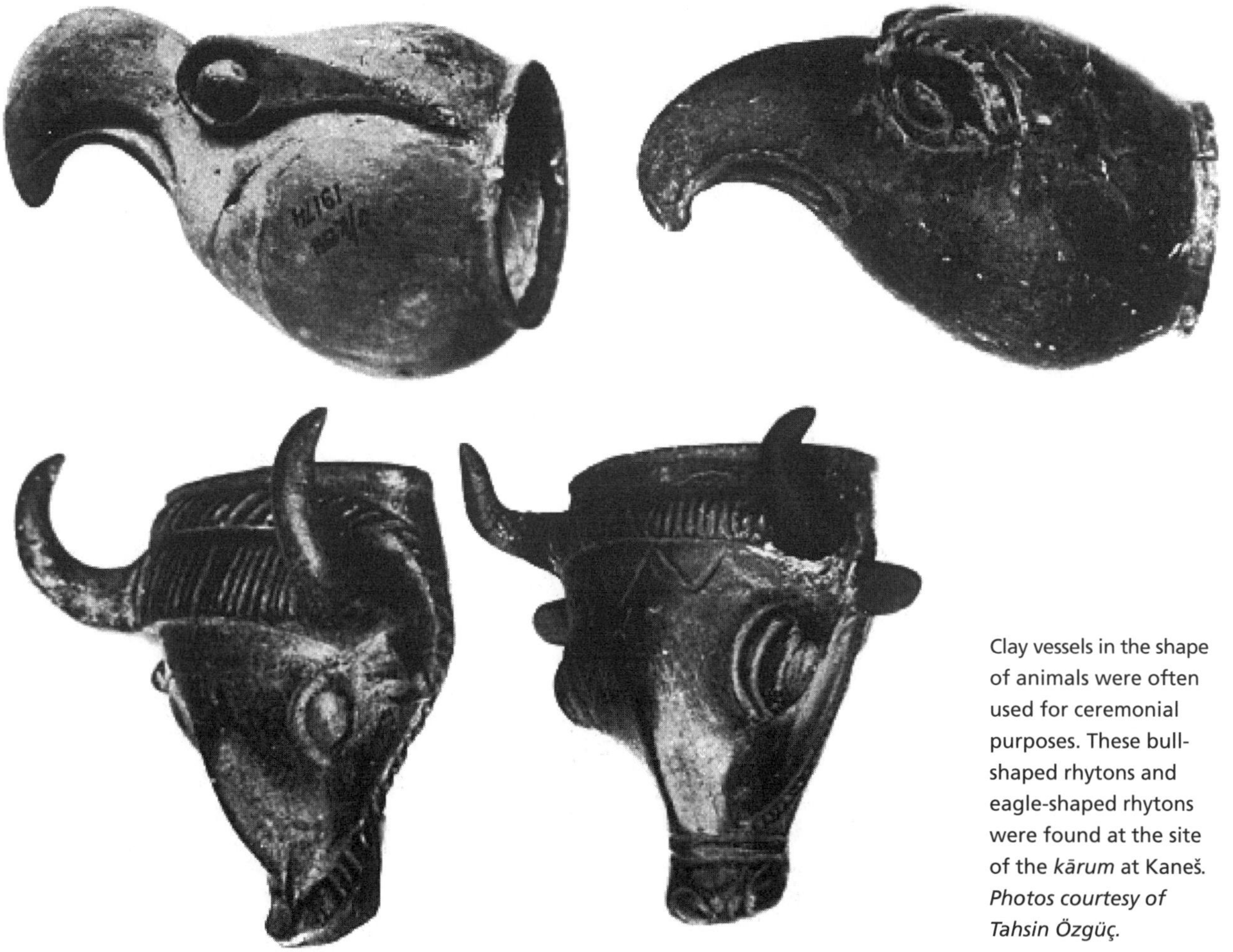

Clay vessels in the shape of animals were often used for ceremonial purposes. These bull-shaped rhytons and eagle-shaped rhytons were found at the site of the *kārum* at Kaneš. *Photos courtesy of Tahsin Özgüç.*

for any reason the gods were unhappy with how the worship was performed, they might invoke sanctions resulting in the most negative effects, from personal sickness to national calamity. Indeed, almost any ill the Hittites interpreted as a manifestation of divine anger. After much effort, for example, Muršili II learned that divine displeasure at a neglected festival and a broken treaty with Egypt had caused plague afflicting Ḫatti.

Descriptions of Hittite festivals are monotonous to read because the largely repetitive ceremonies are described in minute detail. This passage should convey the flavor of these compositions:

> The king and queen, seated, toast the War-God. The *ḫalliyari*-men [play] the large INANNA-instruments and sing. The crier cries out. The cup-bearer brings one snack-loaf from outside and gives [it] to the king. The king breaks [it] and takes a bite. The palace functionaries take the napkins from the king and queen. The crouching (cupbearer) enters. The king and queen, standing, toast the [divinized] Day. The jester speaks; the crier cries out; the *kita*-man cries "*aḫa*" (*KUB* 25.6 iv 5–24).

Our knowledge of native Anatolian mythology (Beckman 1997) derives largely from such texts, for tales of primordial activities by the gods were sometimes recited during a festival as a way of encouraging the gods to maintain the order of the world they had established long before. Thus, priests told two versions of the struggle between the Storm-God and a cosmic serpent during the course of a spring festival (Beckman 1982).

Ritual

In contrast to the festivals, performed at regular intervals, another category of rite—called "rituals"—was intended for use only as the situation required (Frantz-Szabó 1995). Texts describing these ceremonies give us our best view of popular religion because many were not composed in Ḫattuša but were collected by royal scribes throughout the Hittite realm. In most of the ancient Near East, rituals were recorded anonymously, but in Ḫatti such compositions were often named after the practitioner from whom they were elicited. Although the so-called author of a ritual is occasionally said to be a priest, more often female authors—experts in magic—bear the title "old woman," while males are referred to as "seer."

Many Hittite rituals were rites of passage intended to ease the transition of an individual from one stage or station in life to another. Thus, we have many texts describing rituals for birth (Beckman 1983), one for puberty (Güterbock 1969), and several for death (Otten 1958). Rituals for the enthronement of the monarch are alluded to (Kümmel 1967), but no actual text has survived.

The majority of rituals, however, aimed to effect the restoration of a person to his or her proper functioning within a particular sphere of life. The cause of the impairment might be divine anger, but the problem might also be due to *papratar*, a kind of pollution. Whether this pollution was the result of a person's own misdeeds or had been sent by an enemy through sinister magic, it had to be removed and rendered harmless. This was often accomplished by means of analogic magic. A typical incantation reads:

> As a ram mounts a ewe and she becomes pregnant, so let this city and house become a ram, and let it mount the dark earth in the steppe! And let the dark earth become pregnant with the blood, impurity, and sin! (*KUB* 41.8 iv 29–32).

It is interesting to note that most of the analogies used in such magic were drawn from the daily experience of the Hittite peasant.

A ritual could counter a wide range of difficulties. There were ceremonies designed to alleviate such problems as family strife, sexual impotence, and insomnia, and we also know that rituals were performed to ward off plague, military defeat, or evil portended for the person of the king (see Laroche 1971:ch. 7).

Communication

The Hittites believed that communication had to be maintained between the gods and humankind for the world to operate efficiently. On the one hand, as the representative of humankind, the king addressed the gods through a variety of types of prayers (Laroche 1964; Lebrun 1985; de Roos 1995), extracts of which have been quoted above. On the other hand, gods could make their wishes and displeasure known to humans through omens or oracles. Omens were messages from gods to humans, most frequently encountered through dreams (Oppenheim 1956:254–55). Much more important were the oracles, procedures through which humans solicited information from the gods. The archives have preserved countless records of augury, extispicy (divination through the reading of animal entrails), and a curious type of lot oracle (Kammenhuber 1976). These divination techniques were often used as checks on one another. Pleas made by Muršili II in an effort to determine the cause of the plague afflicting Ḫatti underline the need for communication between gods and humans:

> Or if people are dying for some other reason, let me see it in a dream, or let it be established through an oracle, or let a prophet speak it! Or in regard to whatever I communicate [as a possible cause of the epidemic] to all the priests, let them investigate it through incubation! (*KUB* 14.8 rev. 41–44, as restored from duplicates).

Conclusion

In this brief presentation, I have tried to show that the religious conceptions of the Hittites were congruent with their social system and ecological situation. Like the king and other members of the ruling class, the gods stood far above the ordinary Hittite, dispensing favors or punishments according to their pleasure. At the same time, all inhabitants of the Hittite world were interdependent, and the labors of the peasant agriculturalist and pastoralist were the basis upon which all—human and divine—rested.

Bibliography

Alexander, R. L.
1986 *The Sculpture and Sculptors of Yazılıkaya.* Newark: University of Delaware Press.

Archi, A.
1979a Das Kultmahl bei den Hethitern. Pp. 197–213 in *VIII Türk Tarih Kongresi.* Türk Tarih Kurumu Yayınları 4/8 Aukara: Türk Tarih Kurumu Basımevi.
1979b Il dio Zawalli. Sul culto dei morti presso gli Ittiti. *Altorientalische Forschungen* 6:81–94.

Beckman, G.
1982 The Anatolian Myth of Illuyanka. *Journal of the Ancient Near Eastern Society* 14:11–25.
1983 *Hittite Birth Rituals.* Studien zu den Boğazköy-Texten 29. Wiesbaden: Otto Harrassowitz.
1997 Mythologie (bei den Hethitern). *Reallexikon der Assyriologie* 8:564–72.

Beran, Th.
1967 *Die hethitische Glyptik von Boghazköy: I. Teil.* Wissenschaftliche Veröffentlichungen der Deutschen Orient-Gesellschaft 76. Berlin: Gebr. Mann.

Bin-Nun, S.
1975 *The Tawananna in the Hittite Kingdom.* Texte der Hethiter 5. Heidelberg: Carl Winter.

Bittel, K.
1970 *Hattusha: The Capital of the Hittites.* New York: Oxford University Press.
1976 The Great Temple of Hattusha-Boğazköy. *American Journal of Archaeology* 80:66–73.

Brandenstein, C. G. von
1943 *Hethitische Götter nach Bildbeschreibungen in Keilschrifttexten.* Hethitische Texte 8. Leipzig: J. C. Hinrichs.

Carter, C.
1962 *Hittite Cult-Inventories.* Ph.D. dissertation. Chicago: University of Chicago.

Deighton, H.
1982 *The "Weather-God"in Hittite Anatolia.* BAR International Series 143. Oxford: BAR.

Frantz-Szabó, G.
1995 Hittite Witchcraft, Magic, and Divination. Pp. 2007–119 in *Civilizations of the Ancient Near East,* edited by J. Sasson et al. New York: Scribners.

Goetze, A.
1957 *Kleinasien. 2nd. ed.* Handbuch der Orientalistik III.1.3.3.1. Munich: C. H. Beck.

Gurney, O. R.
1958 Hittite Kingship. Pp. 105–21 in *Myth, Ritual and Kingship,* edited by S. Hooke. Oxford: Oxford University Press.
1977 *Some Aspects of Hittite Religion.* The Schweich Lectures 1976. Oxford: Oxford University Press.

Güterbock, H. G.
1950 Hittite Religion. Pp. 83–109 in *Forgotten Religions,* edited by V. Ferm. New York: Philosophical Library.
1954 Authority and Law in the Hittite Kingdom. *Journal of the American Oriental Society,* Supplement 17:16–24.
1960 An Outline of the Hittite AN.TAḪ.ŠUM Festival. *Journal of Near Eastern Studies* 19:80–89.
1964 Religion und Kultus der Hethiter. Pp. 57–73 in *Neuere Hethiterforschung,* edited by G. Walser. *Historia,* Einzelschriften 7. Wiesbaden: Franz Steiner.
1969 An Initiation Rite for a Hittite Prince. Pp. 99–103 in *AOS Middle West Branch Semi-Centennial Volume,* edited by D. Sinor. Bloomington: Indiana University Press.
1969/70 Some Aspects of Hittite Festivals. Pp. 175–80 in *Actes de la XVIIe Rencontre Assyriologique Internationale.* Brussels: Comité belge de recherches en Mésopotamie.
1975 The Hittite Temple According to Written Sources. Pp. 125–32 in *Le Temple et le Culte.* Compte rendu de la 20ième Rencontre Assyriologique Internationale. Istanbul: Institut Historique et Archéologique.
1983 Hethitische Götterbilder und Kultobjekte. Pp. 203–17 in *Beiträge zur Altertumskunde Kleinasiens: Festschrift für Kurt Bittel,* edited by R. M. Boehmer and H. Hauptmann. Mainz: Philipp von Zabern.
1989 Hittite *Kurša* "Hunting Bag." Pp. 113–24 in *Essays in Ancient Civilization presented to Helene J. Kantor,* edited by A. Leonard Jr. And B. B. Williams. Chicago: The Oriental Institute.

Haas, V.
1970 *Der Kult von Nerik.* Studia Pohl 4. Rome: Päpstliches Bibelinstitut.
1994 *Geschichte der hethitischen Religion.* Leiden: E. J. Brill.
1995 Death and the Afterlife in Hittite Thought. Pp. 2021–230 in *Civilizations of the Ancient Near East,* edited by J. Sasson et al. New York: Scribners.

Hoffner, H. A.
1974 *Alimenta Hethaeorum: Food Production in Hittite Asia Minor.* American Oriental Series 55. New Haven, CT: American Oriental Society.

Kammenhuber, A.
1971 Heth. *haššuš 2e ekuzi,* "der König trinkt zwei." *Studi Micenei ed Egeo-Anatolici* 14:143–59.
1976 *Orakelpraxis, Träume und Vorzeichenschau bei den Hethitern.* Texte der Hethiter 7. Heidelberg: Carl Winter.

Kellerman, G.
1978 The King and the Sun-God in the Old Hittite Period. *Tel Aviv* 5:199–208.

Kestemont, G.
1976 Le panthéon des instruments hittites de droit public. *Orientalia* 45:147–77.

Klengel, H.
1975 Zur ökonomischen Funktion der hethitischen Tempel. *Studi Micenei ed Egeo-Anatolici* 16:181–200.

Kohlmeyer, K.
1983 Felsbilder der hethitischen Grossreichszeit. *Acta praehistoricae et archaeologicae* 15:7–154.

Korošec, V.
1974 Einiges zur inneren Struktur hethitischer Tempel nach der Instruktion für Tempelleute (KUB XIII 4). Pp. 165–74 in *Anatolian Studies Presented to Hans Gustav Güterbock on the Occasion of his 65th Birthday,* edited by K. Bittel et al. Istanbul: Nederlands Historisch-Archaeologisch Instituut.

Košak, S.
1976 The Hittite *nuntarrijashas*-Festival (CTH 626). *Linguistica* 16:55–64.

Kümmel, H. M.
1967 *Ersatzrituale für den hethitischen König.* Studien zu den Boğazköy Texten 3. Wiesbaden: Otto Harrassowitz.
1973 Gesang und Gesanglosigkeit in der hethitischen Kultmusik. Pp. 169–78 in *Festschrift Heinrich Otten,* edited by E. Neu and C. Rüster. Wiesbaden: Otto Harrassowitz.

Laroche, E.
1947 *Recherches sur les noms des dieux hittites.* Paris: Librairie Orientale et Américaine.
1948 Tešub, Ḫebat et leur cour. *Journal of Cuneiform Studies* 2:113–36.
1952 Le panthéon de Yazılıkaya. *Journal of Cuneiform Studies* 6:115–23.
1964 La prière hittite: vocabulaire et typologie. *Annuaire de l'École Practique des Hautes Études,* V^e section 72:3–29.
1971 *Catalogue des textes hittites.* Paris: Editions Klincksieck.

Gary Beckman was formerly Associate Professor of Hittite at Yale University and Assistant Curator of the Yale Babylonian Collection. He has written widely on the social and cultural history of the Hittites and has been a collaborator on the Hittite Dictionary Project at The Oriental Institute. He is currently Professor of Hittite and Mesopotamian Studies at the University of Michigan.

Lebrun, R
1976 *Samuha, foyer religieux de l'empire hittite.* Publications de l'Institute Orientaliste de Louvain 11. Louvain-la-neuve: Institute Orientaliste.
1980 *Hymnes et prières hittites.* Homo Religiosus 4. Louvain-la-neuve: Centre d'Histoire des Religions.
1985 Le zoomorphisme dans la religion hittite. Pp. 95–103 in *L'animal, l'homme, le dieu dans le Proche-Orient ancien.* Leuven: Éditions Peeters.
1995 From Hittite Mythology: The Kumarbi Cyle. Pp. 1971–1980 in *Civilizations of the Ancient Near East,* edited by J. Sasson et al. New York: Scribners.

Loon, M. van
1985 *Anatolia in the Second Millennium B. C.* Iconography of Religions XV/12. Leiden: E. J. Brill.

McMahon, G.
1995 Theology, Priests, and Worship in Hittite Anatolia. Pp. 1981–1995 in *Civilizations of the Ancient Near East,* edited by J. Sasson et al. New York: Scribners.

Mora, C.
1987 *La glittica anatolica del II millennio A. C.: classificazione tipologica. I. I sigilli a iscrizione geroglifica.* Studia Mediterranea 6. Pavia: Gianni Iunculano Editore.

Neve, P
1987 Hattuscha, Haupt- und Kultstadt der Hethiter—Ergebnisse der Ausgrabungen in der Oberstadt. *Hethitica* 8:297–318.

Oppenheim, A. L.
1956 *The Interpretation of Dreams in the Ancient Near East.* Transactions of the American Philosophical Society 46/3. Philadelphia: American Philosophical Society.

Otten, H.
1951 Die hethitischen "Königslisten" und die altorientalische Chronologie. *Mitteilungen der Deutschen Orient Gesellschaft* 83:47–71.
1956 Ein Text zum Neujahrsfest aus Boğazköy. *Orientalistische Literaturzeitung* 51:101–5.
1958 *Hethitische Totenrituale.* Institut fur Orientforschung Veroffentlichung 37. Berlin: Akademie-Verlag.

Roos, J. de
1995 Hittite Prayers. Pp. 1997–2005 in *Civilizations of the Ancient Near East,* edited by J. Sasson et al. New York: Scribners.

A Hittite Seal from Megiddo

By Itamar Singer

Peter Neve's excavations in Ḫattuša enriched us with thousands of new seal impressions that will open new vistas in the study of Hittite glyptics (Neve 1993:52–58). The one seal that I discuss here has hardly any importance *per se*, except for its place of discovery—Megiddo, a town with other connections to the Hittite world.

Megiddo (Tell el-Mutesellim) was situated immediately on the best communication avenue between the Egyptian and Hittite spheres of influence after their mid-thirteenth century peace treaty. The charioteer's seal joins other data, including an Akkadian letter uncovered in Boğazköy that mentions the town and a Hittite ivory plaque, pointing to the significance of Megiddo on the political map of the Late Bronze Age. *Photograph courtesy of R. Cleave.*

The seal was found in the excavations of the Oriental Institute of the University of Chicago in the late thirties.[1] It comes from Area CC, Locus 1829, Stratum VII B (Loud 1948:156), which is dated to the thirteenth century BCE. The area is residential, and the structure in which the seal was found has nothing particular to distinguish it from other neighboring houses (Loud 1948:fig. 409).The biconvex seal is made of steatite and measures 19 mm maximum in diameter, 11 mm in thickness. The perforation runs perpendicular to the inscription on face B. Both faces of the seal are framed by a circular border. This type of Hittite seal is dated to the thirteenth century BCE (Gorny 1993:191). A photograph of the seal was published in *Megiddo II* (Loud 1948:pl. 162:7) together with a short comment by I. J. Gelb.[2] Clelia Mora's corpus of Hittite seals includes a sketch drawing based on this photograph and a tentative reading.[3] Collation of the original seal in the Oriental Institute Museum (A 20551)[4] provides, I believe, an improved reading of the name.

Face A depicts a somewhat ill-designed animal, probably a lion, striding to the right (on the impression). Its long, curving tail is similar to that of lions depicted on other seals and the very schematic head seems to represent the open mouth of a roaring lion (so also Mora 1987, but Gelb [see note 2] thought the animal was a dog). Above the animal there is a large "filler" which resembles the floral motif L 152[5] (rather than a bird, as tentatively suggested by Mora). An additional large "filler" is between the animal's legs, and there is a smaller one in front of his chest. Face B has the name of the seal owner running from top to bottom, his title on the left, and the combination "WELL-BEING" and "MAN" on the right. It reads:

L 450—395—312—376; 289; 370; 386 = À-*nu*-VIR^{ZI} AURIGA; BONUS; VIR

"Anu-ziti; Charioteer; Well-being; Man." Two small "fillers" are on each side of the *zi*.

The first V-shaped sign (L 450) usually has its "arms" more closed (see e.g., Gonnet 1991:450), but it seems that the seal carver had difficulties in reproducing accurate signs.[6] The "*a*" vocalism is more often expressed on Anatolian seals with *a* (L 209) or *á* (L 19), but it is quite common on the Hittite seals from Meskene/Emar, especially in initial position.[7] The second sign has only seven strokes, one of them very poorly carved. Nevertheless, its identification with *nu* (L 395) is very probable. Quite often this sign appears with less than the "required" nine strokes, with eight or even with seven (Dinçol and Dinçol 1980:24, no. 8 with further refs.; Dinçol 1983:Taf. XXIII/23 A). AURIGA (L 289) is represented with a large rhomboid attached to two instead of the usual three vertical lines (representing the reins of a chariot). In short, both the inscription and the drawing seem to have been performed by a somewhat inexperienced seal engraver.

The name Anu-ziti is so far unattested, but both its elements are attested in Anatolian names (Laroche 1966:34, 324–25). The main interest of the seal is in the title or profession of the owner, "charioteer," which corresponds to cuneiform *kartappū*

The Hittite seal from Megiddo and impressions in clay (top). The diminutive seal bears a naturalistic design on one face and an inscription on the other. It is made of steatite (soapstone), an easily carved silicate commonly used for seals and other small objects.

(Laroche 1956:29ff.). As I tried to show in a prosopography of Takuḫ-linu of Ugarit (Singer 1983:9ff.), the title was born by official diplomats of Ḫatti and of vassal states. The office was originally connected with horses and chariots (hence the hieroglyphic sign representing reins). Some of the *kartappū* mentioned in texts from Ḫattuša and from Ugarit functioned as special deputies of their rulers in complicated diplomatic missions. For example, Zuzzu was involved in the negotiations preceding the royal marriage between Ramses II and a Hittite princess.[8] Diplomatic envoys were particularly active in the new bond between Ḫatti and Egypt after the signing of the Peace Treaty in 1258 BCE.

Megiddo was an important station on the diplomatic route between the two royal courts. A fragmentary Akkadian letter from Boğazköy demonstrates this with its two-fold mention of the town Makkittā (*KBo* 28.86; Singer 1988). The context leaves no doubt that this is Megiddo in the Jezreel Valley, frequented by Egyptian and Hittite messengers traveling between their respective courts. The text preserves the name of one Hittite messenger only partly, but it can plausibly be restored as Ti[li-Tešub], who is explicitly designated in an Ugaritic text as "the messenger who was sent to Egypt." From other texts we learn that the Hittite and the Egyptian diplomatic missions consisted each of several envoys, probably of different rank and qualification.[9] The best known Hittite connection with Megiddo is the exquisite Hittite ivory plaque found in the "treasury" of the palace in Area AA, now in the Oriental Institute Museum.[10] Stylistic and historical considerations point to a late imperial date for the plaque, coinciding with the heyday of Egyptian-Hittite cooperation in the second half of the thirteenth century BCE.[11] Anu-ziti's seal joins this constellation of indicators of the significance of Megiddo on the political map of the thirteenth century. Perhaps the renewed excavations at Megiddo will provide further evidence for the role of this city in the *Pax Hethitica–Egyptiaca*.

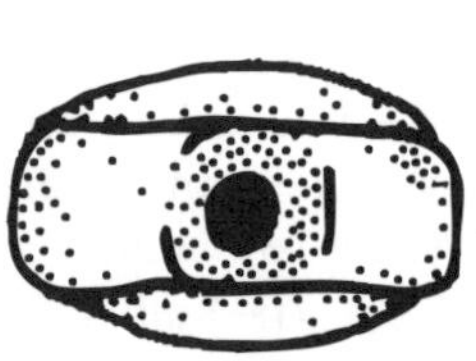

The 19 x 11 mm Hittite seal was a biconvex design with a center perforation.

Notes

[1] This is, so far, the only Hittite stamp seal found in a controlled excavation in Israel. Two silver ring seals were found at Tell el-Farah (Petrie 1930:pl. XXXVI; Macdonald, et al. 1932: pl. LXXIII: 58, 65 and p. 30) and one of bronze at Tel Nami (Singer 1994). In addition, a Hittite bulla was found at Tel Aphek (Singer 1977).

[2] "It belongs to the class of perforated button seals. One side is occupied by the name of the owner written in Hittite hieroglyphic characters, the other by a picture of a dog (or panther, according to Bossert) and a few symbols. The form of the seal, the signs, and the pictorial representations are typically Hittite. The seal most probably dates from the time of the Neo-Hittite Empire (i.e. , ca. 1400–1200 B.C.)."

[3] Mora 1987:266, XI 3. 4.: x?-ma/ i? - VIR?ZI AURIGA

[4] I am indebted to Dr. Emily Teeter and Dr. Raymond Tindel of the Oriental Institute Museum for facilitating my study of this seal and for providing me photographs and impressions, and to Ms. Kate Sarther for the drawing.

[5] L + number refers to the enumeration of hieroglyphic signs in Laroche (1960).

[6] There is a slight resemblance between this sign and the first sign on Ankara Museum 8 B, identified by the publishers as L 447, Na5 (Dinçol and Dinçol 1980:24, Taf. VIII), which is also followed by *nu*, but on our seal the first sign lacks the two "thorns" at the bottom.

[7] Laroche 1981:10; Gonnet 1991:212; Singer 2000: (À-pa-nú; À-pi-la-lu).

[8] *KUB* 21:38 obv. 22; Helck 1963:89. See now Edel (1994 II: 147 ff., 325, 335) for further occurrences of Zuzzu in the Hittite-Egyptian correspondence.

[9] For some of the Hittite missions to Egypt, see Singer (1977:187 n. 18).

[10] Loud 1939:10ff., pl. 11. For artistic evaluations see in particular Barnett (1982:28, 34 and fig. 12) and Alexander (1991). For the cultural-political context see Singer (1988/89), where I suggested an Egyptian ownership of this extraordinarily rich collection of *objets d'art*. (I have to correct now my statement in (1988/89:105), that the two figures at the head of the plaque are Hittite kings. Güterbock (1993) has convincingly demonstrated that the

Artist's rendering of the design of side A shows an animal—probably a poorly executed striding lion—with a long curving tail and open, roaring mouth. The opposite side bears the name of the seal owner—Anu-ziti—as well as his title, "charioteer," and the words "well-being," and "man." The title, "charioteer," marked Anu-ziti as a Hittite diplomatic envoy.

image topped by a winged disk can only represent the Sun-God of Heaven; see also Alexander [1991:164]).

[11] For the late imperial imagery see Alexander (1991:172 ff). Still unaware of my article (1988/89), Alexander (p. 182) mentions the possibility that the Hittite plaque reached Megiddo after the fall of the Hittite Empire. I consider this possibility as most unlikely.

Bibliography

Alexander, R. L.
1991 Šaušga and the Hittite Ivory from Megiddo. *Journal of Near Eastern Studies* 50:161–82.

Dinçol, A. M.
1983 Hethitische Hieroglyphensiegel in den Museen zu Adana, Hatay und Istanbul. *Anadolu Araş timalari/ Jahrbuch für Kleinasiatische Forschung* 9:173–249, Taf. 1–35.

Dinçol, A. M. and Dinçol, B.
1980 *Hethitische Hieroglyphensiegel im Museum für Anatolische Zivilisationen.* Ankara Turizmi, Eskieserleri ve Müzeleri Sevenler Dernegı Yayınları 10.

Edel, E.
1994 *Die ägyptisch-hethitische Korrespondenz aus Boghazköy in babylonischer und hethitischer Sprache.* Band I–II. Opladen: Westdeutscher Verlag.

Gonnet, H.
1991 Légendes des empreintes hiéroglyphiques anatoliennes. Pp. 198–214, pl. I–VII in *Textes syriens de l'Âge du Bronze Récent (Aula Orientalis-Supplementa)*, edited by D. Arnaud. Barcelona: AUSA.

Gorny, R.
1993 The Biconvex Seals of Alişar Höyük. *Anatolian Studies* 43:163–91.

Güterbock, H. G.
1993 Sungod or King? Pp. 225–26 in *Aspects of Art and Iconography: Anatolia and its Neighbors. Studies in Honor of Nimet Özgüç*, edited by M. Mellink, E. Porada, T. Özgüç. Ankara: Türk Tarih Kurumu Basımevi.

KBo
1916– *Keilschrifttexte aus Boghazköi.* Wissenschaftliche Veröffentlichungen der Deutschen Orient-Gesellschaft. Leipzig: J. C. Hinrichs.

KUB
1921– *Keilschrifturkunden aus Boghazköi.* Staatlich Museen zu Berlin, Vorderasiatische Abteilung. Berlin: Akademie Verlag.

Laroche, E.
1956 Noms de dignitaires. *Revue hittite et asianique* XIV/58:26–32.
1960 *Les hiéroglyphes hittites.* Paris: Éditions du Centre National de la Recherche Scientifique.
1966 *Les noms des Hittites.* Paris: Librairie C. Klincksieck.
1981 Les hiéroglyphes de Meskene-Emar et le style "syro-hittite". *Akkadica* 22:5–14.

Loud, G.
1939 *The Megiddo Ivories.* Oriental Institute Publications 52. Chicago: The Oriental Institute of the University of Chicago.
1948 *Megiddo II: Seasons of 1935–39.* Oriental Institute Publications 62. Chicago: The Oriental Institute of the University of Chicago Press.

Macdonald, E., Starkey, J. L., and Harding, L.
1932 *Beth-pelet II (Tell Fara).* London: British School of Archaeology in Egypt.

Mora, C.
1987 *La glittica Anatolica del II millennio A.C.: Classificazione Tipologica.* I. *I sigilli a iscrizione geroglifica.* Pavia: Gianni Iuculano Editore.

Neve, P.
1993 *Ḫattuša: Stadt der Götter und Tempel.* Mainz: Philipp von Zabern.

Itamar Singer is Professor of Hittitology and Ancient Near Eastern Cultures at Tel Aviv University. He received his doctoral degree in 1978 after studies at the Hebrew University, Tel Aviv University, and the University of Marburg. Dr. Singer has written widely on various aspects of Hittite religion, history, and culture as well as on other aspects of ancient Near Eastern history. He has been visiting scholar in many countries.

Petrie, W. M. F.
1930 *Beth-Pelet I (Tell Fara).* London: British School of Archaeology in Egypt.

Singer, I.
1977 A Hittite Hieroglyphic Seal Impression from Tel Aphek. *Tel Aviv* 4:178–90.
1983 Takuḫlinu and Ḫaya: Two Governors in the Ugarit Letter from Tel Aphek. *Tel Aviv* 10:3–25.
1988 Megiddo Mentioned in a Letter from Boğazköy. Pp. 327–32 in *Documentum Asiae Minoris Antiquae (Festschrift Heinrich Otten)*, edited by E. Neu and Ch. Rüster. Wiesbaden: Otto Harrassowitz.
1988/89 The Political Status of Megiddo VII A. *Tel Aviv* 15–16:101–12.
1994 A Hittite Signet Ring from Tel Nami. Pp. 189–93 in *kinattûtu ša dārâti (Raphael Kutscher Memorial Volume)*, edited by A. Rainey. Tel Aviv: Tel Aviv University, Institute of Archaeology.
2000 Hittite Sealings. Pp. 81–89 in *Cuneiform Inscriptions in the Collection of the Bible Lands Museum, Jerusalem: The Emar Tablets*, edited by J. Goodnick Westenholz. Groningen: Styx Publications.

An Urartian Ozymandias

Van Citadel with Toprakkale (Rusahinili) middle distance at left center. The citadel was the initial center of the Urartian Empire. Rusa II set up his throne at the newly founded Rusahinili.

By Paul Zimansky

No "half sunk, shattered visage" reminiscent of Shelley's Ozymandias has yet been found in the highland region around Lakes Van and Urmia,[1] but a forgotten potentate who could have commanded the mighty to look on his works and despair, is emerging from the mists of Anatolian history. A series of independent archaeological discoveries, some old and some quite recent, reveals that the most energetic instigator of building projects in the Iron Age Near East was a ruler who inspired no legends and about whom the written record tells us very little—Rusa II, the last great king of Urartu. The reputations of better known figures such as Solomon, Nebuchadnezzar, and the kings of Assyria rest on the enrichment of pre-existing sites or at best the foundation of a single capital. Rusa, however, built new fortress cities all over his realm, each instance involving manpower, technical skill, and matériel on a scale that the better known figures would be hard pressed to match.

The kingdom that Rusa controlled in the second quarter of the seventh century BCE stretched across the mountainous terrain of eastern Anatolia approximately eight hundred miles from east to west and five hundred from north to south (Kleiss and Hauptmann 1976). Much of this territory was sparsely populated and best suited for pasturage. Urartian settlement was concentrated in pockets beside the lake shores and in isolated locations where river valleys broadened sufficiently to permit intensive cultivation of the alluvium through irrigation. A highly integrated network of fortresses and roads bound these focal points together (Zimansky 1985).

By the time Rusa came to the throne, Urartu had weathered the repeated attacks of the powerful Assyrian Empire for a century and a half. Its artisans had generated their own distinctive style, which can be seen on thousands of surviving bronze and stone artifacts. Its rulers had set up hundreds of monuments

Fragment of stele inscribed with the Annals of Sarduri II, Van Museum. Rusa II left no annals comparable to his eighth-century predecessors. *All photographs courtesy of Paul Zimansky.*

Bulla from Bastam with inscription mentioning Rusa II's building activities at Toprakkale. The text reads: "The same year Rusa, the son of Arghisti, set up the throne in Rusahinili Qilbanikai. Boards and carpenters xx-ed. Rusa(i)-URU.TUR, land of Alaa'ni."

bearing cuneiform inscriptions in the Urartian language. Urartian kings waged annual military campaigns, rounding up booty and captives by the thousands from neighboring populations. They ordained sacrifices of countless animals to a populous pantheon, presided over by a god, Haldi, who seems closely identified with the state (Piotrovsky 1969; Wartke 1993). Much construction had also been undertaken: in addition to fortresses, roads, irrigation projects, their dedicatory inscriptions speak of temples, cult sites, storehouses, and specialized structures whose function is not understood.

While the creative accomplishments of Urartian civilization have been recognized since the nineteenth century, we would have no conception of the personal importance of Rusa II without the testimony of recent archaeological excavations. In fact, other sources of evidence consigned him to obscurity. The dynamics of Urartian history have generally been interpreted through the written record, much of which comes from biased Assyrian reports. The Assyrians are most informative about Urartu in the late ninth and eighth centuries, but singularly laconic in the seventh. The texts of the Urartians themselves, particularly building inscriptions, have nearly the same temporal distribution. Taken together, these historical sources point to 714 BCE as a time of crisis and shift in Urartu's fortunes.

In that year, Sargon II of Assyria invaded Urartu, sending his armies through five Urartian provinces on a mission of destruction. This is the best documented campaign in Assyrian history, thanks to a poetic and lengthy "letter" to the god Aššur, now the pride of the tablet collection of the Louvre (Thureau-Dangin 1912). Here Sargon reported on his actions, apparently quite soon after his return. Although he makes no mention of it in the letter, Sargon's attack appears to have been undertaken when Urartu was reeling from another defeat that was probably even more devastating: the warlike Cimmerians made their first appearance in history by routing Urartian forces and killing a large number of governors in the process. We learn of this not from any public claim, but from letters transmitting intelligence gathered by spies along the Assyrian/ Urartian border to Sargon's court.

The sense that Urartu suffered serious damage at this time is reinforced by Urartian records themselves—not so much in what they say, but by a sharp drop in the number of inscriptions. Most of the documents that survive from Urartu are not clay tablets, but display inscriptions carved in stone, virtually all of which were royally commissioned. They are generally stylized and repetitive. The majority are building inscriptions on blocks that were set into the architecture of structures such as temples, storehouses, and fortresses. Others were written on living rock to record victories in a specific campaign. The latter are particularly useful in gauging the extent of the Empire and understanding something of its historical geography. In essence, Urartian texts appear to act as something of a barometer of royal fortunes. Around 714 BCE, the barometer fell.

Thus, to earlier generations of scholars, it appeared that Urartu's era of greatness was the eighth century, after which the kingdom was more or less in eclipse. To be sure, there are enough seventh-century Urartian inscriptions to make it clear that Urartu survived. Argišti II, the immediate predecessor of Rusa II, actually left monuments farther to the east than any other king. Roughly a dozen inscriptions of Rusa II were found. Post-dating these, several isolated royal display inscriptions were carved in the name of third, rather obscure Rusa, who calls himself the son of Erimena. This is a modest corpus compared to the scores of inscriptions associated with each eighth century ruler, and there are no elaborate annals, such as those of Argišti I or Sarduri II, recording military campaigns.

Archaeological evidence, however, rescues the reputation of Rusa II and dramatically counters the notion that Urartu slipped into an irreversible decline after Sargon's attack. The discoveries came so gradually that their overall import has hardly attracted comment along the way, but it is now clear that Rusa II brought Urartu to a level of architectural magnificence that none of

Bastam from the south. The main fortress is on the ridge in the center of the photograph, to the right of which, below the saddle connecting it to the next ridge, structures of the settlement are visible.

his predecessors attained. Some of the clues to his importance have been known for decades; others are still coming from the ground. The key fact is that there are now five sites founded by Rusa II, each one of major significance. Rusa seems to have done as much building as all of the other Urartian kings put together.

Toprakkale/Rusahinili Qilbanikai

The first of Rusa's enclaves to become known archaeologically was Toprakkale, a fortress on the outskirts of modern Van and the first Urartian site ever excavated. In this case, the issue was not the importance of the site, but the identity of its founder. Urartian inscriptions are generally clear on who built what, giving both the name of the king and his patronymic. Here, however, the evidence is circumstantial. The citadel rock at Van, which lies some 5 km to the west of Toprakkale, was the original center of the Empire, and beside it stood the capital city of Tušpa. Toprakkale is a more defensible site, and it was long believed that the reverses of the late eighth century caused the Urartians to build there to give their Empire a more secure center of government.

The ancient name of Toprakkale, Rusahinili, indicates that it had been built by a king Rusa, and the logic of this argument was that this should refer to Rusa I, Sargon's opponent and the grandfather of Rusa II. A broken inscription found at site of Keşiş Göl, which mentioned an irrigation project to provide water to Tušpa and Rusahinili, was for a long time attributed to Rusa I, but only because it was erroneously assumed to join another block, which bore the name of that king. This identification has now been rejected. New inscriptions have emerged that demonstrate that Rusa II both set up his throne in Rusahinili and moved the god Haldi there, so it seems almost certain that he was also the founder of this Rusahinili. None of the many artifacts found at Toprakkale can be dated to the eighth century (Zimansky 1985:77–78), but several bear inscriptions of Rusa II and other seventh century kings.

Karmir Blur/City of Teisheba

The "City of Teisheba" was the second major site of Rusa to be discovered and is securely identified by a building inscription found *in situ*. Located at modern Karmir Blur, on the outskirts of Erevan, in the Armenian Republic, this is the kind of site archaeologists dream about: violently destroyed and rich in well-preserved remains. Although most of its inhabitants seem to have been spared when the fortress was put to the torch, the collapsing walls created a level of debris meters thick. These nearly

Basalt pylons in palace of Rusa at Kef Kalesi.

Relief of gate-protecting deity from Adilcevaz. Van Museum.

anaerobic conditions enabled biological materials as well as luxury goods to survive. The complete ground plan of the citadel has been unearthed and the functions of the 150 rooms can be determined by their inventories. There were eight wine magazines, each with scores of pithoi large enough for a person to crawl into. The excavator estimates the total storage capacity at 9000 gallons of wine and 750 tons of grain (Piotrovsky 1969:133). There is also an associated town containing houses of both the lower strata of society and the elite (Piotrovski 1969:177–78). Like Toprakkale, Karmir Blur offered cuneiform tablets which show that it was directly administered by the Urartian king (Zimansky 1985:80–84).

Bastam/Rusai-URU.TUR

Around the turn of the century, an inscription in which Rusa II claimed to have built a place called "Rusa's Small City" (Rusai-URU.TUR) was found in a secondary context, built into a bridge in the village of Kasyan, in northwest Iran. In 1968, Wolfram Kleiss of the German Archaeological Institute in Teheran discovered the site to which this referred beside the nearby village of Bastam. Despite its name, Rusai-URU.TUR is one of the largest Urartian enclaves known (Kleiss 1983: 283–84).

"Rusa's Small City" was constructed on a steep spur of rock that controls access to a plain watered by the Aq Chay. The entire eminence was fortified from plain level to summit, the difference in elevation being such that each day it took the German excavation teams half an hour to climb to their trenches from their base camp near the Urartian settlement below. The lower settlement was an extensive city that stretched out for nearly a kilometer along a wadi. Everywhere, the remains speak of architectural magnificence. Again, there are enormous areas of the site given over to storerooms, only a few of which were cleared by the time the Iranian revolution brought the excavations to a close. The stone foundations of the walls, which are still visible from miles away, are grounded on special footings carved into the bedrock, which must have required thousands of human-years of labor to prepare. The small finds at Bastam are not particularly rich, probably because those who conquered the site had the good sense to wait until after they had pillaged it before setting it ablaze. Nevertheless, excavators unearthed more administrative tablets, as well as countless bullae bearing the royal seal of Rusa II (Kleiss 1979, 1988).

Kef Kalesi

A fourth site of unusual prominence was discovered near the north shore of Lake Van in the 1950s and excavated by a Turkish team led by Emin Bilgiç and Baki Öğün (1964). Once again, an inscription in its secondary context provided the key to recognizing the site's prominence. Surveyors found the stone near the village of Adilcevaz in a retaining wall that had slipped into Lake Van (Burney and Lawson 1958). The Adilcevaz inscription mentioned that Rusa had imported captives from the west and settled them here. On the high ground well back from the lake, Charles Burney identified a major citadel at Kef Kalesi, and the Turkish excavators later uncovered a palace and fortress complex. Sculpted pylons, some of which bear inscriptions of Rusa II, make it clear that this was the site from which the Adilcevaz inscription originated, along with some of the fine pieces of Urartian relief sculpture that were found with it.

Ayanis/Rusahinili Eidurukai

Since 1989, Altan A. Çilingiroğlu and a team from Ege University (Izmir) have been excavating perhaps the richest of Rusa's creations. Ayanis, ancient Rusahinili Eidurukai, is located on a rocky outcrop overlooking the eastern shore of Lake Van. The heart of the fortress is a lavishly furnished pillared court, in which there is a well-preserved temple decorated with stone inlay. Carved on the temple's facade is a lengthy inscription, which lists numerous works of Rusa and relates that captives of many of the surrounding lands, including Hatti, Tabal, Mushki (Phyrgia) and Assyria, were brought here when the fortress was created. Each season, more of the extensive magazines and storerooms in the fortress are uncovered, revealing bronzes, bullae, and wall paintings. An extensive settlement containing both public buildings and private houses surrounded the citadel (Çilingiroğlu and Salvini 2001).

In sum, Rusa II gave his name to three fortress complexes—Bastam, Toprakkale, and Ayanis—and founded at least two others of significant size—Kef Kalesi near Adilcevaz and Karmir Blur. These are among the largest and richest Urartian sites. No other Urartian king is known to have created more than one enclave on this scale, and none named more than one site after himself. Something extraordinary was going on during Rusa's reign.

If Rusa was the commanding figure his architectural works suggest, why did he make so little impression on posterity? We know nothing about his personality: there is no portrait, no anecdotal material, no reference to him in Greek historiography or the Bible. Two factors may help to explain this paradox. In the first place, none of the great works of Rusa survived very long after his reign. Secondly, the Urartian Empire itself was structured in such a way that its culture was ephemeral and its legacy unlikely to be transmitted to posterity. Both of these hypotheses require some elaboration, and both are dependent upon recently won archaeological evidence.

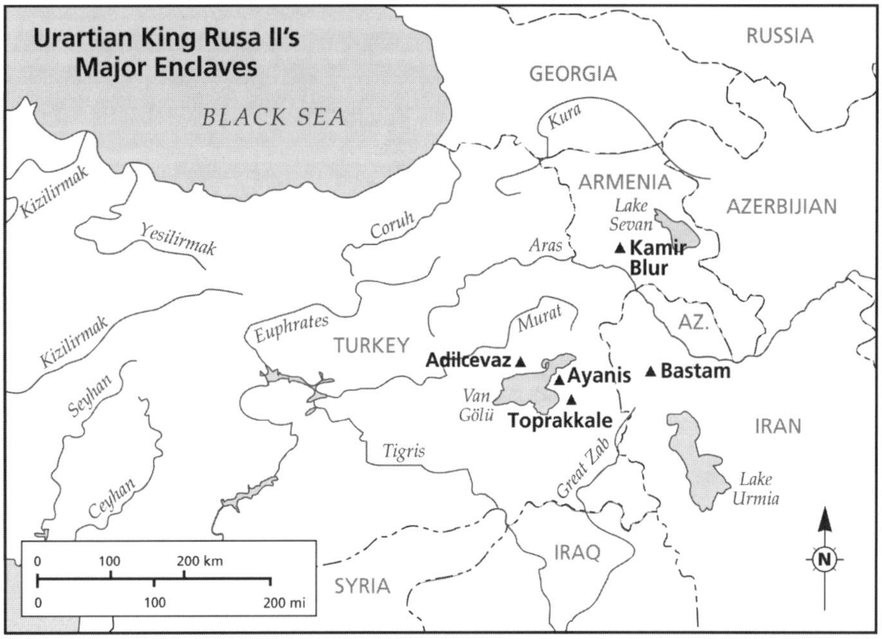

Principal sites known to have been founded by Rusa II. This volume of construction makes Rusa II one of the ancient Near East's greatest builders.

Let us first consider the question of how long the kingdom lasted after Rusa. Until quite recently, the standard answer was that a biblical reference (Jer 51:27) and Neo-Babylonian chronicles proved Urartu was still a power until around 590 BCE. Greek historians record that the Medes were in control of eastern Anatolia by 585 BCE, so there is no possibility of an Urartian kingdom after that.

Stephan Kroll (1984) has recently challenged this sixth century date on the basis of several strands of evidence, the most compelling of which come from excavations at Bastam. There, in several rooms, excavators found the bones of thousands of animals in association with bullae

Royal bulla with the seal of Rusa II from bone rooms at Bastam help with determining the duration of the Urartian kingdom. Thousands of animal bones were found in association with bullae bearing Rusa II's seal. Similar mysterious collections of bones were found at Toprakkale and Karmir Blur. Whatever their genesis, the bones at Bastam were clearly deposited in Rusa II's time and not added to by any subsequent Urartian royalty. Thus the destruction of the city occurred during Rusa II's reign. Allowing about a decade for two obscure successors, the kingdom of Urartu probably dissipated by ca. 640 BCE.

Entrance to staircase cut into living rock on citadel at Toprakkale.

impressed with the seal of Rusa II. A few other sealings with names that sound royal—names that others have argued belonged to late Urartian kings—also came from the same context, but they constitute only a small percentage of the evidence. These sealings were peculiar in that they all had the same iconography, which differed from a royal seal. The owners were given a title, ^{lú}A.NIN-*li*, which may mean "prince," but certainly does not mean "king." Kroll has interpreted the bone assemblages as meat storage of some form, and since there is little likelihood that meat would be kept for decades, the citadel had to have been destroyed in the reign of Rusa II (Kroll 1984:157). Since there is no evidence that the other persons named on the bullae ever ruled, most of these putative later kings now appear simply to have been members of Rusa II's royal family.

Kroll dismissed the other evidence for a prolonged existence of Urartu: the references in Neo-Babylonian chronicles of 609 and 608 BCE were to a geographical region, not a kingdom, and Jeremiah contains many other anachronisms, quite incompatible with its ostensible date of 594 BCE (Kroll 1984:165–8). Allowing for the existence of two obscure Urartian kings after Rusa—Rusa son of Erimena and a Sarduri, who is mentioned by Assurbanipal—Toprakkale and Karmir may have outlasted Bastam by a decade or so, but the kingdom of Urartu was essentially gone by around 640 BCE (Kroll 1984:170).

Having taken part in the excavation of the bones at Bastam myself, I cannot agree with Kroll's interpretation of these as meat storage rooms. The bones were simply too fragmentary, too closely packed, too burned, and too disarticulated to have had flesh upon them when the citadel was destroyed. I believe that the bones themselves were being kept, perhaps because leftovers from the king's meals were tabooed in some way (Zimansky 1988).

In any case, neither the evidence nor my interpretation of it invalidates Kroll's basic point about chronology. Whatever the reason the bones were in these rooms, they were put there in the time of Rusa II and no other king either added to them or removed them. The royal activity that created these assemblages was clearly practiced on a grand scale in Rusa's time. Similar rooms full of bones were found at both Toprakkale and Karmir Blur. If, as seems likely, they were associated with an essential Urartian institution or ideology, one would expect later kings to be represented as well. Although this does not constrict the time frame as tightly as the meat storage hypothesis, Rusa II was in all probability the last ruler of any consequence at Bastam.

The Urartian kingdom was thoroughly destroyed, not simply taken over. None of the great foundations of Rusa II were reoccupied and their toppled mud brick walls soon decayed into amorphous mounds of soil. In the absence of historical records, the agents of Urartu's demise cannot be identified with certainty. The traditional date would implicate the Medes, whereas the earlier one would give a larger role to the Scythians—a nonsedentary people whose reputation in Asia Minor is rather like that of the Cimmerians. If the Medes inherited the territory after a hiatus of some decades, there was little possibility of any direct transmission of institutions and historical memories. We know almost nothing about the Median Empire, except what Greek historians like Herodotus tell us. Their presumption that it had the same sort of structure as the later Achaemenid Empire—which might well have coopted Urartian administrative mechanisms—is highly suspect (Sancisi-Weerdenburg 1988). When Xenophon passed through Urartian territory in 401 BCE, ethnic groups such as the Kurds and the Armenians were prominent, and there was little to remind him of Urartu or its greatest builder.

Another reason that Rusa was so quickly forgotten has to do with the nature of the Urartian cultural tradition. What we really see in the Urartian assemblage is a set of styles, artifacts, and features that pertain to a military elite, rather than to a broad spectrum of the population. The best known Urartian sites are fortresses, and the most characteristic artifacts are bronzes, particularly pieces of royally dedicated equipment. The Urartian religion appears to be a state religion (Salvini 1989), and the god Haldi, who stood at the head of the pantheon, vanishes with the Urartian state. Urartian writing, as noted above, is almost entirely royal.

There obviously was a popular culture, or perhaps a variety of popular cultures within the state. Somebody spoke Urartian, obviously, but there was plenty of room in the interstices of this society for other groups like the Manneans, Kurds, and Armenians to have their own traditions. When the elite government was swept away, presumably by the Scythian invaders in the late seventh century, no unity persisted underneath.

So "nothing beside remains." The memory of Rusa perished, lost not in "lone and level sands," but in the folded terrain around Mt. Ararat. Posterity, at least in the West, has been more impressed by the works of Oriental potentates whose construction projects are more imagined than real, such as those of Semiramis, Ramses, and Solomon. Sargon will be remembered as founder of Khorsabad, even though he never finished it and his efforts at that single site were no greater than Rusa's at Bastam alone. When it comes to creating legends by architectural accomplishment in a land of mud brick and stone, the written word is clearly mightier than the trowel. The imprint of Rusa's majesty and the grandeur of the kingdom he commanded in its latter days survive nevertheless in the soil. It is to archaeologists that he must entrust the restoration of his reputation.

Note

[1] Shelley's poem ends: "And on the pedestal these words appear:/'My name is Ozymandias, king of kings;/Look on my works, ye mighty, and despair,'/ Nothing beside remains./Round the decay/Of that colossal wreck, boundless and bare,/The lone and level sands stretch far away."

Bibliography

Azarpay, G.
1968 *Urartian Art and Artifacts: A Chronological Study*. Berkeley and Los Angeles: University of California.

Barnett, R. D.
1950 The Excavation of the British Museum at Toprak Kale, near Van. *Iraq* 12:1–43

Bilgiç, E. and Ögün, B.
1964 1964 Adilcevaz Kef Kalesi Kazıları [Excavations at Kef Kalesi of Adilcevaz, 1964]. *Anadolu (Anatolia)* 8:65–120.

Burney, C. A.
1957 Urartian Fortresses and Towns in the Van Region. *Anatolian Studies* 7:37–53.

Burney, C. A. and Lang, D. M.
1971 *The Peoples of the Hills: Ancient Ararat and Caucasus*. London: Weidenfeld & Nicholson.

Burney, C. A. and Lawson, G. R.
1958 Urartian Reliefs at Adılcevaz on Lake Van, and a Rock Relief from the Karasu near Birecik. *Anatolian Studies* 8:211–18.

Çilingiroğlu, Altan A. and Mirjo Salvini, eds.
2001 *Ayanis I: Ten Years' Excavations at Rusahinili Eiduru-kai 198-1998*. Documenta Asiana VI. Rome: CNR Isitutuo per gli Studi Micenei ed Egeo-Anatolici.

Diakonoff, I. M.
1984 *The Pre-History of the Armenian People*. Translated by L. Jennings. Delmar, NY: Caravan Books.

Haas, V., ed.
1986 *Das Reich Urartu: Ein altortientalische Symposien*. Xenia: Konstanzer althistorische Vorträge und Forschungen 17. Konstanz: Universitätsverlag Konstanz.

Kleiss, W.
1983 Größenvergleiche urartäischer Bergen und Siedlungen. Pp. 283–90 in *Beiträge zur Altertumskunde Kleinasiens: Festschrift für Kurt Bittel*, vol. 1, edited by R. M. Boehmer and H. Hauptmann. Mainz am Rhein: Philipp von Zabern.
1988 *Bastam II*. Teheraner Forschungen 5. Berlin: Mann.

Kleiss, W., Hauptmann, H. et al.
1976 *Topographische Karte von Urartu*. Archäologische Mitteilungen aus Iran Ergänzungsband 3. Berlin: Dietrich Reimer.

König, F. W.
1955–57 *Handbuch der chaldischen Inschriften*. 2 vols. Archiv für Orientforschung 8. Graz: E. Weidner.

Paul Zimansky received his Ph.D. from the University of Chicago in 1980 and since 1983 has taught in the Department of Archaeology at Boston University where he is an Associate Professor. He has excavated at Nippur (Ira), Bastam (Iran), and 'Ain Dara (Syria). Most recently he has directed excavations at Tell Hamide in northern Iraq and served as co-director of the Tell Abu Duwari project in southern Iraq. He is author of *Ecology and Empire: The Structure of the Urartian State* (Chigago 1985).

Kroll, S.
1976 *Keramik urartäischer Festungen in Iran*. Archäologische Mitteilungen aus Iran, Ergänzungsband 2. Berlin: Dietrich Reimer Verlag.
1984 Urartus Untergang in anderer Sicht. *Istanbuler Mitteilungen* 34:151–70.

van Loon, M. N.
1966 *Urartian Art: Its Distinctive Traits in the Light of New Excavations*. Istanbul: Nederlands Historisch-Archaeologisch Instituut.

Melikisvili, G. A.
1960 *Urartskie klinoobraznye nadpisi*. Moscow: Izdatel'stvo Akademii Nauk SSSR.

Piotrovsky, B. B.
1969 *The Ancient Civilization of Urartu*. Translated by J. Hogarth. Geneva: Nagel.

Salvini, M.
1989 Le panthéon de l'Urartu et le fondement de l'état. *Studi epigrafici e liguistici sul Vicino Oriente antico* 6:79–89.

Sancisi-Weerdenburg, H.
1988 Was There Ever a Median Empire. Pp. 197–212 in *Achaemenid History III. Method and Theory*, edited by A. Kuhrt and H. Sancisi-Weerdenburg. Lieden: E. J. Brill.

Sevin, Veli
1988 The Oldest Highway; Between the Two Regions of Van and Elazığ. *Antiquity* 62/236:547–51.

Thureau-Dangin, F.
1912 *Une relation de la huitième campagne de Sargon*, Textes cunéformes du Louvre 3. Paris: Paul Geuthner.

Wartke, R.-B.
1993 *Urartu: Das Reich am Ararat.* Kulturgeschichte der antiken Welt 59. Mainz: Philipp von Zabern.

Zimansky, P.
1985 *Ecology and Empire: The Structure of the Urartian State*. Chicago: Oriental Institute of the University of Chicago.
1988 MB2/OB5 Excavations and the Problem of Urartian Bone Rooms. Pp. 107–24 in *Bastam II*, edited by W. Kleiss. Teheraner Forschungen 5. Berlin: Mann.

King or God? Imperial Iconography and the "Tiarate Head" Coins of Achaemenid Anatolia

By Elspeth R. M. Dusinberre

The Achaemenid Persian Empire (ca. 550–331 BCE), founded by Cyrus II (the Great), centered on southwest Iran and lower Mesopotamia. Under Darius I (521–486 BCE) it reached its greatest extent, stretching from the Indus River to the Aegean Sea, from Egypt to the modern Central Asian Republics. The Empire encompassed within its boundaries people of many different backgrounds, speaking diverse languages, worshiping multiple deities, living in tremendously varied environments, and practicing widely differing social customs. The challenge for the Achaemenid dynasty was to devise a method of hegemony that would allow these various peoples to function within the conscripts of the new imperial authority. Its task was to devise a system of empire flexible enough to provide for the needs of different peoples and cultural landscapes and to ensure their ability to operate as part of the vast and complex new Empire.[1] Even as the Achaemenid dynasty laid out bureaucracies and put administrative networks into effect, so too it established programs to support and promulgate the ideology of the Empire.

These programs included the manipulation of artistic imagery to bear meaning within an imperial context in ways sufficiently flexible to convey significance to widely disparate local viewing audiences. In peripheral areas with different artistic customs than those of the Persian heartland, traditional local images were reworked to promote imperial ideologies. Official imperial iconography was translated into regional artistic syntaxes to make it intelligible to local viewing audiences. This adaptation of images had a self-reflexive function as well, for the appropriation and manipulation of local iconographies and styles signified the incorporation of these areas into the Empire. By taking on and adapting traditional local imagery, the Achaemenid elite might embed themselves in an artistic framework that reinforced their own goals or sense of authority and power in those regions. Thus the reworking of older imagery displayed multiple levels of significance: spreading imperial ideology to distant parts of the Empire, asserting power over those areas, and incorporating local imagery into official imperial art.

The Nature of the Inquiry

Much of the artwork known to us from Achaemenid Anatolia does not come from scientific excavations. In particular, objects such as seals or coins have tended to appear on the art market without any secure information concerning their provenance, let alone their archaeological context. But because of ongoing archaeological work at Achaemenid-period sites in Anatolia and study of excavated material from the Achaemenid heartland capitals at Pasargadae and Persepolis, the artistic styles and imagery of the western regions of the Achaemenid empire may now be placed within their broader cultural contexts. We can begin to examine "floating" artifacts with a sense of the society in which they functioned.

In this paper, I will first explore some of the developments seen in sculptural and glyptic art at Persepolis at the end of the sixth and beginning of the fifth centuries BCE. Having examined these artistic movements at the center of the Empire, I will then consider how this material may inform our analysis of a particular much-discussed series of coins from Achaemenid Anatolia, the so-called "tiarate head" series. The analytical model used to examine the material from Persepolis may help us ground our study of Achaemenid coins, providing them not with their lost archaeological context but at least with an archaeologically-founded basis for further discussion.

The Achaemenid kings manipulated artistic imagery to equate themselves visually with previous renditions of divinities, reworking iconography in different parts of the Empire to conform to local artistic traditions and milieux. Thus, whereas in Mesopotamia new Achaemenid renderings draw on ancient Mesopotamian traditions of portrayal of deities, in western Anatolia they reflect instead Greek visions of godhead.

An Art of Empire

The official imperial iconography of the Achaemenid Empire was a calculated and refined hybrid of the various imperial and religious images of bygone Mesopotamian powers.[2] It focused on the figure of the king, producing images of an Empire in joyous support and recognition of a king who was visually equated with previous representations of divine figures.[3] This equation of the kingly figure with traditional divine representa-

Aerial view of Persepolis. From Schmidt (1953: pl. 1).

tions was a radical twist to earlier Near Eastern imagery. The significance of the figure encompassed a blend of meanings: he is a superhuman figure; he is a king; he is the Persian hero, a sort of everyman figure. The image portrayed no specific individual, but rather functioned as an embodiment of stable kingship rooted in age-old traditions. The strong visual connections to earlier portrayals of deities lay at the heart of this sense.

I will briefly address here four distinct artistic images from the Persian capital at Persepolis. In each case, the iconography reworked earlier customs, literally setting the figure of the Persian King in positions that in traditional Near Eastern imagery had been occupied exclusively by gods and personifications of cosmic forces. The first three images I will examine belonged to the imperial sculptural program at Persepolis. These reliefs have been discussed and interpreted already by M. C. Root (1979); but material subsequently available for analysis allows us to reconsider her work and the interpretation of these sculptural representations. I will address this new material in my analysis of a fourth image. The artistic material preserved in the form of seal impressions on the Persepolis Fortification tablets opens up an entire new arena of evidence in our consideration of Achaemenid iconography. The addition of this new image set to the sculpted reliefs previously available for study lets us press further our understanding of the significance of Achaemenid representations of kingship (for greater detail, see Dusinberre 1979a, 1976b).

The Apadana reliefs from Persepolis showed processions of peoples from twenty-three subject lands of the empire, bearing gifts and advancing towards a figure of the king enthroned.[4] The imagery of the Apadana reliefs were strongly invested with religious overtones, due to the use of particular Mesopotamian tropes such as the hand-over-wrist gesture (Root 1979:227–84). The

The King enthroned. Treasury. From Schmidt (1953: pl. 121).

significance of leading a petitioner forward by the hand was absolutely critical in the Apadana representations. The image of pious petitioners brought before enthroned authority derived simultaneously from antique Mesopotamian scenes of presentation to deities and from Egyptian portrayals of presentation before Osiris for judgment in the Underworld. But at Persepolis, we see the figure of the king in the traditional position of the deity, lending the image a new multivalent meaning of simultaneous kingship and divinity within a context of universal empire.

Another key image was that of the archetypal hero figure combating monstrous adversaries, found in certain door jambs at Persepolis. Although this figure may have represented an entirely distinct hero figure, it is far more likely that it was the king as archetypal "Persian man," as Darius called himself in an inscription (see below and Root 1979:303–8 with references). In some instances, the hero grappled with lions and bulls; in others, he combated fabulous monsters with lions' bodies but also horns, wings, scorpion tails, eagle claws, and sometimes birds' heads. Here the hero figure was taken out of the realm of the human world. Ancient Mesopotamian precedents show genii or Gilgameš figures grappling with lions or fantastic composite monsters. Assyrian iconography never showed kings combating monsters, but rather preserved the critical distinction that they struggle only with real animals like lions, bulls, or ostriches. Achaemenid imagery, however, drew from this antique imagery of the supernatural world. The Persian hero-king was visually equated with divine figures.

A similar visual process may be recognized in the image of the king on high, supported by figures who hold him aloft above their heads. The words of Darius I help to interpret this image.

> If now thou shalt think that "how many are the countries which King Darius held?" look at the sculptures (of those) who bear the throne, then thou shalt know, then shall it become known to thee: the spear of a Persian man has gone forth far; then shall it become known to thee: a Persian man has delivered battle far indeed from Persia (DNb: see Kent 1953; Lecoq 1997).

The Achaemenid representation of the King carried by the peoples of the realm reproduces ancient Mesopotamian and Egyptian images of subject peoples, but with an important difference: these subjects retain their harmony and support the figure of the King as if willingly (Root 1979:131–61). Moreover, the image of the King held aloft resonates with religious tones. The "Atlas" posture of the figures carrying the King is universally associated before the Achaemenid period with cosmic celebration/uplifting. A similar metaphor of an enthroned figure borne aloft by rejoicing subjects is expressed poetically in the biblical Psalm 22:3: "Yet Thou (Yahweh) art holy, enthroned on the praises of Israel." The image of the Achaemenid King is a polysemous image, an image that retools the past and reconfigures the new dynast so as to cloak him in ancient images of history and worship.

New Material Evidence: The Persepolis Fortification Tablets

Root (1979) stopped short of an emphatic statement that the artistic program at Persepolis presents the King as a divine figure.

Persian hero combating horned lion-headed monster. Palace of Darius. From Schmidt (1953: pl. 145A).

Persian hero combating horned lion-headed monster. Throne Hall. From Schmidt (1953: pl. 114A).

But the seal impressions on the Persepolis Fortification tablets, only now available for study, represent a vast corpus of glyptic art that lets us alter and refine our interpretation of Achaemenid art (see Garrison and Root 2001). The discovery on the Fortification tablets of seal impressions demonstrating the same concept of King as divine figure—this time translated into the artistic language of glyptic representation—is exciting in itself. More than that, their existence presses Root's interpretation further and clarifies the true force behind the sculptural representations at Persepolis.

The Oriental Institute's excavations at Persepolis in the early 1930s exposed, in addition to architecture adorned with sculpted reliefs, two archives of sealed tablets: the Persepolis Treasury tablets and the Persepolis Fortification tablets. Erich Schmidt published seventy-seven seal impressions on the former in 1957. Richard Hallock published the texts of over 2,087 tablets from the Fortification archive in 1969. Scholars at the University of Michigan and Trinity University are currently engaged in publication of the more than 1,400 ancient seals known through multiple impressions ratifying these Fortification tablets.[5]

Excavators unearthed the Fortification tablets in two small chambers, possibly archival rooms, at the northeast corner of the fortification wall surrounding the Persepolis terrace (Herzfeld 1941, 1934; Hallock 1973; Schmidt 1957; Sami 1955; Britt Tilia 1978; Garrison and Root 2001). The clay tablets record the disbursal of foodstuffs during the years 509–494 BCE from the royal storehouses in the regions of Fars and Elam to various people from different geographical and social backgrounds, including members of the royal family, courtiers, priests, administrators, artists, and agricultural workers. The tablets often include date formulae and are usually ratified by the seals of the individuals or offices named in the texts, impressed on the clay of the tablet. The Persepolis Fortification documents and their seal impressions thus provide an enormous corpus of glyptic evidence, in which the use of specific seals is linked to texts that also document crucial information on the personnel involved in transactions. The seals of both recipients and suppliers appear on these documents; the tablets and sealings document a broad cross-section of people who received food supplies, as well as officials of the bureaucracy involved in the transactions. This range of social backgrounds represented in the archive makes it of particular use in considering the social significance of the various developments evident in the glyptic art preserved, including both iconographic and stylistic phenomena.

The Persepolis Fortification sealings include yet another example of the equation of King with the divine. (For greater detail see Dusinberre 1997a). The impressions show a kingly figure wearing a crenelated crown, combating or controlling animals or monsters, and standing on animals that serve as pedestals under his feet. Artistically, the concept of animals acting as pedestals that carry aloft a divinity is an ancient one in the Near East. Divine figures standing on animals that represent essential qualities of the divinity are a well-known tradition in Mesopotamian and eastern Anatolian art. Similarly, in Egypt the divine ruler (Pharaoh) is sometimes depicted standing on pedestal animals. Before the Achaemenid period, such supporting animals seem to have been the representational prerogative solely of divinities. Under the patronage of the early Achaemenids, however, glyptic artists adapted this imagery to express the complex concept of a king (see illustration on page 162). This additional evidence in the

The king on high. Council Hall (left) and throne hall (right). From Schmidt (1953: pl. 78A [left] and 107 [right]).

Fortification sealings demonstrates again the fundamental importance in imperial Achaemenid iconography of the King portrayed occupying a position traditionally reserved for a deity. The images preserved on the Fortification tablets reveal the translation of the same concept into the artistic vocabulary of widely disparate artistic milieux: sculpted reliefs on royal walls and the glyptic art of the seals individuals used to ratify documents.

Artistic Circles at Persepolis

One of the most interesting, and perhaps surprising, features of the Fortification corpus is the concurrent use of many different glyptic styles (Garrison 1988, 1990). The simultaneity of these manifold styles demonstrates several important points about the meanings and uses of artistic style in the Persian heartland. At Persepolis, multiple artistic workshops operated at once. The patrons of these artists had a broad range of styles from which to choose when selecting seals for personal or official use. These circumstances at Persepolis may shed light in turn on the multiple artistic styles in use through the Empire, deriving from local workshops serving a particular clientele, and to some extent being cross-fertilized by distinctively regional artistic traditions (see Dusinberre 2002).

Garrison's seminal study on the various artistic styles represented in the seals preserved on the Fortification tablets characterized eight significant stylistic categories (1988, Garrison and Root 2001). The Modeled Style is a direct outgrowth and continuation of traditional Neo-Assyrian and Neo-Babylonian modeled styles. The Fortification Style represents an active local tradition in glyptic art—previously not recognized in other parts of the Empire—thriving at Persepolis at the end of the sixth/beginning of the fifth centuries BCE. The Court Style is that style traditionally associated with Achaemenid glyptic art, perhaps best represented in the impressions on the Persepolis Treasury tablets. The label derives from Boardman (1970b) who, though he did not analyze the style in detail, used the term to describe a class of Achaemenid seals that he thought showed iconographic connections to architectural relief sculpture at Persepolis (see also Schmidt 1957). In addition to these three styles, the seal impressions fall into five other categories. Mixed Styles I includes those seals with designs sharing stylistic characteristics of the Modeled Style and the

Drawings of seal impressions. Top: Persepolis Fortification seal 164*. Middle: Persepolis Fortification seal 9*. Bottom: Persepolis Fortification seal 16*. Courtesy of M.C. Root and M.B. Garrison.

Fortification Style. Mixed Styles II comprises seals sharing the characteristics of the Court Style and the Fortification Style. The Broad and Flat Style is self-explanatory; seals in this style are often carved rather coarsely. The Linear Style consists of a fairly wide range of various linear styles. Two relatively small but ultimately very interesting groups of seals do not fit into any of these stylistic categories. One group is termed "Anomalous Styles." It represents contemporary styles *not* local to the heartland court and region. In addition, some Fortification tablets were ratified with antique seals.

The existence at Persepolis of at least eight glyptic styles—most being produced simultaneously by workshops presumably operating in the Persepolis region—creates an exciting impression of a lively and creative artistic environment. The Fortification archive provides scholars with the opportunity to explore many issues, including those of patronage, seal-use patterns, stylistic developments, and connections between glyptic art and art in other media. Examination of one specific case in the glyptic art preserved at Persepolis lays the groundwork for a consideration of the implications of iconography and style in Achaemenid coinage of the western empire.

Circles of Style

The various glyptic styles in concurrent use at Persepolis represent multiple local stylistic phenomena within the context of a court environment. The distinct styles represent particular categorizations of stylistic attributes, but they were permeable in some important ways. Mixed Styles I and II demonstrate the potentially shifting boundaries between stylistic categories, the existence, as it were, of a spectrum of stylistic variation in glyptic art at Persepolis. This has profound implications for our understanding of Achaemenid culture and of the multi-valence of artistic style and iconography in the Achaemenid empire. The imperial Court Style is important in this context precisely because it was *not* imposed on the court circle: although people high in the administrative echelon might choose to have seals made in the Court Style, it was not *de rigueur* for anyone who wanted to impress the king to have a seal carved in the Court Style. Instead, the simultaneity of different styles in use at Persepolis suggests an environment that allowed for subtle manipulation of seal style and iconography to emphasize particular messages.

Artistic style clearly projected value-laden meaning and identity in the Achaemenid world. I pick one out of many examples for discussion here: the seals of Parnaka, impressions of which are preserved on the Persepolis Fortification tablets (Root 1991; Garrison and Root 2001). Parnaka was the uncle of Darius I and the chief administrator at Persepolis, overseer of all interactions (Root 1991:22; also Garrison 1988). His first seal bore Assyrianizing imagery carved in the local Fortification Style (PFS 9*). On June 6, 500 BCE, he replaced it with a new one carved in the masterful and archaizing Modeled Style (PFS 16*) based on the same Neo-Assyrian and Neo-Babylonian precedents that informed the seal's iconography (Porada 1947). Neither seal was carved in the imperial Court Style.

Parnaka's second seal is a telling example of the association of style with geographical and traditional identity, consciously employed to convey a specific message to the viewer. The seal shows the hero figure grappling with two lions; its style and iconography derived directly from Neo-Assyrian palace reliefs, including the stance of the lions, the robe of the hero, and the manner in which musculature is indicated on all three figures. This choice likely reflects an association of Parnaka and his family with antique Mesopotamian traditions. Indeed, according to Herodotus his grandson Tritantaechmes was, in the latter years of Darius' reign, satrap at Babylon. This position was considered the most powerful one in Asia.[6] The style and imagery of Parnaka's seal thus bear a message of power and of ascribed identity that goes beyond the raw potency of the image itself to refer solidly and directly to the foundation of his family's power specifically in Assyria.

The artifacts from Persepolis discussed here demonstrate the multifold significance of artistic imagery in the Achaemenid heartland. We have seen the reworking of ancient artistic traditions to equate the King with the divine on the sculptural reliefs. The discovery in the Fortification sealings of the same concept translated into the medium of glyptic art underscores this message. Moreover, the Fortification sealings let us consider the use and significance of different styles that convey meaning in a manner linked to, but distinct from, the iconography of a given image.

Excavated vs. Unexcavated: Interpreting "Floating" Objects

The analytical model used in the study of excavated glyptic art at Persepolis serves productively in the interpretation of the iconography and style even of unexcavated objects from elsewhere in the Empire. Studies of the art of Achaemenid Anatolia have often focused on unprovenanced artifacts bearing significant artistic symbols: coins and the so-called Graeco-Persian sealstones.[7] Most of the seals generally studied are not from controlled excavations, but nonetheless lie at the heart of the typological work done on the seal corpus (e.g., J. Boardman 1970a: 303–58, 1970b). Even in Boardman's seminal study of pyramidal stamp seals (1970b), fully 75% are unprovenanced; of the remaining seals that do claim some provenance, almost half come from Sardis. But even the excavated material that has been embraced in this and other discussions has not been particularly focused upon as contextualized material. The seals are treated as isolated works of art, without particular social context. Furthermore, ancient seal impressions available in published form, such as the Persepolis Treasury sealings, the Ur sealings, many of the Nippur Murašu sealings, were generally not factored into the analysis, though Boardman (1970a:305) does allude to the Treasury tablets. The social significance of the art has scarcely been addressed. Because there has seemed to be little to work with beyond formal description, scant attention has been given to interpretive frameworks for considering how this artistic imagery conveyed symbolic meaning.[8]

A similar problem has limited the study of coins, as much the greater number of coins available for study has not been found in controlled scientific excavations. The designs on seals may reflect the personal choices of individual artists and patrons, but they were intended for public viewing and designed to signify particular meaning to a very broad audience. So, too, coins bear imagery designed to convey meaning in a public capacity. They are widely circulating objects. Each face is a small discrete surface that may be decorated with a selection of emblems designed to represent the issuer in a manner meaningful to both issuer and viewer. Because of their size and their artistic function as recognizable representations, coins parallel the artistic function of seals. Thus coins, even when lacking a known archaeological context, may nonetheless contribute to a discussion stemming from an analysis of the symbolic system represented by seals and sealings from excavated contexts. The enormous corpus of the Persepolis Fortification sealings now suggests ways of legitimately querying even such unexcavated material. The Fortification archive at last offers us a model for analyzing "floating" objects.

"Graeco-Persian" seal with facing sphinxes. Lydian inscription: "*manelim*." From Boardman (1970a; no. 834).

"Graeco-Persian" seal with Persian warrior. From Boardman (1970a: no. 884).

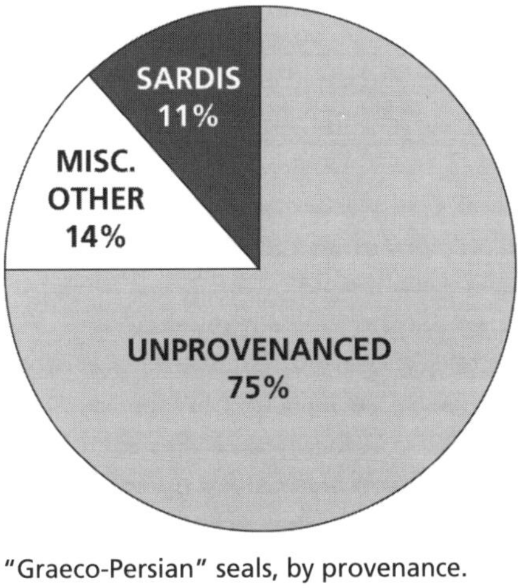

"Graeco-Persian" seals, by provenance. Percentages drawn from Boardman (1970b).

The king with attendants. Palace of Darius.

Achaemenid Imagery in the West: The Archer Coins

In this section, I will offer a fresh interpretation of the imagery of imperial Achaemenid coins, based on the foregoing analysis of artistic iconography and style in the Persian heartland. I will examine a specific case, the so-called tiarate head coins, demonstrating their position in the artistic program of the Achaemenid Empire. We will see that the coinage of the western Empire fits directly into the ideologies expressed in the artistic imagery of imperial sculpture and seals.

The most familiar coinage of the Achaemenid Empire—the imperial issue, gold darics and silver *sigloi*—bear on the obverse an image of a figure wearing the Persian court robe and dentate crown, carrying a

Siglos. Type iiia archer. From Kraay (1966: pl. 183 no. 619, obverse and reverse).

bow and sometimes other weapons. The coins are hence generally designated "archers." (For an excellent discussion of these coins see Carradice 1987; see also Descat 1989; Naster 1962; Price 1989; Root 1988, 1989; Stronach 1989). Whereas most Greek cities changed their types frequently, the issues of Athens and Corinth, as well as those acknowledged to be the official issues of the Achaemenid empire, retained their major symbols despite subtle variations in design. This constancy of image had several ramifications, including not only a long-lived circulation of individual coins and correspondingly worn appearance when they are found in modern times, but also a very high degree of recognition of image among ancient viewers (the two points are of course related). (See Carradice [1987:90–91] for a discussion of wear and the use-life of certain coins.) How well Achaemenid coins functioned as recognized signifiers of the might of the Persian King is clear from the ancient literary sources: when King Agesilaus of Sparta withdrew from the Troad in 394 BCE, he claimed to have been driven from Asia by the King's thirty thousand archers (Plutarch, *Artaxerxes* 20. See also Carradice 1987:76.) It is the King's *gold* archers to which he refers, used by Artaxerxes II to foment revolt in Greece against Sparta.

The meaning of the archer symbol itself is complex. The reliefs and inscriptions at the royal tombs at Naqsh-i Rustam demonstrate the importance of the bowman in Achaemenid Persian ideology: not only is a figure explicitly named "bow-bearer" prominently represented in a position of honor behind the King, but the accompanying texts make clear the significance of this weapon and perhaps even a specific position of honor associated with it (Kent 1950 DNd and DNc). He is labeled "Aspathines, bow-bearer, holds the battle-ax of Darius the King," and he carries a bowcase slung over his shoulder and a battle-ax in his right hand. The other figure shown bears a spear and is labeled "Gobryas, a Patischorian, spear-bearer of Darius the King." In the inscription accompanying the figural relief, Darius himself proclaims his military prowess:

> Trained am I both with hands and with feet. As a horseman I am a good horseman. As a bowman I am a good bowman both afoot and on horseback. As a spearman I am a good spearman both afoot and on horseback. (DNb; see Kent 1953; Lecoq 1997.)

And yet despite the emphasis on the virtues of the warrior, the King is shown in the relief wearing the so-called Persian robe, or court attire, rather than military garb. This implied duality underscores the multifold significance of Achaemenid kingship, where King-as-warrior, King-as-courtly-presence, and King-as-superior-being are embodied in the person of the King. Nylander (1992) includes a brilliant discussion of these multiple functions of the king and their effect on kingly behavior in war and otherwise.

The significance of the archer coins probably reflects more than the ideological importance of the bow in Achaemenid assessment of virtue. The earliest type of archer coin minted clearly suggests the idea of a *divine* figure holding a bow: only the upper half of the figure is portrayed, emerging from a crescent in the standard manner of representing Ahuramazda. The format recalls earlier Assyrian portrayals of the god Aššur and contemporary Achaemenid images of Ahuramazda, both on seals and wall reliefs. (For a discussion of the archer types and the possible figures they may portray, with annotated bibliography, see Harrison 1982a: esp. 14–38.) And yet the crenelated crown worn by the figure links him to representations of the King in an almost symbiotic association. The figure represents an image of divine kingship, in this case founded not on ancient Mesopotamian iconography, but on the imperial ideology of the Achaemenids themselves. We see here, apparently, a multivalent symbol similar to the polysemous reliefs carved on the walls at Persepolis and into the living rock at Naqsh-i Rustam.

This multifold meaning is made both more specific and more complex in the archer coins that portray the full figure of the bowbearer. Here a figure moves to the right, carrying both bow and spear and wearing a crenelated crown and the "Persian" robe or court dress. It is an image designed to convey in one symbol the full significance of the King we have seen represented in sculpted reliefs in the Persian heartland.

It has been a matter of some puzzlement to scholars that the production of *sigloi* should have petered out in the fourth century, apparently replaced increasingly in western Anatolia by what have been considered issues by local satraps (regional governors) (Carradice 1987:93). While gold darics continued to be minted, the *sigloi*—the small change, the coins that were used the most (as their extreme wear shows)—do not. The so-called satrapal issues exist only in silver and bronze, without gold examples: they must therefore have taken the place of the *sigloi* that were no longer minted.

This development has interesting implications, which we probably do not yet fully understand. Usually the satrapal issues are viewed as the result of increasing satrapal independence and the establishment of new local satrapal mints. I would like here to propose an alternative interpretation in which the coins do not attest to a weakening of imperial rule. I would propose they conform ingeniously to the symbolic message of the original *sigloi*, bearing a similar imperial message of conflated kingship and divinity, but couched in stylistic terms that would have increased their impact on the local viewing audience.

Achaemenid Imagery in the West: The Tiarate Head Coins

The so-called tiarate head series were silver and bronze coins minted in western Anatolia in the fifth and especially fourth centuries BCE. Their ascription to Anatolian satraps derives from the fact that some of the coins bear inscriptions naming western satraps as well as their preponderance in coin hoards found in Anatolia (for these coins, see, e.g., Carradice 1987; Casabonne 1996, 1998, with references). The provenance of these coins is beyond the scope of this paper. Instead, we turn to a possible interpretation of the imagery impressed on the coins' surfaces. As explained before, these objects generally become available for study without a secure archaeological context that might provide some basis for understanding their social significance. We are forced, therefore, to contextualize them with different strategies. Here I offer an interpretation based on the *archaeological* evidence available in Achaemenid glyptic and sculptural art from the Persian heartland.

The tiarate coins bear on their obverse a bearded head. The head sports the "Median" headgear, or so-called tiara (hence the modern name of the coin). This is a soft cap with side and back flaps, the kind of headgear a Persian warrior would wear into battle (Herodotus I,132.1; 12.4; V, 49.3; VII, 66.2; VIII, 120; Xenophon *Cyropaedia* VIII, 3.13; Strabo XV, 3.15 and 3.19). With few exceptions, (Erhart 1979; Cahn 1975) the bearded head is shown in profile. The style of the head is subtly modeled and highly veristic, with intricate plastic volumes showing the folds of the headgear and the configuration of facial muscles, and with great attention to detail in the carving of beards and eyes as well as long aquiline noses. It is a style that is essentially Greek.

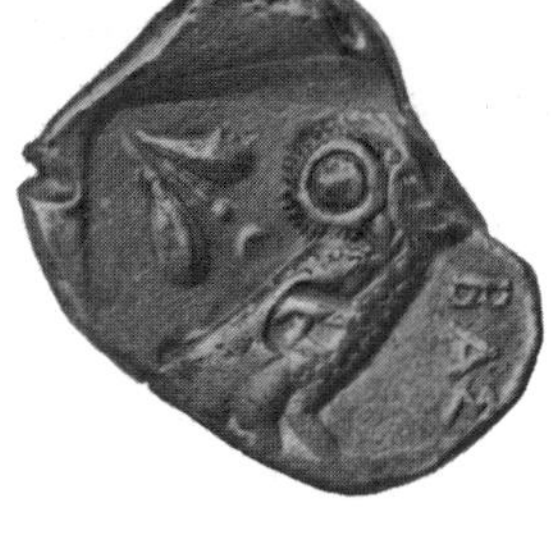

Tiarate head coin. From Kraay (1966:pl. 184 no. 621 obverse and reverse).

Tiarate head coin. From Kraay (1966:pl. 184 no. 622 obverse and reverse).

The coins have often been called portraits, either of specific Persian kings or of the specific Persian satraps or local dynasts assumed to be responsible for their issuing (Harrison 1982a:81–96). Some scholars have claimed to be able to recognize in the facial characteristics of the heads distinctive features attributable to particular individuals. Moreover, some of the coins are inscribed on the reverse with the names of satraps known to us through Greek literary sources. Many scholars have assumed these inscriptions assign a name to the figure whose portrait appears on the obverse. But recent analysis has shown these assignations to be erroneous. When names are inscribed, they appear on the reverse of the coins rather than the obverse where the head is shown, undermining any sense that the name refers to the figure on the other side of the coin. Moreover, satrapal or dynastic names appear also on coins that do not include images that could in any sense be described as portraits. The presence of the name, therefore, is insufficient evidence to claim the tiarate heads are portraits of individuals. And to clinch the matter, the facial characteristics even of heads on coins labeled with the same name vary widely from one coin to the next (Morkholm and Zahle 1976). These heads are not portraits of specific individuals, but rather represent a composite of features in a general stereotyped image. In the words of one scholar, they are "more or less hellenized images of oriental rulers, idealized to almost divine dignity" (Schwabacher 1968:116). The heads on the tiarate coins, then, represent generalizing and idealized portrayals of a Persian in military garb. They do not serve as veristic likenesses of specific satraps.

Unlike the archer coins, the tiarate head coins bear a figural reverse instead of a simple incuse punch. Whereas the obverse always show the tiarate head, the reverse of these coins shows considerable variation from issue to issue. These include motifs of particular Greek cities: the owl of Athens and the *kithara* of the Chalcidicians. But while the coins display the motifs of Greek cities, they also bear the Greek inscription "of the King." The imagery, the style of carving, and the language of inscription leave little room for doubt that the intended audience of the coins was Greek. Like the *sigloi*, these coins served as a convenient medium for payment—"small change," appropriate for paying people for humdrum services rendered. We know some Achaemenid coins were used to pay Greek soldiers in the west. These factors reinforce the argument suggested by the imagery on the coins. Although the iconography and style of the reverse proclaim these issues to be of Greek cities, the inscription changes the meaning profoundly:

this is the coinage of the King. And the flip side of this coin shows a figure wearing the headgear Persians wore into battle: the garment that people on the western fringes of the Empire, or mercenary soldiers, were perhaps most likely actually to have seen Persians wearing.

The reverse imagery of some of the coins helps clarify the issue. One depicts a kneeling archer with bow and spear, a many-oared galley (a symbol of Sidon) perched on its beak, and the legend "of the King" in Greek. The style of these figures is that of the Achaemenid archer coins. The inscription on the coins makes their message clear: these are the King's lands; this is the King's money. The iconography of the currency bears the same message, couched in an artistic style intelligible to the local audience.

Tiarate head coin. From Kraay (1966:pl. 184 no. 623 obverse and reverse).

Athenian tetradrachm. From Kraay (1966:pl. 119 no. 363 obverse and reverse).

The issue of style is an important one here and ties in with the previous discussion of Parnaka's second seal (PFS 16*). The use of an artistic style may carry multiple meanings. Style may be manipulated in a manner appropriate to communicate with the receiver, but an image used is also a signal of a certain identification by the patron or issuer. In the case of the tiarate head coins, I would suggest, the latter message is one of cultural appropriation. Like the presence at Pasargadae, in the Persian heartland, of the Takht—a building constructed in recognizably Ionian masonry technique (Nylander 1970; Stronach 1978)—so the styles of the coins, seals, and sculpture provide forceful demonstrations of the power of the Empire to appropriate the cultural attributes of its various peoples. Parnaka's second seal, I would hold, is Assyrianizing partly in order to demonstrate his appropriative capacity for the cultural attributes of Assyria. The tiarate heads on our coins are represented in a Greek style not just to make the imperial message easier for Greeks to understand, but also to demonstrate the power of the King to take up and use the cultural attributes of the peoples at the periphery of the Empire.

Conclusion

Debate has raged for years about the identity of the individuals represented on the tiarate coins.[9] The divergence of interpretations demonstrates the problematic nature of such an assignation to a specific individual. I think another interpretation is more likely. The heads of the tiarate coins are carved in a fully Greek style and are a coin emblem used in Greek contexts only to display gods. They show the head of kingship, alluding to divinity by allusion to heads on Greek coins. But these Anatolian issues deployed on the western fringe of the Empire in a western (Greek) style display the head of a Persian equipped for war. The Greeks would have recognized this war gear.

I would suggest the obverse of these coins conveys a message parallel to that of the *sigloi* they seem to have replaced. For the *sigloi* and darics showed a figure representing both kingship and divinity, carrying his bow and spear far from the Persian heartland. On the tiarate head coins, too, we see a militant Persian figure. The Apadana reliefs at Persepolis show the peoples of the realm bearing significant gifts to the King. In particular, examples of the military costume are prominently—almost emphatically—displayed in the procession. This costume seems to have served specifically as a symbol for the King-as-warrior (see Root 1979: 227–284, esp. 279–282, on "Median" garb). The same image appears on the reliefs of the Nereid Monument in Xanthos, Lycia, in a context at the western reaches of the Empire. Just as weaponry was an important symbol of kingship, this "Median" costume was tremendously significant. On the tiarate head coins, the garment is particularly charged: in addition to its symbolic value, it bears particular meaning for its local audience. Those small-change soldiers on the edges of the Empire who had actually *seen* the king would have seen him as a warrior.

The significance of the tiarate head coins is thus extraordinarily intricate. They portray the king as warrior, reinforcing the relation of the intended receivers to the Empire in terms of this aspect of kingship. At the same time, they appropriate the iconography and artistic style of the Greek sphere to equate the king with the divine. Rather than being portraits of a specific local governor, these coins represent a manipulation of iconography and style to bear an extremely complex message. They form part of a consistent program of the Achaemenid kings to appropriate and rework local artistic traditions so as to equate kingship with the divine, an imperial system of images building on the burgeoning creativity of local artistic environments.

Notes

[1] This was clearly a matter of concern to the empire-builder Darius I: see Herodotus III, 38 for a story involving his awareness of and interest in the differing attitudes of disparate peoples in the Empire, and in his own words, DB 1.17-20, 4.70, 4.88-92, DNa esp. 15-47, DNb (Kent 1953; Lecoq 1997). For examples of multilinguality practiced in official sendings, see Greenfield and Porten (1982); von Voigtlander (1978). See also Tuplin (1987). M. C. Root (1990) lays out imperial texts that characterize the diversity of the Empire.

This introduction is adapted from Dusinberre (2002).

[2] On the background and symbolism of Achaemenid art, see esp. Root (1979), Dusinberre (1997a). For the architectural relief sculptures at Persepolis and Pasargadae, see also Schmidt (1953), Stronach (1978), Cook (1983), Herzfeld (1941), Krefter (1971), Richter (1946), Root (1990), Roaf (1983), Farkas (1974), Nylander (1970).

[3] In this study, I argue that the imperial Achaemenid artistic iconography equates the king with the divine. Whether the king himself or any of his subjects actually considered him to be divine or semi-divine is of course an entirely different issue.

[4] The reliefs were planned, but not completed, during the final years of the reign of Darius I. The original central panel, showing the King enthroned, was later removed to the Treasury and replaced with a different panel. This later change does not affect the argument here, dealing as it does with the construction of imperial iconography to convey imperial ideology. See Root (1979), Schmidt (1953).

[5] Garrison and Root (2001), Schmidt (1957), Porada (1961), Garrison (1988). For the tablets, see also Cameron (1948, 1958, 1965), Hinz (1960), Hallock (1950, 1960, 1969). Hallock published the texts of an additional 33 tablets (1978). Hallock had read and transliterated an additional 2,586 texts, most of which are referenced in Hinz and Koch (1987). A number of studies have dealt directly with the Fortification archive; see, e.g., Lewis (1990), Garrison (1988, 1990, 1996), Koch (1990, 1992). Most recently, see Garrison and Root (1996, 2001), and Root (1996). I am deeply grateful to Margaret Cool Root of the University of Michigan for allowing me access to the Persepolis Fortification sealings and for providing constant inspiration and advice. I am also grateful to Mark B. Garrison of Trinity University for his generosity and help with these and many related issues. Their work on the Fortification sealings has been undertaken with the kind permission of The Oriental Institute and with the aid of generous support from the National Endowment for the Humanities, the John Simon Guggenheim Memorial Foundation, the Samuel H. Kress Foundation, and several units of the University of Michigan: the Kelsey Museum of Archaeology, the Horace H. Rackham School of Graduate Studies, the Office of the Vice-President for Research, and the College of Literature, Science, and the Arts; Vassar College; and Trinity University.

[6] Herodotus I, 192.2. The Greek conflation in the Achaemenid period of Assyria and Babylonia is interesting in light of the impossibility of distinguishing these artistic styles in the glyptic of the preceding centuries. I am indebted to Matthew Stolper, Amélie Kuhrt, and Pierre Briant for sharing with me their thoughts and knowledge on the matter of the satrapy of Babylonia in the reign of Darius.

[7] See, e.g., Furtwängler (1903), Moortgat (1926), Maximova (1928), Richter (1946, 1952), Nikoulina (1971), Farkas (1974). Some scholars have considered this issue essentially less interesting than other approaches to the material. See, e.g., Seyrig (1952), Boardman (1970a, 1970b, 1976), Richter (1949); see also Young (1946); cf. Root (1991). Even on the level of descriptive typology, the term "Graeco-Persian" has been used for the classification of alarmingly diverse-looking material. The most precise definition offered of "Graeco-Persian" style is "often sketchy, with undisguised use of the rotating drill" (Richter 1949). But the diverse seals frequently gathered together under the heading "Graeco-Persian" simply do not form one stylistically or iconographically homogeneous entity. See the plates in Starr (1975) and (1977). For a re-analysis, cf. Root and McIntosh (1994) and Dusinberre in press.

[8] In part, discussion has generally been limited by the assumptions underlying ethnically-determined attributes. So, e.g., Furtwängler (1903:12): "Despite all the variations in detail, a common spirit runs through this oriental art. It is the spirit of despotism and subordination. When we now turn to the Greeks, however, we may breathe in freedom, the freedom of the manifold life and joyous beauty." One criterion of determining the social significance of these artifacts and the ethnicity of their artists has traditionally been qualitative. Generally, seals that appear high in quality and in naturalism have been attributed to Greek artists. It is assumed that these Greek artists will have been working for Persian patrons. It is also assumed no Greek would want an image of a Persian or indeed a Persian-influenced image on his seal; but a Greek artist might be forced to craft such an image for a wealthy barbarian patron. "Graeco-Persian" seals that seem stilted, lacking in volume and naturalism, are attributed on the other hand to Persian artists. These Persian artists presumably worked within a "Graeco-Persian" milieu of exposure to Greek artists, but without the ability or sensibility to achieve the same results. In these discussions, "Persian" seems to mean an ethnic Persian, without much consideration for what "Persian" might mean when speaking of a range of producers and consumers of glyptic art across a vast empire.

[9] Imhoof-Blumer (1885:4–5, 24), Jenkins (1959), Schwabacher (1968), Olçay and Mørkholm (1971), Jenkins (1972), Mørkholm and Zahle (1972), Cahn (1975), Kraay (1976:271), Mørkholm and Zahle (1976:85), Hurter (1979), Harrison (1982), Cahn (1985). A not dissimilar discussion has centered on the palace reliefs; see Root (1979:92–95), including an analysis of previous scholars' work. J. Borchhardt's (1983) arguments are, I think, rather undermined by his lack of distinction between different forms of headdress.

Bibliography

Amiet, P.
1973 La glyptique de la fin de l'Elam. *Ars asiatiques* 28:3–22.

Babelon, E.
1893 *Les Perses Achéménides*. Paris: Rollin et Feuardent.

Boardman, J.
1970a *Greek Gems and Finger Rings: Early Bronze Age to Late Classical*. London: Thames and Hudson.
1970b Pyramidal Stamp Seals in the Persian Empire. *Iran* 8:19–46.
1976 Greek and Persian Glyptic in Anatolia and Beyond. *Revue Archéologique* 1976 (1):45–54.

Bodenstedt, F.
1976 Satrapen und Dynasten auf Phokäischen Hekten. *Schweizer Münzblätter* 26:69–75.

Borchhardt, J.
1983 Bildnisse achaimenidischer Herrscher. *Archaeologische Mitteilungen aus Iran Ergänzungsband* 10:207–23.

Britt Tilia, A.
1978 *Studies and Restorations at Persepolis and Other Sites of Fars*. Instituto Italiano per il Medio ed Estremo Oriente, Reports and Memoirs 16 Rome: IsMEO.

Cahn, H.
1975 Dynast oder Satrap? *Schweizer Münzblätter* 25:84–91.
1985 Tissaphernes in Astyra. *Archäologischer Anzeiger* 1985(4):587–94.

Calmeyer, P.
1976 Zur Genese altiranischer Motive IV. "Persönliche Krone" und Diadem. *Archaeologische Mitteilungen aus Iran* n.F. 9:45–95.

Calmeyer, P. and Shahbazi, A. S.
1976 The Persepolis "Treasury Reliefs" Once More. *Archaeologische Mitteilungen aus Iran* n.F. 9:151–56.

Cameron, G. G.
1948 *Persepolis Treasury Tablets*. OIP 65 Chicago: The Oriental Institute of the University of Chicago.
1958 Persepolis Treasury Tablets Old and New. *Journal of Near Eastern Studies* 17:161–76.
1965 New Tablets from the Persepolis Treasury. *Journal of Near Eastern Studies* 24:167–92.

Carradice, I.
1987 The "Regal" Coinage of the Persian Empire in Coinage and Administration in the Athenian and Persian Empires. *Biblical Archaeology Review* 343:73–93.

Cook, J. M.
1983 *The Persian Empire*. London: Dent.

Descat, R.
1989 Notes sur l'histoire du monnayage Achéménide sous le regne de Darius I. *Revue des études anciennes* 91:15–32.

Dusinberre, E. R. M.
1997a Imperial Style and Constructed Identity: A "Graeco-Persian" Cylinder Seal from Sardis. *Ars Orientalis* 27:99–129.
1997b Satrapal Sardis: Aspects of Empire in an Achaemenid Capital. Ph.D. dissetation. Ann Arbor: University of Michigan.
2002 *Satrapal Sardis in the Achaemenid Persian Empire*. Cambridge: Cambridge University Press.
in press Greco-Persian Art. In *The Archaeology of Anatolia: An Encyclopedia*, edited by G. K. Sams.

Erhart, K. P.
1979 *The Development of the Facing Head Motif on Greek Coins and Its Relation to Classical Art*. New York: Garland.

Farkas, A.
1974 *Achaemenid Sculpture*. Leiden: E. J. Brill.

Furtwängler, A.
1903 *Die antiken Gemmen: Geschichte der Steinschneidenkunst im klassischen Altertum*. Berlin: Gesecke & Devrient.

Garrison, M. B.
1988 Seal Workshops and Artists at Persepolis: A Study of Seal Impressions Preserving the Theme of Heroic Encounter Preserved on the Persepolis Fortification and Treasury Tablets. Ph.D. diss., University of Michigan, Ann Arbor.
1990 Seals and the Elite at Persepolis: Some Observations on Early Achaemenid Persian Art. *Ars Orientalis* 20:1–30.
1996 A Persepolis Fortification Seal on the Tablet MDP 11 308 Louvre Sb 13078. *Journal of Near Eastern Studies* 55:15–35.

Garrison, M. B. and Root, M. C.
1996 *Persepolis Seal Studies. An Introduction with Provisional Concordances of Seal Numbers and Associated Documents on Fortification Tablets 1–2087*. Leiden: E. J. Brill.

Garrison, M. B., and Root, M. C.
2001 *Seals on the Persepolis Fortification Tablets, Vol. I: Images of Heroic Encounter*. Chicago: The Oriental Institute of the University of Chicago.
in press a *Seals on the Persepolis Fortification Tablets, Vol. II: Nono-Heroic Images of Human and Human-Creature Activity*. Chicago: The Oriental Institute of the University of Chicago.
in press b *Seals on the Persepolis Fortification Tablets, Vol. III: Studies of Animals, Animal-Creatures, Plants, and Abstract Devices*. Chicago: The Oriental Institute of the University of Chicago.

Greenfield, J. and Porten, B.
1982 *Bisutun Inscription of Darius I: Aramaic Version*. London: Corpus Inscriptionum Iranicarum, 5.

Hallock, R. T.
1950 New Light from Persepolis. *Journal of Near Eastern Studies* 9:237–552.
1960 A New Look at the Persepolis Treasury Tablets. *Journal of Near Eastern Studies* 19:90–100.
1969 *Persepolis Fortification Tablets*. OIP 92 Chicago: The Oriental Institute of the University of Chicago Press.
1973 The Persepolis Fortification Archive. *Orientalia* 92:320–23.
1978 Selected Fortification Texts. *Cahiers de la Délégation Archéologique Française en Iran* 8:109–36.

Harrison, C. M.
1982a Coins of the Persian Satraps. Ph.D. diss., University of Pennsylvania, Philadelphia.
1982b Persian Names on Coins of Northern Anatolia. *Journal of Near Eastern Studies* 41:181–94.

Herzfeld, E.
1934 Recent Discoveries at Persepolis. *Journal of the Royal Asiatic Society* 1934:231.
1941 *Iran in the Ancient East*. Oxford: Oxford University Press.

Hill, G. F.
1922 *Catalogue of the Greek Coins of Arabia, Mesopotamia and Persia*. BMC 28. London: British Museum.

Hinz, W.
1960 Zu den Persepolis Täfelchen. Zeitschriften der Deutschen Morgenländischen Gesellschaft 110:236–51.

Hinz, W. and Koch, H.
1987 *Elamisches Wörterbuch*. AMI Ergänzungsband 17. Berlin: D. Reimer.

Hurter, S.
1979 Der Tissaphernes-Fund. Pp. 97–108 in *Greek Numismatics and Archaeology: Essays in Honor of Margaret Thompson*, edited by O. Mørkholm and N. M. Waggoner. Wetteren: NR.

Imhoof-Blumer, F.
1885 *Porträtsköpfe auf antiken Münzen hellenischer und hellenisierter Völker.* Leipzig: Teubner.

Jenkins, G. K.
1959 Recent Acquisitions of Greek Coins by the British Museum. *Numismatic Chronicle* 1959:38–39.
1972 *Ancient Greek Coins.* London: Barrie and Jenkins.

Kent, R. G.
1950 *Old Persian: Grammar, Texts, Lexicon.* Chicago: The Oriental Institute of the University of Chicago.

Koch, H.
1990 *Verwaltung und Wirtschaft im persischen Kernland zur Zeit der Achämeniden.* Wiesbaden: L. Reichert.
1992 *Es kündet Dareios der König...: Vom Leben im persischen Grossreich.* Kulturgeschichte der Antiken Welt 55 Mainz: Verlag P. von Zabern.

Kraay, C. M.
1966 *Greek Coins.* London: Thames and Hudson.
1976 *Archaic and Classical Greek Coins.* Berkeley: University of California.

Krefter, F.
1971 *Persepolis Rekonstruktionen.* Berlin: Gebr. Mann.

Lecoq, P.
1997 *Les inscriptions de la Perse achéménide: traduit du vieux perse, de l'élamite, du babylonien et de l'araméen, présenté et annoté par Pierre Lecoq.* Paris.

Lewis, D. M.
1990 The Fortification Texts. Pp. 1–6 in *Achaemenid History IV: Center and Periphery*, edited by H. Sancisi-Weerdenburg and A. Kuhrt. Leiden: E. J. Brill.

Martin, T. R.
1985 *Sovereignty and Coinage in Classical Greece.* Princeton: Princeton University Press.

Maximova, M.
1928 Griechisch-persische Kleinkunst in Kleinasien nach den Perserkriegen. *Archäologischer Anzeiger* 43:648–77

Metzler, D.
1971 *Porträt und Gesellschaft: Studien über die Entstehung des griechischen Porträts.* Münster: [D. Metzler].

Moortgat, A.
1926 Hellas und die Kunst der Achaemeniden. *Mitteilungen der Deutschen Orientalischen Gesellschaft* 2:3–39.

Mørkholm, O.
1959 A South Anatolian Coin Hoard. *Acta Archaeologica* 30:184–201.
1974 A Coin of Artaxerxes III. *Numismatic Chronicle* 1974:1–4.

Mørkholm, O. and Zahle, J.
1972 The Coinage of Kuprlli: A Numismatic and Archaeological Study. *Acta Archaeologica* 43:57–113.
1976 The Coinages of the Lycian Dynasts Kheriga, Kherêi and Erbbina: A Numismatic and Archaeological Study. *Acta Archaeologica* 47:47–90.

Naster, P.
1962 Les sicles persiques à la demi-figure dans leur contexte numismatique et archéologique. *Bulletin de la societé française de numismatique* 17/6.

Nikoulina, N. M.
1971 La glyptique "grecque-orientale" et "gréco-perse." *Antike Kunst* 14 (2):90–106.

Noe, S. P.
1956 *Two Hoards of Persian Sigloi.* ANSNNM 136. New York: American Numismatic Society.

Nylander, C.
1970 *Ionians in Pasargadae: Studies in Old Persian Architecture.* Uppsala: Uppsala Universitet.
1992 Darius III—The Coward King: Point and Counterpoint. Pp. 145–59 in *Alexander the Great: Reality and Myth*, edited by J. Carlsen et al. Rome: L'Erma de Bretschneider.

Olçay, N. And Mørkholm, O.
1971 The Coin Hoard from Podalia. *Numismatic Chronicle* 1971:1–29.

Porada, E.
1947 Suggestions for the Classification of Neo-Babylonian Cylinder Seals. *Orientalia* 16:145–65.
1961 Review of Schmidt, Persepolis II. *Journal of Near Eastern Studies* 20:66–71.

Price, M.
1989 Darius I and the Daric. *Revue des études anciennes* 91:9–14.

Richter, G. M.
1946 Greeks in Persia. *American Journal of Archaeology* 50:15–30.

Richter, G. M. A.
1949 The Late "Achaemenian" or "Graeco-Persian" Gems. *Hesperia Suppl.* VIII:296.
1952 Greek Subjects on "Graeco-Persian" Seal Stones. Pp. 189–94 in *Archaeologica Orientalia in Memoriam Ernst Herzfeld*, edited by George C. Miles. Locust Valley: J. J. Augustin.
1965 *The Portraits of the Greeks*, Vol I. London: Phaidon Press.

Roaf, M.
1983 Sculptures and Sculptors at Persepolis. *Iran* 21:1–164.

Robinson, E. S. G.
1947 A Hoard of Persian Sigloi. *Numismatic Chronicle* 1947:173–74.
1958 The Beginnings of Achaemenid Coinage. *Numismatic Chronicle* 1958:187–93.
1960 Two Greek Coin Hoards. *Numismatic Chronicle* 1960:31–36.

Root, M. C.
1979 *The King and Kingship in Achaemenid Art: Essays on the Creation of an Iconography of Empire.* Acta Iranica 19. Leiden: E. J. Brill.
1985 The Parthenon Frieze and the Apadana Reliefs at Persepolis. *American Journal of Archaeology* 89:103–20.
1988 Evidence from Persepolis for the dating of Persian and Archaic Greek Coinage. *Numismatic Chronicle* 1988:1–12.
1989 The Persian Archer at Persepolis: Aspects of Chronology, Style, and Symbolism. *Revue des études anciennes* 91:33–50.
1990 Circles of Artistic Programming: Strategies for Studying Creative Process at Persepolis. Pp. 115–39 in *Investigating Artistic Environments in the Ancient Near East*, edited by A. C. Gunter. Washington, D.C.: Arthur M. Sackler Gallery, Smithsonian Institution.
1991 From the Heart: Powerful Persianisms in the Art of the Western Empire. Pp. 1–29 in *Achaemenid History VI. Asia Minor and Egypt: Old Cultures in a New Empire*, edited by H. Sancisi-Weerdenburg and A. Kuhrt. Leiden: E. J. Brill.

1996 The Persepolis Fortification Tablets: Archival Issues and the Problem of Stamps Versus Cylinder Seals. In *Archives, Sealings and Seals in the Hellenistic World,* edited by M.-L. Boussac and A. Invernizzi. Turin.

Root , M. C. and McIntosh, E. R.
1994 What is Graeco-Persian Art? Perspectives on the Construct and a Case Study from Sardis. Paper presented at symposium, Culture and Ethnicity in the Hellenistic East: Issues, Problems, and Approaches. Ann Arbor, Michigan.

Sami, A.
1955 *Persepolis Takht-i Jamshid.* Shiraz: Persepolis and Ma'arefat Bookseller.

Schlumberger, D.
1953 L'argent grec dans L'Empire Achéménide. Pp. 3–62 in *Trésors monétaires d'Afghanistan,* edited by R. Curiel and D. Schlumberger. Paris: Impr. Nationale.

Schmidt, E.
1953 *Persepolis I: Structures, Reliefs, Inscriptions.* Oriental Institute Publications 68. Chicago: The Oriental Institute of the University of Chicago.
1957 *Persepolis II: Contents of the Treasury and Other Discoveries.* Oriental Institute Publications 69. Chicago: The Oriental Institute of the University of Chicago.
1970 *Persepolis III: The Royal Tombs and Other Monuments.* Oriental Institute Publications 70. Chicago: The Oriental Institute of the University of Chicago.

Schwabacher, W.
1957 Satrapenbildnisse: Zum neuen Münzporträt des Tissaphernes. Pp. 27–32 in *Charites Studien zur Altertumswissenschaft, Festschrift Ernst Langlotz,* edited by K. Schauenburg. Bonn: Athenäum-verlag.
1968 Lycian Coin-Portraits. Pp. 111–24 in *Essays in Greek Coinage Presented to Stanley Robinson,* edited by C. M. Kraay and G. K. Jenkins. Oxford: Clarendon.

Seyrig, H.
1952 Cachets Achéménides. Pp. 195–202 in *Archaeologica Orientalia in Memoriam Ernst Herzfeld,* edited by George C. Miles. Locust Valley: J. J. Augustin.
1959a Le roi de Perse. *Syria* 36:52–56.
1959b Antiquités syriennes: divinités de Sidon. *Syria* 36:48–56.

Starr, C. G.
1975 Greeks and Persians in the Fourth Century B.C. A Study in Cultural Contacts before Alexander Part I. *Iranica Antiqua* 11:39–99.
1977 Greeks and Persians in the Fourth Century B.C. Part II. *Iranica Antiqua* 12:49–116.

Stronach, D.
1978 *Pasargadae: A Report on the Excavations Conducted by the British Institute of Persian Studies from 1961 to 1963.* Oxford: Clarendon.
1989 Early Achaemenid Coinage: Perspectives from the Homeland. *Iranica Antiqua* 24:255–79.

Thompson, W. E.
1965 Tissaphernes and the Mercenaries at Miletos. *Philologus* 109:294–97.

Tuplin, C.
1987 The Administration of the Achaemenid Empire. Pp. 109–66 in *Coinage and Administration in the Athenian and Persian Empires,* edited by I. Carradice. *Biblical Archaeology Review* 343.

Vickers, M.
1986a Early Greek Coinage, A Reassessment. *Numismatic Chronicle* 1986:1–44.
1986b Persepolis, Athenes, et Sybaris: Questions de monnayage et de chronologie. *REG* 99:248–53.

von Gall, H.
1974 Die Kopfbedeckung des persischen Ornats bei den Achämeniden. *Archaeologische Mitteilungen aus Iran* 7:145–61.

von Voigtlander, E. N.
1978 *The Bisutun Inscription of Darius I: Babylonian Version.* London: Corpus Inscriptionum Iranicarum, 2/I.

Young, G. M.
1946 A New Hoard from Taxila Bhir Mound. *Ancient India* 1:33.

Elspeth R. M. Dusinberre is an Assistant Professor in the Classics Department of the University of Colorado at Boulder. She is interested in cultural interactions in Anatolia, particularly in the ways in which the Achaemenid Empire affected local social structures in Anatolia and in the give-and-take between Achaemenid and other cultures. She has worked at Sardis, Gordion, and Kerkenes Daği in Turkey, as well as at sites elsewhere in the eastern Mediterranean.

Lydian Houses, Domestic Assemblages, and Household Size

By Nicholas Cahill

One of the main foci of excavation at Sardis in western Turkey has been an immense building of mudbrick and stone, the "Colossal Lydian Structure." Built in the late seventh century BCE, the structure apparently forms part of a massive fortification and gate. It is roughly 20 m wide at the base, exposed for a length of some 160 m, and in places still stands up to 7 m high.[1]

Excavations to the east of the fortification between 1984 and 1993 uncovered parts of two Lydian houses dating to the mid-sixth century BCE. While the great depth of these structures and the presence of well-preserved Roman houses above them limited their exposure, what they lacked in extent, they made up for in preservation. The floors of these spaces—an area of only some 163 m^2—held nearly 300 pottery vessels, hundreds of objects of iron, bronze, glass, stone, terracotta, bone, faience, silver and other materials, as well as foodstuffs and other organic materials, constituting some of the most complete domestic assemblages, not only at Sardis, but at any other site in this part of the world.[2]

This exceptional preservation resulted from the deliberate destruction of the fortification. Its superstructure was dumped over the sides, burying the stub of the fortification and the houses in brick debris. The "brick fall" stood out as a distinctive and colorful stratum, made up largely of whole bricks and large chunks, including both red low-fired bricks and unfired green and brown mudbricks. Excavated on both sides of the fortification, it was apparently used to landscape the stub of the demolished fortification, creating a more uniform and even grade.

Drawing of painting on Orientalizing *dinos* from yard.

A violent military attack—and its attendant burning and slaughter—probably brought about this thorough-going destruction. Parts of the fortification were severely burned, reddening and spalling the masonry and leaving quantities of ash and charcoal at its foot. The houses and their contents were also intensely burned. The stratigraphy and distribution of the brick fall showed that it was deposited deliberately, rather than being the result of a natural catastrophe like an earthquake or

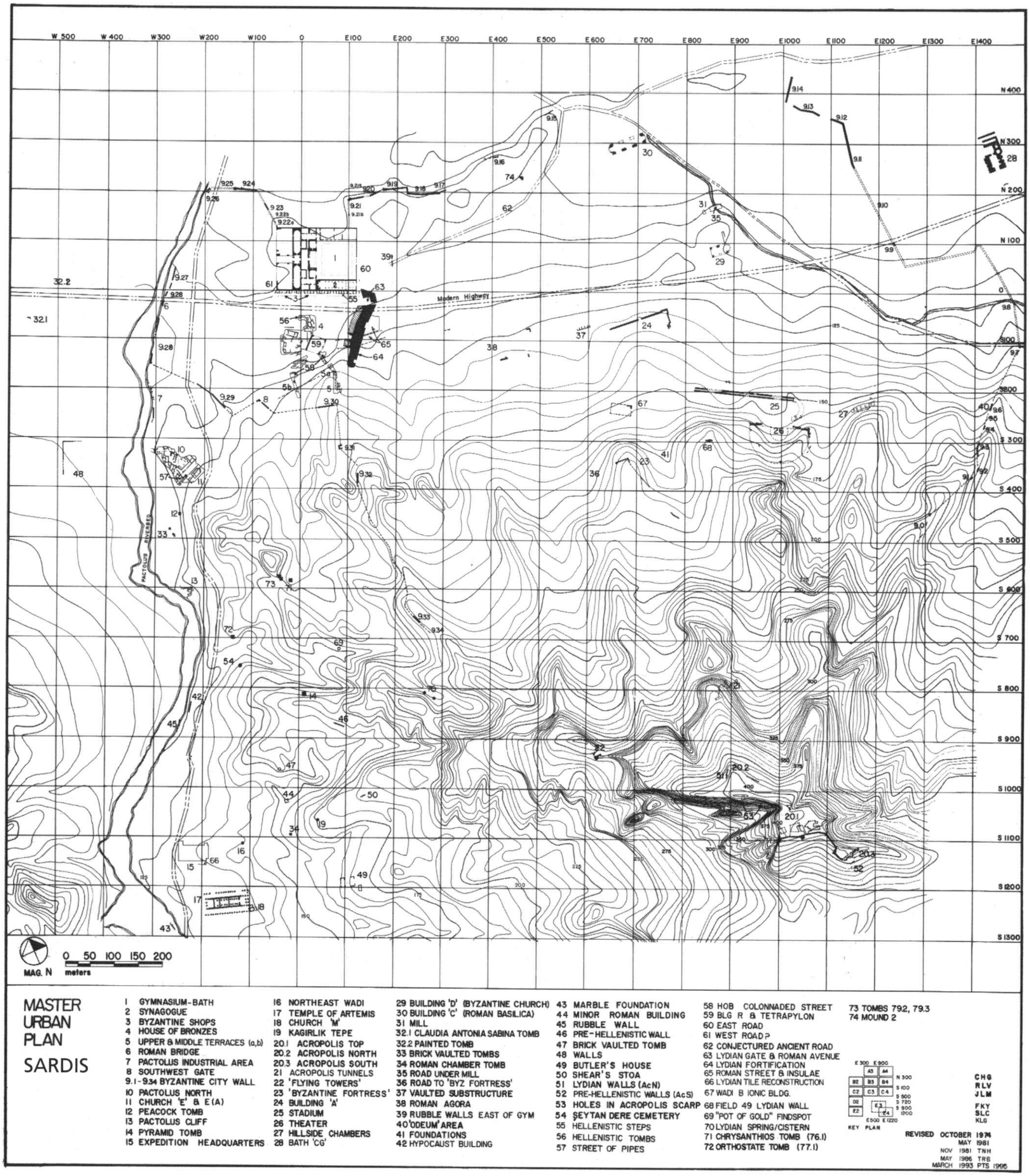

gradual deterioration after abandonment. The skeleton of a soldier, still clutching a stone and bearing injuries apparently sustained in battle, as well as an iron and bronze helmet emerged from the brick fall stratum on the west side of the structure; a second skeleton was found in one of the houses, probably another casualty.

Local and imported Greek pottery date the destruction to the middle of the sixth century BCE. The pottery comes from the brick fall itself (sherds) and from the house floors (whole pieces), whose undisturbed and uneroded state shows that they must have been burned and buried at the same time that the fortification

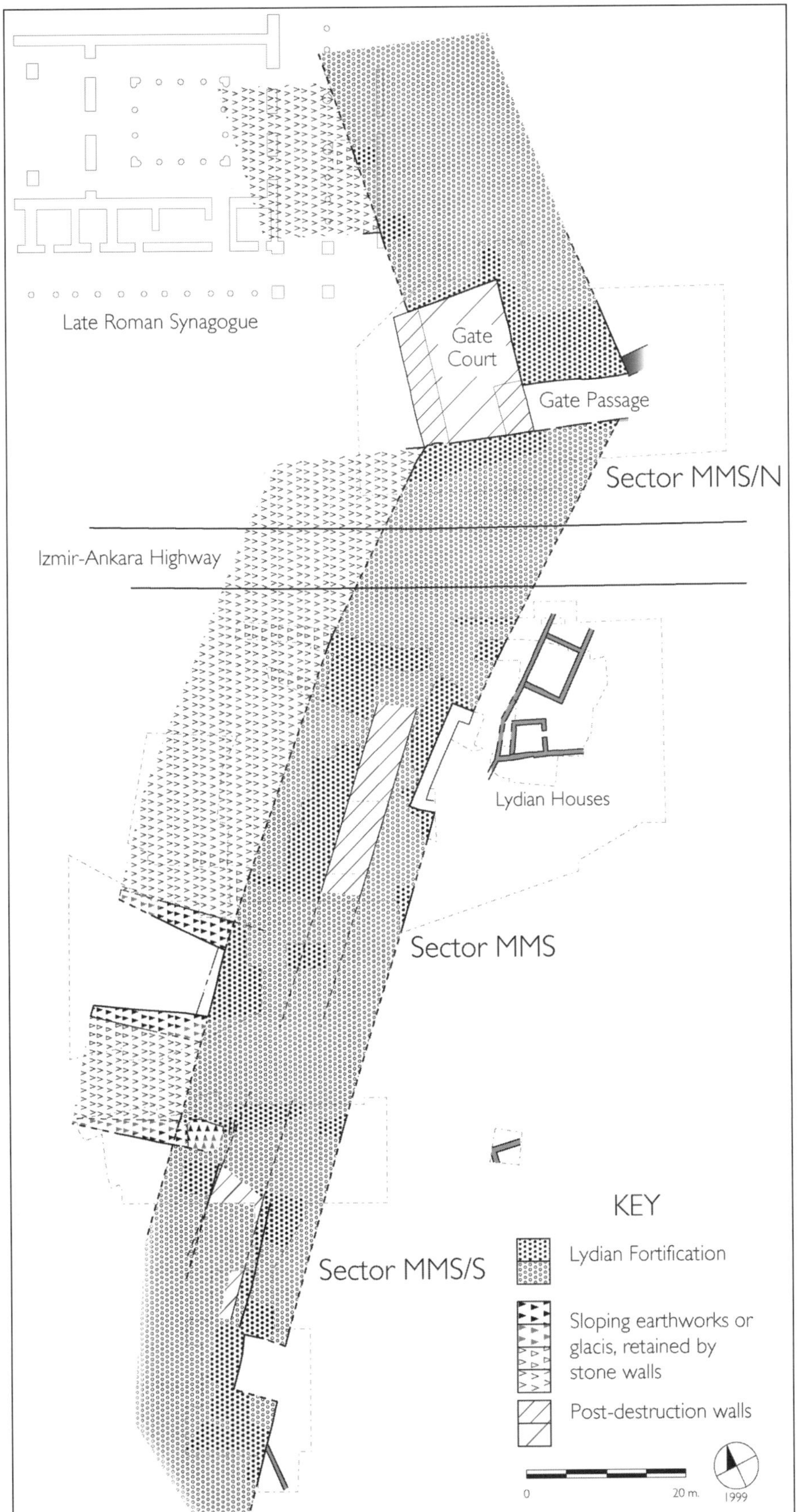

Simplified Plan of Lydian fortification and houses.

was destroyed. Attic black-figure vessels, including a Komast cup, one complete and two fragmentary Little Master cups, fragments of a Tyrrhenian amphora and other sherds, are closely datable to the years around 550 BCE; other imported and local pottery is consistent with this date. Carbon-14 analysis of burned barley from a house floor yielded a date of 570±50 years BCE. The obvious context for a military attack in the middle of the sixth century is the capture of Sardis by Cyrus the Great around 546 BCE.[3] The assemblage thus provides an important and welcome fixed point in the chronology of archaic Lydian material culture.

Archaeologists exposed five areas of the houses of the east side of the structure, although only one room could be completely excavated without destroying the well-preserved Roman remains above. At the south, part of a room contained a post support, showing that this was roofed space (Area 1 on the top plan to the right). North of this room were at least four more rooms or spaces. A small room about 3.5 X 3.5 m was likely used as a kitchen (Area 3). Around this was an open courtyard, of which an L-shaped portion has been exposed (Areas 4 and 6). A narrow corridor-like space ran between the kitchen and the west wall of the house (Area 2). Finally, a room at the north served as a workshop for making glass objects (Area 5). The rooms continued to the north, east, and south; on the west an open passage separated them from the fortification.

The architecture and pre-destruction stratigraphy suggest that we have two distinct houses here. The house to the north, including in its final phase Areas 2 through 6, is the earlier, probably built in the early sixth century BCE. To the south of this house was originally just an open area. Sometime in the first half of the sixth century, the house was remodelled. Its southern wall was torn down and rebuilt and a new house was built to the south. The kitchen

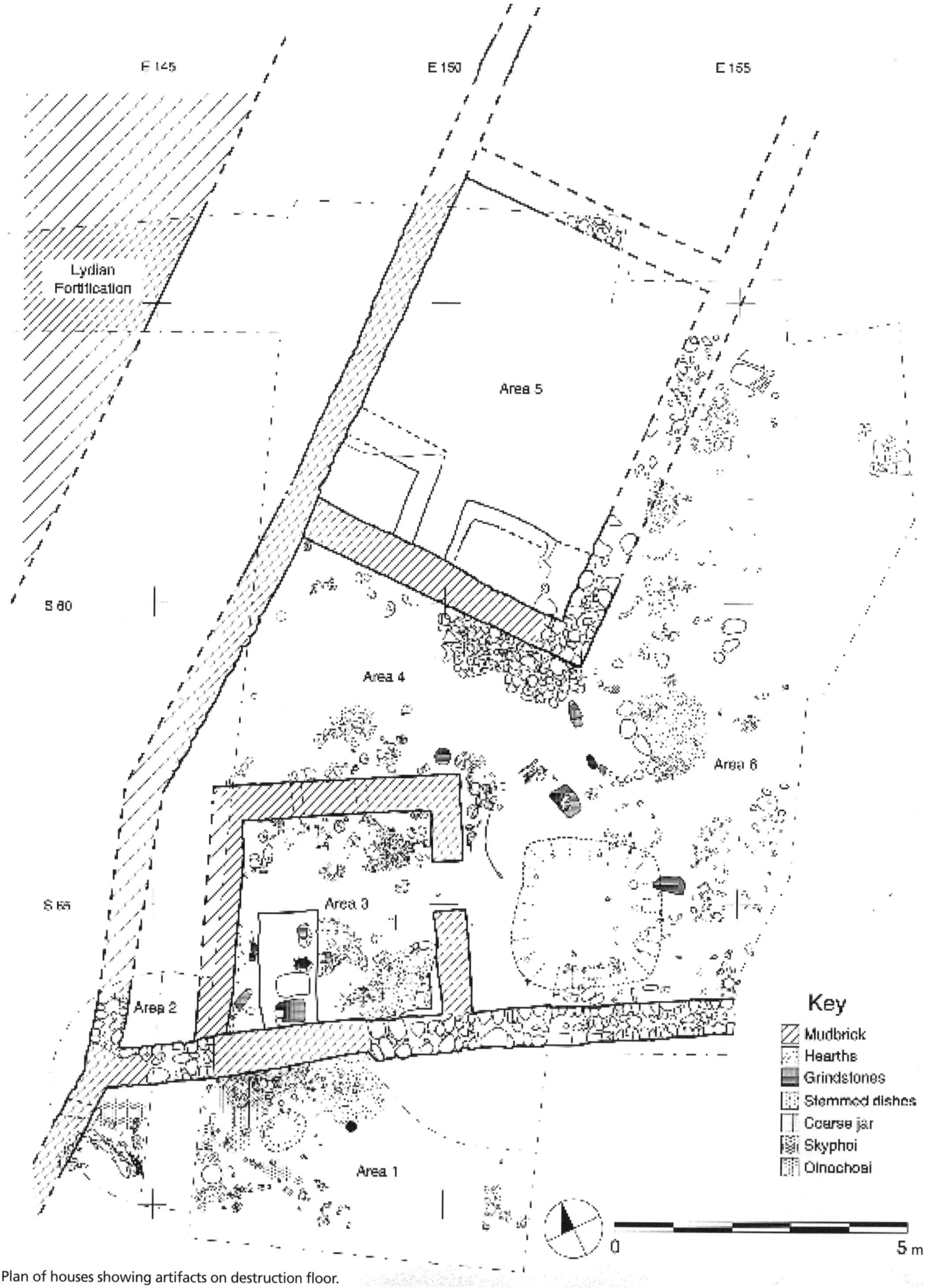

Plan of houses showing artifacts on destruction floor.

and glass workshop were also later subdivisions of the original house, both belonging to the sixth century. Probes have revealed earlier strata dating as far back as the first half of the seventh century or earlier, but the nature of the previous occupation remains uncertain.

Areas 3 (kitchen) and 4 (yard) during excavation, from the east.

North House: Kitchen (Area 3)

The northern house is the better-explored area, with four spaces partly or completely exposed. Of these, the kitchen is the only completely excavated room. An open hearth occupied its southeast corner and consisted of about 14 cm of grassy ash. At first, we thought this ash was burned dung, and looked to the East, where wood and charcoal are hard to come by, for parallels for cooking on dung (Greenewalt et al. 1990:148). The paleobotanists, M. Nesbitt and D. Samuels, are now more hesitant about this identification and suggest that the ash may be burned straw instead. In either case, cooks used this hearth for both baking and cooking stews. At least two breadtrays, flat low-fired clay pans with burnished top surfaces, were found on it, together with two cooking stands, which would have supported cooking pots, seven of which were found in the northern part of the room.

Food preparers ground grain into flour or meal on two sets of grindstones set into a low bench in the southwest corner of the room. The people doing the grinding would have knelt or squatted in the rather narrow space between the bench and the wall, gaining leverage from the wall behind. Between the two grindstones, an unfired clay tray served to hold grain or meal. The grain was probably stored in a large cookingware amphora found fallen and shattered between the bench and the hearth. The amphora contained barley grains, rachis and husk fragments, as well as various other burnt organic material.

Against the south and west walls stood some sort of shelves or fixtures, of which only the iron nails and brackets remained. An unusual vessel in the shape of a duck had fallen from the southern shelf. This had a sipping spout on one side and a filling spout equipped with a strainer on top. Similar in principle to many Phrygian pots, the vessel might have been used for drinking beer, as described by Archilochos (Fr. 42 West), Xenophon (*Anabasis* 4.5.26), and others. A lamp and globular *lekythos* had fallen from the shelf over the grinding bench; this same shelf might also have held the cookingware amphora.

Twenty-three stemmed dishes were piled on the floor in the northeast corner of the room. Some piled upside down and some right side up, they may have been stored in a basket of which no trace remained. These were among the most common Lydian pottery shapes, and the vessels in this group were all essentially identical, ranging in diameter from 19–23 cm. The interiors of most of the plates were worn from use; they presumably served as the standard plate for eating. The stem might have served as a handle for holding the plate while reclining at the table. The dishes were notable, among other reasons, for the graffiti incised on eighteen of them. A number of monograph-like signs are repeated on several vessels, but in different "handwritings", such as a sign that looks like a snake and another that appears like a figure 8 with a bar crossing the center. There are also possible alphabetic graffiti, including alpha and Lydian digamma, and a marvelous figural hound chasing a deer. The meaning of these graffiti is unclear: are they personal monograms, family monograms, or what? Such marks are not rare on Lydian pottery, but seem especially common on this shape.

Another shelf or fixture stood against the northern wall, again attested by a cluster of nails. A number of vessels must have fallen from this shelf, including seven cooking pots, two more cooking stands, two *oinochoai*, a table amphora, three *skyphoi*, a *kantharos*, a ring *askos*, four lydions, a *lekythos*, two lamps, a lid, and two coarse bowls. Nearby was a large iron swinging handle, probably from a bucket. An iron knife and two bone buttons lay on the floor near the center of the room.

Grinding bench with grindstones in use.

Courtyard (Areas 4–6)

The kitchen opened onto an unroofed yard, of which about 68 m^2 have been excavated in an L-shaped area. Towards the center of the area sat another hearth, partly ringed by stones like the hearth in the kitchen. One or two cooking pots were broken on it, containing carbonized wheat (?), probably for making porridge.

Another group of cooking vessels was set up just outside the door of the kitchen: three cooking stands, four cooking pots, a cooking pot lid, and a long iron spit. The cooking pots rested on the stands when the house was destroyed, but they were empty, and there was no trace of charcoal or burning. They were probably being stored here for use on the hearth in the center of the yard.

One of the more enigmatic features of this area was an open pit, roughly 2.6 m in diameter and 1.3 m deep, covered with planks. The pit was either empty at the time of destruction or contained mainly perishable substances. The bricky fill of the pit contained a number of artifacts, including loom weights, lydions and *askoi*, part of a vessel with a phallic spout, and three possible touchstones. These probably fell into the pit during the destruction of the house. Such pits have sometimes been interpreted as food storage pits, and, indeed, this pit did produce remains of wheat and/or barley. However, damp and exposed to vermin, an unlined, subterranean pit in the middle of an unroofed courtyard would be a rather poor choice for grain storage, and I doubt that this was its main use (see Gallant 1991:96).

Two lower and two upper grindstones sat not far from the hearth, and against the north wall of the kitchen excavators uncovered a basalt grinding bowl and a limestone rubbing stone, its sides worn smooth from grinding and its ends battered from pounding. A cooking pot fallen from a shelf nearby retained clumps of barley husks, the cast-off chaff from dehulling barley to make "pearl barley" for porridge and other uses (see Pliny, *Nat. Hist.* 18.14.22).

Shelves against the walls stored many of the vessels from the yard, probably protected by a simple roof cantilevered out from the wall. A number of these vessels were worn, partial, and reused: a hydria neck reused as a stand for an *oinochoe*, *oinochoai* without neck or handles, a few partial roof tiles, and the bottom of a column krater. Residents probably reused worn-out and broken table vessels for other purposes here in the open yard. For example, a hydria whose neck had been broken off in antiquity contained at least 3.5 kg of iron "rustballs"—shapeless lumps of iron about 1–3 cm in diameter. These might be some byproduct of the smelting of iron, awaiting reprocessing.

Among these worn-out and reused vessels were a number of antiques. Most notable among these was an orientalizing *dinos* decorated with dog-headed sea monsters. Although it had been broken, perhaps deliberately, and scattered widely in the destruction, it was nevertheless almost complete. It had been repaired in antiquity and was probably at least a generation old, but still in use, when the house was destroyed. An aquatic theme was also found on another orientalizing vessel in the shape of a boat. This showed a procession of cows on one side and a dog chasing a hare on the other, while below the "waterline" fish swim among seaweed growing from the floor. This vessel was recovered, half preserved, from a pile of rocks dumped against the north wall of the yard; it had evidently been discarded here sometime before the destruction of the house.[4] This area also included imported ceramics: fragments of two Attic black figure Little Master cups, a Tyrrhenian amphora(?), and other fragments.

Many more vessels were scattered in the eastern part of the yard—where they had apparently been thrown and smashed in the ransacking of the house—bringing the total for the yard to more than 130 vessels. The inventory included one complete and one partial Myrina amphora, a small Wild Goat style oinochoe, at least three waveline hydrias, four to six oinochoai, two spool-shaped objects with orientalizing decoration, nine lydions, and four lamps. Two or three *pithoi* were found in the northern portion of the excavated area. Their contents have not been identified, but if they stood in an open space, they were probably not used for storing foodstuffs. In some respects the courtyard assemblage complemented that of the kitchen. For instance, while the kitchen contained twenty-three stemmed dishes, but only six *skyphoi*, the yard had twenty-five skyphoi, but only eight stemmed dishes, some of which were fragmentary and being reused for other purposes.

Area 1 (southern house) during excavation, from the south.

Scattered in the southern part of the yard were about 105 loom weights. They can be divided into six or seven groups on the basis of weight and shape. Most were pyramidal, although there were a few rectangular and one ovoid weight; the groups ranged in weight from an average of 42 g to an average of 280 g. The variety suggests that different kinds or, perhaps, more complex types of cloth were being woven here, demanding warp threads weighted at different tensions.[5] The weights may have represented the equipment of at least three looms. Unfortunately, because they were scattered throughout the southern part of the yard, their distribution does not reveal whether or how they may have been set up on looms or stored at the time of destruction.

Finally, the area just north of the door to the kitchen provided a gruesome witness of the fate of these houses: the torso, left arm, and part of the left leg of a middle-aged, arthritic man, undoubtedly a victim of Cyrus' troops. Although, like the rest of this area, the bones of the burned and fragile skeleton had been buried and sealed by the destruction debris dumped from the fortification, there were no traces of the missing parts. The skeleton's poor preservation makes it nearly impossible to say whether the missing parts had been carried off (e.g., by animals) or whether the victim had been mutilated by Cyrus' troops, a common Near Eastern practice (Greenewalt, Ratté, and Rautman 1993:25–26; Greenewalt et al. 1990:150, n. 22).

Glass Workshop (Area 5)

To the north of the yard, a room about 6 X 4.3 m may have had two doors, one in its north wall and perhaps one on its east. Unlike the other areas, this room had been intentionally dug out to slightly below floor level after the destruction and then backfilled with the dug-out debris. The ancient excavators probably intended to recover the precious contents of the room: its fill retained ca. 3.5 kg of opaque red cuprite glass cullet. This rather rare and costly material has been found in roughly contemporary contexts at Nineveh, Persepolis, and elsewhere, and its manufacture is described in Akkadian glass-making texts (Brill and Cahill 1988; Oppenheim et al. 1971). The raw glass was probably not manufactured on the site, but was likely being softened and worked into finished artifacts. One of the few of these that survived was a glass "melon bead" made of different colored glasses.

In the southern corners of the room were two mudbrick platforms or blocks with low, narrow benches on two sides. The vertical surfaces and the interior walls of this room were plastered with mud plaster and painted with a gold micaceous paint, and its edges were reinforced with wooden boards. The surfaces of the low benches had been covered with blackened clay and may have functioned as working areas for glass.

The inclusion of light industry in a primarily domestic context was relatively common at Sardis and throughout the ancient Mediterranean world. Many houses in both Greece and elsewhere included spaces for cottage industry, and, indeed, most manufacture was probably carried out in an essentially domestic context.[6]

Southern House (Area 1)

Though excavations exposed a much smaller area of the southern house—only 22 m^2—the finds represented many of the same activities. Shelves or other furnishings were built against the north and west walls. The structure against the west wall left a scatter of nails, mostly aligned, in the destruction debris; it had been supported by wooden beams or posts set into slots in the mudbrick wall. The shelf against the north wall left no hardware. Instead, a prodigious pile of broken pottery, that spilled onto a group of vessels, which were found *in situ* on the floor adjacent to the wall, provided ample witness to its existence.

The floor against the north wall held a hearth, with a cooking pot smashed on it. Nearby was a cooking stand and, next to it, a cooking pot filled with barley and its lid. A fragmentary breadtray rested on the cooking stand, and an iron grater, perhaps a cheese grater, lay nearby. The cooking assemblage parallels those in the house to the north, but contains fewer examples of each type, at least in the space excavated.

The southern house offered yet more storage for foodstuffs. A large coarse gray jar full of tiny chickpeas had fallen from a shelf, and, in addition to the cooking pot full of barley, a bag or basket of barley rested on the floor near the west wall of the house. Finally, a few heads of carbonized garlic lay against the house wall, from which they had perhaps hung in a braid as in a modern house.

Eating and drinking vessels existed in somewhat smaller numbers than in the northern house, but the similarities are still clear. A pile of thirteen stemmed dishes rested on the floor against the north wall of the area, the same relative location but only about half the number of the northern house. These stemmed dishes were more diverse than those from the northern kitchen, however. Four dishes were small, only 12–14 cm in diameter, and painted with a burnished yellow slip rather than the usual black bands on red streaky slip. One was of medium size, 15.5 cm in diameter, while the other eight were similar in size and decoration to those from the kitchen to the north.

The shelf above these objects held about thirty-four more vessels, including a large strainer or colander, three lamps, four *lekthoi*, four lydions, and six *oinochoai*. On the floor was a fine waveline amphora. Imports from this shelf included a complete Attic black-figure komast cup and a Little Master cup (N. Ramage 1986).

The small area excavated against the west wall of the room offered more pots and other artifacts, mostly fallen from a shelf. These included vessels for serving wine (a large column krater, a hydria, and two oinochoai) and cooking implements such as another cooking stand and a set of ten iron spits. Two clusters of small artifacts associated with cosmetics and personal ornamentation joined these, perhaps stored originally in a box that had disintegrated. These included five lydions, two Corinthian *aryballoi*, a small cosmetics(?) plate, fourteen spindle whorls, a disk shaped ivory or bone earring, three silver ornaments, glass beads, a faience hawk, seventy-eight knucklebones,

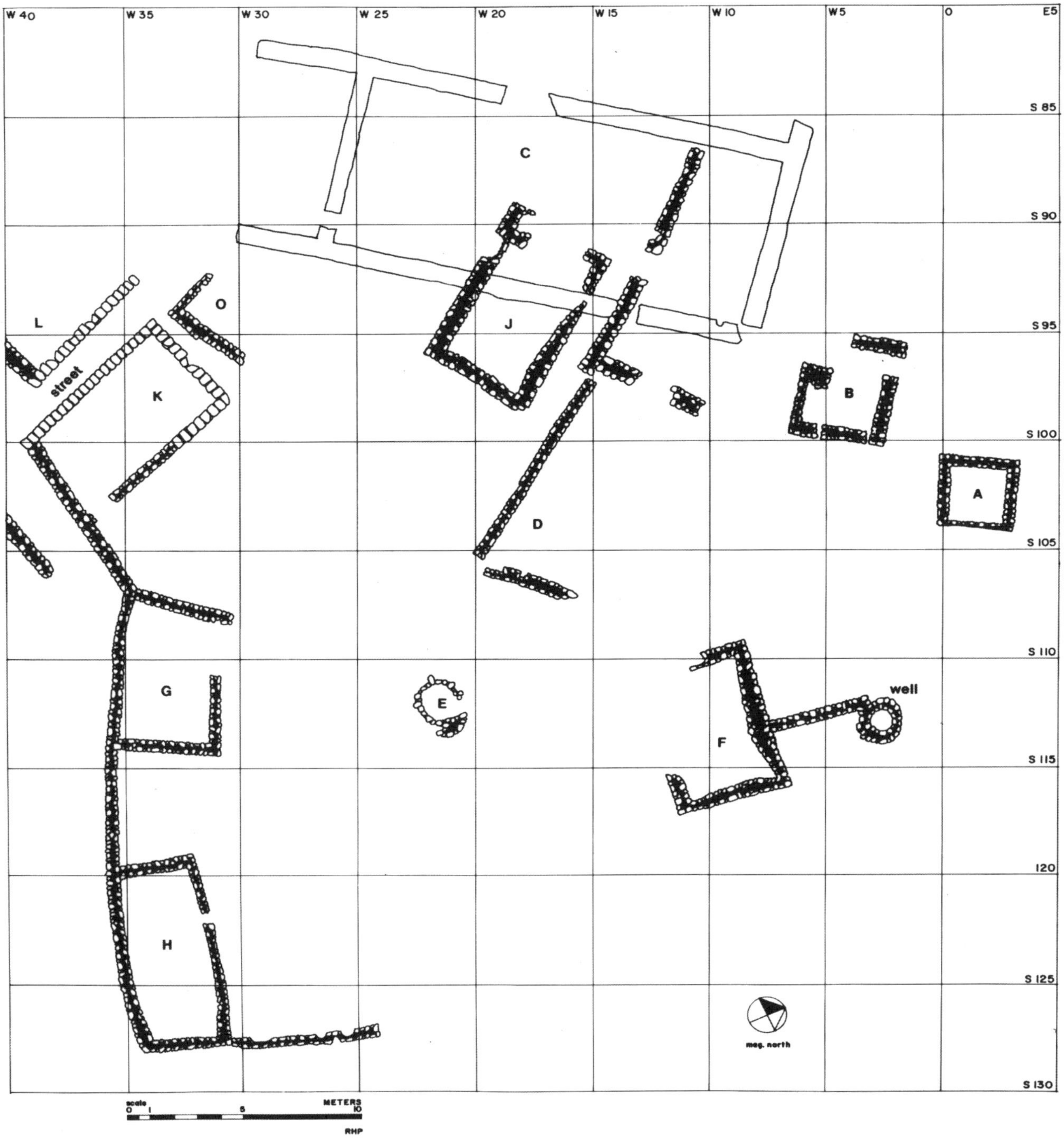

Sector HoB: Lydian buildings from Lydian Levels II (buildings G, H, J, K, L, and O) and III (buildings A, B, D, E, and F).

and other small objects. It is tempting to interpret these as a woman's toiletry and personal effects, but the collection also included objects that do not necessarily belong to a feminine assemblage, such as a horse trapping and a touchstone for assaying the purity of gold. A deep Roman foundation had cut into the floor just east of here, undoubtedly removing many more objects.

Towards the center of the space, excavators uncovered a pithos and, scattered nearby, forty-six loom weights, perhaps fallen from a loom. Iron and bronze hardware found among these may well have belonged to the loom itself. A telling difference between this cluster of loom weights and those scattered in the courtyard was that nearly all the weights of this cluster were the same size, weighing between 210 and 269 g (a bit smaller than the largest size of loom weight in the northern house). At least in this space, then, the residents seem to be weaving only a single, coarser type of cloth, rather than the variety and finer weaves woven in the northern house.

Overview

It would be impossible—and, I believe, ultimately unproductive—to ask how "typical" these houses were of Lydian houses. Even to begin establishing types, norm, and degrees of variation would require many more houses fully exposed in different parts of the city so that their size, structure, and contents could be compared. Such an endeavor lies at the heart of any study of the ancient house and household, but it is unfortunately impossible at most sites.

The assemblages from these houses nevertheless present some surprises. First, there is the sheer quantity of pottery, grindstones, and other materials. The partly-excavated northern house alone contained some 200 eating, drinking, and cooking vessels. This large inventory included thirty-one stemmed dishes, thirty *skyphoi*, seventeen lydions, seventeen cooking pots, sixteen *oinochoai*, ten lamps, eight cooking stands, and some seventy-eight other vessels. This is many times more than has been found in excavated houses at Sardis itself or at other sites.

Of course, the preservation of this area is exceptional and that clearly accounts, on one level, for the large numbers. But are we to conclude, then, that most ancient houses contained such a profusion of pots and other artifacts, and that it is merely poor preservation that leaves us with the paltry assemblages found in houses at other sites? Or is there an unusually heavy concentration of people, activities, or some other factor in this house? If so, is this typical for Lydia or is it anomalous even at Sardis?

The extraordinary number of artifacts has led some members of the expedition to suggest, perhaps lightheartedly, that this building was not a house but something more in the nature of a restaurant or "soup kitchen," i.e., that the pottery and other artifacts were not intended for domestic, but commercial use. While this is not impossible, the mixture of activities in these spaces, including storage, preparation, cooking, serving and eating of food, weaving, and storage of personal effects, makes their identification as houses, in some sense of the word, much more likely. The questions, rather, are how Lydian houses were organized and what constituted a Lydian household, i.e., what the Lydians meant by "house."

We know little about the size and composition of Archaic Lydian households. Household size is not of course a fixed number; it varies through cycles as children are born, grow, move out; as parents and relatives join the households of their children, age, and die; and as kin come and go. Household composition also includes varying numbers of slaves and other unrelated members (Gallant 1991:11–33). Estimating the size of ancient households is therefore hazardous at best. Archaeologists often estimate household size from the area of the house, using some standard of people per square meter derived from ethnographic analogies.[7] This begs important questions by assuming standard numbers of people per square meter, as if all cultures were the same. And since we don't have the full extent of either of these houses, we could not use this method in any case. Literary texts may shed some light on household size, but while we have relatively good sources from Greece and some Near Eastern cultures, very few documents illuminate such questions for Archaic Lydia. Demographic reconstructions also require assumptions that are often problematic, as do ethnographic analogies and other methods.

Despite the paucity of sources, many scholars have concluded that a modal household size in ancient Greece, pre-industrial Europe, a number of Near Eastern cultures, and in other situations more or less analogous to Archaic Sardis, ranged from four to six people, plus slaves (always an uncertain factor)—a single nuclear family, with an occasional addition of relatives. This seems to be a fairly common form of household organization and has generally been the explicit or implied model for Lydian Sardis.[8]

How do the contents of these houses fit with this model of the Lydian household? It seems a good assumption that a household maintains possessions appropriate for its needs. This should be particularly true of objects for food preparation, cooking, and everyday eating vessels, which make up the majority of the assemblage. So when we have such extraordinary preservation, we should be able to draw conclusions about the size and composition of a household from the quantities of vessels and other artifacts. I should emphasize that we have very few full household assemblages anywhere to which we can compare these, either in the archaeological or literary records. Arguments from what seems "reasonable" are very risky, but it is worth at least speculating about these important issues.

The quantity of pottery recovered from the southern house seems more or less consistent with a household of four to six people. There are eight large stemmed dishes, five smaller ones, four cooking pots, two cooking stands, and enough loom weights for one loom. Although the assemblage is incomplete, what we have seems appropriate for a single-family household.

This is not true for the northern house, however. The group of twenty-three virtually identical stemmed dishes is particularly striking. The number of stemmed dishes, moreover, is roughly equivalent to the number of *skyphoi* in the excavated portion of the house (thirty-one total). Other eating and drinking vessels are found in similar numbers. We might suggest that on the order of two dozen people could be served simultaneously. Even if we are conservative and cut the number in half, to eleven or twelve people, we still have twice the modal household size that has been argued or assumed for most ancient cultures.

The large number of grindstones in this house also demands explanation. Grindstones were relatively expensive, made of imported granite and shaped to create an exact fit between upper and lower stones. Grinding was also a slow and labor-intensive task, one that left telltale injuries on the bones of Neolithic and later women (Molleson 1994). To grind the flour for a large household would have taken a significant length of time—a modern experimenter took two minutes to grind ca. 15–20 ml of grain, or more than one and one-half hours to grind a daily ration of about one liter for one person (Samuel 1989). Even if ancient women were much more efficient at it than modern academics, grinding still remained a time consuming labor. Four complete sets of grindstones recovered from the northern house therefore represented a significant investment in both time and money. For them to be all in use simultaneously there must have been at least four working women in the house.

Finally, the 105 or more loom weights of different sorts from the courtyard, representing the equipment of perhaps three looms, suggests that at least three women could have woven simultaneously here. Every type of artifact that we can meaningfully quantify points to a household significantly larger than a nuclear family.

We may contrast these numbers with assemblages from another site with relatively well-preserved domestic contexts, Olynthus in northern Greece, dating to the mid-fourth century BCE. The largest number of pottery vessels in any of the 100-odd houses excavated at Olynthus was 106—only half the number here (the House of Many Colors: Robinson 1946:183–206; Cahill 2002:85–97). The largest number of grindstones in a house at Olynthus was seven, or three sets of upper and lower stones; and this again was a unique occurrence; most houses had only one set.[9] Omitting one house that engaged in large-scale weaving for the market, the largest number of loom weights in any house at Olynthus was 133. High numbers typically ranged from thirty to sixty weights per house. Although both preservation and, just as important, mending were not nearly as complete as at Sardis, this is probably offset by the fact that whole houses were excavated, while ours is only partially dug—and that is the maximum for the entire excavated area (Cahill 2002:169–79).

How should we understand the large number of artifacts in this building? The household might have included a large number of slaves or other unrelated household members, swelling numbers beyond the nuclear family "core." If so, the fact that the stemmed dishes and other eating utensils seem to be stored and, perhaps, used in common, rather than being spatially segregated, suggests that the household was at least eating as a single unit, or the great quantity might suggest some type of extended household: a parent with offspring and perhaps their family or a number of siblings sharing the same enclosure, perhaps with slaves and other non related members of the household, sharing a common kitchen and cooking and eating communally. In the final analysis, we might need to expand our notions of "house" and "household" to include some wider form of organization.

Other Lydian houses at Sardis offer both similarities and contrasts. At Sector HoB, some 100–200 m to the west of our houses and on the other side of the fortification, a number of buildings were excavated that dated from the eighth through the sixth centuries BCE and later into the Hellenistic and Roman periods. The most coherent Lydian level, Lydian II, is dated to the mid-seventh century BCE, about a century earlier than the houses at the foot of the fortification (Buildings G, H, J, K, L, and O).[10]

Buildings G, H, J, and K are roughly comparable in size, about 6–8 m X 3–4 m; building L, incompletely excavated, may be of a similar size. They are similar in their features as well, with benches built against their shorter walls and small stone "bins" or platforms built near one end of a longer wall, often with an adjacent oven. Slots in the stone walls may have held wooden uprights supporting built-in furniture like shelves. Buildings G, H, and K are linked by a perimeter wall, suggesting an identification of this area as a market or bazaar with one-room shops built against it.[11] One might instead interpret this constellation as the individual rooms of a single large compound house, stressing the domestic nature of this area over the commercial. While there is considerable evidence for light industry in this area, this is perfectly compatible with a primarily domestic use, similar to the glass workshop in the northern house discussed above. Moreover, the ovens, cooking pottery, loom weights, and other domestic utensils found in the buildings suggest that they were primarily domestic in function.

Their residents apparently abandoned the buildings in a hurry, perhaps in advance of a flood to which this area is susceptible, leaving a number of vessels and other artifacts *in situ* on the floors. Thus, the circumstances of abandonment are quite different from those of the houses near the fortification, and the final assemblages are much smaller and not easily comparable.

One important point of comparison, A. Ramage has pointed out, is that the sector HoB units seem to be parallel in function, each with its own cooking and storage facilities (if that is what the small "bins" were used for), benches, and other features. They might, therefore, be independent households linked by commercial ties (stressing the industrial quality of the area) or they might be "sub-houses" of separate or semi-separate households within a single compound, linked by family or other social ties—siblings for instance. By contrast, the rooms of the northern house near the fortification are specialized—one room serves as a kitchen for a group larger than a nuclear family; another as a glass workshop—and there is much less duplication of features, assemblages, and activities.

Alternatively, these buildings may represent a group of non-related households sharing certain common tasks like food preparation and perhaps other work as well. This would be somewhat similar to the situation at the Early Phrygian Terrace Buildings at Gordion. There, rows of identical units, measuring ca. 11.5 X 21 m, each contained facilities for food preparation and weaving remarkably similar to those found at Sardis. Grinding benches stood at the back of the main room, a short distance from the back wall, just as our bench does. These benches, however, contained between five and eighteen grindstones, many more than the two on our bench. Ovens and other cooking facilities occupied the anterooms of these terrace buildings. Excavators unearthed loom weights and spindle whorls by the hundreds, together with hundreds of pots, other domestic equipment, and foodstuffs (DeVries 1980).

While the facilities, equipment, and activities in the Terrace Buildings were quite similar to those in our houses, the overall situation was quite different. The Terrace Buildings were engaged in production, weaving, and cooking on a very large scale, much larger than the cottage industries of the Sardis houses. Keith DeVries proposes that they were specialized productive units, worked by groups of women (slaves?)—perhaps about twenty-five per Terrace Building—to supply the needs of the palace compound on the citadel of the city. But it is worth noting that production again took place in a sort of semi-domestic context. Each building contained a mixture of activities appropriate for a house—weaving, cooking, and grinding—rather than having each activity take place in a separate building or workshop. Although on a much larger scale, the organization of work here in this palatial situation adhered to a domestic model.

We may therefore consider houses like those at Sardis as occupying several points in a series of continua. One scale is household size and composition, from a small nuclear family, to an extended household, to a group of (presumably) non-related co-residents like the workers at Gordion. Another scale is that of productive activities, ranging from the day-to-day necessities of food preparation and textile production for a family unit, to engagement in these same activities on a larger scale for consumption outside the household, to specialized craft production, like the glass workshop, and an articulation with the extra-household economy. The term "house" can describe many locations on this landscape of human occupation. By examining the landscape contents as well as the architecture in extraordinary situations like at Sardis, we can add important dimensions to our portrait of ancient households.

Notes

[1] Preliminary reports have appeared in *BASOR*, *AJA*, and *AASOR*: Greenewalt, Cahill, and Rautman 1987; Greenewalt, Rautman, and Cahill 1987; Greenewalt et al. 1990; Greenewalt 1994 and 1995.

[2] These figures, and all the figures for assemblages presented here, are preliminary estimates as of the time of writing. Mending and study of fragments is still continuing, and will probably change the quantities slightly.

[3] For more detailed information on the skeleton and helmet, see Greenewalt and Heywood (1992) on the two complete Attic cups and the date of destruction, see N. Ramage (1986), and on the date of the capture of Sardis, see Cargill (1977), Burstein (1984), and Greenewalt (1992).

[4] Compare another boat-shaped vessel from a grave at Sardis (Greenewalt 1987); another boat vase, perhaps from the Sardis region, is now in the Manisa Museum.

[5] On the warp-weighted loom, see Hoffman (1964); Barber (1994) gives a good account of ancient weaving.

[6] For instance, Greek pottery was manufactured primarily in domestic settings. See Blondé and Perreault (1992) and Arafat and Morgan (1989).

[7] E.g., Naroll 1962 and Kolb 1985. Wallace-Hadrill (1994:90–117) estimates the size of Roman households at Pompeii and Herculaneum and takes a properly skeptical view of the procedure.

[8] See Hanfmann (1983:87) and Gallant (1991:11–33) for classical Greece. One source of information not often cited in studies of Anatolian households is funerary epitaphs. Bryce notes that Lycian "tomb families"—people who had the right to be buried in a tomb together with its owner—generally included the owner's wife and children, occasionally extended to include the owner's grandchildren, servants, and retainers (Lycian *prñnezi*) and other persons: essentially a nuclear family with occasional additions (Bryce 1979, 1986). Lydian epitaphs are less numerous, well-understood, or well studied as those of Lycia, but suggest similar configurations, see McLaughlin (1985:290–317).

[9] One house at Olynthus (A 6) had twelve grindstones, as well as an olive crusher and other equipment for processing agricultural produce, but this household seems to be doing such processing professionally, rather than simply for household use.

[10] Hanfmann 1966:8–15 and 1983:29–31, 71–73; and A. Ramage 1978:7–8. A. Ramage is writing a final publication of these buildings, including their contents and functions. In the succeeding phase, Lydian III, dating to the sixth century BCE, the excavated structures were smaller and somewhat less organized.

[11] The area is often described as the "Lydian Market," and sometimes identified with the agora described by Herodotus (5.101) in his account of the Ionian Revolt in 499 BCE (e.g. Hanfmann 1970:28, 1980:106, and 1983:29–31). However, the Pactolus River, which Herodotus describes as flowing through the agora of Sardis, could not have flowed through this part of the site, as it is separated by high natural ridges from the present and ancient course of the stream. The thick beds of water-laid sand and gravel that separate the occupational strata here are, according to Sullivan (Greenwalt et al. 1985:540–55), perhaps the result of flooding of the Hermus River, which may have flowed much closer to the city than it does at present, perhaps just along the northern edge of the city.

Bibliography

Akurgal, E.
1983 *Alt-Smyrna I: Wohnschichten und Athenatempel.* Türk Tarih Kurumu Yayınları. V. Dizi, Sa. 40. Ankara: Türk Tarih Kurumu Basimevi.

Arafat, K. and Morgan, C.
1989 Pots and Potters in Athens and Corinth: A Review. *Oxford Journal of Archaeology* 8:31–46.

Barber, E. W.
1994 *Women's Work: The First 20,000 Years.* New York: W. W. Norton.

Blondé, F. and Perreault, J. Y., eds.
1992 *Les ateliers de potiers dans le monde grec aux époque géometrique, archaïque et classique.* Bulletin de Correspondence Hellénique Suppl. 23. Paris: École française de'Athènes.

Bryce, T. R.
1979 Lycian Tomb Families and their Social Implications. *Journal of the Economic and Social History of the Orient* 23:296–313.
1986 *The Lycians in Literary and Epigraphic Sources. The Lycians: A Study of Lycian History and Civilisation to the Conquest of Alexander the Great 1.* Copenhagen: Museum Tusculanum Press.

Burstein, S. M.
1984 A New *Tabula Iliaca*: The Vasek Polak Chronicle. J. Paul Getty Museum Journal 12:153–62.

Cahill, N. D.
2002 *Household and City Planning at Olynthus.* New Haven: Yale University Press.

Cargill, J.
1977 The Nabonidus Chronicle and the Fall of Sardis. *American Journal of Ancient History* 2:97–116.

DeVries, K.
1980 Greeks and Phrygians in the Early Iron Age. Pp. 33–49 in *From Athens to Gordion: Papers of a Memorial Symposium for Rodney S. Young*, edited by K. DeVries. University Museum Papers 1. Philadelphia: The University Museum, University of Pennsylvania.

Gallant, T. W.
1991 *Risk and Survival in Ancient Greece.* Stanford: Stanford University Press.

Greenewalt, C. H., Jr.
1987 A Lydian Canoe-shaped Vessel from Sardis. In *Akurgal'a Armağan: Festschrift Ekrem Akurgal*, edited by C. Bayburtluoğlu and T. Özgüç. Anadolu/Anatolia. Ankara.
1992 When a Mighty Empire was Destroyed: The Common Man at the Fall of Sardis, ca. 546 BC. *Proceedings of the American Philosophical Society* 136:247–71.

Greenewalt, C. H., Jr., Cahill, N. D., Dedeoğlu, H., and Herrmann, P.
1990 The Sardis Campaign of 1986. *Bulletin of the American Schools of Oriental Research* Supplement 26:137–77.

Greenewalt, C. H., Jr., Cahill, N. D.,and Rautmann, M. L.
1987 The Sardis Campaign of 1984. *Bulletin of the American Schools of Oriental Research* Supplement 25:13–54.

Greenewalt, C. H., Jr., and Heywood, A. M.
1992 A Helmet of the Sixth Century B.C. from Sardis. *Bulletin of the American Schools of Oriental Research* 285:1–31.

Greenewalt, C. H., Jr., Ratté, C., Sullivan, D. G., and Howe, T. N.
1985 The Sardis Campaigns of 1981 and 1982. *Bulletin of the American Schools of Oriental Research* Supplement 23:53–92.

Greenewalt, C. H., Jr., Ratté, C., and Rautman, M. L.
1994 The Sardis Campaigns of 1988 and 1989. Pp. 1–43 in *Annual of ASOR, Vol. 51.* Atlanta: Scholars Press.
1995 The Sardis Campaigns of 1990 and 1991. Pp. 1–36 in *Annual of ASOR, Vol. 52.* Atlanta: Scholars Press..

Greenewalt, C. H., Jr., Rautman, M. L., and Cahill, N. D.
1987 The Sardis Campaign of 1985. *Bulletin of the American Schools of Oriental Research* Supplement 25:55–92.

Hanfmann, G. M. A.
1959 Excavations at Sardis, 1958. *Bulletin of the American Schools of Oriental Research* 154:5–35.
1966 The Eighth Campaign at Sardis. *Bulletin of the American Schools of Oriental Research* 182:2–54.
1983 *Sardis from Prehistoric to Roman Times: Results of the Archaeological Exploration of Sardis, 1958–1975.* Cambridge, MA: Harvard University Press.

Hoffmann, M.
1964 *The Warp-weighted Loom: Studies in the History and Technology of an Ancient Implement.* Studia Norvegica 14. Oslo: Universitetsforlaget.

Kolb, C. C.
1985 Demographic Estimates in Archaeology: Contributions from Ethnoarchaeology on Mesoamerican Peasants. *Current Anthropology* 26:581–99.

McLauchlin, B. K.
1985 *Lydian Graves and Burial Customs.* Ph.D. diss. University of California at Berkeley.

Molleson, T.
1994 The Eloquent Bones of Abu Hureya. *Scientific American* 271/2:70–75.

Narroll, R.
1962 Floor Area and Settlement Population. *American Antiquity* 27:587–89.

Ramage, A.
1978 *Lydian Houses and Architectural Terracottas.* Archaeological Exploration of Sardis Monograph 5. Cambridge, MA: Harvard University Press.

Ramage, N.
1986 Two New Attic Cups and the Siege of Sardis. *American Journal of Archaeology* 90:419–24.

Robinson, D. M.
1946 *Excavations at Olynthus, Part 12: Domestic and Public Architecture.* Johns Hopkins University Studies in Archaeology 36. Baltimore: Johns Hopkins University.

Samuel, D.
1989 Their Staff of Life: Initial Investigations of Ancient Egyptian Bread Baking. Pp. 253–90 in *Amarna Reports V*, edited by B. Kemp. London: Egyptian Exploration Society.

Wallace-Hadrill, A.
1994 *Houses and Society in Pompeii and Herculaneum.* Princeton: Princeton University Press.

Nicholas Cahill is Associate Professor of Greek and Roman Art in the Department of Art History at the University of Wisconsin-Madison. He received his Ph.D. from the University of California-Berkeley in 1991. He has published a book entitled "*Settled in an Orderly Fashion*": *Household and City Organization at Olynthus* (Yale UP, 2000), as well as numerous articles. He has conducted archaeological fieldwork in Turkey, Israel, Greece and Great Britain and has held fellowships from the Fulbright and American Council of Learned Societies.

Gordion: The Rise and Fall of an Iron Age Capital

Aerial view of Gordion.

By Mary M. Voigt

Current research at Yassihöyük, the archaeological site identified as ancient Gordion,[1] is focused on changes in settlement form, economy, and political organization through time. This paper summarizes ideas about the size and organization of Gordion generated by seven recent field seasons directed by the author (Sams and Voigt 1990, 1991, 1995, 1996, 1997, 1998, 1999; Voigt 1994), building on the far more extensive excavations conducted by Rodney Stuart Young and his colleagues, G. Roger Edwards and Machteld Mellink between 1950 and 1972 (Voigt 1996 with references). The resultant picture of Gordion's settlement organization for any single chronological period is highly schematic and speculative, based on archaeological data that has not been analyzed completely. Nevertheless, the collected images provide a basis for asking a series of historical questions that can be answered through the (re)analysis of data already on hand as well as new, limited field work. In this way, this paper summarizes past research and sets a direction for future work at the site.

The Archaeological Sample

Gordion can be divided into three distinct topographic zones: a high mound (Yassihöyük) that was at least partially fortified during much of its history (the "Citadel Mound"); a low area to the south of the Citadel Mound that was also fortified during some periods (the "Lower Town"); and an unfortified area on the low slopes across the present bed of the Sakarya River to the north and west of the Citadel Mound (the "Outer Town"). Each of these zones has a long and complex history, so that the names are intended only as descriptors of the modern topography of the site; they do not specify the function of each zone throughout the 4,000 year occupation of Gordion.

Our information varies significantly both by zone and by occupation phase. In general, excavation at Gordion has focused on the Citadel Mound and especially on the eastern half of the Citadel where Rodney Young cleared more than two hectares down to the Early Phrygian Destruction Level (the "Main Excavation Area"). Young and Machteld Mellink also carried out limited soundings beneath the Destruction Level, which exposed Bronze Age and Early Iron Age deposits (Gunter 1991). These data are supplemented by the Yassihöyük Stratigraphic Sounding excavated in 1988–89, which was intended to provide a better understanding of depositional processes in the Main Excavation Area as well as better chronological control (see also Voigt 1994; Sams and Voigt 1990, 1991). The resulting stratigraphic sequence (YHSS)—composed of ten chronological phases—extends from the Middle Bronze Age to Medieval times.

The Yassihoyuk/Gordion Stratigraphic Sequence (YHSS): 1988–1996

PERIOD NAME	YHSS PHASE	TENTATIVE DATE (BCE)
Medieval	YHSS 1	?
Roman	YHSS 2	1st cent BCE–AD 3rd cent
Late Hellenistic (Galatian)	YHSS 3A	3rd cent–189
Early Hellenistic	YHSS 3B	ca. 330–3rd century
Late Phrygian (Achaemenid)	YHSS 4	after 550–ca. 330
Middle Phrvgian	YHSS 5	after 800–ca. 550
Early Phrygian Destruction Level	YHSS 6A	ca. 800
Early Phrygian	YHSS 6B	ca. 950–800
Early Iron Age	YHSS 7	ca. 1100–950
Late Bronze Age	YHSS 8-9	ca. 1400–1200
Middle Bronze Age	YHSS 10	ca. 2000–1400
Early Bronze Age	—	ca. 2300–2000

The size of the Yassihöyük Stratigraphic Sounding is minuscule when compared with the area excavated by Young during seventeen seasons. For comparative purposes, we can use a minimum figure of ca. 2.0 ha for Young's Main Excavation Area, which chronologically spanned YHSS Phases 1 to 6A. In 1988–89, we cleared around .01 ha of phases 1-6A, or 0.15 percent of the area cleared by Young and his colleagues. For the Late Bronze Age, the 1988–89 area compares more favorably to the maximum area cleared by Young and Mellink in the Megaron 12 and Megaron 10 soundings (Gunter 1991:1–4).

On the western half of the Citadel, Young excavated limited areas within the so-called Southwest and South Trenches, with sample size decreasing rapidly as he moved down from Medieval to Middle Phrygian times. Excavation since 1989 on the Northwest Quadrant of the Citadel Mound has taken advantage of Young's work, which removed the Medieval occupation, allowing exposure of Roman through Middle Phrygian remains. Again the sample is small, but extremely valuable for our understanding of the sixth through the third centuries BCE (YHSS phases 5–3). In the South Trench, Young cleared most of the excavated area down to the Middle Phrygian occupation, leaving one block at the level of a Roman house. This block has now been excavated as Operation 17, providing a stratigraphic control for the rest of the trench and a sequence for the western half of the Citadel parallel to the YHSS to the east.

Interest in the Lower Town during the 1950s and 1960s focused on an investigation of the Küçük Höyük fortification system (YHSS 5) conducted by Mellink (1991:653). Mellink also tested one area within the Lower Town walls, exposing domestic architecture. In 1993, we began work in two areas inside the Lower Town walls, uncovering remains dating from Middle Phrygian to Roman times (YHSS 5-2).

While Young never investigated the broad plain to the north of the site (the "Outer Town"), he and members of his staff noted the presence of cut stone blocks churned up during dredging of the Sakarya River, and Ellen Kohler was particularly intrigued by agricultural field marks on aerial photographs taken in 1950. In 1987, William Sumner conducted the first surface survey in this area, finding scatters of sherds and other artifacts over an area of ca. 1 km^2. Since that time, more systematic survey coupled with limited test excavations have documented an occupation of this area beginning in the seventh century BCE (YHSS 5: Table 2).[2] Estimates of the size of the settled area in this part of the site are highly impressionistic, based more on the test excavations than on the surface collection of ceramics, which await detailed study.

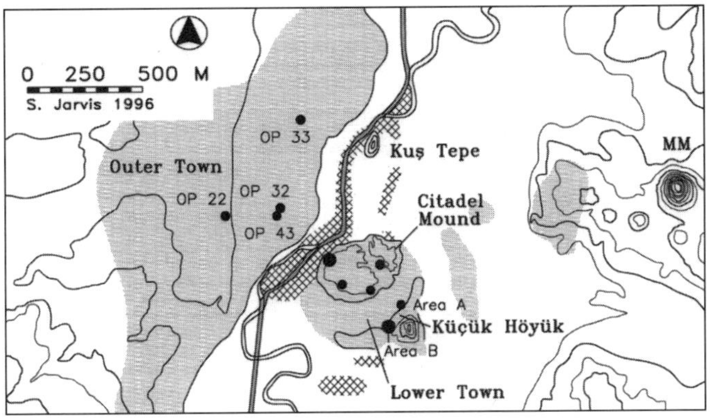

Map of Yassihoyuk/Gordion
- Settlement areas based on surface remains
- Settlement areas based on cores and river bank cuts
- • Excavation areas 1993–1995
- = Sakarya River course 1950 — Modern dredged river course

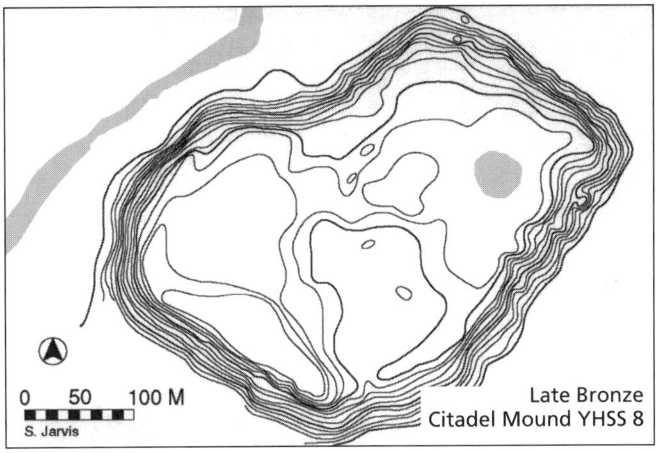

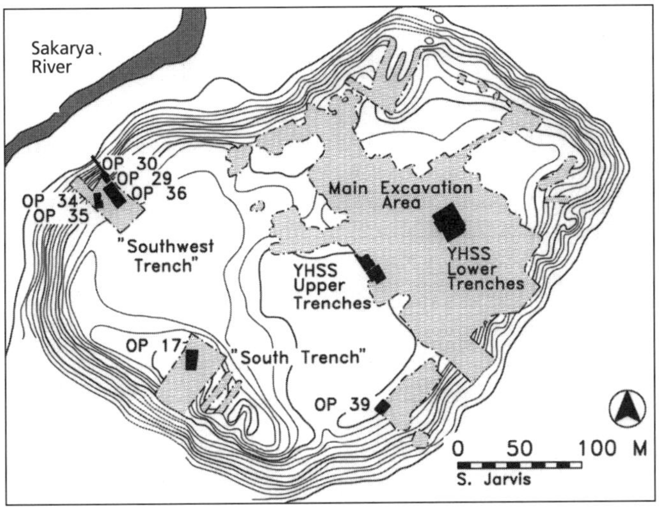

Map of the Citadel Mound showing excavated areas.
- Excavated areas 1900–1972
- Excavated areas 1988–1995

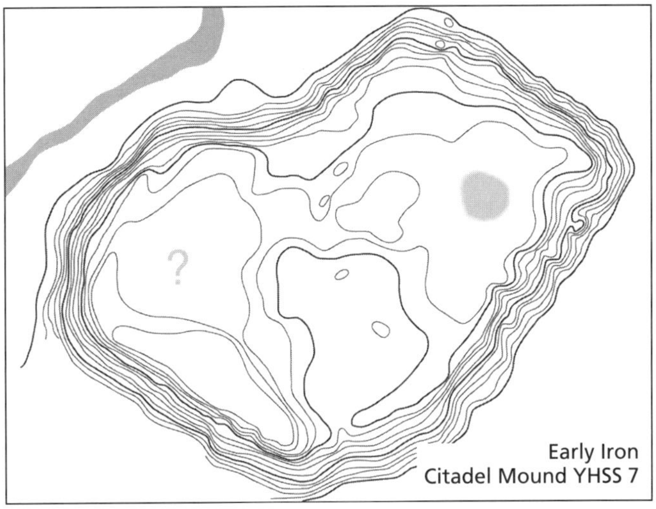

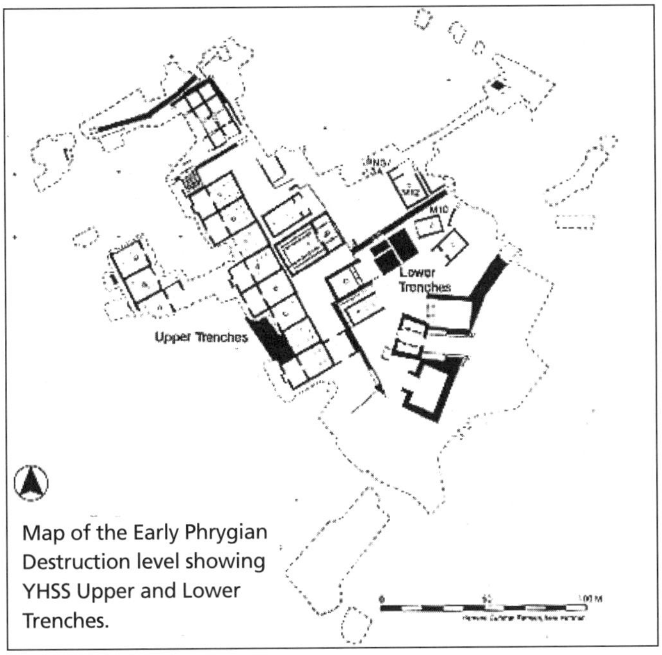

Map of the Early Phrygian Destruction level showing YHSS Upper and Lower Trenches.

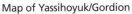

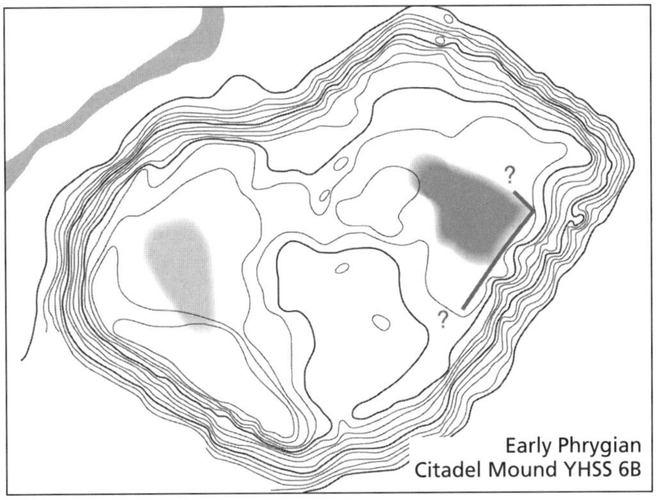

Schematic reconstructions of settlement organization...

CITADEL MOUND KEY
- Monumental buildings
- Domestic buildings
- Fortification walls
- Road between East and West mounds

Size of Excavated Area through 1997, by Phase* Key Sources: Gunter 1991; Voigt 1994; Gordion Archives

PHASE	SIZE OF SAMPLE	LOCATION OF EXCAVATED AREAS
Early Bronze Age	120 m^2	1950–1972: Main Excavation Area (MEA) on eastern half of Citadel Mound, soundings in Meg 12, Tr PN-3/3A
YHSS 10 Middle Bronze Age	ca. 60 m^2 10 m^2	1950–1972: MEA, soundings in Megarons 10, 12 1988–89: Lower Trench Sounding (LTS, sounding within Operation 14)
YHSS 9-8 Late Bronze Age	ca. 105 m^2 126 m^2	1950–1972: MEA Soundings in Megarons 10, 12 1988–89: LTS, Operation 14 and 11
YHSS 7 Early Iron Age	135 m^2 270 m^2	1950–72: MEA, soundings in Megarons 10, 12 1988–89: Entire Lower Trench Sounding
YHSS 6B Early Phrygian	ca. 3000 m^2 370 m^2	1950–72MEA, Early Phrygian Building and nearby areas 1988–93: Entire Lower Trench Sounding, extended to the south in 1993
YHSS 6A Early Phrygian Destruction Level	ca. 2 hectares 75 m^2 5 m^2	1950–1972: Eastern Citadel Mound (MEA) 1988–93: Upper Trench Sounding (UTS), Terrace Building 2A Western Citadel Mound, Operation 12 sounding
YHSS 5 Middle Phrygian	ca. 2 ha ca. 1290 m^2 ? 100 m^2 16 m^2 115 m^2 260 m^2 20 m^2	1950–1972: Main Excavation Area Western Citadel Mound, Middle Phrygian South Trench Lower Town Fortifications 1988–96: UTS Operations 1, 2 Western Citadel Mound, Operation 12 Lower Town Area A Lower Town Area B Outer Town Operation 22
YHSS 4 Late Phrygian	ca. 2 ha ca. 1290 m^2 150 m^2 110 m^2 140 m^2 150 m^2 310	1950–1972: Eastern Citadel, Main Excavation Area Westem Citadel Mound, South Trench 1988–96: Eastem Citadel, UTS Operations 1, 2, 7 Western Citadel Mound, Operation 17 Northwest Quadrant Lower Town Area A Area B Outer Town, Operations 37,43
YHSS 3 Hellenistic	ca. 2 ha ca. 1290 m^2 150 m^2 110 m^2 365 m^2 160 m^2 310 36 m^2	1950–1972: Eastern Citadel, Main Excavation Area Westem Citadel Mound, South Trench 1988–96: Eastern Citadel, UTS Operations 1, 2, 7 Western Citadel Mound, Operation 17 Northwest Quadrant Lower Town Area Area B Outer Town, Operation 38
YHSS 2 Roman	? ca. 1290 m^2 ca. 1175 m^2 150 m^2 110 m^2 365 m^2 175 m^2 310 36 m^2	1950–1972: Eastem Citadel, Main Excavation Area Westem Citadel Mound, South Trench Southwest Trench 1988–96: Eastern Citadel, UTS Operations 1,2,7 Western Citadel Mound, Operation 17 Northwest Quadrant Lower Town Area A Area B Outer Town, Operation 38
YHSS 1	? ca. 1175 m^2 150 m^2	1950–1972: Eastern Citadel, Main Excavation Area Southwest Trench 1988–89: Eastern Citadel, UTS Operations 1,2,7

* The size of the area on the eastern half of the Citadel Mound excavated by Rodney Young are approximations. Not only were digging units irregular in shape, but the trench plan for the last years of excavation has not been formally plotted. The very rough estimate of the size of the Main Excavation Area used here is based on a map of the extant trench boundaries in 1987 (i.e. after at least 15 years of erosion). These 1987 boundaries have been added to plans of the Early and Middle Phrygian elite quarter in order to distinguish open spaces between architectural units from unexcavated areas.

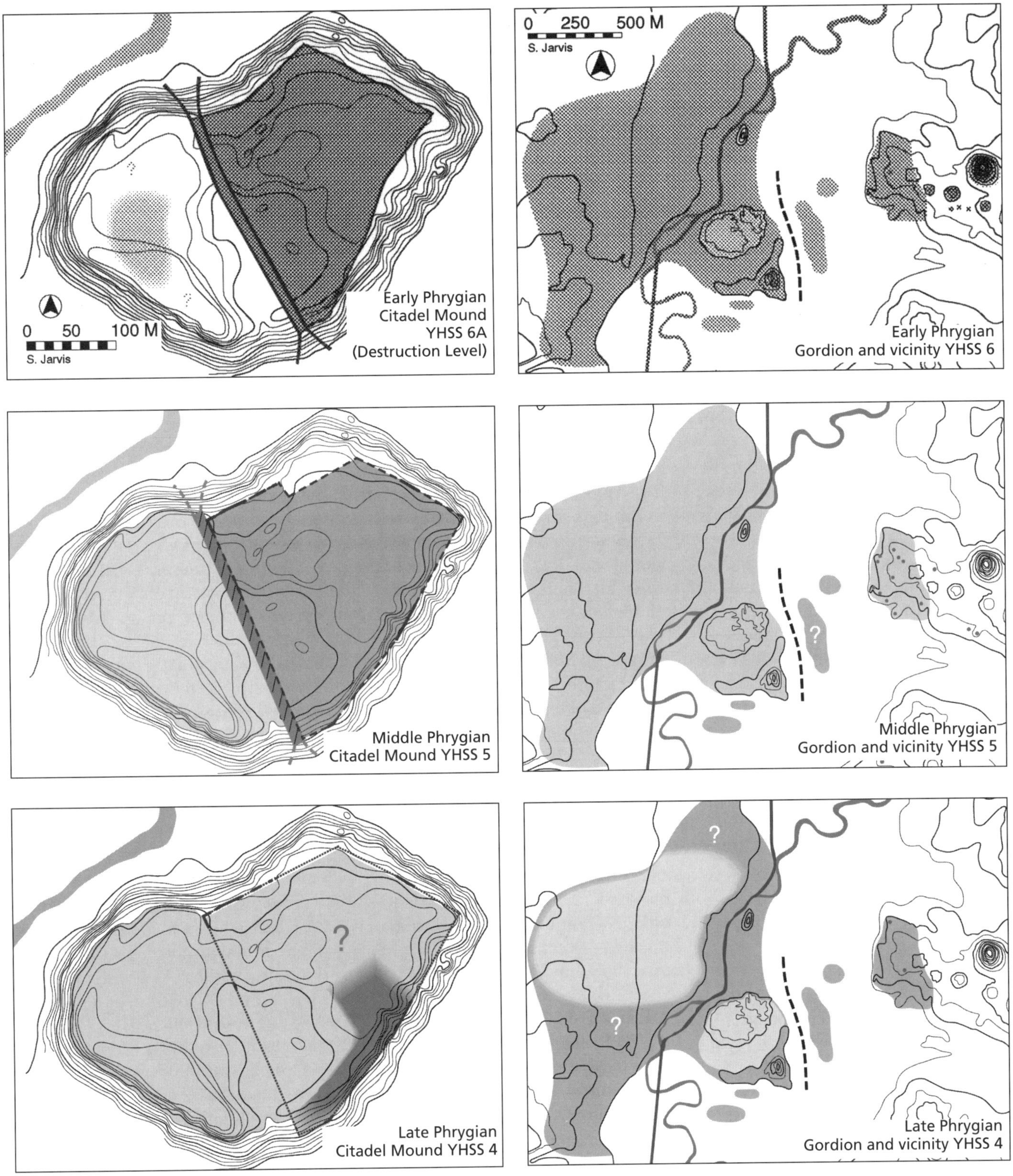

Schematic reconstructions of settlement organization...

CITADEL MOUND KEY

- Monumental buildings
- Domestic buildings
- Fortification walls
- Road between East and West mounds

GORDION AND VICINITY KEY

- Area Occupied During YHSS Phase
- Cemetaries
- Total Settlement Area Based on Surface Remains and Cores
- Reconstructed Ancient Sakarya River Course
- Sakarya River Course 1950
- Modern Dredged River Course

Settlement History

Early Bronze Age

Early Bronze Age Gordion is known from a series of closely spaced soundings on the eastern half of the Citadel. Mellink has used the stratigraphy from these trenches to reconstruct a "lower mound surrounding a prominent citadel" similar to Troy I or Demirci Höyük (1991a:110; Gunter 1991:Plan 11). Builders of the second-millennium settlement apparently erected it on the lower part of the Early Bronze Age settlement. Yet, whether or not there was a Middle or Late Bronze Age citadel above that of the Early Bronze Age will remain a mystery since the construction of the Early Phrygian elite quarter—at latest—apparently removed these levels.[3] Thus, we know almost nothing about the Early and Middle Bronze Age settlements beyond their ceramics, and have made no attempt to provide even a schematic plan for these periods.

Late Bronze Age

Information on the Late Bronze Age (YHSS 9-8) is better and more diverse. During this time, Gordion was probably small in size, but was still of some importance within its region, both politically and economically, perhaps a minor center. Our architectural sample for this period consists of a single house with associated cylindrical pits (Voigt 1994). Nevertheless, Robert Henrickson's analysis of the ceramics indicates that Gordion supported specialized potters using local clay sources to turn out forms typical of the Hittite Empire (see 1994 and this volume). Sealings and a seal support that Hittite connection, and a stamp with a personal name on a ceramic storage vessel suggests that at least some members of the population were acquainted with Hittite hieroglyphs. This seal impression raises the possibility that local leaders were affiliated with the Hittite state (Voigt and Hendrickson 2000; see also Guterbock 1980; Sams and Voigt 1990).

Twelfth Century BCE

In the twelfth century BCE, residents apparently briefly abandoned Gordion. The arrival of new settlers with a very different economy and material culture marks the beginning of the Iron Age, or YHSS 7 (Voigt and Henrickson 2000). The excavated area for this period is small, but is filled with houses surrounding an open area. These settlers built the earliest houses in shallow rectangular pits, with walls erected on a framework of reeds and branches covered with mud plaster. They sometimes faced the pit or interior walls with flat stones or orthostats (Voigt 1994). Ceramic form and technology suggest household production, and the faunal remains are compatible with a less intensive economy than that of the Late Bronze Age (Henrickson 1994). Within his period there are significant changes in subsistence, architecture, and ceramics that are not yet satisfactorily explained, but overall there is evidence of cultural continuity from the beginning of the Iron Age into historic times. Based on what we know from archaeological and documentary sources, we have argued that the initial Iron Age/ YHSS 7 settlement—a place we can only describe as a rather isolated village—manifests the migration of Phrygian speakers into the Gordion area (Voigt and Henrickson 2000).

Tenth Century BCE

By the tenth century, Gordion had gained importance and was the home of a leader who could mobilize labor to construct public and, indeed, monumental architecture. During YHSS 6B, or the beginning of the Early Phrygian period, builders cleared the area that had been devoted to houses and exterior workspaces in Phase 7, and transformed it into an open court that was eventually surrounded by elevated stone structures (Voigt and Henrickson 2000; fig. 6). Beyond this architectural complex stood a fortification wall, with an entrance structure leading up to the court. Within a short period, the Phrygians began what was to be an ongoing program of remodeling, that concluded the construction of a new fortification system with an entry structure built of multi-colored stone ("the Polychrome House"). The foundations of one of the surviving stone structures inside the fortress has been called the Post and Poros Building (PAP; Voigt and Henrickson 2000:fig. 7). The Phrygians built the PAP of white stone with wooden elements in the foundations and frame. There is evidence for carved moldings around windows and/or doorways and probably a pitched roof topped with an acroterion (an ornamental projection creating bases for sculpted figures). Sculpted orthostats of the same distinctive stone (and presumably from the PAP or another contemporary structure) have been compared by G. Kenneth Sams to orthostats from North Syrian sites dated to the later tenth or early ninth century BCE. Thus, as the Phrygian rulers extended their territory, they constructed relatively elaborate formal structures in which they emulated styles originating in the older kingdoms to the East.

Ninth Century BCE

During the eighth century, Gordion consisted of a walled area with large residential and service buildings that housed the rulers of the Phrygian capital (YHSS6A; see also Sams 1995). A fire that has been securely dated to ca. 830–800 BCE by radiocarbon preserved buildings and their contents, providing a rich picture of court life. Some residents of the elite quarter engaged in specialized production. Two large, multi-roomed structures with evidence for large scale food storage and preparation as well as textile production might indicate a state-controlled textile industry (DeVries 1990). Craft specialists are also inferred from the nature of ceramic production.

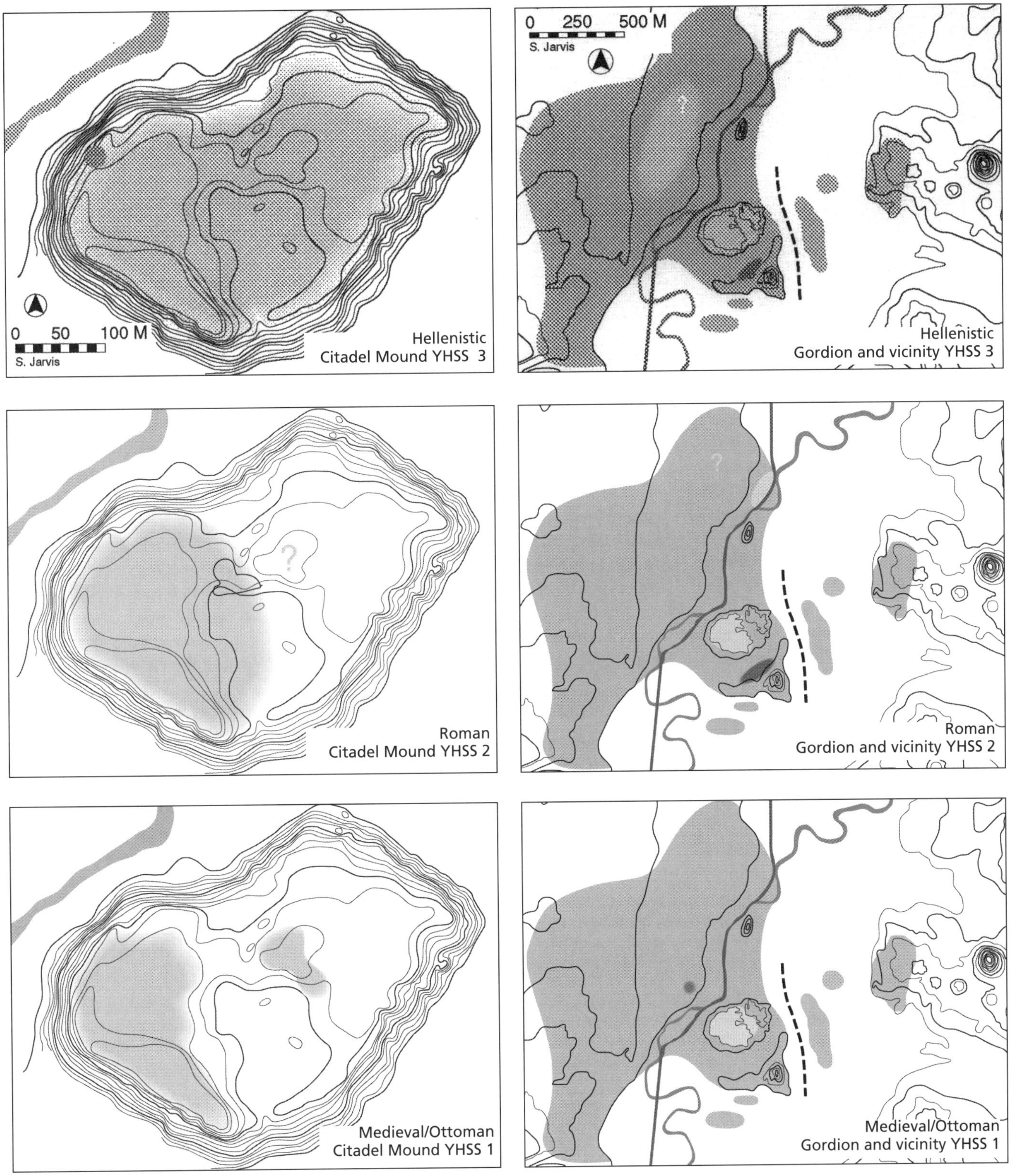

Schematic reconstructions of settlement organization...

CITADEL MOUND KEY

- Monumental buildings
- Domestic buildings
- Fortification walls
- Road between East and West mounds

GORDION AND VICINITY KEY

- Area Occupied During YHSS Phase
- Cemetaries
- Total Settlement Area Based on Surface Remains and Cores
- Reconstructed Ancient Sakarya River Course
- Sakarya River Course 1950
- Modern Dredged River Course

Rodney S. Young excavated more than two hectares of this palace quarter between 1950 and 1973. On three sides, the walls enclosing the quarter lay near the outer edge of the Citadel Mound, and presumably near the edge of the Early Phrygian settlement. The southwestern wall, however, ran through the center of the mound. Only a deep and restricted sounding conducted in 1993 hints at what lay to the west, beneath approximately half of the area of the present Citadel Mound. Operation 12, located near the southwestern edge of the Citadel Mound, reached an outside surface with a hearth and characteristic Early Phrygian ceramics. Thus, the ninth century settlement extended well beyond the palace quarter, though its total size remains unknown. Even if the entire area beneath the Citadel Mound welcomed occupation at this time, Early Phrygian Gordion was probably relatively small. It may have been a royal and ceremonial center with only a limited dependent population.

Middle Phrygian Period

When the city was rebuilt soon after the late ninth century fire, the Phrygians expanded and embellished it in a clear assertion of continuing political power (YHSS 5). In the central area, they created two separate high mounds, with stone buildings set on thick layers of fill dredged from the river and carted from the surrounding plain. A broad street with cobble paving ran between the mounds, as if to divide the two elevated surfaces with their clear functional differentiation.

On the Eastern Mound, builders duplicated the earlier palace quarter, with minor changes in building plans, but major changes in the fortification system and construction techniques (Voigt 1994:fig. 25.4). Young's excavations showed that the stone or mudbrick and wood structures of the Early Phrygian (YHSS 6A) period gave way to Middle Phrygian structures with deep rubble foundations set into the fill layer, and ashlar walls of white, red, and green stone.

The Western Mound supported Middle Phrygian domestic structures which were less heavily built but still substantial, with pebble mosaic floors in houses to the southwest (Operation 12). On the northwestern corner of the Citadel Mound, a Canadian team led by T. Cuyler Young, Jr. excavated a test trench in 1994 that established the presence of massive clay and rubble foundations (Sams and Voigt 1996). While the edge of the settlement is eroded in this area, I would argue based on mound topography and the structure of the foundations that the Western Mound probably was walled, and may have had a roadway leading up through the walls in this area.

Gordion reached its maximum size during this Middle Phrygian period (YHSS 5, ca. 800–550 BCE), extending over all or parts of an area of more than one square kilometer. Approximately twenty-five hectares lay within the fortified Citadel and the Lower Town to the south. As part of the Middle Phrygian construction project, a low fortified area anchored by a tall fortress (the Küçük Höyük) rose to the south of the twin mounds. In 1995, deep soundings in two areas of the Lower Town both came down upon Middle Phrygian structures on a deep layer of nearly sterile "fill." Taken together with this data, the modern topography of this area indicates that there was an elevated platform extending out from the fortification walls toward the Citadel. On this platform to the east (Area A), Phrygians erected large stone structures similar in construction to those on the eastern high mound: ashlar blocks rested on rubble foundations set into artificial fill (Voigt *et al.* 1997:6–7, figs. 3–5).

To the west (Area B), inhabitants built mud-walled houses with cobble foundations set into shallow trenches (Voigt et al. 1997:7–8, figs. 6–8). A second, low fortified area may have taken shape to the north of the Citadel. Heavy ashlar walls that now form rapids within the bed of the Sakarya River extend away from the Citadel and appear to converge on Kus Tepe, a small oval mound that is similar in form to the Küçük Höyük.

To the north and west of the fortified areas, on sloping land above the alluvial plain, lay an extensive area with domestic structures. Surface survey has documented and excavation has confirmed occupation as early as the seventh century (Sams and Voigt 1995). We have not yet fully surveyed this area so that exact estimates of settlement area for each period are still uncertain and the map shown here with occupation throughout the Outer Town area should be seen as provisional.

Late Phrygian Period

The Late Phrygian period (YHSS Phase 4) corresponds to the time when Gordion had been incorporated into the Achaemenid Empire. People again occupied all three topographic areas of the site, and the city seems to have changed little in overall size or economic importance. On the other hand, with a loss of political power, the area devoted to public buildings shrank. On the eastern high mound, two relatively elaborate buildings excavated by Rodney Young date to the fifth and fourth centuries: the Mosaic Building and the Painted House (Young 1953; Mellink 1980), and some of the Middle Phrygian ashlar buildings remained in use. However, in most areas of the Eastern Mound, Middle Phrygian buildings were modified or used as quarries for building materials. Inhabitants cut poorly built semi-subterranean houses and workshops ("cellars") into clay and rubble foundations (Voigt 1994). Better built domestic structures (usually semi-subterranean) stood on the Western Mound and in the Lower and Outer Towns (Voigt and Yound 1999:223–35, figs. 26–38). Though the size of the Outer Town is again uncertain, all soundings in this part of the site have produced several phases of Late Phrygian architecture. The Late Phrygian houses and courtyards differed in details of construction, plan, and contents from one part of the site to another, reflecting variation in wealth, the kinds of activities conducted, and perhaps ethnicity.

Hellenistic Period

After Gordion fell to Alexander, it retained some of its former importance, but changed significantly in architecture and settlement form. As a result of work in the Lower Town during 1994, we know that this area was no longer used for housing during the Hellenistic period (YHSS 3) but instead became a cemetery (Voigt 1996a). The Outer Town's size at this time is not certain, but surface materials suggest that it was not as extensive as in the Middle and Late Phrygian times. Thus, total settlement size certainly declines, with low-lying areas completely or partially abandoned. Excavations by Young had already shown that the area between the two high mounds of Middle and Late Phrygian times was filled in at the beginning of the Hellenistic period, producing an elevated area equivalent to the top of the present Citadel Mound; differences in settlement density between the Late Phrygian and Hellenistic periods are also possible.

Whatever its size, Hellenistic Gordion was a place of some importance, especially during the second half of the third century when Gordion was occupied by immigrant Celts. Monumental stone structures dated to this period lay on the northwest corner of the Citadel Mound, the most substantial (public?) Hellenistic building yet recovered at Gordion (Sams and Voigt 1999: plans 4–7, photos 7–10).

The settlement suffered destruction when its Celtic population fled before a Roman army under Consul Manlius Vulso (189 BCE). Houses dated to the early second century that were abandoned in haste, and often burned, have been found archaeologically across the entire Citadel Mound. Gordion is described as an "oppidum" or hillfort during the Galatian occupation, but no fortification walls have been discovered, and it is possible that this description simply refers to the location of the settlement on top of a high and defensible mound.

Roman Period

Settlers returned to Gordion in the first century CE, perhaps because it controlled the road connecting Roman cities at Pessinus and Ankara. Settlement during YHSS 2 was apparently limited to the Citadel Mound. A large area cleared on the western part of the mound contained substantial buildings bordering a paved street (Voigt *et al.* 1997:figs 20–21). The Lower Town cemetery continued in use, with both cremation and inhumation practiced (Sams and Voigt 1996).

Medieval or Early Ottomon Period

The final occupation on the site dates to Medieval and early Ottomon times (YHSS 1) when the settlement extended over much of the Citadel Mound. Ceramic samples are small so that precise dates for this phase have not yet been determined. Large, buttressed, stone walls tentatively assigned to YHSS 1 may indicate that during part of this phase, there was again a small fortress on the top of the Citadel. Burials assigned to this period have been found in the Outer Town (Sams and Voigt 1997).

Conclusion

This picture of changing settlement patterns is provisional. We are not yet ready to make population estimates for each phase since careful plotting of ceramic distributions within the Outer Town remains unfinished. Nevertheless, it is clear that Gordion changed in size and form throughout the first millennium BCE.

One of the unexpected outcomes of our restudy has been a series of challenges to long-standing assumptions about Phrygian Gordion. When we began work in 1988, the date assigned to the Early Phrygian Destruction Level (YHSS 6A) was 700 BCE based on readings of fragmentary texts. The fire itself was attributed to invading Kimmerian nomads who literally destroyed Midas and his kingdom. By the late 1990s it was difficult to reconcile this reconstruction with the picture provided by survey and limited excavation, which showed that Middle Phrygian Gordion was far larger than its predecessor. Not only was the rebuilt citadel grand in scale, representing a huge investment in labor, but the rebuilding process started almost immediately after the fire!

What seemed to be an impossible set of contradictions was resolved through a reexamination of old evidence and the use of radiocarbon and dendrochronology to provide new absolute dates independent of documentary sources. In January 2000, DeVries, Sams and Voigt met to reconsider the date of the Destruction Level. We agreed that the ceramic evidence from the burnt palace quarter supported a date *before* 700 BCE, and placed the destruction conservatively in the mid-eighth century. Peter Kunihom, of the Malcolm and Carolyn Wierner Laboratory for Aegean and Near Eastern Dendrochronology at Cornell University, had a long-term interest in chronological questions at Gordion and had already analyzed a set of dendrochronological samples from the burned level. He offered to fund the analysis of a group of short-lived radiocarbon samples (five pots of seeds representing three plant species recovered from the Destruction) at the University of Heidelberg. The results surprised everyone: all of the calibrated dates fell between 830–800 BCE. We have just begun a thorough restudy of the artifacts from the Destruction Level, but work carried out by DeVries thus far provides strong confirmation of the radiocarbon dates. Overall, the results of new research at Gordion provide an example of the kinds of results that can be obtained when large data sets from older, large-scale excavations are combined with small, precisely-collected stratigraphic samples.

Acknowledgements

From 1950 to 1972 excavations at Gordion were directed by Rodney Stuart Young. Since 1988, an integrated program of excavation and regional surface survey has been under the direction of Mary M. Voigt; this work was supported by funds from the National Endowment for the Humanities (a federal agency), the National Geographic Society, the IBM Foundation, the Kress Foundation, the Royal Ontario Museum, the Social Science and Humanities Council of Canada, and generous private donors. G. Kenneth Sams has served as Director of the Gordion Project since 1988. All modern archaeological research at Gordion (1950–2001) has been sponsored by the University of Pennsylvania Museum of Archaeology and Anthropology.

Notes

[1] The identification of modern Yassihöyük with the Gordion of ancient sources is based on geographical location and archaeological sequence rather than any kind of text or inscription from the site itself. For the relevant historical sources on Gordion, see Körte (1902), Voigt (1996).

[2] The Outer Town would appear to be an ideal area for the use of remote sensing methods as a means of investigating intra-site settlement patterns. Lamentably, in 1995, when Lewis Somers tested the effectiveness of both resistivity and magnetometry, both proved spectacularly ineffective due to the nature of soils and rocks in the Gordion area.

[3] This conclusion is based on the fact that the uppermost Early Bronze Age strata in Trench PN-3 lie immediately beneath the floor of Early Phrygian Megaron 10. The Phrygian fondness for mining ancient mounds as construction material is well-documented by the YHSS 5 or Middle Phrygian "clay" fills, which sometimes contain large quantities of Bronze Age sherds and other artifacts.

Bibliography

Dandoy, J., Selinsky, P., and Voigt, M. M.
2002 Celtic Sacrifice. *Archaeology* 55:44–49.

DeVries, K.
1990 The Gordion Excavation Seasons of 1969–1973 and Subsequent Research. *American Journal of Archaeology* 94:371–406.

Gunter, A. C.
1991 *The Bronze Age (Gordion Excavation Final Reports III)*. University Museum Monograph 73. Philadelphia: University of Pennsylvania Museum of Anthropology and Archaeology.

Guterbock, H. G.
1980 Seals and Sealings in Hittite Lands. Pp. 51–36 in *From Athens to Gordion*, edited by K. DeVries. University Museum Papers 1. Philadelphia: University of Pennsylvania Museum.

Henrickson, R. C.
1994 Continuity and Discontinuity in the Ceramic Tradition at Gordion during the Iron Age. Pp. 95–129 in *Proceedings of the Third International Anatolian Iron Age Symposium (Van 1990)*, edited by D. French and A. Çilingiroğlu. British Institute of Archaeology at Ankara Monograph No. 16. Ankara: British Institute at Ankara.

Körte, G. and Körte, A.
1904 *Gordion: Ergebnisse der Ausgrabung im Jahre 1900*. Jahrbuch des Kaiserlich Deutschen Archäologischen Instituts, Vol. 5. Berlin: Georg Reimer Verlag.

Mellink, M.
1980 Archaic Wall Paintings from Gordion. Pp. 91–98 in *From Athens to Gordion*, edited by K. DeVries. University Museum Papers 1. Philadelphia: University of Pennsylvania Museum.
1991a Comments on Sections of the Bronze Age Mound. Pp 109–110 in *The Bronze Age (Gordion Excavation Final Reports lll)*, edited by A. C. Gunter. University Museum Monograph 73. Philadelphia: University of Pennsylvania Museum of Anthropology and Archaeology.
1991b The Native Kingdoms of Anatolia. Pp. 619–65 in *Cambridge Ancient History* Vol 3. 2nd ed. Cambridge: Cambridge University Press.

Sams, G. K.
1989 Sculpted Orthostates at Gordion. Pp. 447–54 in *Anatolia and the Ancient Near East*, edited by K. Emre, et al. Ankara: Turk Tarih Kurumu.
1995 Midas of Gordion and the Anatolian Kingdom of Phrygia. Pp.1147–159 in *Civilizations of the Ancient Near East*, Vol. II., edited by J.M. Sasson et al. New York: Scribner's Sons.

Sams, G. K. and Voigt, M. M.
1990 Work at Gordion in 1988. *Xl Kazı Sonuçları Toplantısı* 1:77–105.
1991 Work at Gordion in 1989. *Xll Kazı Sonuçları Toplantısı* 1:455-70.
1995 Gordion Archaeological Activities, 1993. XVI *Kazi Sonuçları Toplantısı* 1:369–92.
1997 Gordion 1995. *XVIII Kazı Sonuçları Toplantısı* 1:407–475
1998 Gordion 1996. *XIX Kazı Sonuçları Toplantısı* 1:681–701
1999 Gordion Archaeological Activities, 1997. *XX Kazı Sonuçları Toplantısı* 1:559–76.

Voigt, M. M.
1994 Excavations at Gordion 1988–89: The Yassihoyuk Stratigraphic Sequence. Pp. 265–93 in *Anatolian Iron Ages 3: Proceedings of the Third Anatolian Iron Ages Colloquium (Van. 1990)*, edited by D. French and A. Cilingiroğlu. British Institute of Archaeology at Ankara Monograph No. 16. Ankara: British Institute of Archaeology at Ankara.
1996 Gordion. Pp. 426–31 in *The Oxford Encyclopedia of Near Eastern Archaeology*. New York: Oxford University Press.

Voigt, M. M., DeVries, K., Henrickson, R. C., Lawall, M., Marsh, B., Gürsan-Salzman, A., and Young, T.C., Jr.
1997 Fieldwork at Gordion; 1993–1995. *Anatolica* 23:1–59.

Voigt, M. M. and Young, T. C., Jr.
1999 From Phrygian Capital to Achaemenid Entrepot: Middle and Late Phrygian Gordion. *Iranica Antiqua* 34:191–241.

Voigt, M. M. and Henrickson, R. C.
2000 Formation of the Phrygian State: The Early Iron Age at Gordion. *Anatolian Studies* 50:37–54.

Young, Rodney S.
1953 Progress at Gordion, 1951–1952. *The University Museum Bulletin* 17/4:3–39.

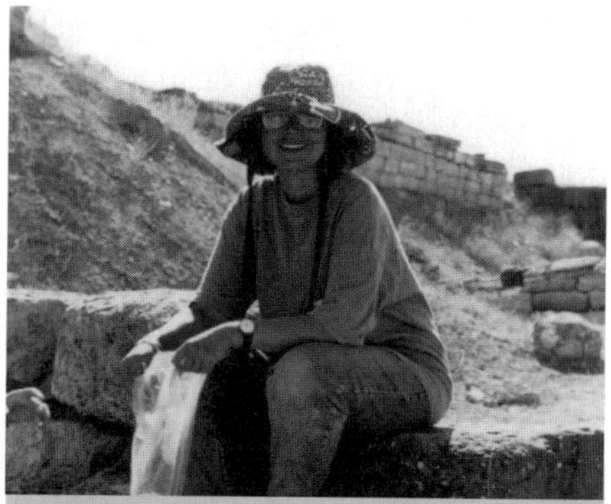

Mary M. Voigt, Chancellor Professor of Anthropology at The College of William and Mary, has been Director of Excavation and Survey of the Gordion Project since 1988. Her research seeks to document the rise of the Phrygian state in the early 1st millennium BCE, the effect of the Persian conquest of Gordion, and the nature of the migration by ethnic Celts to Gordion. She has recently published on the archaeological documentation of ethnicity, migration, urban organization, and ritual practices.

New Research on the City Plan of Ancient Aphrodisias

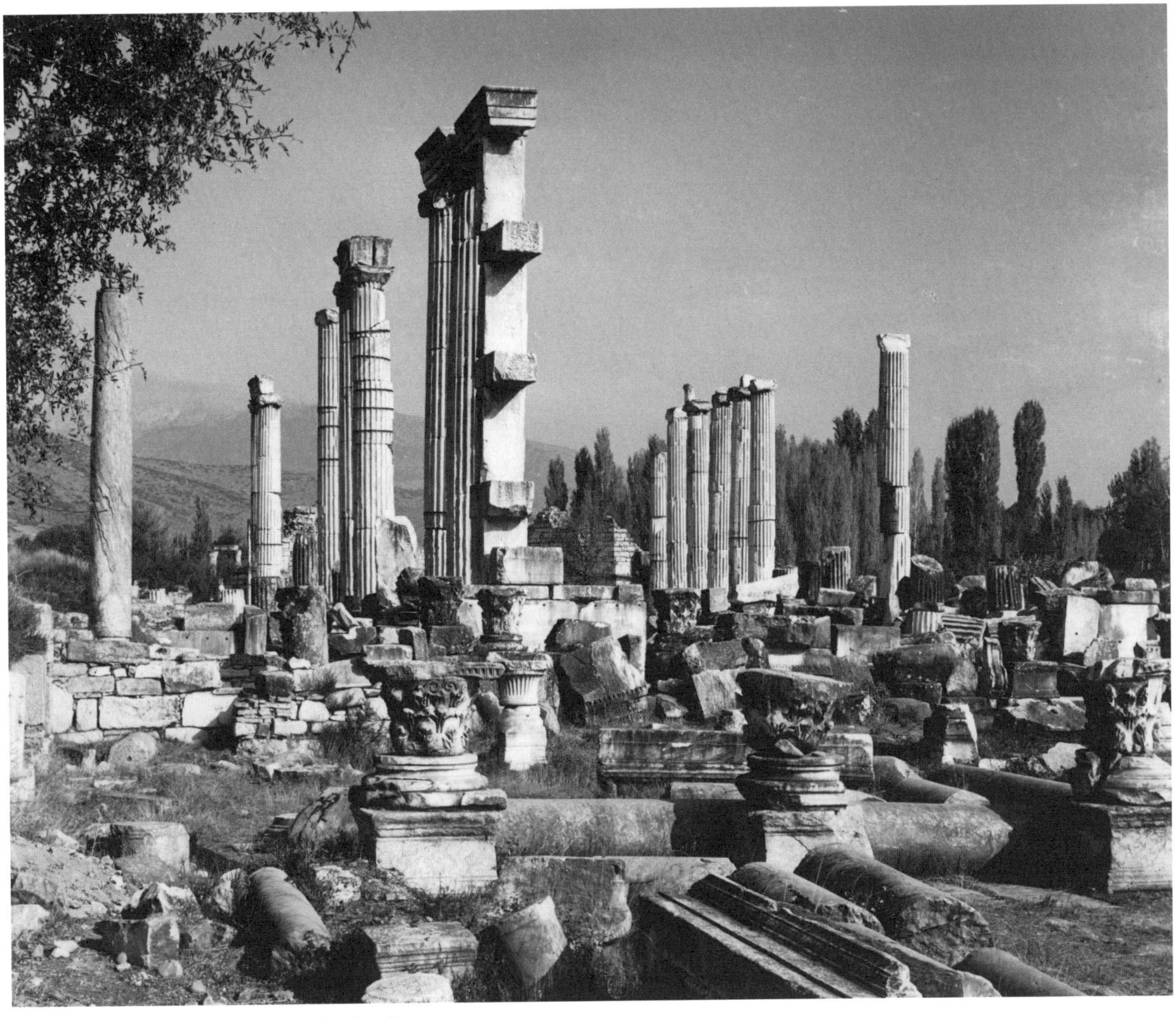

View of the Sanctuary and Temple of Aphrodite.

By Christopher Ratté

The Carian city of Aphrodisias lies in the Maeander River basin, in a fertile valley 100 miles southeast of the port of Izmir. Famous in antiquity for its sanctuary of Aphrodite, the city's patron goddess, Aphrodisias enjoyed a long and prosperous existence from the first century BCE through the sixth century CE. Today, many of the city's ancient monuments remain standing, and excavations have unearthed rich corpora of public statuary, inscriptions, and other artifacts. The great beauty and extraordinary preservation of this site combine to bring the civic culture of the Graeco-Roman world vividly and dramatically to life.

The site and monuments of Aphrodisias have been known to travelers and scholars for several hundred years.[1] The British botanist and sometime epigrapher, William Sherard visited the site and copied a number of inscriptions at the beginning of the eighteenth century. In the nineteenth century, the Society of the Dilettanti carried out an architectural

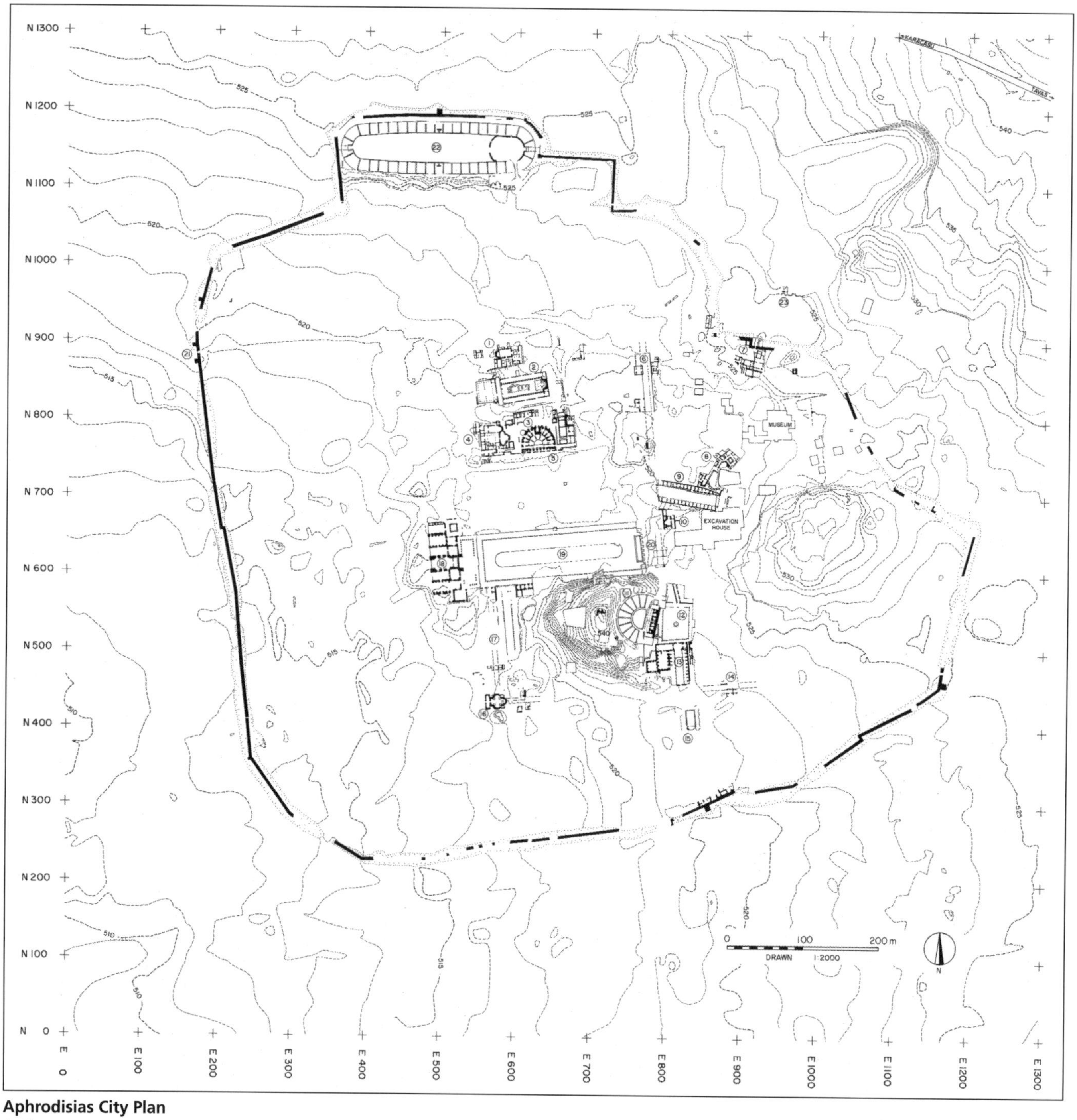

Aphrodisias City Plan

1. House
2. Temple of Aphrodite–Church
3. Sculptors' Workshop
4. Bishop's Palace
5. Bouleuterion and North Agora
6. Tetrapylon and N–S Street
7. Water Channel Area
8. Atrium House
9. Sebasteion
10. Cryptoporticus House
11. Theater
12. Tetrastoon
13. Theater Baths
14. Gaudin's Fountain and E–W Street
15. Gaudin's Gymnasium
16. Triconch Church
17. Basilica
18. Hadrianic Baths
19. Portico of Tiberius
20. Agora Gate
21. West Gate
22. Stadium
23. Nymphaeum

study of the Temple of Aphrodite. French and Italian teams undertook limited excavations in the early twentieth century. The site nevertheless remained largely unexplored until 1961, when New York University sponsored excavations. Kenan Erim inaugurated the work and supervised it for the first thirty years. Erim concentrated his efforts on the excavation of the central part of the city, with spectacular results.

The heart of the city was the Sanctuary of Aphrodite, situated on the northern edge of the city-center.

The earliest evidence for the existence of the Sanctuary dates to the sixth century BCE, but the marble Temple of Aphrodite is a much later structure, probably not begun until the first century BCE (Theodorescu 1987, 1990). Before the Hellenistic period, Aphrodisias probably consisted of little more than a rustic sanctuary and, perhaps, a small village. The growth of the city was closely tied to its relations with Rome, especially from the 30s BCE onward, when Aphrodisias came under the personal protection of Octavian/Augustus, the first Roman emperor.[2] In the first century, city planners renovated the Sanctuary of Aphrodite as part of the development of a monumental civic center to the south, consisting of two large public squares and assorted civic buildings. On the southern edge of the city center lies the Theater, also renovated in the late first century BCE.[3]

Trench (Nag 95.1) excavated in 1995 in the southwest corner of the Northern Agora exposed the foundations of the heretofore unaccounted for western colonnade. This view to the west shows the foundation of the southern colonnade and its northern turn at the western limits of the agora.

The monumental development of the central part of Aphrodisias continued through the first two centuries CE, the most prosperous period in the history of the site. Later, toward the end of the third century, Aphrodisias became the capital of the new Roman province of Caria. The fourth century, however, was a period of greater insecurity, marked by the construction of fortifications surrounding the city on all sides. At the end of the fifth century, the temple of Aphrodite was converted into a Christian church. Aphrodisias survived as a Late Antique city through the sixth century, and as a medieval village throughout the fourteenth century, when the site was finally abandoned (Roueché 1989).

Thanks to Erim's intensive investigations of Aphrodisias's city center, we enjoy a richly detailed picture of the history of the city's principal monuments, of its internal civic culture and external relations both with neighboring cities and with Rome, and of the remarkable local sculpture industry. Since Erim's untimely death in 1990, the Institute of Fine Arts in cooperation with the Faculty of Arts and Science at New York University has continued research at Aphrodisias. After study seasons in 1991 and 1992, NYU began a new program of fieldwork in 1993, under the joint direction of myself, Field Director since 1993, and Prof. R. R. Smith, Project Director since 1991 (Smith and Ratté 1995, 1996, 1997).

This program has two parts: first, study and recording of the earlier excavations, in preparation for final publication; and second, new investigations designed to clarify the urban and regional contexts of the excavated monuments.

Trench AN 3 was dug to test the results of a geophysical sounding. It exposed a street flanked by some kind of public building.

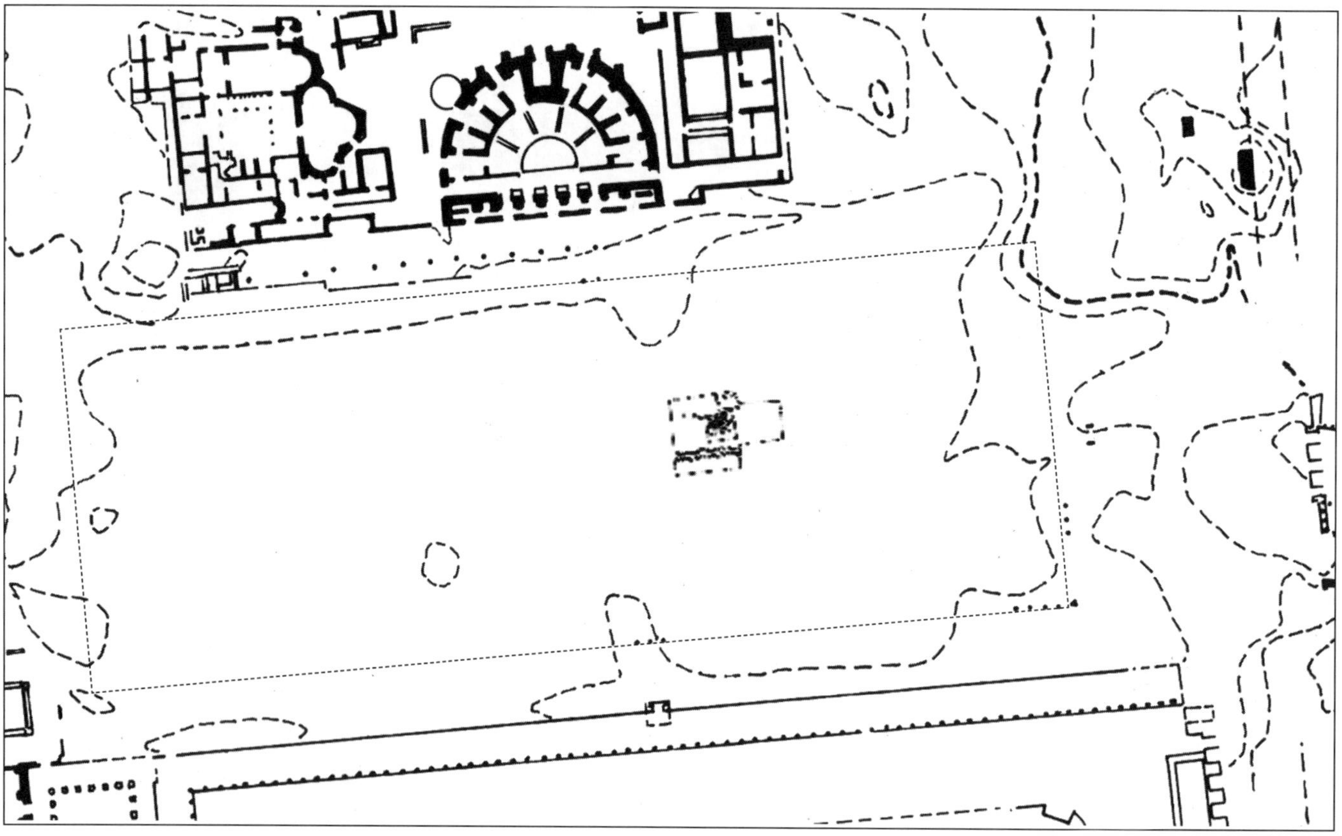

Plan of North Agora.

Previously, the area between the city center and the fortifications of Aphrodisias had remained almost totally unexplored. Thus although the city center was in some ways reasonably well-understood, its relationship to its urban matrix was very poorly understood; and although many of its public civic and religious monuments had been studied with care, little was known of the residential and industrial parts of town. Even in the city center, attention had been focused more on individual buildings than on the connections between them; more on their character as architectural monuments, than on their larger urban presence.

To fill in this major gap in our knowledge of Aphrodisias, the current fieldwork emphasizes research on the city plan and its development through a combination of limited new excavation, detailed graphic and photographic recording, and extensive surveying.

Current Excavations

A trench dug in 1995 in the southwest corner of the North Agora may serve as an example of the kind of excavation now being carried out. The North Agora was Aphrodisias's principal public square, a large open area bordered on the north by a row of public buildings, of which the most important was the Bouleuterion or Council House. Although portions of the colonnades that defined the north, east, and south edges of the Agora are still standing, its western limit was unknown. In 1995, we tackled this problem by digging a trench along the line of the south colonnade of the Agora, at the point where the topography seemed to indicate that the colonnade should turn to the north.[4] This hunch turned out to be correct: the foundations of the south colonnade ran from east to west, and turned to the north just short of the west edge of the trench. This discovery gives us for the first time the line of the Agora's western edge; its larger significance becomes apparent when the new trench is plotted on a plan of the entire Agora, revealing for the first time that the Bouleuterion is precisely centered on the Agora's north side.

Similar small scale excavations in the Sanctuary of Aphrodite have clarified the boundaries of the Sanctuary and its relationship with the public buildings to the south. Investigation of another group of buildings in the southwest corner of the city center has shed new light on the plan of the Civil Basilica and confirmed the existence of a major street intersection southwest of the Basilica (at the location of the later Triconch Church). Projects such as these have much improved our understanding of the relationships between the excavated buildings of Aphrodisias and, in general, our appreciation of the careful planning of the central part of town.

Until recently, however, it was not clear whether the rational planning of the Agora and associated structures extended to surrounding areas. In short, was this scheme limited to the Agora, or was the layout of the Agora only one component of a larger urban plan?

Geo-physical Survey

In order to answer this and other questions, beginning in 1995, archaeologists conducted a geophysical survey of the large unexcavated area between the Sanctuary of Aphrodite and the Stadium on the northern edge of the city. At the time of writing surveyors have covered a total area of approximately 100,000 m^2. Lew Somers of Geoscan Research has supervised two different kinds of surveys: an electrical resistivity survey of the entire 100,000 m^2 area and a magnetometer survey of a 40,000 m^2 part of this area.[5]

Among the most interesting results of the resistivity survey, which was more successful than the magnetometer survey, is the clear appearance of a grid pattern of light grey stripes, which are low resistivity areas, or areas with low concentrations of stone. Test excavations carried out at three locations showed—as suspected—that these low resistivity stripes are streets. One trench uncovered both the street, with a large covered drain running down the middle and, on the east side of the street, part of what appears to be a house complete with a peristyle court. The room between the courtyard and the street is an elaborate latrine.[6]

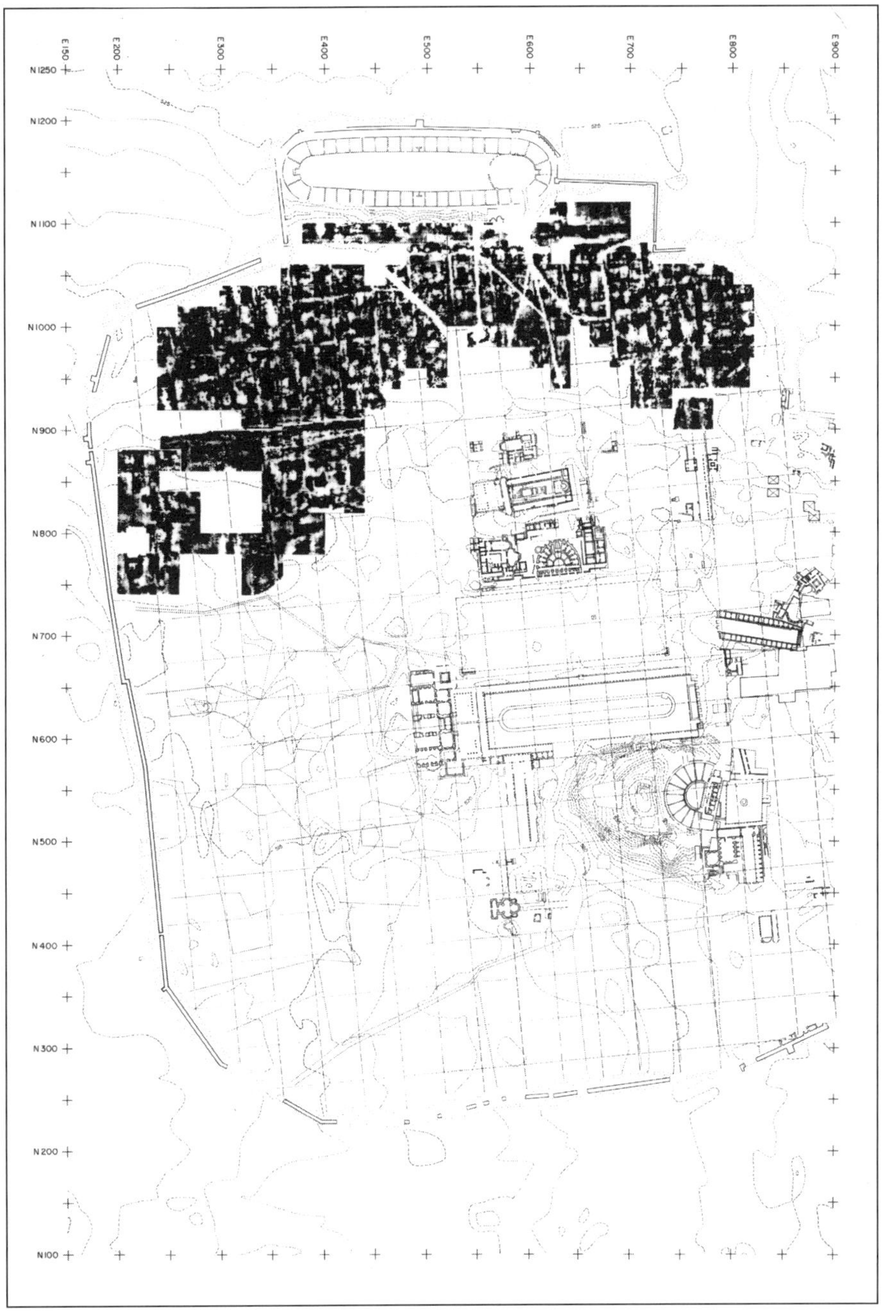

Resistivity survey map plotted on city plan; dashed lines show lines of streets restored on the basis of the resistivity survey.

The resistivity survey thus clearly shows that a planned residential neighborhood occupied the area north and west of the Sanctuary of Aphrodite. Individual city blocks are 35.5 m, or perhaps 120 Ionic feet, wide and 39.0 m, or 132 Ionic feet, long. The extra length of 12 feet may have been left for an alleyway running between back-to-back houses.[7] Each block was probably occupied by four 60 X 60 foot housing plots. The maximum number of houses of this size that could have fit inside the city walls is approximately 1200. These calculations would suggest that the population of ancient Aphrodisias numbered roughly 10,000 inhabitants.[8]

In any case, the resistivity survey more concretely shows that the rational planning of the city-center was in fact not an isolated undertaking, but part of a larger urban design that included the domestic as well as the public sectors of town. When the results of the survey are plotted on the larger city plan, it is apparent that the streets detected in the survey area have the same orientations as the main axes of the Agora and that both areas were in fact laid out on the same grid. Thus, the Bouleuterion and the North Agora are bisected along their shared longitudinal axis by the line of a street; both the North Agora and the so-called South Agora are also bisected by street lines along their east–west axes; and a number of public building complexes, such as the Baths and the Civil Basilica, are exactly one block wide.

The newly revealed city plan of Aphrodisias conforms to established traditions of Classical and Hellenistic Greek city-planning. Its basic planning unit is the residential housing block, and a number of blocks in the center of the city were left free from the start for public use. Aphrodisias does not, however, have the central axes typical of Roman city-planning, both in the western Mediterranean region and in eastern Roman colonies such as Corinth (Romano 1993).

The date of this new plan is uncertain. It is unlikely to be earlier than the second century BCE, the date of the earliest coins and inscriptions attesting the name of Aphrodisias and its existence as a proper city, and it may be as late as the monumental development of the city center in the late first century BCE (Reynolds 1982; 1985). Excavation might decide this issue, if datable material could be found in association with the earliest buildings laid out on the grid—more likely houses outside the city center than the monumental buildings of the Agora.

The results of recent research have transformed our understanding of the city plan of Aphrodisias and, thus, of the urban setting and context of the monuments excavated between 1961 and 1990. But the significance of these discoveries goes well beyond the study of Aphrodisias alone, for like the sculpture from the site, the urban plan of this city is unusually well-preserved and, thus, provides valuable new evidence for Graeco-Roman urbanism in the Late Hellenistic and Early Imperial periods. In future years, we plan both to continue to reexamine the excavated buildings of the city-center, and to extend the resistivity survey to the unexcavated areas on the east, west, and south edges of town. We hope in these ways not only to clarify our understanding of the original city plan of Aphrodisias, but also to study its change over time. These are the kinds of subjects and perspectives that help us understand this city not only as a collection of isolated structures, but as a complex and evolving whole, whose streets and open areas, whose houses, shops, and workshops, were as much a part of its urban landscape as its temples and its other public monuments.

Addendum

Since this article was written, the resistivity survey of the unexcavated parts of Aphrodisias has been extended to the southern half of the city. An additional 70,000 square meters have been surveyed, and the results show the ancient street grid extended southward all the way to the city wall.

Notes

[1] For a general account of the history of the site and excavations, see Erim (1986).

[2] See the inscription published by Reynolds (1982:96–99), especially a letter concerning Aphrodisias from Octavian to a subordinate, in which Octavian says, "This one city I have taken for my own out of all Asia."

[3] On the development of the city center, see Gros (1996). Dedicatory inscriptions from the doorway of the Temple, one of the stoas of the Agora, and the stage building of the Theater all name a single individual, Gaius Julius Zoilos, a citizen of Aphrodisias and freedman of Octavian's, who played an important role in cementing good relations between his native city and the new Roman leader. See Reynolds (1982:156–64), Smith (1993:4–13). The hill into which the Theater is carved is in fact a prehistoric settlement mound: see Joukowsky (1986).

[4] The grid coordinates of this trench are N661/E532.

[5] For a brief description of these and other methods of geophysical prospection, see Bevan (1995).

[6] The grid coordinates of this trench are: N1007-1010/E524-539.

[7] One hundred twenty feet is a standard measurement in ancient surveying, also found in Classical Greek cities on the western coast of Turkey, such as Miletus (fifth century BCE) and Priene (fourth century BCE); on these and other cities, see Hoepfner and Schwander (1994). In addition to the alleyways running through the blocks, both the east–west and the north–south streets between the blocks were also apparently 3.5 m or 12 feet wide.

[8] This estimate assumes an average number of 8–10 inhabitants per household; for the houses at Olynthus, which are comparable in size, Hoepfner and Schwander suggest an average of ten inhabitants, including slaves (1994:72).

Bibliography

Bevan, B.
1995 Geophysical Prospecting. *American Journal of Archaeology* 99:88–90.

Christopher Ratté is Associate Professor of Classics and Fine Arts at New York University and co-director of the current research project, begun in 1991, for the documentation, analysis, and publication of the excavations at Aphrodisias, and the proper conservation and restoration of the excavated monuments form the site.

Erim, K. T.
1986 *Aphrodisias: City of Venus Aphrodite.* N.Y.: Facts on File.

Gros, P.
1996 Les nouveaux espaces civiques du début de l'Empire en Asie Mineure: les examples d'Ephèse, Iasos, et Aphrodisias. Pp. 111–20 in *Aphrodisias Papers* 3. Ann Arbor: University of Michigan.

Hoepfner, W. and Schwander, E.-L.
1994 *Haus und Stadt im klassischen Griechenland.* 2nd ed. Berlin: München: Deutscher Kunstverleg.

Joukowsky, M.
1986 *Prehistoric Aphrodisias.* Providence and Louvain: Brown University.

Reynolds, J. M.
1982 *Aphrodisias and Rome.* London: Society for the Promotion of Roman Studies.
1985 The Politeia of Plarasa and Aphrodisias. *Revue des Etudes Anciennes* 87:213–18.

Romano, D. G.
1993 Post-146 B.C. Land Use in Corinth and Planning the Roman Colony of 44 B.C. Pp. 9–30 in *The Corinthia in the Roman Period,* edited by T. E. Gregory. Ann Arbor: University of Michigan.

Roueché, C.
1989 *Aphrodisias in Late Antiquity.* Journal of Roman Studies monograph 5. London: Society for the Promotion of Roman Studies.

Smith, R. R. R.
1993 *Aphrodisas I: The Monument of C. Juilus Zoilos.* Mainz: P. von Zabern.

Smith, R. R. R. and Ratté, C.
1995 Archaeological Research at Aphrodisias in Caria, 1993. *American Journal of Archaeology* 99:33–58.
1996 Archaeological Research at Aphrodisias in Caria, 1994. *American Journal of Archaeology* 100:5–33.
1997 Archaeological Research at Aphrodisias in Caria, 1995. *American Journal of Archaeology* 101:1–22.

Theodorescu, D.
1987 Le temple d'Aphrodite. Pp. 87–99 in *Aphrodisias de Carie,* edited by J. de la Genière and K. Erim. Paris: Editions Recherche sur les Civilisations.
1990 La restitution de l'Aphrodision. Pp. 49–65 in *Aphrodisias Papers,* edited by C. Roueché and K. T. Erim. Ann Arbor: University of Michigan.

Index

A

Abraham 69
Abu Hureyra 10
Acemhöyük 39, 43, 103
Achaemenid Empire 154, 157–68
Adad-nirari I 53
Adilcevaz 152–53
Afyon 13
Aegean Sea 157
Ahura-mazda 165
Akkadian 62, 114
Alabaster 36
Alaca Höyük 36, 44, 65, 123, 129
Aladağ 39
Alalakh 35, 53, 94
Alexander the Great 195
Aleppo 35, 135
Alişar Höyük 1
Almond 9–10
Amanus mountains 35–36
Ammisaduqa 52
Amphora 175–78
Amuq 5, 38–40
Animal husbandry 12
Anitta, King 36–37, 46, 49, 62–63, 103
Ankara 195
Annales school 2
Anum-Ḫirbe 61, 116
Aphek, Tel 145
Aphrodisias 197–202
Aphrodite 197
Appu 113
Aramaic 73
Arameans 71
Ararat, Mt. 155
Archaeobotany 5–15
Argišti I 150
Argišti II 150
Armenia 151, 154–55
Arnuwanda I 65, 101, 106, 115
Arnuwanda II 67
Arnuwanda III 68
Artaxerxes II 165
Arzawa 67
Asia Minor 1
Asmar, Tell 28, 32
Ašmunikal 65
Aššur (city) 39, 45, 47, 59, 61
Aššur (god) 150, 165
Assurbanipal 154
Aššuwa 1, 36, 108
Assyria 53, 66–67, 102–3, 149, 153, 162
Assyrian Colony period 38, 45–47, 52, 59, 103
Assyrians 46–47, 49, 59, 61, 64, 73, 103, 159
Aşvan 8
Ayanis 153
Azitawanda 73

B

Babylon 50, 52, 64, 71, 113, 162
Babylonian literature 113
Banat, Tell 19
Barley 7–13, 178, 180
Bastam 150–55
Battle of Kadesh 63, 67–68
Bee 112
Beycesultan 5
Bitter vetch 12, 13
Black Sea 39, 59
Boğazköy/Boğazkale-Ḫattuša 1, 14, 35–36, 38–40, 43–44, 47–51, 54, 61, 69, 73, 77–97, 99, 105, 107, 113, 116, 125–26, 128–29, 133, 135, 145.
Brak, Tell 21
Bronze 173
Bronze Age 7, 188
Early 11–12, 14, 19–33, 37, 39, 44, 190, 192
Middle 21, 37, 39, 44, 53, 190, 192
Late 14, 35–40, 44, 51, 54, 72, 123–29, 145, 188, 190, 192
Bullae 103–4, 150, 153–54
Büyükkale 49, 78–80, 95, 97, 100
Byzantines 1, 69

C

Çadır Höyük
Canaan 69, 71, 73
Cape Gelidonya 36
Caria 197, 199
Çatal Höyük 3, 5
Cattle 113
Çayönü 10, 15
Celts 195
Ceramic production 192
Ceyhan River 63
Chalcolithic period 35, 38–39
Chickpea 7, 10, 12, 180
Chronology 52, 60
Chuera, Tell 19
Cilicia 38
Cimmerians 150, 154, 195
Classical period 12, 15, 21
Coins 157–68
Copper 37, 38
Cremation 195
Cuneiform 104
Cyrus the Great 157, 175, 180

D

Dabʿa, Tell el 53
Darias I 157, 159–60, 162, 168
David, King 70
Deforestation 14
Demirci Höyük 192
Dendrochronology 195
Diet 13

E

F

G

H

I

J

K

Y

Z